The Economic World View

Studies in the Ontology of Economics

The beliefs of economists are not solely determined by empirical evidence in direct relation to the theories and models they hold. Economists hold 'ontological presuppositions', fundamental ideas about the nature of being which direct their thinking about economic behaviour. In this volume, leading philosophers and economists examine these hidden presuppositions, searching for a 'world view' of economics. What properties are attributed to human individuals in economic theories, and which are excluded? Does economic man exist? Do markets have an essence? Do macroeconomic aggregates exist? Is the economy a mechanism, the functioning of which is governed by a limited set of distinct causes? What are the methodological implications of different ontological starting points? This collection, which establishes economic ontology as a coordinated field of study, will be of great value to economists and philosophers of social sciences.

USKALI MÄKI is Professor of Philosophy at the Erasmus University of Rotterdam. He is an editor of the *Journal of Economic Methodology* and member of the Executive Board of the International Network for Economic Method. His recent publications include being an editor of and contributor to *The Handbook of Economic Methodology* (1998), *Economics and Methodology: Crossing Boundaries* (1998), and *Fact and Fiction in Economics* (forthcoming).

The Economic World View

Studies in the Ontology of Economics

Edited by
USKALI MÄKI

CAMBRIDGE
UNIVERSITY PRESS

PUBLISHED BY THE PRESS SYNDICATE OF THE UNIVERSITY OF CAMBRIDGE
The Pitt Building, Trumpington Street, Cambridge, United Kingdom

CAMBRIDGE UNIVERSITY PRESS
The Edinburgh Building, Cambridge CB2 2RU, UK
40 West 20th Street, New York, NY 10011–4211, USA
10 Stamford Road, Oakleigh, Melbourne 3166, Australia
Ruiz de Alarcón 13, 28014 Madrid, Spain
Dock House, The Waterfront, Cape Town 8001, South Africa
http://www.cambridge.org

© This collection Cambridge University Press 2001

First published 2001

Printed in the United Kingdom at the University Press, Cambridge

Typeset in 10/12pt Times   System 3b2   [CE]

A catalogue record for this book is available from the British Library

Library of Congress Cataloguing in Publication data

The economic world view: studies in the ontology of economics / edited by Uskali Mäki.
    p.   cm.
   Includes bibliographical references and index.
   ISBN 0 521 801761 – ISBN 0 521 00020 3 (pb)
   1. Economics – Philosophy. 2. Economics – Methodology. 3. Economic man. 4. Macroeconomics. 5. Microeconomics. I. Mäki, Uskali.

HB72.E2664 2001
330.1 – dc21   00–045499

ISBN 0 521 80176 1 hardback
ISBN 0 521 00020 3 paperback

For KEKLU

Contents

Contributors

Fred Bennett was, until his recent retirement, Director of Financial Analysis for Industry Canada. He is now completing a doctorate in philosophy at the University of Ottawa, and has published articles in the area of political philosophy.

Nancy Cartwright is Professor in the History and Philosophy of Science at the London School of Economics (since 1991), as well as Professor of Philosophy at the University of California at San Diego (since 1998). She is the director of the Centre for the Philosophy of the Natural and Social Sciences at the LSE and Fellow of the British Academy. Her research interests include history and philosophy of physics and economics, causal inference, and objectivity in science. Cartwright's publications include *Nature's Capacities and Their Measurement* (1989), *How the Laws of Physics Lie* (1983), and *The Dappled World: A Study of the Boundaries of Science* (Cambridge University Press, 1999). She co-authored the book *Otto Neurath: Philosophy between Science and Politics* together with J. Cat, L. Fleck, and T. Uebel (Cambridge University Press, 1995). Research projects in which she is currently involved include 'Measurement in Physics and Economics'.

John B. Davis, Professor of Economics and International Business, teaches International Trade and International Economics at Marquette University. He is the author of *Keynes's Philosophical Development* (Cambridge University Press, 1994), editor of *New Economics and Its History* (1998), and co-editor of *The Handbook of Economic Methodology* (1998). Among the journals he has published in are *Cambridge Journal of Economics, Economic Journal, Review of Political Economy, History of Political Economy, Economics and Philosophy, The European Journal of the History of Economic Thought*, and *Journal of Economic Methodology*. He has been a visiting scholar at Cambridge University and Duke University. He is President-Elect of the History of Economics Society, and has been the editor of the *Review of Social Economy* since 1987. Currently he is working on a book to be published by Routledge on theories of the individual in economics.

John Dupré, formerly Professor of Philosophy at Stanford University, is currently Professor of Philosophy at Birkbeck College, University of London, and Senior Research Fellow at the University of Exeter. He works on the philosophy of science, with special interests in the philosophy of biology and of economics. He is the author of *The Disorder of Things: Metaphysical Foundations of the Disunity of Science* (1993) and the editor of *The Latest on the Best: Essays on Evolution and Optimality* (1987).

Russell Hardin, professor and former chair of politics at New York University, is the author of *Liberalism, Constitutionalism, and Democracy* (1999), *One for All* (1995), *Morality within the Limits of Reason* (1988), and *Collective Action* (1982). He was for many years the editor of *Ethics*. He is currently at work on a book on problems of the rationality and epistemology of ordinary mortals.

Shaun P. Hargreaves Heap teaches at the University of East Anglia. He has also taught at Concordia University in Montreal and the Sydney University. His research is in macroeconomics and in philosophy and economics. His publications include *Rationality in Economics* (1989), *The New Keynesian Macroeconomics* (1992) and *Game Theory: A Critical Introduction* (with Y. Varoufakis, 1995) and articles in the *Economic Journal*, the *Journal of Post-Keynesian Economics* and *Kyklos*. His current research is on the economics of the media.

Daniel M. Hausman is Professor of Philosophy at the University of Wisconsin, Madison. His work has focused on the philosophy of economics and the problem of causation. In addition to numerous journal articles he has published *Capital, Profits and Prices: An Essay in the Philosophy of Economics* (1981), *The Inexact and Separate Science of Economics* (Cambridge University Press, 1992), *Essays on Philosophy and Economic Methodology* (Cambridge University Press, 1992), *Economic Analysis and Moral Philosophy* (Cambridge University Press 1996; with Michael S. McPherson), *Causal Asymmetries* (Cambridge University Press, 1998), *The Philosophy of Economics: An Anthology* (editor) (Cambridge University Press, 1984; 2nd ed. 1994) and *Economic Methodology: Crossing Disciplinary Boundaries* (edited with R. Backhouse, U. Mäki, and A. Salanti) (1998). He is the former co-editor of the journal *Economics and Philosophy*.

Kevin Hoover is Professor of Economics at the University of California, Davis. He is Chairman of the International Network for Economic

Method and an editor of the *Journal of Economic Methodology*. He is the author of numerous articles on topics in monetary economics, macroeconomics, and economic methodology in journals such as *American Economic Review* and the *Journal of Economic Literature*. He is the author of *The New Macroeconomics* (Blackwell), and *Causality in Macroeconomics* (Cambridge University Press).

Harold Kincaid is Professor of Philosophy at the University of Alabama at Birmingham. He received his Ph.D in 1983 from Indiana University. He is the author of *Philosophical Foundations of the Social Sciences* (Cambridge University Press, 1996), *Individualism and the Unity of Science* (1997), and numerous articles on topics in the philosophy of the social sciences.

Uskali Mäki is Professor of the philosophy of science and of economics in particular at Erasmus University, Rotterdam. His research interests cover topics in the philosophy of economics, such as realism, idealization, explanation, rhetoric, the sociology and economics of economics, and foundations of New Institutional and Austrian economics. He has published in journals such as the *Journal of Economic Literature*, *Philosophy of the Social Sciences*, *Studies in the History and Philosophy of Science*, *Economics and Philosophy*, *Cambridge Journal of Economics*, *Perspectives on Science*. He is a co-editor of the *Journal of Economic Methodology* and of *The Handbook of Economic Methodology* (1998), *Economics and Methodology: Crossing Boundaries* (1998), and *Rationality, Institutions and Economic Methodology* (1993).

Scott Meikle is Reader in Philosophy at the University of Glasgow. He is the author of *Aristotle's Economic Thought* (1995) and *Essentialism in the Thought of Karl Marx* (1985), and is currently preparing a book on Marx's relationship to the Anglo-Scottish Enlightenment and the Aristotelian tradition in European philosophy.

Alan Nelson is Professor and Chair of the Department of Philosophy at the University of California, Irvine. He has also taught at UCLA, Pittsburgh, and Stanford, and has been a Fellow of the Zentrum für Interdisziplinäre Forschung in Bielefeld. He has published widely in the philosophy of science with special attention to the philosophy of economics and to seventeenth-century science.

John O'Neill is currently Professor of Philosophy at Lancaster University. He has written widely on the philosophy of economics, ethics, political philosophy and the philosophy of science. His publications include *The Market: Ethics, Information and Politics* (1998) and *Ecology, Policy and Politics: Human Well-Being and the Natural World* (1993).

Philip Pettit is Professor of Social and Political Theory at the Research
School of Social Sciences, ANU and also holds a regular Visiting
Professorship in Philosophy, Columbia University, New York. He is
the author of several books including, most recently, *The Common
Mind: Essays in Psychology, Society and Politics* (1993, 1996) and
Republicanism: A Theory of Freedom and Government (1997, 1999). He
is also the author of a large number of articles, including pieces in
*Mind, Philosophical Review, Journal of Philosophy, Ethics, Philosophy
and Public Affairs, Economics and Philosophy* and other major journals. Born in Ireland, he taught at universities there and in Britain
before moving to Australia in 1983.

Alexander Rosenberg is Professor of Philosophy and Director of the
Honors Program at the University of Georgia, Athens. His academic
speciality is the philosophy of science, especially the philosophy of
biology and of social and behavioural sciences. In addition to
numerous journal articles, he has published several books, including
Instrumental Biology or the Disunity of Science (1994), *Economics:
Mathematical Politics or Science of Diminishing Returns?* (1992),
Philosophy of Social Science (1988, 1995 enlarged edition), *The
Structure of Biological Science* (Cambridge University Press, 1985),
Hume and the Problem of Causation (1981), and *Microeconomic Laws*
(1976). He has taught at Syracuse University, the University of
California, Riverside, and has been a visiting professor at the
University of Minnesota and the University of California, Santa
Cruz. In 1994–5, he was a visiting lecturer in philosophy at Oxford
University.

Don Ross is Professor of Economics at the University of Cape Town, and
Convenor of UCT's Programme in Philosophy, Politics and Economics. He is the author of over twenty articles, mainly on the
philosophical foundations of economics, of game theory and of
cognitive science, and has published three books. The most recent of
these is *What People Want: The Concept of Utility from Bentham to
Game Theory*. He is currently writing a book on equilibrium explanation in history.

Jochen Runde is Lecturer in Economics at the Judge Institute of Management Studies and Fellow of Girton College, Cambridge. Most of his
previous research has been in the methodology of economics, focusing
particularly on probability, uncertainty and decision theory, causality
and causal explanation, idealization and abstraction, and rational
choice theory. He is currently working on aspects of Austrian
Economics and the Information Theoretic Approach to Economics,
competing conceptions of social structure, tacit knowledge, credit-risk

assessment in the UK banking industry, and case studies of the development of large multinational corporations.

Esther-Mirjam Sent is Assistant Professor in the Department of Economics and Faculty Fellow in the Reilly Center for Science, Technology, and Values at the University of Notre Dame. She has published articles in the *Cambridge Journal of Economics, Journal of Economic Methodology, History of Political Economy, Journal of Economic Behavior and Organization*, and *Philosophy of Science*, among other journals. Her book *The Evolving Rationality of Rational Expectations: An Assessment of Thomas Sargent's Achievements* (Cambridge University Press, 1998) was awarded the 1999 Gunnar Myrdal Prize of the European Association for Evolutionary Political Economy. She has recently started a research project on Herbert Simon.

Jack J. Vromen is currently Assistant Professor of Philosophy of Economics and member of EIPE (Erasmus Institute for Philosophy and Economics) at Erasmus University, Rotterdam. His main research interests are related to evolutionary and institutional economics. In addition to articles on these topics, he has published a book *Economic Evolution: An Enquiry into the Foundations of New Institutional Economics* (1995) which was awarded the 1995 Gunnar Myrdal Prize of the European Association for Evolutionary Political Economy.

Preface

What is the world made of? How does the world work? Is it governed by causes? What is the nature of causality? Are some states of the world necessary and some others impossible? Do universals exist? Do minds exist? Do human beings have a free will? Are there social wholes irreducible to their parts? These are examples of questions that philosophers and scientists keep asking and answering, and have kept asking and answering for centuries. They are concerned with the most fundamental components in our general world views. Some of the time, these questions and answers have been explicit, while much of the time they are implicit. Such questions and answers, at various levels of specificity, are ever-present also in economics: they are presupposed and they are implied in the acts of economic reasoning, both theoretical and empirical. The purpose of this book is to help start making them explicit. To make such elements of economic reasoning explicit is to examine the ontology of economics. It is to study the basic world views of economics.

The economic world view suggests an intellectual challenge from two perspectives. It tends to be part of our everyday experience that economic considerations (those related to money and the market, cost and benefit calculations, etc.) have been growing in importance in our social lives. The academic world has also been witnessing, not only the growing importance of economic constraints on academic life, but also the growing importance of economics as a discipline, both as a resource for studying social phenomena and as a target of study itself. In both cases, questions arise as to what exactly it is that is growing in importance. What exactly is the economic realm made of?

I believe the study of economic ontology is a prerequisite for understanding economics as a scientific discipline. It is thus intended and hoped that this volume will help define a field of study – the ontology of economics, or economic ontology – so as to give it a relatively distinct identity with a set of paradigmatic issues and ways of pursuing insights into them; to help turn it into a collectively coordinated and cumulative endeavour. Economic ontology is a field to which both economists and philosophers of economics and other social sciences can and should contribute. The parallel recent development in general social theory proceeds under the heading of 'social ontology'; it is a project in which social scientists and philosophers of society participate. It is hoped that, in the context of economics and its philosophy, *The Economic World View* will inspire more systematic efforts of the same sort in the future.

When Barry Smith, editor of the prestigious philosophy journal *The Monist*, a few years ago asked me to guest edit a special issue and to propose a topic, I did not hesitate long: it had to be on the ontological foundations of economics. It seemed to me that there was a gap in the otherwise rapidly growing literature on economic methodology and the philosophy of economics: a systematic and collectively coordinated project on economic ontology was missing. Scattered remarks and contributions had been appearing here and there, but no self-consciously collective and coordinated effort existed. I suggested the title, 'The Metaphysics of Economics' and started working. I worked quite hard, and the harvest was good. Eight first-rate papers were published. Those eight papers, four of them rewritten, are included in the present volume.

It was clear that *The Monist* project had to be followed up. Editing a larger volume of contributions was an obvious idea. I spread the message, and once again the harvest was good. Several people proposed contributions and started writing. I gave comments on the drafts that were submitted, and many of the contributors generously served as anonymous referees on other contributors' papers. In such respects it was a genuinely collective endeavour. Under the pressure of the procedure, another ten papers survived, several of them having gone through many rounds of revision.

There are several people whose help and support I want to acknowledge. Barry Smith's invitation played a crucial role. Patrick McCartan at Cambridge University Press was very encouraging from the beginning, while Chris Harrison's role was invaluable at the end. Many of the contributors have been extremely helpful in reviewing each other's papers; also, several others acted as referees, assessing the submissions to *The Monist*. At the final stages of the project, the assistance of Frank Hindriks and Judith de Putter has been indispensable. Many thanks to them all. This project has been supported by the Foundation 'Vereniging Trustfonds Erasmus Universiteit Rotterdam' in the Netherlands and the Academy of Finland research project 'Economics as a Target and Tool of Science Studies'.

Uskali Mäki, Rotterdam, May 2000

Part I

The what, why, and how of ecomonic ontology

1 Economic ontology: what? why? how?

USKALI MÄKI

So you're an economist? You study everything that can be gauged by the measuring rod of money? You view human interaction in terms of supply and demand in the market? You depict human action as seeking self-interest in a calculative manner? Is this indeed your view of the world? If you are an economist and somebody has attempted, or might attempt, to embarrass you with such questions, you should read this book. If you are a non-economist inclined to raise such questions, you too should study the essays collected in this volume. If you are a philosopher interested in the peculiar characteristics of the 'dismal science', this is a book to read. The book examines aspects of the economic world view from a variety of perspectives by raising shamelessly deep questions. This is a book in the ontology of economics.

1 What?

What is the economy made of? What are its constituents and how do they hang together? What kind of general principles govern its functioning, and its change? Are they causal principles and, if so, what is the nature of economic causation? What drives economic actors, and what mental capacities do they possess? What is utility, or well-being? What is uncertainty, or risk? Do aggregates exist? Do individual preferences and social institutions exist, and in what sense? Are (any of) these things historically and culturally invariant universals, or are they relative to context? These are some questions about the economy. The answers that an economist will provide in response to such questions will include concepts such as scarcity, rationality, preference, well-being, expectation, choice, information, probability, strategy, convention, contract, wealth, division of labour, market, exchange, money, equilibrium, coordination, mechanism, and so on. These answers are seldom sufficiently detailed and refined to give us a precise idea of what exactly is presupposed about the world in posing and answering the questions. The ontology of economics takes as its task to offer detailed analyses and refinements of such basic concepts.

The study of economic ontology is concerned with what may be called 'the economic realm': the economic realm consists of those parts or aspects of the universe which are set apart as constituting the subject matter of economics. We may think of the economic realm as being distinguished from other realms (the physical realm, the biotic realm, the realm of aesthetics) by virtue of being composed of certain types of entities or properties – such as 'that part of individual and social action which is most closely connected with the attainment and with the use of the material requisites of wellbeing' (Marshall 1920, p. 1) or 'human behaviour as a relationship between ends and scarce means which have alternative uses' (Robbins 1935, p. 16). This suggests that the economic realm has definite boundaries which separate it from other realms. On the other hand, the history of the discipline suggests that such boundaries are not completely sharp and fixed and that there are rival and evolving perceptions of how to draw them. The contents and confines of the economic realm are 'essentially contestable' as a popular phrase has it, and they change along with the rest of the discipline of economics (see Kirzner 1976). The question then arises whether the varying circumscriptions of the economic realm are endeavours to discover something about the objective constitution of the world, or whether they are subjective impositions of structure on the social world.

The economic realm is connected to other realms in various ways. The possibility of the existence of the economic realm presupposes the existence of the physical, the biotic, and the psychic realms. How exactly this dependence is to be characterized is itself an ontological issue; is it a matter of reduction, or supervenience, or is some sort of emergence involved? The functioning of the economic realm is shaped by the realms of morality and politics. The exact character of this dependence – and the question whether the realms of morality and politics are made of stuff that is different from that of the economic realm – are likewise among some of the major ontological issues related to economics. We may say that the justification of the discipline of economics requires a claim to relative autonomy, but this does not yet give us a precise idea of what such autonomy amounts to.

The contents and confines of the economic realm are suggested by the ontological commitments that economists hold. A set of such commitments has the nature of a *Weltanschauung*, a fundamental world view with a focus on a selection of economically relevant aspects of the world. Joseph Schumpeter (1954) used the word 'vision' to capture very much the same idea. There is a sense in which those commitments have a foundational status: they are more fundamental than other elements in one's belief system in that they are not as easily corrigible and that they are presupposed rather than derived by the reasoning within the belief system. The ontological commitments have the character of *absolute presuppositions* as R. G. Collingwood called them. He viewed them as the ultimate and unquestioned presuppositions in terms of which all the relative suppositions are to be justified (Collingwood 1940). Ludwig Wittgenstein called them *hinges* on which our ordinary thoughts and judgements turn, and the *riverbed* within which our thought flows (Wittgenstein 1969, §§97–9, 341–3). Adopting a metaphor from constitutional economics, we may also view the ontological commitments as providing part of the *constitutional framework* of a belief system. In this spirit, James Buchanan refers to elements of a research programme which are 'rarely, if ever, challenged by those scholars who work inside the intellectual tradition . . . These central elements are taken as presuppositions, as relatively absolute absolutes, and, as such, they become, themselves, the constraints (the constitution) within which the scientific discourse is conducted' (Buchanan 1991, pp. 13–14). Thus there is something basic or fundamental about the ontological presuppositions in our belief systems.

It is in the nature of such a constitutional framework that it determines the boundaries of a discipline or a line of research. Among the ontological or metaphysical core principles of economics, including constitutional economics, Buchanan lists individual autonomy, rationality of choice, and spontaneous market coordination. 'Unless those who would be participants in the scientific dialogue are willing to locate the exercise in the choice calculus of individuals, there can be no departure from the starting gate . . . The principle of spontaneous coordination of the market is *the* principle of our discipline' (Buchanan 1991, pp. 14, 22). Buchanan thus takes such principles as defining the boundaries of a research field or programme. Such ontological principles have social consequences: they effectively help identify the genuine participants in a programme and exclude others as non-participants. 'There is simply no common basis for scientific argument, and ultimately agreement, with those who choose to perceive social interaction either in purely conflictual or purely idealistic visions. These visions are, indeed, alternative "windows" on the world' (p. 18). Legitimate membership in the conversations of the economics profession thus requires that the world is being viewed through shared ontological 'windows'.

Another feature characteristically ascribed to the fundamental commitments is implicitness. The constitutional world view they work with or the ontological windows through which they view the world are articulated by practising economists themselves only seldom and incompletely, if at all; such explicit articulation is characteristically not regarded as one their preoccupations *qua* economists. In contrast, making explicit what tends to be implicit is exactly the preoccupation of this book. Buchanan says that 'the process through which individuals choose among such windows remains mysterious' (p. 18). It is one purpose of this book to start demystifying the process of choosing such ontological windows. It is a prerequisite of this demystification that we understand what those windows are like. One has to start *looking at* the ontological windows instead of merely *looking through* them. This is also acknowledged by Buchanan in his remark about the insiders and outsiders: 'External intellectual challenges to the whole enterprise tend to be directed at these elements in the core of the program. The ongoing research within the constraints can, of course, proceed without concern for these external criticisms, but practitioners need to be aware of the core-imposed limits on the persuasive potential of the internalized analytical exercise' (p. 14). It is a purpose of this volume to help practitioners in economics be 'aware of the core-imposed limits' of what they can successfully do as such practitioners. A more ambitious goal would be to try to help economists to make well-argued constitutional choices, that is, reasoned choices of the constitutional framework within which they do their work, or of the windows through which they view the world – or at least help them to be aware of that larger framework and to design arguments for the constitution they have ended up working with, whether as a matter of choice or perhaps as a matter of some path-dependent academic process. The possibility of constitutional choice implies that ontological constitutions are not fixed, that in principle they can be changed at will. Constitutional change may also – and often does – occur without much reflection; as Wittgenstein puts it, the riverbed within which our thought flows can itself change in response to the flow of thought (Wittgenstein 1969, §97).

In some cases and for some purposes, we had better distinguish between two aspects of the ontology of economics: the ontological convictions of an economist and the ontological presuppositions of an economic theory. Questions about the economic world view can often be transformed into questions about economic theories, taking on the general form, 'What does theory T presuppose concerning P?' For example, 'What exactly does theory T presuppose about the capacities and dispositions of economic agents, or of the market mechanism?' A refined account of the presuppositions of theory T does not necessarily serve as an adequate account of the ontological convictions of an economist using T: deep in her heart, the economist may not fully believe in the world view presupposed by T. This means that the two are contingently related: they may or may not coincide. In cases where they do not coincide, there is a tension between them that may function as a dynamic force driving theory development: the economist may be motivated by an urge to resolve the tension by attempting to modify the theory. Chapter 17 by Esther-Mirjam Sent and chapter 19 by Uskali Mäki contain discussions of the role that the ontological convictions of economists play in their attitudes towards theories. Alex Rosenberg's chapter 10 and Jack Vromen's chapter 11 stress the importance of distinguishing between economic theories and economists' convictions.

The ambition of articulating and making explicit the ontological underworld of economic beliefs tends to run counter to a strong reading of Collingwood's belief that the absolute presuppositions of a belief system are not and cannot be transparent to those whose thoughts are based on them. He believed that it is only with hindsight that we can clearly see what the basic commitments were, in other words that it is only after the period in intellectual history building upon those elements is over that we can make those building blocks fully explicit. I admit that the task of explicating the presuppositions may be easier with hindsight, but it is one of the (explicit) presuppositions of the endeavour exemplified by the present volume itself that the explication of contemporary commitments is not impossible. I should perhaps add that the explication of the presuppositions of theories may be an easier task than the explication of the ontological convictions of economists.

The attempt to understand economics as a scientific discipline requires the examination of its ontology. Such an examination is also legitimate from a more general point of view. Ontology is a branch of philosophy that is once again enjoying a respectable status. It is generally understood as the study of being as being, of the most general characteristics of all things, whether actual, possible, or even impossible, whether physical, mental, or social. The concerns of this book for the most part are not this abstract or global. The focus is on ontological issues that are characteristic of economics, whether or not they are shared by other disciplines and other realms. This is a book devoted to studies in local or regional ontology. Yet, it is obvious that ontological categories of various levels of generality are relevant to understanding economics. The articulation of the world view of economics involves various kinds of categories: those which are predominantly and specifically economical; those that are more general in their applicability but not universally applicable; and those that apply to virtually all domains. This division is somewhat artificial as the fact is that there is a continuum of categories rather than sharply distinct sets. Thus we get a continuum of sets of categories in an ascending order of generality, such as the following: money, market, firm, price; preference, belief, rationality, choice, rule, welfare; evolution, aggregate, equilibrium; quality and quantity, probability, essence, causal power, mechanism, existence, objectivity. The contributions to this volume characteristically combine such levels. Kevin Hoover's chapter 12 examines the existence of aggregates; chapter 9 by John O'Neill discusses the essence of markets; Russell Hardin's chapter 4 examines the normative values at the core of rational choice theory; Jochen Runde analyses probability and belief in chapter 8; Scott Meikle's chapter 3 sets out to characterize the economic realm in terms of quality and quantity; and chapter 13 by Don Ross and Fred Bennett argues for the objectivity of both micro and macro economics in terms of real patterns.

A final remark on the sense of 'ontology' relevant to this book is in order. 'Ontology' and 'metaphysics' are often used synonymously, but the relevant concept of ontology is not given by the familiar pejorative usages of 'metaphysics'. This book is about local or special metaphysics of an honourable and prestigious kind, of the kind that has recently enjoyed a resurgence and rehabilitation both in philosophy and in the special sciences. The present book is not about metaphysics in the logical positivists' sense of unverifiable nonsense nor in Karl Popper's sense of unfalsifiable non-science. In economic ontology, the relevant questions are neither, 'Is it meaningful?' nor, 'Is it scientific?' Using the verifiability and falsifiability criteria, most if not all of science would turn out to be meaningless and non-scientific. The relevant questions in economic ontology are, 'What are the underlying presuppositions?' and, 'How do the presuppositions constrain and determine belief?' as well as, 'How does and can one justify or criticize the presuppositions?' There is no absolute break between ontological presuppositions and other claims of science; there is rather a continuum of claims of various degrees of generality and corrigibility.

2 Why?

There are several interrelated reasons for why the study of economic ontology is desirable. One has to do with the boundaries of the discipline of economics and of the economic realm. Another has to do with the grounds of the beliefs that economists hold; their ontological commitments are among these grounds, along with conventional empirical evidence. Yet another has to do with the reliability and appropriateness of the methods economists use; as a general rule, methods should match the nature of the reality they are used to investigate. Let me briefly elaborate on these three reasons.

Consider first the issue of boundaries. Supposing one holds that the economic realm is constituted by categories such as money, the market, and calculative self-interest, or something weaker, such as instrumental rationality, the question arises as to the boundaries of the realm so circumscribed. For example, one may ask, as Shaun Hargreaves Heap does in chapter 6, whether phenomena related to self-worth (or trust, care, and esteem) belong to the economic realm by way of reduction to preferences and self-seeking calculation. Likewise, does the notion of market apply to science, or religion, and to which aspects of them? And what exactly does one presuppose about the ultimate nature of the constituents of certain regions of social life when proposing an economics of politics and marriage, of crime and church-attendance? Are those presuppositions defensible as some economists believe, or not, as many non-economists suspect? How do ontological arguments about the way the world is constituted bear on the ongoing dispute around 'economics imperialism' – the expansionistic tendencies of economics in the social sciences?

The second set of reasons is related to the idea that ontology plays a role in justifying economists' beliefs and the lines of research they pursue. The famous Duhem–Quine thesis suggests that empirical tests are unable to fully determine the merits and demerits of any particular hypothesis or theory so as to reliably discriminate it from its rivals. All theories or theory-choices are underdetermined by evidence: there is slack between theory and empirical evidence. This implies that there must be other determinants to fill in the gap, so to speak. Various social factors have been proposed to serve as such determinants of beliefs or theory choices, such as the pursuit of fame and fortune by scientists, or the social interests of the scientific community. The suggestion here, in no way a novel one, is that ontological commitments are one determinant of theory choice and theory development in science, economics included. The general world views held serve as constraints that any successful theory-candidate has to meet as a minimum condition of acceptability. If economists view the world through metaphysical windows, this suggests that there are limits to the power of conventional empirical testing. Buchanan puts it rather strongly: 'How can empirical evidence be made convincing when such evidence must, itself, be perceived from only one vantage point at a time? The naïveté of modern empirical economists in this respect verges on absurdity' (1991, p. 18). If modern economists are naïve in not recognizing the role of ontological windows and riverbeds in theory choice, the study of economic ontology may help them in growing up. The role of ontology in shaping the fate of theories is addressed in chapters 17 and 19 by Sent and Mäki as well as in Rosenberg's chapter 10.

There is a related thought that is worth exploring. It is a major task of economic ontology to uncover the ontological presuppositions of *economic theories*. The fact that *economists* hold those theories may then be at least partly explained by the fact that they hold exactly those presuppositional commitments. However, as suggested in the previous section, the situation is not always that simple. It may often be the case that the ultimate ontological convictions of an economist and the ontological presuppositions of the theories he holds are not perfectly tuned with one another. In a situation of such a mismatch between the ontologies of an economist and of a theory, one way to rectify ontological harmony in one's beliefs is to treat the theory instrumentalistically. The very fact that economists are attracted by an instrumentalist interpretation of theory may in some cases provide partial evidence for the existence of such a mismatch. According to the intstrumentalist view, a theory is not really to be believed to give us a truthful picture of what the world is like, it is rather to be used as a useful tool for whatever purposes there may be. Thus the study of economic ontology may help explain why economists hold certain views of the nature of economic theory – and perhaps help them drop those views. Philip Pettit's chapter 5 seeks to show how economists might try to avoid an instrumentalist view of the notion of *homo economicus*.

The third reason for examining economic ontology is that theories and methods need justification and that one way of attempting to justify them is to argue that they somehow conform to the structure of the world. The issue around a given method can often be phrased as one concerning its appropriateness for addressing certain parts or aspects of reality. Social scientists inspired by hermeneutics argue that quantitative, formal, and causal modelling is not appropriate for studying the human realm; some method of understanding the meaningfulness of human behaviour is required to accommodate the specific nature of the human realm. A weaker line of reasoning would be to admit that there are causes out there and social phenomena are causally determined, but that the method adopted by economists from mechanics, namely that of the decomposition and composition of causes, employing idealizing assumptions and their relaxations, is not appropriate in social sciences. This is because the interactions between the causes are significant enough to undermine the model of vector addition which underlies the method. This is a venerable issue which is often discussed in terms of metaphors such as those of mechanism, machine, and organism. Such metaphors can be expressions of major ontological convictions, or, more weakly, signals of entertaining a way of looking at the social world. Chapters 14, 15, 16, and 18 by Nancy Cartwright, Daniel Hausman, John Dupré, and Alan Nelson address these fundamental issues.

3 How?

One can pursue economic ontology in a variety of ways. They differ from one another in regard to the aims pursued, the theoretical resources employed, and the relationships envisaged between the substance of economics and general ontological doctrines. chapter 2 by Harold Kincaid deals with some of these issues.

Economic ontology may be practised as an exercise in direct description of what is believed to be the fundamental nature of the economy, or it may be viewed as an exercise in describing or prescribing the ontological presuppositions underlying theoretical accounts of economic phenomena or the ontological convictions held by economists. In the first guise, it is an attempt to directly represent economic realities, while in the second mode, it is directly about economics and only indirectly about the economy.

Another distinction is that between descriptive and revisionary ontology (Strawson 1959). We may pursue a description of the ontological categories and presuppositions that we, or some others, work with. Given that much of the ontological underworld in our belief systems is implicit and hidden, the task of articulating it in explicit and systematic form may not be easy. Descriptive ontology in this sense is a challenging project. Revisionary ontology, on the other hand, is an attempt to change, rather than just describe, the prevailing ontological categories and presuppositions of a belief system: it is a matter of constitutional revision. Examples of the latter include John Dupré's criticism of the ontology of mechanism in chapter 16; the suggestions to revise the ontology of economic agency in chapter 7 by John Davis; and Philip Pettit's re-articulation of the self-seeking economic man in terms of virtual reality in chapter 5.

Most of the contributions to the present volume belong to descriptive rather than revisionary ontology. It is to be noted that these two endeavours do not exclude one another. In particular, if one wants to do revisionary ontology, say, in order to replace the prevailing ontological windows of certain branches of economics, one had better have accomplished an analysis in descriptive ontology so as to be in possession of an adequate account of the categories and presuppositions that underlie those parts of economics. Some critical writing on economics that has such a revisionary character is clearly not based on an adequate descriptive ontology. It is difficult to do good descriptive ontology. It is more difficult to do good revisionary ontology, based as it should be on sound descriptive ontology.

These perspectives are connected with others, such as those of *a priori* and *a posteriori* approaches to economic ontology. One can do economic ontology in an *a priori* fashion by starting from some general philosophical ontology, then try to apply it to parts of economics in pursuit of description. If the fit is poor, one may then switch to a revisionary gear and propose that the ontological presuppositions of economics had better be changed so as to establish a better fit between economics and general ontological doctrine. Economic ontology in this mode may become an exercise in *a priori* imposition. Alternatively, one may proceed by way of empirical case studies in descriptive economic ontology so as to develop, in an *a posteriori* fashion, an accurate account of the actual ontological presuppositions of particular economic theories and the actual ontological commitments of particular economists. By comparing these to one another and to the ontologies of other social sciences and scientists, one may then possibly end up with identifying interesting mismatches and using them to develop arguments of a revisionary kind.

4 The menu

Convinced as we are that we will be well nourished in a good company, we are now asked to sit down to the meal and take a look at the menu. The next two chapters in this starter section deal with the methodology and substance of economic ontology. In chapter 2, Kincaid agreeably argues for a continuity between metaphysical arguments and the substance of economics, while chapter 3 by Meikle reflects on the departure of the world of economics from the ordinary commonsense world.

The first main course will be served in part II, devoted to the concept of the economic actor. Given the individualist leanings of much of economics, the individual actor is a major component amongst the furniture of the economic world. One's vision of the rest of the economy very much depends on the properties attributed to economic actors – and so does one's belief in the reality of such actors. Hardin's chapter 4 examines the normative value of the actor's own welfare involved in rational choice theory and contrasts this with other views. In chapter 5, Pettit suggests a new way of thinking of the reality of *homo economicus* driven by self-regarding desires, given that it runs counter to our commonsense picture of human beings. Hargreaves Heap, in chapter 6, argues that economists should not exclude self-worth and expressive rationality in their representation of economic actors. Chapter 7 by Davis explores the idea of conceiving of economic actors as genuine agents, equipped with causal powers which have magnitude and duration. The final chapter 8 in this section by Runde discusses attributions of belief and concepts of risk and uncertainty in terms of the ontology of probability.

Part III provides dining experiences in areas that lie beyond the sphere of the individual actor, addressing ontological key issues in micro, macro, and evolutionary economics. In chapter 9, O'Neill explains how we can safely talk about the 'essence' of markets – and, one might want to add, of many other things, just as economists do on a daily basis. Rosenberg's chapter 10 seeks to identify the major components in the ontology of micro economics, such as equilibrium, individualism, and the intentional or folk psychological notions of preference and expectation. In chapter 11, Vromen examines the ontological commitments of the Nelson and Winter type evolutionary theory and argues that neoclassical economists such as Alchian and Friedman may share them even if their theories do not fully implement them. Moving on to the realm of macro, in chapter 12 Hoover makes the case that aggregates can be viewed as real once we are careful with the character of aggregates and what their reality consists in. The final chapter 13 of the section by Ross and Bennett suggest that the objectivity of the economic realm can be defended in terms of 'real patterns', using examples from macro and micro economics to make the case.

The chapters of part IV address the deep ontological issues related to economic causation. They continue the long tradition of thinking of society in terms of a mechanics of causes and effects. In chapter 14, Cartwright imagines the economy made of machines equipped with causal powers that run them. In the next chapter, Hausman raises doubts about whether the causes will retain their identity and characteristic tendencies as they act jointly – which would be required for the composition of causes. The final chapter 16 of the section by Dupré questions the suitability of the metaphor of mechanism in economics and argues for a pluralistic ontology for economics.

14   The what, why, and how of economic ontology

The final part V serves the dessert by exhibiting some of the methodo-logical implications of ontological arguments in economics. Sent's chapter 17 examines the ontological desideratum of treating economic agents, economists, and econometricians symmetrically, and traces the difficulties met by Thomas Sargent in establishing this symmetry. In chapter 18 by Nelson, the claim is made that the method of idealization in economics should not be conceived after the model of Newtonian mechanics, since economic systems, unlike mechanical systems, do not satisfy the principle of continuity. The final chapter 19 by Mäki proposes an ontology of theory choice where economists' convictions about the way the world works sometimes function as constraints on what they accept and reject.

References

Buchanan, James (1991) *The Economics and the Ethics of Constitutional Order*, Ann Arbor: University of Michigan Press.
Collingwood, R. G. (1940) *An Essay on Metaphysics*, Oxford: Clarendon Press.
Kirzner, Israel (1976) *The Economic Point of View*, Kansas City: Sheed and Ward.
Marshall, Alfred (1920) *Principles of Economics*, 8th edition, London: Macmillan.
Robbins, Lionel (1935) *An Essay on the Nature and Significance of Economic Science*, 2nd edition, London: Macmillan.
Schumpeter, J. A. (1954) *History of Economic Analysis*, New York: Oxford University Press.
Strawson, Peter (1959) *Individuals. An Essay in Descriptive Metaphysics*, London: Methuen.
Wittgenstein, Ludwig (1969) *On Certainty*, Oxford: Blackwell.

2 The empirical presuppositions of metaphysical explanations in economics

Metaphysical explanations and analyses are common fare among commentators on economics. Philosophers, economists and historians of economic thought often evaluate, criticize, support or explain the practice of economics by invoking very general metaphysical facts. In what follows I raise some skeptical questions about this practice on two interrelated grounds. First and foremost I argue that analyses of economics on allegedly general metaphysical grounds often rest on much more substantive, empirical and contingent matters of fact – on substantive issues in economics itself – than their advocates acknowledge. Second, defending or criticizing economics on general metaphysical grounds tends to ignore the complexity of economic research. Economists employ theories for different purposes in different contexts with different interpretations. Metaphysical diagnoses of success or failure generally must ignore this diversity and instead wrongly treat modern economics as a homogeneous whole. The moral I draw from these two points is not that metaphysical considerations play no role, but that to understand their role we must pay much more attention to empirical, local details of economic explanation.

I support these claims by looking at three cases where economics has been evaluated by appeal to broad metaphysical considerations. Section I below looks at a common argument among philosophers that goes like this: Modern economics is a more or less dismal failure by the standards of the natural sciences. Why is that? Neo-classical theory is essentially committed to certain predicates or kinds. The best explanation for the failure of neo-classical theory is that those essential predicates or kinds do not cut nature at the joints – in short, they are not natural kinds. This

"The Empirical Presuppositions of Metaphysical Explanations in Economics," Harold Kincaid, *The Monist*, vol. 78, no. 3, pp. 368–85. Copyright © 1995, THE MONIST, La Salle, Illinois 61301.

metaphysical argument is quite popular, and my concern shall be with the argument form, not all its specific instantiations.

Section II takes up a related argument, this time one coming from an economist and one more closely tied to fundamental issues in the field. In a very interesting history of the productive-nonproductive distinction in economics, Helen Boss has implicitly endorsed the following argument: Fundamental to any economic theory is a decision about what phenomena to count as economic (or as production *vs.* consumption, etc.). But any such distinction does not cut nature at the joints, for the economic and social world is characterized by "netness" – a thoroughgoing interdependence that makes any such distinctions arbitrary. Thus every economic theory rests essentially on subjective imposition, largely determined by the normative views of the economists. I argue that metaphysical facts such as "netness" by themselves do not warrant Boss's conclusions; at issue, again, are substantive economics questions undecided by general metaphysical facts. Once again the real issues are substantive economic ones.

Finally, Section III turns to a different use of metaphysical principles in economics, namely, to argue *for* the legitimacy and future prospects of the neo-classical tradition. Here my target is appeal to individualist metaphysical principles. A great many economists have taken there to be (1) some obviously true facts about the relations of individuals to social wholes that (2) warrant reductionist approaches to theory construction in economics. I argue that neither is the case. The obvious metaphysical principles about parts and wholes really rest on quite specific and controversial economic assumptions. Moreover, the truth of those assumptions by themselves do not support reductionist programs. Only by the addition of further nontrivial economic assumptions can we get any plausible implications for how economics can or must proceed.

I

A common view among philosophers of economics is that modern economics has failed to meet the standards of the natural sciences. The real puzzle is to explain that fact, particularly given the success with which economics has applied advanced mathematics to its domain. One standard explanation is a metaphysical one: the basic categories of economics do not pick out natural kinds. Hence we hear Rosenberg claiming that "reasons and actions are not natural kinds"; that this claim is an "inference to the best explanation,"[1] an explanation of the fact that

---

[1] Alexander Rosenberg, *Sociobiology and the Preemption of Social Science* (Baltimore: Johns Hopkins University Press, 1980), p. 115.

economic theory has "not been improved, corrected, sharpened, specified, or conditioned . . . None of these things have been done because
they cannot be done."[2] Nelson locates the problem most directly in the
basic notion of a "commodity" – "economics *never* gets it right because
commodity is not a natural kind";[3] he takes a similar conclusion to hold
for other key economic concepts as well. Both Rosenberg and Nelson
believe that at least part of the problem with economic kinds is their lack
of universality. Nelson: "economics is not universal, for we are supposing
that there are societies to which it does not apply in virtue of their not
having any commodities"; hence "economics is not universal and does
not express relations among natural kinds."[4] Rosenberg: the basic
categories of economics refer to "states of members of the species *Homo
sapiens*, states which can only be defined . . . by components of a
spatiotemporally restricted particular individual," something that must
rule out the universality that scientific laws require.[5] Similar conclusions
on broadly similar reasoning are reached by others, like Dupré, who view
natural science quite differently than does Rosenberg. So Dupré claims
that "most of economic theory [is] an unpromising candidate for
epistemologically respectable science" because of its "indeterministic
metaphysical grounding" – in short, because economic categories do not
pick out stable kinds.[6]

Of course, if economics does not pick out natural kinds, we cannot
expect it to do what good science does: provide laws, predict with
precision and predict the unexpected, unify diverse phenomena, and so
on. We thus have an explanation for why economics fails. These
explanations are indeed metaphysical, for they appeal to facts about the
basic structure of reality to explain what economics can and cannot do.

Arguments of the kind sketched above rest on three basic claims:
(1) that there is a fact that needs to be explained, in this case, the "fact"
that neo-classical economics has been a dismal failure, (2) that there are
specific *essential* categories of neo-classical theory, and (3) that the
hypothesis that those categories do not pick out natural kinds is a
better explanation for the alleged fact cited in (1) than any alternative

---

[2] Alexander Rosenberg, *Economics: Mathematical Politics or Science of Diminishing Returns* (Chicago: University of Chicago Press, 1992), p. 149.

[3] Alan Nelson, "Are Economic Kinds Natural Kinds?" in Savage, W., ed., *Scientific Theories* (Minneapolis: University of Minnesota Press, 1990), p. 130.

[4] Cited in n. 3 above, p. 129, p. 130.

[5] Cited in n. 1 above, p. 131.

[6] John Dupré, "Could There Be a Science of Economics?" in French, P., Uehling, T., and Wettstein, H., eds., *Midwest Studies in Philosophy* (Notre Dame, IN: University of Notre Dame Press), vol. XVIII, pp. 374–5.

explanation. There are serious obstacles to establishing these claims, some general and some specific. I shall begin with the former.

Any argument about the success or failure of modern economics or about its essential presuppositions assumes that there is one theory at issue. That assumption, however, seems questionable. As writers such as Kuhn have pointed out, focusing on the theory of a given area overly simplifies scientific practice. For our purposes the most questionable simplification is the assumption that we can identify the essential predicates of a theory. Real science seems to be much messier. Different individuals work with different versions of a theory for different purposes. Details are added and dropped, basic notions are given different readings, and so on. Economics seems to be no exception in this regard. Sometimes these differences come because a shared but very general and abstract formulation of neo-classical theory has to be interpreted to be applied; other times economists work with different fundamental postulates, no matter how broadly construed. So basic predicates like rationality get different readings depending on the application and economist;[7] allegedly fundamental axioms are dropped depending on the context. For example, Hausman's careful attempt to sort out the essential components in neo-classical theory identified profit maximization as central, yet an important body of recent work on the theory of the firm is willing to give that up in favor of maximization by individuals inside the firm.[8] These difficulties in identifying essential predicates multiply when we note that neo-classical theory does not exhaust modern economics. Much applied work, for example, arguably proceeds largely independently of the postulates typical of abstract general equilibrium theory.

We can see how these metamethodological worries come out in practice by pointing out one implicit assumption at work in Rosenberg's argument. Rosenberg argues that belief-desire psychology does not pick out natural kinds and that this explains the failure of modern economics. That diagnosis makes a crucial assumption: that economics is essentially about *individual* behavior. Putting aside the question where macro-economics fits in, for much of neo-classical *microeconomics* the basic or primitive entities – those whose internal structure is left unexplained – are aggregates or social entities such as firms, households, aggregate market demand and so on. The fundamental laws of supply and demand

---

[7] See Kenneth Arrow, "Economic Theory and the Hypothesis of Rationality," in Eatwell, J., Milgate, M., and Newman, P., eds., *The New Palgrave* (New York: W. W. Norton).

[8] See Daniel Hausman, *The Inexact and Separate Science of Economics* (Cambridge: Cambridge University Press, 1992).

arguably make claims about markets as a whole and have in large part been tested by evidence about aggregate quantities. Moreover, at least some of those tests arguably proceed independently of any very strong assumptions about individual behavior.[9] So even if the categories of belief-desire psychology were not natural kinds, that would not by itself explain the alleged failure of economics, at least when it came to the laws of supply and demand as generally interpreted by economists.

If "the" neo-classical theory is a misnomer, then we should have doubts both about steps (1) and (2) above. Any assessment of the neo-classical tradition will have to be piecemeal, looking carefully at case-by-case evidence. Such assessments are impossible without taking sides on substantive issues in economic research, and it is unlikely that this diverse work is a success or failure across the board. Thus there is unlikely to be any general fact to explain or any single factor that explains all.

Even if we were convinced that there was a single entity "modern economics" that was largely a failure and which was committed to a well-defined set of essential categories, I still do not think the metaphysical diagnoses would be reasonable. The evidence for these diagnoses is that they are supposedly the best explanations of the facts at issue. However, the evidence for that claim is thin. There are at least the following problems:

(a) To be the best explanation, a metaphysical diagnosis must rule out or at least show implausible the obvious competing hypotheses explaining the failure of neo-classical economics. There are numerous such competitors – for example, the difficulties of testing with nonexperimental evidence, the lack of incentives in the profession for data gathering, the complexity of the phenomena at issue, the closeness of political and moral values to the issues economists investigate, the role of ideology, the relative scarcity of resources compared to the natural sciences, and so on. These factors and complexes of them have to be ruled out before the metaphysical account wins the day. That of course is a big task, but it is one that cannot be avoided if we want to infer to the best explanation.

(b) Metaphysical explanations of scientific success and failure have their own problems. In particular, we have good evidence from the natural sciences that theories without natural kinds can be successful – can produce accurate predictions, explain new phenomena, open up fruitful domains of inquiry, etc. – for significant periods of time and that theories

---

[9] As I argue in *Philosophical Foundations of the Social Sciences: Analyzing Controversies in Social Research* (Cambridge: Cambridge University Press, 1995), ch. 7.

with natural kinds can similarly fail. Biology and genetics more specifically made enormous strides over a long period of time working with a notion of the gene that ultimately proved not to be a natural kind; much was learned about patterns of inheritance and the mechanism of gene expression despite the fact that there was no single entity corresponding to the notion of "gene" employed. Likewise, theories of continental drift floundered for decades, despite the fact that their basic categories are now counted as picking out natural kinds. These are just a few of the many examples from the history of science apparently showing that successful science does not entail that real kinds have been found and that finding real kinds does not guarantee scientific success.[10]

(c) The notion of natural kinds on which these diagnoses depend is itself troublesome. Both Rosenberg and Nelson see an important tie between natural kinds and one criterion for lawfulness, namely, universality. The idea is that natural kinds ground laws, that laws are separated from accidental generalizations by the universality of the former, and that good science is science that produces laws. These claims are philosophically controversial. Universality in the syntactical sense seems not to matter at all, since any statement referring to particulars can be transformed into one that does not. Important parts of the natural sciences do refer to particulars – geology, evolutionary biology, molecular biology, ecology and the like refer to processes characterizing this planet. Laws, moreover, seem neither sufficient nor necessary for explanation, as an exhaustive philosophical literature argues.[11] No doubt there is some important role for the distinction between laws and accidental generalizations, between kinds and other groupings, and between universal and particular statements. But the moral of the philosophical challenges to these notions seems to be that we cannot evaluate entire areas of research by pointing out that their statements do not have the right form – it takes a much more detailed look at actual empirical work.

Given this plethora of obstacles, it would be rash to conclude that lacking natural kinds is the best explanation for the alleged failure of economics.

Thus every step of the no-natural-kinds diagnosis relies on specific empirical assumptions, ones that are far from necessary and certain. Those assumptions are both economic and historical: they involve taking

---

[10] See Larry Laudan, "A Refutation of Convergent Realism," *Philosophy of Science*, vol. 48 (1981), 218–49.

[11] See Bas van Fraassen, *The Scientific Image* (Oxford: Clarendon Press, 1980), for a survey of the standard objections.

a stand on where and what neo-classical axioms are essential to explanation, on the empirical success of those specific applications, on the role of aggregate *vs.* individual-level variables, on the relative importance of various obstacles to economic theorizing, on the relative scope of neo-classical explanations, and so on. So the claim that economics has no natural kinds turns out to rest crucially on substantive claims within economics itself.

The proper moral to draw, however, is not that these no-natural-kinds diagnoses are a dead end. It is rather that (1) the arguments for them will have to appeal much more directly and convincingly to specific economic considerations and (2) that any successful claim about a lack of natural kinds is likely to be much less broad in scope. Thus while I am skeptical about the claim that "commodity" is no natural kind or that economic predicates do not pick out stable entities, it may well be that less global claims are reasonable explanations for particular failures in economics. In applied work on supply and demand there is the constant worry, for example, about particular commodity groupings – about when and where commodities can be aggregated and treated as a single entity such as "food."[12] There is also the worry that specific empirical findings are confounded by changes in taste, income, etc. These are worries about natural kinds and about stability, but when they are justified, it is on the basis of quite specific empirical considerations. Moreover, we should not expect these debates to be as black and white as the philosophers have pictured them – we should expect them to ask whether specific economic variables are *stable enough* for the purposes at hand, whether some aggregation procedure allows *sufficient integration* given the assumptions of the study in question, and so on. What is stable or a kind for one set of purposes in one context with one set of evidence may not be so in another situation.

II

Philosophers are not, of course, the only ones to offer metaphysical explanations. Economists offer them as well. In this section I want to look at some arguments given by an economic historian tracing out the role of the productive–nonproductive distinction in the history of economic thought. The arguments again allegedly raise doubts about economic natural kinds.

---

[12] For an overview of the issues involved, see Angus Deaton and John Muellbauer, *Economics and Consumer Behavior* (Cambridge: Cambridge University Press, 1980).

The productive–nonproductive distinction has a long, if troublesome, history. In discussing that history up to the present, Helen Boss presents an argument, metaphysical in nature, for a startling conclusion about economics. The conclusion is that "The productive/unproductive distinction turns out to be more than a trivial error," for "the boundary problem must be faced by all";[13] yet "there are as many boundaries as there are sovereign boundary drawers. There can be no 'correct' boundary."[14] So economic theories rest on an ultimate subjective imposition. The apparent upshot is that the distinction between the economic and noneconomic is value laden and with it the enterprise of economics itself.[15]

Boss reaches this conclusion after convincingly pointing out again and again the inconsistencies and arbitrariness of specific uses of the productive–nonproductive distinction throughout the history of economic thought. However, she is ultimately after bigger game and not content to point out specific problems with specific economic theories. There is, Boss implies, a larger moral. Attempts to draw the productive–nonproductive distinction are doomed to fail, because they commit the "input–output fallacy": they treat certain activities as essential to a productive process and yet deny that those activities are productive themselves. However, according to Boss, the economic and social world exhibits "netness," a thoroughgoing interdependence. Attempts to separate consumption and production, market and nonmarket, rent seeking and profit seeking, and more generally the economic and noneconomic in any sharp way fail time and time again, because they require a dichotomous distinction between what is continuous and interdependent.

Obviously Boss's argument has much in common with the arguments of the previous section. Both raise doubts about the scientific qualifications of economics on the grounds that it does not pick out natural kinds. Similar reasoning is advanced by the many who describe economic disputes as paradigm disputes in which order is ultimately imposed on the economic world, not found.[16] Whether they rest on philosophical premises about intentionality or claims about interdependence in the social world, all these arguments are of a piece in that they doubt the

---

[13] Helen Boss, *Theories of Surplus and Transfer: Pirates and Producers in Economic Thought* (Boston, MA: Unwin Hyman, 1990), p. 5.

[14] Ibid., p. 277.

[15] I qualify my interpretation here because Boss herself is not entirely clear on how far she wants to push this claim, on exactly what value ladenness involves, on exactly what her points say about the prospect of science in economics and so on.

[16] See, for example, Richard Wolff and Stephen Resnick, *Economics: Marxian versus Neo-Classical* (Baltimore, MD: Johns Hopkins University Press, 1987).

prospects of economic science because of some alleged very general facts about the nature of social reality. Economics rests on a dubious metaphysics.

Boss raises complex and difficult issues, ones that I cannot fully sort out here. However, something less than complete clarity will suffice to show that Boss's pessimistic conclusion is not inevitable and that the real issues depend upon substantive empirical questions of social research, not on the broad considerations about economic kinds she cites. Boss's basic argument is that the social world is an interdependent world, so that imposing any distinction between the economic and noneconomic or between production and consumption is arbitrary and ultimately reflects a theorist's value judgements. The premise of this argument is questionable, and the inference drawn from it does not follow.

To evaluate Boss's claims we must first get clearer on what netness involves. Some distinctions will help. Economic and noneconomic processes might be either *causally* or, for lack of a better word, *existentially* dependent. Causal dependence is a relatively clear notion, at least to the extent that causality itself is. One entity, event, kind, etc. is causally dependent upon another just in case its properties are in part causally produced by the latter. "Existential" dependence is a noncausal relation. The left sides of objects, for example, cannot exist without the right sides and are thus mutually dependent. Biological processes depend on chemical processes, but the relation is apparently not one of causation, for the processes do not involve two separate entities. Both kinds of dependence can be categorized according to whether they are *weak* or *strong*: strong dependence is a matter of necessity, weak dependence a contingent rather than inevitable fact. Furthermore, causal dependence varies along several dimensions. The causal factors involved may be *additive* or *nonadditive* causes. Additive causes are ones where the joint effect of economic and noneconomic causes are a simple function of their separate effects. Noneconomic causes can also be *minor* or *integral*. In the former case the economic causes produce most of the effects in question; in the latter they do not. Obviously netness can take on different forms depending which of these various categories are involved.

The idea of netness, construed causally, entails Boss's conclusions only with the help of further assumptions that are controversial and that involve taking a stand on fundamental empirical matters. If all social phenomena are amenable to economic explanation, then netness does not raise problems for drawing a line between the economic and the social, for the social is economic. Of course, the idea that the economic approach – as exemplified in rational-choice explanations – can be applied to all sorts of human behavior is one with many adherents. This economic imperialism may ultimately be shown to be a dead end. But if it is, it will be on empirical grounds. There is no metaphysical inevitability here.

Let us assume that the above empirical question was settled against the economic imperialists. Nonetheless, netness alone does not entail that any distinction between the economic and noneconomic is arbitrary, on either the causal or existential interpretation of netness. The reason is that neither causal nor existential dependence entails *explanatory* dependence. To see how this can be, consider first the case where every economic process is causally dependent on noneconomic processes. If those noneconomic causes are minor and/or additive, we can legitimately leave them out of our economic explanations. We can do so because we can either ignore their effects because they are sufficiently small or because we can subtract them. Natural science is predicated on such practices, and even though ultimately all physical bodies are interconnected by gravity, no one claims that this netness entails that geology or biology, for example, is based on arbitrary divisions.

Of course, noneconomic causes might be neither minor nor additive. Yet again there are substantive questions of economic theory at issue here, questions that cannot be settled simply by pointing out that the social and the economic are interconnected. In explaining the distribution of income, for example, we can at least in principle make a distinction between economic factors like investment in human capital and noneconomic factors like discrimination. Innumerable studies try to subtract the effects of the latter from the former; there are *prima facie* plausible reasons for thinking that in a competitive market the influence of discrimination will be driven to a minimum. So causal netness gets us to Boss's subjectivist conclusion only by ruling out these possibilities. Again substantive economic presuppositions are at work.

In this connection we should note that the "input-out fallacy" is no *fallacy* at all. Boss's claim is that if a factor is a necessary input to a productive process, then it must itself be considered productive of economic value. No doubt many or most attempts to draw the productive–nonproductive distinction were badly motivated. But the failure was not one of logic. The gravitational attraction of the Earth is a necessary precondition for most economic processes, but treating it as non-economic, nonproductive causal influence is of course eminently reasonable. One such counterexample is all it takes to show that excluding necessary factors is no error in *reasoning*. It takes specific and nontrivial economic arguments to determine which factors influencing the production process can be legitimately ignored.

What about existential netness? Does it fare any better in establishing the arbitrariness of the economic–noneconomic distinction? Apparently it does not, for such dependence arguably holds between all the special sciences and physics. Biological processes, for example, depend upon physical processes. If we followed Boss's reasoning, we would be led to the conclusion that biological categories were arbitrary impositions. Of course we should not swallow that conclusion but rather reject the reasoning that led to it. Explanation is always *qua* description, and we can thus explain one process in multiple and separate ways under different descriptions. To take Boss's examples, one thing, a highway, or one activity, work, may be both productive and nonproductive (consumption) at the same time. Highways contribute to lower transportation costs for corporations and are at the same time consumed by happy campers on vacation. Work is not just toil and trouble but can also be fun, a commodity to be consumed. However, there is no inconsistency or arbitrariness in making such distinctions here, for we might well have good grounds for believing that *qua* its contribution to productive economic output the highway or work is productive and *qua* its contribution to preference satisfaction it is not. Of course there are practical obstacles to drawing these distinctions. Yet we have no *a priori* reason to think any attempt to make these distinctions is doomed.

Behind Boss's general argument there perhaps lies another argument that is also worth dispelling, for doing so will add more grist to my mill. The argument is this:

Specifying any particular economic theory involves a decision about its domain of application. Different economic theories pick out different domains, and often there are equally good reasons for these commitments. Thus the sphere of the economic rests on a fundamental and arbitrary imposition of economic categories onto reality.

I see this argument in the background of Boss's discussion, because she ultimately argues that the productive–nonproductive distinction is closely tied to issues about where to draw the line between the economic and noneconomic. She argues that every economic theory involves commitments about the latter, and yet that this line can be drawn in many different ways, making this fundamental decision about domain a subjective imposition. This version of Boss's argument is akin to the arguments of the last section, for it too traces the difficulties of economic science back to a lack of objective natural kinds.

A look at the natural sciences shows fairly convincingly that this argument must be flawed. A first hint that something is wrong comes from the fact that there are cases in the natural sciences where important categories can be applied in divergent incompatible ways. The concept of a "species," for example, plays an important role in biology and yet is rendered differently by evolutionary biologists, ecologists, and paleontologists. Arguably this situation results not because two of these groups are confused, but because the complex set of facts about individual organisms can be divided up in multiple ways depending on the explanatory interests involved.[17] This does not mean that biology is inherently value laden but only that complex causal systems can be individuated in various ways. That openness does not entail that these individuations are inherently subjective, for not just any grouping counts as a species and there are definite and motivated criteria for the specific species concepts which biologists use.

A more fundamental objection to this argument is that decisions about domains can be rationally motivated and need not be value laden impositions. Any sophisticated look at the history of the natural sciences will surely show that the object of explanation for most disciplines has altered in sometimes subtle and sometimes drastic ways. That does not make natural science categories inherently arbitrary, for domain change and redescription can be motivated by a piecemeal process that is rationally warranted at each step.[18] So the mere fact that every economic theory must define its domain does not of itself entail that the economic–noneconomic distinction is arbitrary and value laden.

Of course, what is not inevitable in theory may be common in practice. Boss does a terrific job of exposing many such specific miscues – cases where economists distinguish the productive and nonproductive or the economic and noneconomic on arbitrary, inconsistent, or otherwise weakly warranted grounds. Here, however, her arguments are really economic; they argue from within, rather than from without, and on substantive economic grounds rather than on some very general quasi-metaphysical facts about the nature of the social or economic realm.

Once again, what looked like a metaphysical explanation depends for its success – if and when it is successful – on concrete questions of economic theory and investigation. It is not the very general metaphysical facts that are doing the work.

III

I want to finish my argument by looking at methodological individualism. Methodological individualism is often expressed and/or motivated by appeal to very general ontological principles, principles that seem

[17] See Philip Kitcher, "Species," *Philosophy of Science*, vol. 51 (1984), 308–33.
[18] For a discussion of how this goes, see Dudley Shapere, *Reason and the Search for Knowledge* (Dordrecht, Holland: D. Reidel, 1984).

undeniable. In what follows I try to show that those principles are not undeniable but rest on quite specific and contestable economic assumptions and that those principles support individualist methodology only with the help of other substantive economic assumptions. Moreover, much modern economics, even that with pristine neo-classical credentials, does not exemplify individualism at all. Once again metaphysical diagnoses tend to mistakenly treat modern economics as a homogeneous whole.

Individualism has seemed so powerful a doctrine because it seems supported by two "metaphysical commonplaces": that society is composed solely of individuals and does not act independently of them.[19] These metaphysical principles are generally thought to be undeniable *and* to have important methodological implications – for example, that any macrolevel theory is reducible in principle to individualist accounts. These two metaphysical commonplaces certainly seem reasonable at first glance. We can formulate them more precisely by borrowing work from the philosophy of mind where physicalists claim that the physical exhausts what there is – every entity is either an entity described by physics or some sum thereof – and that the mental supervenes on the physical – in other words, once the physical facts are set, so too are the mental facts. Transferred to the case of economics or the social sciences more generally, the individualist metaphysical commonplaces are that individuals exhaust the economic world and that once all the facts about individuals are set, then so too are all other aggregate economic facts.

These metaphysical principles are not as trivial as they look. In fact, they are open to multiple readings, and which reading is correct, if any, is a matter of substantive economics, not grand metaphysics. As stated, the exhaustion principle is arguably false for the obvious reason that a society, an economy, or economic entity such as a corporation is populated by more than individuals – it includes material goods. However, once we recognize that fact, much larger controversies lurk. If these material goods are means of production, how are they to be described? In physical-technological terms? As a particular quantity of capital? As so many hours of embodied labor? How we answer the question is of course taking sides on some fundamental economic issues, namely, whether capital can coherently be considered a factor of production, etc. Thus the apparently obvious principle that society is made up of individuals turns out to raise deep and controversial economic issues.

---

[19] As asserted, for example, by J. N. Watkins, "Methodological Individualism: A Reply," in O'Neill, J., ed., *Modes of Individualism and Collectivism* (London: Heinemann, 1973).

The supervenience principle is in the same boat. Here we have to ask what exactly is the supervenience base – on just what facts about individuals do the macroeconomic facts depend? Answering that question is again taking a position on important substantive economic issues. Consider, for example, the overall pattern of income distribution, an aggregate relationship. On what facts about individuals does that aggregate relation supervene? In other words, which individual variables suffice to determine the aggregate relationship? Are human capital variables sufficient? Or are factors such as race, sex, sector, and other more social variables involved? Clearly there are fundamental issues in economic theory involved here. Moreover, there is nothing special about this particular example. When, for example, we ask what microeconomic facts determine the macroeconomic facts we have to take a stance on the role of expectations and their nature. So the commonplace metaphysical truth of supervenience is no truism. It can be spelled out in different ways; which version is correct is a controversial economic issue.

Even if the exhaustion and supervenience principles were obvious metaphysical truths, the reductionist claims based upon them would nonetheless require further economic assumptions. The reduction of one theory to another requires a bridge law showing that the descriptions or terms in the theory to be reduced are co-extensional with some term or terms in the more fundamental theory. Moreover, these linkages must be established in a way that allows the more fundamental theory to replace the explanations of theory to be reduced. Exhaustion and supervenience do not *entail* that such conditions will be met. To use a commonsensical example, chairs are surely physical objects and the facts about chairs supervene on the facts about molecules. Yet that does not mean we can define "chair" in physical terms, for there may be indefinitely many physical ways to make a chair. To use a philosopher's term, "chair" is multiply realizable. Even when the requisite one-to-one linkage can be found, it may not suffice for reduction. For example, defining an antibody as "anything with such and such structure and eliciting an immune response" does not suffice to reduce immunology to biochemistry, for it invokes unreduced facts about the immune system. The upshot is that reducibility requires extra assumptions, ones empirical in nature.

In economics those assumptions again involve specific, contingent assumptions about how the economic world works, assumptions that in no way follow from some general metaphysical truth. Consider, for example, what it would take to reduce explanations in terms of corporations to ones about individual behavior. We would need to show that there is some fixed set of ways that individual behavior can bring about corporate behavior and that we could list and explain, at least in principle, all those individual behaviors. It might well be that we will eventually produce such an account. Yet surely that is an open issue, one that depends on contingent and currently unknown facts about the relation between corporate and individual behavior. If we think firms maximize because *economic selection* has forced them to, then we might wonder whether there is any fixed set of individual behaviors that must be involved, for economic selection of corporations might not "care" about individual-level detail, allowing an open-ended number of processes at that level. The current diversity of individual-level mechanisms offered by recent work on the firm might further support that prospect.[20] At any rate, it should be clear that reducibility here rests on much more than exhaustion and supervenience; it rests on quite specific empirical matters to be decided by the course of economic inquiry.

Similar points can be made about reduction elsewhere in economics. Reducing aggregate-level business cycle theory to some less aggregative account assumes more than simply that lower-level facts fix higher-level ones. It also assumes that patterns at the most aggregate level are brought about by some fixed set of less aggregative variables. Whether that holds might well depend on the level of aggregation involved: large-scale macroeconomic processes might result from some fixed set of processes describing the labor market, credit markets, and so on while those processes themselves might result at different times from indefinitely many distributions of individual preferences, endowments, etc. I point out these abstract possibilities for one reason: they again make it clear the metaphysical commonplaces of exhaustion and supervenience will not by themselves suffice to support reduction. It is the subsidiary economic assumptions that decide the issue.

Mention of corporations and aggregate macroeconomic variables leads naturally to the second point I want to make about individualist metaphysics. Commentators inside economics and out identify methodological individualism as a central tenet of modern economics, sometimes even economics from its inception. Yet that claim threatens grossly to oversimplify modern economic practice. Modern economics is not exhausted by neo-classical theory, and much work outside the neo-classical tradition is explicitly anti-individualist. More important, work that does fall into the neo-classical tradition is often not individualist in nature. Microeconomics typically treats the firm and the household as fundamental entities, unexplained in individualist terms. Much supply-and-demand analysis is about aggregate market behavior as is the data testing

---

[20] For some off the possibilities, see Oliver Williamson and Sidney Winter, eds., *The Nature of the Firm* (New York: Oxford University Press, 1991).

it; these results neither derive from nor directly support strictly individualist neo-classical accounts of individual consumer behavior. Talk of *the* metaphysics behind modern economics once again leads us astray. Thus we have yet another reason for the conclusion reached above, namely, that any evaluation of the metaphysical underpinnings of modern or even neo-classical economics will have to be much more attuned to local empirical detail.

So appeals to individualist metaphysics, like the metaphysical arguments of the previous sections, carry little force on their own; if they are compelling, it will be because of other substantive economic facts. Of course, the three examples discussed in this paper are only a small batch of evidence. But they should make us wary of the claim that economics rests on metaphysical "assumptions that are not themselves subject to empirical confirmation."[21] Metaphysical assumptions abound in economics, but they are intimately tied to specific economic issues and must be evaluated accordingly.[22]

References

Arrow, Kenneth (1987) "Economic Theory and the Hypothesis of Rationality," in Eatwell, Milgate, and Newman, *The New Palgrave*, pp. 25–38.
Boss, Helen (1990) *Theories of Surplus and Transfer: Pirates and Producers in Economic Thought*, Boston: Unwin Hyman.
Deaton, Angus and Muellbauer, John (1980) *Economics and Consumer Behavior*, Cambridge: Cambridge University Press.
Dupré, John (1993) "Could There Be a Science of Economics?" in French, Uehling, and Wettstein, *Midwest Studies in Philosophy*, Volume XVIII, pp. 374–5.
  (1993) *The Disorder of Things: Metaphysical Foundations of the Disunity of Science*, Cambridge, MA: Harvard University Press.
Eatwell, J., Milgate, M., and Newman, P., eds. (1987) *The New Palgrave: Utility and Probability*, New York: W. W. Norton.
Fine, Arthur (1986) *The Shaky Game: Einstein, Realism and the Quantum Theory*, Chicago: University of Chicago Press.
French, P., Uehling, T., and Wettstein, H., eds. (1993) *Midwest Studies in Philosophy*, Volume XVIII: *Philosophy of Science*, Notre Dame, IN: University of Notre Dame Press.
Hausman, Daniel (1992) *The Inexact and Separate Science of Economics*, Cambridge: Cambridge University Press.

[21] John Dupré, *The Disorder of Things: Metaphysical Foundations of the Disunity of Science* (Cambridge, MA: Harvard University Press, 1993).
[22] I would like to thank Uskali Mäki and an anonymous referee for helpful comments on this paper.

Kincaid, Harold (1996) *Philosophical Foundations of the Social Sciences: Analyzing Controversies in Social Research*, Cambridge: Cambridge University Press.

Kitcher, Philip (1984) "Species," *Philosophy of Science*, 51, 308–33.

Laudan, Larry (1981) "A Refutation of Convergent Realism," *Philosophy of Science*, 48, 218–49.

Nelson, Alan (1990) "Are Economic Kinds Natural Kinds?" in Savage, *Scientific Theories*, pp. 102–36.

O'Neill, J., ed. (1973) *Modes of Individualism and Collectivism*, London: Heinemann.

Rosenberg, Alexander (1980) *Sociobiology and the Preemption of Social Science*, Baltimore: Johns Hopkins University Press.

(1992) *Economics: Mathematical Politics or Science of Diminishing Returns*, Chicago: University of Chicago Press.

Savage, Wade, ed. (1990) *Scientific Theories*, Minneapolis, MN: University of Minnesota Press.

Shapere, Dudley (1984) *Reason and the Search for Knowledge*, Dordrecht, Holland: D. Reidel.

van Fraassen, Bas (1980) *The Scientific Image*, Oxford: Clarendon Press.

Watkins, J. N. (1973) "Methodological Individualism: A Reply," in O'Neill, *Modes of Individualism and Collectivism*, pp. 166–78.

Williamson, Oliver and Winter, Sidney, eds. (1991) *The Nature of the Firm*, New York: Oxford University Press.

Wolff, Richard and Resnick, Stephen (1987) *Economics: Marxian versus Neo-Classical*, Baltimore, MD: Johns Hopkins University Press.

3 Quality and quantity in economics: the metaphysical construction of the economic realm

SCOTT MEIKLE

There is a feeling today, more or less vague but nonetheless real, that accountants, economists, and others who deal mainly with money, inhabit a different world from everyone else.[1] This 'economic world' maps roughly onto the ordinary world of things, people, and the activities of life, but it comes subtly adrift at important points in ways that produce bafflement. Economists often insist that they live in the 'real world', with the heavy implication that their critics and detractors live in a world of dreams, and though this insistence is sometimes enough to silence opposition, it is seldom accepted as wholly convincing or satisfactory.

My purpose here is to argue that this feeling that the economic world is strange has substantial grounding of a kind not to be be brushed aside as inexpert 'folk economics'. The feeling presupposes a contrast between a commonsense world and an economic world, and if there is such a contrast to be drawn, it ought to be possible to say something about these worlds and how and why they differ. I shall take it that the commonsense world is the world as it is ordinarily thought of and spoken about, and by 'ordinary' thought and speech I mean those conducted in terms of the concepts of the natural language we all use. The economic world, accordingly, is the world as it is thought of and spoken about using economic concepts.

In order to limit and define the task I shall consider two ordinary concepts which have fundamental places in our common conceptual scheme for dealing with the world and its contents, that of a thing and that of an activity. Ordinary English has been partly penetrated by economic or market conceptions, but by considering old and fundamental concepts there may be some hope of navigating around this

---

[1] I am grateful to Geoff Kay, Pat Shaw, Chris Martin, Uskali Mäki, Jimmy Lenman, and David Wiggins for commenting on earlier drafts of this paper.

obstacle. These ordinary or natural language concepts have logical features which characterize them and connect them with other concepts in the scheme, and this tissue of characteristics and connections I shall refer to as the metaphysics of natural language. In order to find forms of expression suitable to serve the purposes of economic thought, economists have, since the eighteenth century when economics first emerged as a discrete science, reformed the metaphysics of the ordinary concepts of a thing and an activity, and I shall chart those reforms in sections I and III, and consider some of the consequences for understanding that they have had in sections II, IV, and V.

The ordinary concepts of thing and activity, and their corresponding economic ones of utility and labour, evidently contest the same ground as elements of alternative or rival ways of handling certain portions and aspects of the world of ordinary experience. In order to get some grip on the confusions that arise in this contest, I shall draw contrasts between modern market thinking and pre-modern thought which did not suffer from this modern difficulty. MacIntyre has illuminated aspects of modernity by means of contrasts with pre-modernity in the philosophies of knowledge, ethics, and politics, and it may be that the same is possible in metaphysics and in thought about matters that are today called 'economic'.

Aristotle's philosophy sticks very closely to the metaphysics of natural language. He saw it as the task of philosophy as he understood it to discover the logical characteristics of the concepts in common use in the natural language and the connections they have with other concepts in the scheme. This is a descriptive conception of the philosophical task rather than a reforming one, or 'revisionary' one as Strawson put it. Wittgenstein was alarmed at the relaxed habits which mainstream anglophone philosophy has got into regarding attempts to reform the metaphysics of natural language, which some in that tradition have disdained as the 'metaphysics of the Stone Age'. Whether or not one is inclined to share Wittgenstein's general alarm, there is, I think, good reason for caution about such reforms in the case of economics. Aristotle's accounts of the ideas of a thing and an activity provide insight into just what our ordinary ideas of these things are, both in classical Greek and in English. That is one reason why Aristotle is a useful author to consider here. Another is that pre-modern European thought was conducted largely through the medium of the Greek and Latin inheritance, principally the Aristotelian inheritance, and so the Aristotelian tradition is rich in providing food for thought if one is looking for ways of getting perspective on familiar modern ideas concerning which, where they differ from traditional or ordinary ideas, there is a tendency unreflectively to suppose them to be the results of scientific improvement. A third reason is that Aristotle's own thought in *Nicomachean Ethics* (*NE*) 5.5 and *Politics* (*Pol*) I, 8–10, dealing with matters that today are referred to as 'economic', has had a profound influence on the ideas of modern critics of the market, especially Marx and Keynes.

I

Our ordinary idea of a thing includes the idea that things fall into kinds. There are, for example, organic things and inorganic things, and each of these kinds falls into other kinds, and each of them into yet others. This ordinary idea has been philosophically explicated in the Aristotelian manner by Wiggins in the following way: things are naturally occurring entities, or artifacts (substances in Aristotelian jargon), which persist through change, and whose identities are bound up with the continuity of the path they trace through space and time, and with their membership of natural kinds, into which they fall in virtue of their composition, properties, structure, origin, typical or nomological behaviour, and so forth. The notion of identity itself (in logical notation '='; the expression '$a = b$' says that a and b are the same thing), as Wiggins has argued, is primitive in the sense that it cannot be strictly analysed or dismantled into more basic ideas, because there are no ideas more basic than it into which it may be analysed. Furthermore, the notion of identity, primitive as it is, presupposes the objects themselves that are the same or different, together with the kinds into which these objects fall. Everything that we can talk about or identify is a thing in this, that, or the other kind. By reference to the kind it can be said what identity and difference criterially amount to – what it takes for a and b to coincide or be identical. In the case of the particulars of ordinary experience the objects and kinds that are presupposed are continuants or substances and the kinds into which these fall. With these kinds come ways of coming into being, acting, interacting, and passing away, in the light of which identities are to be adjudicated.[2]

The attempt, beloved of philosophers of empiricist sympathies backed by Humean anti-substance metaphysics, to analyse identity in terms of properties (that is, '$a = b$' if they share all their properties) fails because it gets things back to front. The fact that a and b share properties follows

---

[2] See D. Wiggins, *Sameness and Substance* (Oxford 1980), 49–55. For an examination of what is involved in the disputes over substance between empiricists like Hume and Russell, and the Aristotelians or rationalists, see D. Wiggins, 'Substance', in A. C. Grayling (ed.), *Philosophy: A Guide Through the Subject* (Oxford 1995), 214–49.

from the identity of *a* and *b* (they are the same thing), and the identity is not something constructed out of that community of properties. Identity is a primitive notion transcending any philosophical reduction, so it is not analysable at all, and the best we can do is to uncover and describe the actual practices and criteria that are used in individuating and reidentifying things of the different kinds that there are, in order to enhance the understanding we already have of sameness or identity as ascribed to things. These practices and criteria vary with the kind of thing; those for one kind of living entity differ from those of another, and from those for non-living entities, from those for the different kinds of artifacts that there are, and from those for such a thing as a republic. Thus the notion of identity itself involves the notions of the things there are, and of their kinds, so that the notion of a thing, entity, or substance, lies at the core of our language, and our equipment for thinking about reality. It is not an idea that is very likely to be a suitable subject for reform.

The notion of value in use found in the classical political economists, Smith, Ricardo, and Marx, is coherent with the ordinary idea of a thing through the notion of an artifact, or things that exist because we have made them. The classical notion of value in use is that of a useful thing, and in the overwhelming majority of cases the thing is designed and made to have just those qualities which make it useful for a purpose, and it is said to have value in use in virtue of that fact. 'Useful' can be treated as a two-place predicate, with the form 'x is useful for y', where x is a thing and y a purpose, and the classical notion of value in use fits that form because it is tied to the notion of purpose.[3] The purposes served by useful things are of different kinds, and accordingly these things too fall into different kinds according to the purposes they serve, for which they are fitted in virtue of their natural properties, which properties they were deliberately constructed to have in order that they might serve those purposes. So useful things are necessarily heterogeneous, and the kinds into which they fall are incommensurable.

The classical notion of value in use remained part of the foundation of thought about matters that today we call 'economic' from Aristotle through to Smith, Ricardo, and Marx. But it became recalcitrant as

---

[3] The full statement of usefulness involves a three-place relation: x is useful to y in respect of z. Here, however, we are concerned with the purpose which a certain sort of use value is made in order to serve. A pen (x) is made to be useful for writing (z), and that is the same for any person y, so as regards the use value of pens, y can be disregarded and the predicate 'useful' can be treated as a two-place predicate. This is not to say that a particular y might not use a pen for getting coins out of washing-machines.

economic thought developed in the nineteenth century, and the classical notion of value in use was eliminated and replaced by the notion of utility. Bailey makes no mention of useful things, or value in use, in the early chapters of the *Critical Dissertation* in which he sets up his conceptual apparatus.[4] Mill, in his *Principles of Political Economy*, retains the term, but smudges the distinction between value in use and price in a way that causes value in use to lose some of its conceptual independence. He defines wealth as 'all useful or agreeable things, which possess exchangeable value'.[5] Jevons shifts the focus decisively away from usefulness in consumption towards usefulness in buying and selling, and as a consequence an independent notion of value in use is entirely lost. Jevons was convinced that most of what was wrong with economics in his time was due to the presence of qualitative notions, and he was concerned to replace these with quantitative notions wherever it seemed possible to him. Utility, or what had earlier been called 'value in use', was at the top of his list. He writes, in the preface to *The Theory of Political Economy*, that concerning economics

I have long thought that it deals throughout with quantities . . . I have endeavoured to arrive at accurate quantitative notions concerning Utility, Value, Labour, Capital, &c . . . Mathematical readers may think that I have explained some elementary notions, that of degree of utility, for instance, with unnecessary prolixity. But it is to the neglect of economists to obtain clear and accurate notions of quantity and degree of utility that I venture to attribute the present difficulties and imperfections of the science.[6]

The classical notion of usefulness, or value in use, was an obstacle to these ambitions for quantification, and Jevons introduces instead a notion of usefulness, 'utility', which is severed from the idea of things that are useful for particular purposes, which is a heterogeneous notion capable of only limited quantification. His notion of utility is that of a generic 'usefulness' which is not discriminated into species, and which may inhere indiscriminately in things of any kind at all. This is a 'usefulness' that is unconnected with the actual usefulness of a thing, or

---

[4] S. Bailey, *A Critical Dissertation on the Nature, Measures, and Causes of Value* (London 1825).

[5] J. S. Mill, *Principles of Political Economy* (New York 1969), 9. Mill's work was the standard textbook until it was replaced by Marshall's *Principles of Economics*.

[6] W. S. Jevons, *The Theory of Political Economy* (London 1879), vii–viii. Jevons begins the preface to the second edition by explaining that 'certain new sections have been added, the most important of which are those treating of the *dimensions of economic quantities*. The subject, of course, is one which lies at the basis of all clear thought about economic science. It cannot be surprising that many debates end in logomachy, when it is still uncertain . . . what kind of quantity *utility* itself is.' (Italics in original.)

with the purpose it was made to serve, and it is indifferent to the physical constitution of things of that kind in virtue of which they are useful for a purpose. This undifferentiated 'usefulness' is an economic construct which, unlike the ordinary concept of usefulness, is common to all things. Usefulness, by this device, had been made into something uniform, homogeneous, and measurable, just like money or exchange-value, with which it could then be aligned or confused. The impression is given that the difficulty posed for economic thought by the recalcitrant fact that things fall into incommensurable kinds has been overcome. The differences of purpose which those things of different kinds are useful for, have been put out of the picture and replaced by the single purpose of exchanging them, that is, their usefulness in use has been subordinated to their usefulness in exchange or buying and selling. Things are regarded only or primarily as exchangeable items, and one differs from another only or primarily in the magnitude of its value in exchange.

Jevons's concept of utility is not, as it might appear, a refinement of the concept of value in use, in the way that the concept of velocity is a refinement of the concept of speed. Before the development of mechanics, the concept of speed allowed descriptions of the movement of a moving body, and comparisons of one moving body with another in respect of speed. But there was no precise way of saying how much speed a moving thing had, or how much faster its movement was than that of another moving thing, until the notion of speed was refined into the quantitative notion of velocity, that is, so many units of length per unit of time. Velocity is a refinement of the ordinary notion of speed, because there is a conceptual continuity between the two notions which makes it possible to say that velocity is a quantitative version of speed. But that is not how Jevons's notion of utility relates to the classical notion of value in use and to the ordinary idea of a thing. These are simply different concepts, and where value in use relates to the constitution of a thing in virtue of which it is useful for the specific purpose which things of that kind are meant to serve, Jevons's notion of utility does not.

By the time Marshall wrote, some twenty years after Jevons, it had become possible to dismiss value in use without argument, and a thing's usefulness came to be understood almost entirely as its usefulness in buying and selling. Marshall writes:

'The word *value*' says Adam Smith 'has two different meanings, and sometimes expresses the utility of some particular object and sometimes the power of purchasing other goods which the possession of that object conveys.' But experience has shown that it is not well to use the word in the former sense. The value, that is the exchange value, of one thing in terms of another at any place and time, is the amount of that second thing which can be got there and then in exchange for the first. Thus the term value is relative, and expresses the relation between two things at a particular place and time.[7]

Marshall offers no argument, but merely the assertion that there is no useful place in economics for the idea of value in use, though doubtless he was right. Wicksteed was more forthcoming: 'What we really have to do is to put out of consideration the concrete and specific qualitative utilities in which they [i.e. useful things] differ, leaving only the abstract and general quantitative utility in which they are exchanged.'[8] The notion of the usefulness of things for purposes of life other than buying and selling (Wicksteed's 'concrete and specific qualitative utilities'), no longer occupies a position of prominence in economics. In the voluminous index of Schumpeter's *History of Economic Analysis* it does not rate an independent entry, though there are two columns of entries under 'Value', all of which concern value in exchange or price.

The classical approach to the analysis of economic value, or price, was based on the distinction between value in use and value in exchange, and in turn the notion of value in use was based on the ordinary idea of a thing. The artifacts that Smith, Ricardo, and Marx were interested in, were conceived as a sub-class of natural things, whose differentiating characteristic is that they occur, not by nature, but by virtue of human efforts or 'labour'.[9] So products were seen as things continuous with the natural world, and not as radically separated from it, even though their chief interest was the money those things could be bought and sold for. These established conceptual dispositions were redrawn in a revolutionary way with the introduction of the notion of utility. The natural constitution of things, their having a certain composition, certain properties, structure, their membership of natural kinds, and their being useful for specific purposes, were now to be 'put out of consideration' as Wicksteed enjoined, and we are not to think of things, but of abstract entities, utilities. It is, of course, precisely the differences being set aside here that ordinarily concern people. The trouble with humans, as Evelyn Waugh's Titoist quartermaster complained about wartime refugees, is that 'They all want sumpin' different'. These differences are the point, in ordinary life. It is a serious matter to be told that we must think of things in a way that is different from how we know them to be, and it is

---

[7] A. Marshall, *Principles of Economics* (London 1898), 8. Bailey had followed the same course much earlier. In his *Critical Dissertation* (see n. 4) of 1825, he omits altogether any consideration of the usefulness of things for any other purpose than that of exchange.

[8] Philip A. Wicksteed, *The Common Sense of Political Economy* (London 1933), ii, 714.

[9] For a treatment of artifact identity see Wiggins, *Sameness and Substance*, ch. 3, sections 3 and 4.

something which, if we do it, might be expected to have consequences. In this economic account of the nature of things, a major point of connection was severed between the 'economic realm' and the natural realm of things, people, and their activities, as we ordinarily think of them.[10]

The natural realm, as it will, keeps pushing through these metaphysical revisions, as it does in the problem of aggregation. Leontief observes that in trying to deal with the problem of determining the magnitude of artificial aggregative objects such as 'output of consumer goods' and 'average price level of agricultural goods', 'the reduction in qualitative variety is attained at the cost of ever increasing quantitative indeterminacy', so that the economist 'winds up either with a system of quantitatively well-defined relationships between qualitatively ill-defined variables or with a set of quantitatively indeterminate – or at least loosely described – relationships between sharply defined variables'.[11] The problem of aggregation is insoluble in principle, because the heterogeneity of things is not negotiable.

I have discussed nineteenth-century economists because it was they who engineered the metaphysical reform. Economists have since moved from cardinal *ex post* utility to ordinal *ex ante* utility expressed in preferences. In doing so they have not reversed the reform, but merely continued with it, while forgetting that there is a problem about heterogeneity and that there was a reform which was meant to solve it.

II

The loss of a clear grasp of the ordinary idea of a thing, which accompanies this metaphysical reform, has serious consequences, two of which will be considered in this section. Firstly, it makes difficult or impossible the formulation of an adequate conception of wealth, that is, a conception sufficiently rich to allow making the pertinent and intelligible distinction that is in fact made between wealth as money and wealth as useful things. Secondly, it frustrates framing questions about the end aimed at by market economy, considered as a system, which are

---

[10] This severence and others like it have come with costs attached. For example, the practice of calculating GDP by measuring movements of money in market transactions, to the exclusion of considerations from the ordinary world such as well-being, and the stock of physical and intellectual capacities, now has increasingly insupportable costs, even in terms which economics is prepared to countenance. See, for example, Will Hutton's discussion in *The Guardian*, 11 March 1996, p. 15.

[11] W. Leontief, 'The Problem of Quality and Quantity in Economics', in his *Essays in Economics: Theories and Theorizing* (Oxford 1966), 55–6, and 46. See also his remarks on the 'production function', 46ff.

intelligible and which are in fact asked.[12] Marx and Keynes held that the
end of the market system is the accumulation of money rather than the
accumulation of useful things, and whether they were right or wrong in
this claim, the distinction between the alternatives is intelligible, pertinent, and worthy of consideration. However, if the end of 'economic
activity', ambiguous as that expression is, is identified as utility, then it
appears that the distinction cannot be drawn, or at any rate it is not clear
how or whether it can be drawn, and as long as that remains so the
distinction cannot be given consideration, and neither can theories like
those of Marx and Keynes which rest on it.

Keynes retained a grip on the ordinary idea of a thing, and on the
derivative idea of a useful thing. In his discussion of the choice of units in
the *General Theory*, he writes that the 'national dividend', as defined by
Marshall and Pigou, 'measures the volume of current output or real
income and not the value of output or money-income'. It depends on net
output, that is, 'on the net addition . . . to the resources of the community available for consumption or for retention as capital stock'. The
distinction he draws between volume of output or real income, and value
of output or money income, is a distinction between wealth as useful
things and wealth as money, and the distinction is the foundation of
those social and economic policies known as Keynesianism. He enters it
as 'a grave objection . . . that the community's output of goods and
services is a non-homogeneous complex which cannot be measured,
strictly speaking, except in certain special cases', and he adds with
unconcealed sarcasm that 'on this basis an attempt is made to erect a
quantitative science'. The heterogeneity and incommensurability of
things, and other conceptual difficulties which must be faced by attempts
at making economics a quantitative or exact science, are, he says,
generally dismissed by economists as 'conundrums' because businessmen
don't worry about them: 'They are "purely theoretical" in the sense that
they never perplex, or indeed enter in any way into, business decisions
. . . which are clear-cut and determinate in spite of the quantitative
indeterminacy of these concepts'.[13] This is so because business, in
Keynes's view, is concerned above all with wealth as money. He writes:

The distinction between a cooperative economy and an entrepreneur economy
bears some relation to a pregnant observation made by Karl Marx, – though the

[12] I shall resist here the not-very-strong temptation to enter into a discussion of preferences.
There is little reason to acquiesce in the strategy of circumventing discussion of the
possibility that market economy might have a systemic end, by the device of insisting
that ends be discussed only in relation to the preference schedules of individual choosers.
[13] J. M. Keynes, *The General Theory of Employment Interest and Money* (London 1936),
38–9.

subsequent use to which he put this observation was highly illogical. He pointed out that the nature of production in the actual world is not, as economists seem to suppose, a case of C-M-C', i.e. of exchanging commodity (or effort) for money in order to obtain another commodity (or effort). That may be the standpoint of the private consumer. But it is not the attitude of business, which is a case of M-C-M', i.e. of parting with money for commodity (or effort) in order to obtain more money.[14]

Keynes is dealing here with the two types of economy, the 'cooperative', neutral monetary economy, or non-market economy which prevailed throughout history until modernity, a version of which the Soviets tried unsuccessfully to establish, and the market economy, or 'disembedded' economy as Polanyi called it.[15] It is a distinction that absorbed Keynes. For the present, however, I want to concentrate on the distinction between C-M-C, in which the end aimed at is useful things (C), and M-C-M, in which the end is money (M). Keynes says here that he found the distinction in Marx, though he might also have got it from Aristotle, whom he read, and who first made the distinction in *Politics* book one.[16] Marx himself took it from Aristotle and made it the cornerstone of his analysis of market economy.[17] The distinction has far-reaching implications, most of which Aristotle himself drew at least in outline.

Oikonomikê (literally 'running a household') was Aristotle's name for the art of providing ourselves with the things we need.[18] It 'must either find ready to hand, or itself provide, such things necessary to life, and useful for the community of the family or the polis' (*Politics,* 1, 1257b27–30). Acquiring them is itself an art, the art of acquisition or *chrêmatistikê*: 'Of the art of acquisition then there is one kind which is by nature a part of *oikonomikê*' (1256b27f.; 1256a10–13). In this art, money is a means to getting useful things, C-M-C. But there is another kind, *chrêmatistikê* in the bad sense, which aims, not at acquiring useful things,

[14] *The Collected Works of John Maynard Keynes* (London 1971), xxix, 81

[15] See *Trade and Market in the Early Empires*, ed. K. Polanyi, C. Arensberg, and H. Pearson (Glencoe, Illinois 1957).

[16] On Keynes's relation to Aristotle see A. Fitzgibbons, *Keynes's Vision: A New Political Economy* (Oxford 1988), 91, 126, 131, and A. Carabelli, *On Keynes's Method* (London 1988). See also J. Coates, *The Claims of Commonsense: Moore, Wittgenstein, Keynes and the Social Sciences* (Cambridge 1996).

[17] See especially *A Contribution to the Critique of Political Economy* (London 1971), 27, 42, 50, 68, 117, 137, 155, and also *Capital*, i (London 1976), 65–6, 150–1, 162. The distinction, and the notation which is due to Marx, are to be found passim in the *Contribution*, in *Capital*, and throughout the three volumes of *Theories of Surplus Value*.

[18] A fuller account of Aristotle's ideas can be found in my *Aristotle's Economic Thought* (Oxford 1995). Needless to say, there are neo-classical 'economic' interpretations of some of Aristotle's ideas, and these are examined mainly in chapter 6 of that book.

but at getting money, M-C-M. It too is concerned with acquisition, and because of that people confuse it with the first art, but it is really quite different because its end is different: 'The source of the confusion is the near connection between the two kinds of wealth-getting; in either, the instrument is the same, although the use is different, and so they pass into one another; for each is a use of the same property, but with a difference: accumulation is the end in the one case, but there is a further end in the other' (1257b34ff.). According to Aristotle's theory of action, actions are defined by their ends, and if two activities have different ends they are different activities. Natural *chrêmatistikê* (C-M-C) aims at getting useful things. Unnatural *chrêmatistikê* (M-C-M), which includes not only trade (*kapêlikê*) but any other activity when it is pursued for the sake of money, aims at getting money.

Having distinguished these ends, Aristotle must give two definitions of wealth, one as C and one as M. Wealth properly speaking (true wealth, *ho alêthinos ploutos*, 1256b30f.; or natural wealth, *ho ploutos ho kata phusin*, 1257b19f.), is 'the stock of things that are useful in the community of the household or the polis' (1256b30f., and 36–7). Wealth 'of the spurious kind' is money (it is perhaps possible here to glimpse one of the more practical reasons why the early anglophone moderns, Hobbes, Locke, & co., found Aristotle so objectionable). The distinction contrasts sharply with the definitions of wealth to be found in the economics that followed classical political economy, where it became usual in definitions of wealth to elide the distinction between useful things and price. Mill, as we saw earlier, elides it by defining wealth as 'all useful or agreeable things, which possess exchangeable value'. Defining wealth in economics nowadays means defining and measuring capital, and the issue at stake in the capital controversy of the 1950s and 1960s was whether wealth should be defined as a stock of heterogeneous goods or as sums of money, and it may be regarded as a reprise within economics of the problems Aristotle is tackling here.

Aristotle also distinguishes possession or the capacity to use wealth, from ownership or the capacity to exchange it. 'Wealth as a whole', he writes in the *Rhetoric*, 'consists in using things rather than owning them; it is really the activity – that is, the use – of the property that constitutes wealth', and he adds that the 'definition of security is present possession in such a way that the owner has the use of the goods, and that of ownership is the right of alienation, whereby gift or sale is meant' (*Rhet.* 1361a19ff.). In contrast Marshall, taking no account of the distinction between possession and ownership, defines wealth, not in terms of use, but in terms of exchange or rights of transference: 'a person's wealth' consists in 'those material goods to which he has (by law or custom) private rights of property, and which are therefore transferable and exchangeable', and 'those immaterial goods which belong to him, are external to him, and serve directly as the means of enabling him to acquire material goods'.[19] Cairncross sees no substantial distinction, but only one of viewpoint, between wealth and capital, both of which he regards as involving exchange; 'Social capital . . . includes not only trade capital, but also non-commercial assets that possess a money value . . . The distinction between social capital and wealth is one of standpoint. Capital is an agent in production . . . Wealth is a fund upon which we can draw in consumption'.[20] Samuelson gives no definition of wealth in the eighth edition of his textbook *Economics*.

C-M-C' behaviour begins and ends with useful things. Its aim is to acquire a useful thing that is needed; once it is acquired, exchange reaches a natural terminus, and that thing leaves circulation and enters consumption. M-C-M' behaviour has no natural terminus. In this form of behaviour 'money is the starting-point and the goal' (1257b22f.), and since there is no difference of quality between one sum of money and another, the only possible difference being one of quantity, this quantitative growth of money is the only aim that M-C-M' can have. But if M can be advanced to become M', so can M' be advanced to become M'', and so on without limit: 'there is no limit to the end it seeks; and the end it seeks is wealth of the sort we have mentioned . . . the mere acquisition of money' (1257b28f.); 'it is concerned only with getting a fund of money, and that only by the method of conducting the exchange of commodities' (1257b21ff.), 'all who are engaged in acquisition increase their fund of money without any limit or pause' (1257b33f.). Roll observes that 'Aristotle's long discussion of the two arts of [*chrêmatistikê*] . . . was not just an attempt to drive home an ethical distinction. It was also a true analysis of the two different forms in which money acts in the economic process: as a medium of exchange whose function is completed by the acquisition of the good required for the satisfaction of a want; and in the shape of money capital leading men to the desire for limitless accumulation.' [21] In M-C-M' the particular natures of the useful things falling under C are not especially important because C is not an end, but merely a means to M, and here it may be possible to discern why the idea of a useful thing should eventually have proved otiose in modern economics.

True wealth has a limit because, being the stock of things that are

[19] A. Marshall, *Principles of Economics*, 125.
[20] A. Cairncross, *Introduction to Economics* (London 1960), 67–8.
[21] E. Roll, *A History of Economic Thought* (London [1938] 1961), 35.

useful in a community, a natural limit is reached when there are enough of them for the purposes of the citizens in living well and having a flourishing life, 'for the amount of property which is needed for a good life is not unlimited'. There is a limit in the art of *politikê*, or the running of a community or *politeia*, 'just as there is in the other arts; for the instruments of any art are never unlimited, either in number or size, and wealth may be defined as the number of instruments to be used in a household or in a polis' (1256b32ff.). Wealth is limited, as the means to any end are limited, and wealth is a set of means for the flourishing of the citizens. 'Limit' (*peras*) is an important idea in Aristotelian thought, and it is a serious matter for Aristotle that in the pursuit of wealth as money 'there is no limit of the end it seeks'. True wealth consists in 'those goods . . . necessary for life and useful for the community of the city or household', and they are limited to those needed to attain the ends of those communities. The pursuit of wealth as money has no limit imposed from without because it is not a means subordinate to an end, as the pursuit of wealth as useful things has, and since it is a quantitative thing it has no limit of its own, so it has no limit at all. C-M-C′ is an institution or form of behaviour with a limit built into its form. But it is in the nature of M-C-M′ that it has no limit built into its form ('there is no limit to the end it seeks', 1257b28f.). For that reason those who pursue it are engaged in a form of activity whose end is of such a kind that it has no limit. Whether or not they are personally greedy is beside the point; the point is that the end of the activity they are engaged in has no limit or terminus.

Wealth, according to Aristotle, is a set of instruments or means for the activities of life, not the end to which all the activities of life are directed. If the members of a polis 'associated in nothing more than military alliance and the exchange of goods, this would not be a polis', because a polis is a partnership in living well (*Pol.* 3, 1280b17–23, 29–35). The specification of what it is to live well, of the good life, is derived from an analysis of human nature, given in *De Anima*, which provides a basis for identifying what provisions and arrangements are best for creatures with the needs and capacities humans have to flourish as things of their kind. Wealth, or true wealth, is a set of means for that flourishing. Aristotle means more by 'living well' than is meant today by the 'standard of living'. Activities and relationships are the greater part of living well, and means are subordinate to them as means are to ends.

The Aristotelian theoretical structure, its concepts, distinctions, supporting analyses, and overall conceptual dispositions, has carried great weight with modern critics of market economy, because it holds out the possibility, which it itself partly realizes, of an integrated set of definitions of wealth, human nature, and human well-being, that are drawn up, not in economic terms, but in terms that are theoretically independent of economics. This independence allows such a theory to act as a standard against which it may be possible to test how well or badly market economy, and its dedicated science of economics, are doing in serving human good. Market economy will always pass the test if it is judged by the accounts of human nature, human good, and wealth, offered by economics and its associated utilitarian philosophy.

III

Activities are ordinarily thought to have a point or purpose, and as those purposes differ so activities differ. In Aristotle's theory of action, which sticks closely to the ordinary idea, this is expressed by saying that actions are discriminated into kinds by their ends.[22] Each kind of activity, studying mathematics, fattening beef, practising medicine, going for a walk, administering justice, or playing football, has an end for the sake of which it is pursued. They are different kinds of activity because they have different ends, and other differences between them, differences in the sorts of movements called for, the instruments used, and the blends of human capacities required, are what they are because of those differences of end. Some have ends which are distinct from the activities aimed at bringing them about, as the end of performing a surgical operation is to make someone well again. The end of others is simply to engage in the activity, like going for a walk. Activities of different kinds cannot be added up because they are incommensurable. Although they all take time, it is an irreducible fact that an hour of studying maths is not an hour of the same thing as an hour of walking or performing surgery. They share duration and perhaps some features that are accidentally common, but that is all, and it isn't much because activities are distinguished by their ends.

The heterogeneity and incommensurability of different kinds of activity posed a difficulty for economic thought in arriving at the kind of conception of activity or 'labour' it needed. Smith had spoken of labour as a quantity, implying commensurability between kinds, and found the idea difficult but failed to identify the difficulty.[23] Ricardo formulates it clearly early in chapter 1 of the *Principles*: 'In speaking, however, of

---

[22] See *NE* 3, 1115b22, and *Met.* Θ 1050a22–4. This remains in the Aristotelian tradition. When Aquinas asks if 'human acts receive their species from their end?', he answers that they do, *Summa Theologiae*, I–II q. 1 a. 3.

[23] A. Smith, *Wealth of Nations*, ed. E. Cannan (London 1904), vol. i, 33.

labour, as being the foundation of all value . . . I must not be supposed
to be inattentive to the different qualities of labour, and the difficulty of
comparing an hour's or a day's labour, in one employment, with the
same duration of labour in another.' But his response is unconvincing:
'The estimation in which different qualities of labour are held, comes
soon to be adjusted in the market with sufficient precision for practical
purposes.'[24] This clearly will not do. The theory was that labour-value
underpins market-value, but arriving at a coherent idea of labour-value
was made difficult by the fact that there are different kinds of labour,
which are incommensurable because of the differences in kind. Ricardo,
like Smith before him, tries to surmount the obstacle by introducing
market estimations of different labours, and these are supposed to do the
commensurating. But this is to underpin labour-value with market-value,
and that is the wrong way round for the theory. As long as nothing was
done about this the classical theory of economic value was resting on a
circularity.

Economic thinkers at that time were not so ready to dismiss conceptual
difficulties as 'conundrums', and in seeking a solution the device they
adopted was to adjust the metaphysics of the idea of activity by
eliminating the cause of the problem, kinds. They didn't do things by
halves, and around the reform an entire theory of action was made up, or
adapted from one that had been made earlier, in which there were no
kinds of activities but only individual actions, and only one end to which
all actions were to be considered means. Activities differed, not by end,
but only in their efficacy in promoting the single end they were all
supposed to share, utility. Since there was only one end, there could be
only one kind of activity, not many as is ordinarily thought. For that
reason, the specific ends or purposes of distinct activities drop out of the
picture. The notion of kinds is removed by the reform, just as the notion
of kinds among useful things was removed by the metaphysical reforms
to the idea of a thing. (In deciding whether this was problem-avoidance
or problem-evasion, account must be taken of the fact that kinds still
thrive in ordinary thought and speech, where the reforms continue to be
entirely ignored.)

So the ground was cleared for the economic version of the idea of
activity. Activities count alike in economics, and they can be added up or
aggregated. 'Labour' is regarded, not as a set of activities differentiated
into kinds by differences of end and quality, but as a quantity, indifferent
to ends, whose instances are commensurable and addable because they

---

[24] D. Ricardo, *The Principles of Political Economy and Taxation*, ed. P. Sraffa (Cambridge
1986), 20. Smith had adopted the same solution in the *Wealth of Nations*.

form a single kind, and are all expenditures of a single undifferentiated capacity, the capacity for labour. Labour is seen as the negative correlate of utility, disutility, and as such it is not differentiated into kinds any more than utility is.

The work of Halévy and Macpherson, among others, shows convincingly enough that modern anglophone utilitarianism was historically an integral part of the development of economic thinking itself, and that it is an expression in philosophical idiom of the economic view of the world.[25] Utilitarianism provided philosophical and ethical infrastructure for the new economic view of the world which had been developing along with market economy itself in the previous couple of centuries before Bentham.[26] Modern utilitarian philosophy is not neutral in respect of economics, and its theory of action is inadmissible as a philosophical witness for the defence in the case that can be brought against economics, that the world of things and activities it portrays is not the world of common understanding, that it is at odds with that world and with the metaphysics of natural language.

IV

The suppression of kinds among activities entails the suppression of the specific ends of activities, and many of the objections made to utilitarian philosophy and economic thinking have been aimed at positions that are consequences of this metaphysical reform. The weakness of the first draft of utilitarianism, subsequently known as act-utilitarianism, was that if actions fall into only one kind, then actions must be ethically evaluated individually, not by kinds since there are supposed to be none. This was soon shown to be an unworkable basis for ethics, if by ethics we mean something that is supposed to tell you how to live, and rule-utilitarianism was devised to meet the difficulty. Halévy's 'philosophic radicals' did not adopt utilitarian ethics because it was consequentialist, but because they wanted to hold that there was only one kind of action. Earlier versions of utilitarian thought like that of Protagoras were inspired by other things, but modern anglophone utilitarianism was inspired by economics.

[25] The economic background to this revisionist movement in philosophy is the subject of a classic treatment by Elie Halévy, *The Growth of Philosophic Radicalism* (London 1928). Much of C. B. Macphersons's work is directly or indirectly relevant here, but particularly his paper 'The Economic Penetration of Political Theory', collected in *The Rise and Fall of Economic Justice* (Oxford 1987).

[26] For an account see ch. xiii, 'The Augustan Debate over Land, Trade and Credit', in J. G. A. Pocock, *The Machiavellian Moment: Florentine Political Thought and the Atlantic Republican Tradition* (Princeton 1975).

More recent concern about utilitarian thinking has focused on its insensitivity to the real point of activities, and to the ways in which performances of activities are appraised. This insensitivity follows from the utilitarian insistence on the commensurability of values, to which Bernard Williams has drawn attention, and that in turn follows from the elimination of kinds from among activities.[27] The idea of an activity, as distinct from an action, is an important element in the metaphysical structure of the ordinary concepts we bring to bear when we think and speak about the affairs and agency of ourselves and others. The elimination of kinds tears the idea of an activity out of the scheme of ordinary concepts and destructures ordinary thought and sensibility about behaviour. Without it we would lose the idea of a calling or vocation, and be unable to make discriminations, appraisals, and judgements that are ordinarily thought important.

Performances are appraised as good or bad instances of a kind of activity, and the criteria applied in such appraisals vary from one kind of activity to another. The criteria by which a surgeon may be judged to have done well will probably be unknown to any but medical people, and they are different from those by which an advocate, architect, musician, academic, or footballer may be judged to have done well, which in each case involve subtleties of discrimination that are not quickly or easily learned. When we don't know or understand the criteria by which performances of an activity are appraised we are not in a position to judge them, and we occupy the role of the ignoramus. The utilitarian theory that there is a single standard for appraising performances in any kind of activity rationalizes that sort of ignorance. All the world's greatest hits sound alike on the didgeridoo.

This is a point of practical conflict between the ordinary world and the economic world which has recently become acute as a result of the introduction of market thinking into the management of non-commercial activities in the public sector. The ends of some activities have come to be protected by codes of ethics which preserve those ends and prescribe the fitting conduct of the activity; for example, the Hippocratic oath, collegiality and the disinterested pursuit of truth, and others that are less determinate like the spirit of sport. According to the economic view, however, kinds have been discontinued and with them the specific ends in relation to which activities fall into kinds. So there is no reason in theory to acknowledge the existence of codes of ethics which protect specific ends, or to take them seriously, even if there might be practical reasons for paying them lip-service when managing people who believe in them.

---

[27] See for instance B. Williams, *Morality* (Cambridge 1972).

Practitioners of those arts, in trying to defend those codes of value, the ends they embody, the kinds of relationships they need, and the supply of means required for their pursuit, find themselves forced onto the wrong foot. They are put in the position of having to defend what they see as the end of the activity they practise, as if it were either (i) a means to a further end altogether which has no specific connection with the activity or with the human good embodied in its end but only the generic connection that everything is supposed to have with utility, or (ii) as if it were part of an all-inclusive end, commensurable with all other parts of that end, and tradeable with them.[28] In this position they find it difficult to argue with the accountants and economists, who see in their case the expression either of a dream world, or of the self-interest of a particular interest group sometimes disparaged as 'trade-union attitudes'.[29] Since their activities are supposed to be commensurable, the economist is apt to suppose them to be quantifiable too. Consequently practitioners of those activities are also often forced into the apologetic dilemma arising from the enforced quantification discussed by Bernard Williams: 'Again and again defenders of such values are faced with the dilemma, of either refusing to quantify the value in question, in which case it disappears from the sum altogether, or else of trying to attach some quantity to it, in which case they misrepresent what they are about and also usually lose the argument, since the quantified value is not enough to tip the scale.'[30]

Aristotle's chief concern about the introduction of money into Greek society and culture was precisely its capacity to sow confusion in thought about ends. Plato had worried about the effects of too much buying and selling because 'trade fills the land with wholesaling and retailing, breeds shifty and deceitful habits in a man's souls and makes the citizens distrustful and hostile' (*Laws*, 705a), and Aristotle probably shared those sentiments. But Aristotle's main worry concerned the effects that M-C-M has on all the other activities that make up the life of the polis. He noticed that those not themselves involved in trade tend to use the arts they practise as a way of getting money, and that this can have an adulterating effect on the conduct of any kind of activity. His worry arose from the fact that getting money is a distinct art with a distinct end,

---

[28] J. S. Mill couldn't decide whether such activities were means to happiness or parts of it.

[29] A standard professional response often provoked by considerations of this kind mentions 'corporatism', so it is apt to cite Marx: 'The bourgeoisie has stripped of its halo every occupation hitherto honoured . . . It has resolved personal worth into exchange value, and in place of the numberless indefeasible chartered freedoms, has set up that single, unconscionable freedom – Free Trade', *The Communist Manifesto*, in Marx and Engels, *Collected Works* (London 1975–), vol. vi, 487.

[30] See B. Williams, *Morality*, 103.

and when it becomes connected with the conduct of another art A (as it always does since there is no distinct activity of making money other than the coining or printing of legal tender) it does not leave the conduct of art A unaffected. It introduces another end so that a conflict of ends arises, as a result of which something must happen to the specific end of art A; it can be subordinated and compromised by becoming merely a means to the end of money-making.[31]

The general form of the problem can be illustrated with the example of medicine, not because medicine is any more susceptible to the problem than any other kind of activity, but just for the sake of an example. The end of medicine is health. But if social arrangements are such that the medical profession pursues it also for the sake of money, then health is no longer its only aim. The practitioners will now be pursuing two ends at the same time. Those ends can be combined in different proportions by individual practitioners. In the best case the practitioner will give the greatest priority to health and the least to money. Even in this case the aim is still not simply health, but a minimum compromise between health and the other end. In the worst case the practitioner gives the greatest priority to money and the least to health. In this case he cannot disregard health altogether, because the pursuit of money here is parasitic on the pursuit of health, and there is a threshold in the pursuit of health below which he cannot go and still effectively use the art for the pursuit of money. He is using the medical art as a means to another end altogether. In both the best and the worst cases, and at every point on the spectrum between them, the practitioners are no longer pursuing health alone, and they will not always do the same things they would have done if they had been.

Aristotle criticizes the Sophists for pursuing money rather than philosophy. What they do looks like philosophy because it 'turns on the same class of things as philosophy', but it differs in its end since the end of philosophy is not making money, and activities that have different ends are different however similar they may appear (*Metaphysics* Γ, 1004b17ff.). He concludes that what the Sophists do 'is, as we said, a kind of money-making', rather than a kind of philosophy (*De Sophisticis Elenchis*, 165a23, 171b28). Many walks of life are intended as targets of the criticism. Artisans like the maker of the Delphian knife produce inferior things which cannot do what they are meant to do properly because they were made for sale rather than use (*Pol.*, 1252b1–5), and the professional arts like medicine are targets too. Aristotle generalizes

---

[31] For a more detailed account of the difficulty and Aristotle's view of it, see my *Aristotle's Economic Thought*, ch. 4 (1), 68–81.

the point: those not involved in commerce but who want to pursue money 'try to do so by some other means, employing each of the faculties in an unnatural way [and] make all these faculties means for the business of providing wealth [*chrêmatistikê*, that is, money-getting], in the belief that wealth is the end and that everything must be directed to the end' (*Pol.*, 1258a8–14).[32] Aristotle's worry is that commerce and its values could penetrate into all the activities that make up the life of the polis or society, corrupting them, causing a confusion of ends which would make it difficult for the community to order its activities properly, and obscuring any clear view of the end or point of social living, of what it is to live well.

This kind of worry is rife today when almost all activity is regulated by money, though many modern writers are less acutely aware of this ambiguity in the conduct of activities than Aristotle was, even though they live in a market economy where the situation is much worse, and he didn't. The utilitarian reform of the metaphysics of the ordinary idea of activity is well adapted to the modern market situation, because it gives the impression of avoiding the kind of concern Aristotle had about the ambiguous conduct of activities. The suppression of specific ends removes the conflict of ends in favour of the end of pursuing money, for which the single end of 'utility' looks suspiciously like a euphemism.[33]

Aristotelian metaphysics, unlike utilitarian metaphysics, is not amenable to eliding category distinctions, distinctions between kinds, or distinctions between ends, and because of this Aristotle is led to establish a strict line of demarcation between the ordinary and the economic worlds. He begins his thinking about matters that we would call 'economic' with a distinction between value in use and value in exchange

---

[32] *Chrêmatistikê* is often translated nowadays in ways that blur the very distinction Aristotle is drawing between the two arts of wealth-getting, getting wealth as useful things and getting wealth as money. Rackham, in the Loeb edition of the *Politics* (London 1926), at times translates it as 'business', so that at 1257b35 Aristotle's distinction becomes an opaque one between 'the two arts of business'. Carnes Lord makes it even more misleadingly a distinction between the two 'forms of expertise in business', *Aristotle: The Politics* (Chicago 1984).

[33] Utilitarians might deny that they are committed to the view that the common currency of utility is money, but as Bernard Williams observes, 'they are committed to something which in practice has those implications: that there are no ultimately incommensurable values'. Williams adds that it is not an accidental feature of the utilitarian outlook that the presumption is in favour of the monetarily quantifiable and against other values, 'because (for one thing) utilitarianism is the value system for a society in which economic values are supreme; and also, at the theoretical level, because quantification in money is the only obvious form of what utilitarianism insists upon, the commensurability of value', Williams, *Morality*, 103.

(1257a6–13), the former falling into the category of quality and the latter into that of quantity. When he subsequently comes to define wealth and acquisition (*chrêmatistikê*) he gives two definitions of each, one in terms of value in use (C) and one in terms of value in exchange (M). He first defines and distinguishes wealth as useful things and wealth as money, and then he transposes each of them into an end of action, distinguishing two forms of behaviour C-M-C and M-C-M. So he is quite systematic in separating the ordinary world from the economic world, and this gives Aristotle's analysis a certain transparancy. Economic thought today is expressed in terms which, in effect if not by design, merge the ordinary world and the economic world rather than hold them apart, and this gives it a certain opacity.

Aristotle's pre-modern clearheadedness in keeping the ordinary world separate from the economic world has not endeared him to commercial society, and anglophone moderns from Hobbes onwards have given him an infamous reputation as an enemy of science and a defender of aristocratic privilege which is entirely unfounded. Marx and Keynes were sailing against a well set tide in taking the Aristotelian course rather than the utilitarian one. They got from Aristotle a vantage point from which it could be seen just how strange the economic world is: a world of exchange value and M-C-M, in which wealth is money not useful things, in which there is only one kind of activity not many, and in which there is only one kind of useful thing.

V

In defence of these metaphysical reforms it might be said that they are technicalities required for a special scientific purpose, and that this is their justification. Such a defence can work only on the condition that the special scientific purpose (SSP) be defined in a way that clearly demarcates the special terrain to which it applies in order that the use of the technicalities may be restricted to that terrain, and prevented from contesting with ordinary concepts for the role of favoured terms for describing the world of ordinary experience. Definitions of the SSP generally fail to meet the condition. Robbins famously defines economics as 'the science which studies human behaviour as a relationship between ends and scarce means which have alternative uses'.[34] Such a definition bridges the distinction between the ordinary world and the economic world, and this makes it useless as part of a defence of the metaphysical reforms as technicalities required for an SSP. Indeed, in defining

[34] L. Robbins, *The Nature and Significance of Economic Science* (London 1932), 15.

economics in terms that represent it as a branch of practical reason, Robbins commissions the very confusion of the ordinary and economic worlds that the defence is meant to defend against.

There is point in looking for ways of keeping economic discourse apart from ordinary discourse if the aim is to prevent the reformed concepts competing with ordinary language for the description of ordinary experience. But if part of the aim is to enter into such a contest with a view to winning it, then we are not dealing primarily with an SSP at all, but with an attempt to change how things and activities are ordinarily described and thought about. If that were the case, then a definition of the sort offered by Robbins would be a contribution to the contest, and its strength would be that it builds on the difficulty everyone has in keeping the ordinary world and the economic world apart by merging them and making it even more difficult to unravel them. If this has been the strategy it has been effective in creating confusion, and it has produced some grotesque results in other areas of scholarship. In some historical work on the ancient world, for instance, authors have stocked antiquity with entrepreneurs, banks, interest-rates, money markets, and other market phenomena that didn't exist, largely because of a failure to make adequate safeguards for maintaining a distinction between the language of the economic world and that of the ordinary world, so that such authors have unreflectively resorted to economic or market language for describing any form of social behaviour in any kind of society and in any period of history.[35]

Not all schools of economic thought have muddied the waters in this way. Marx and Keynes didn't, and Adam Smith himself maintained a substantial separation between the ordinary world and the economic world. Smith knew perfectly well that market economy was a recent phenomenon. He identified it as the fourth of his historical stages, the 'stage of commerce', and he was not led to read back into non-market societies the concepts, behaviour, and institutions of a market economy. He also held that 'consumption' or useful things (C) 'is the sole end and purpose of production', and since he was aware that business pursues M not C and that there are dangers in this, he thought that business needed public regulation.[36] Provided business was regulated properly, however, he believed that the totality of business operations produced an outcome for the society that was characterized by improving C. Smith could not

---

[35] See M. I. Finley, *The Ancient Economy* (London 1985). The same kind of anachronism is found in anthropology; see C. Meillassoux, 'Essai d'interpretation du phénomène économique dans les sociétés traditionelles d'auto-subsistence', *Cahiers d'études africaines*, 4 (1972), 38–67.

[36] A. Smith, *Wealth of Nations*, vol. ii, 159.

have formulated either position if he had merged the ordinary and the economic worlds in the way that economics now does.

Little more has been done here than scratch the surface of what it is that underlies the common feeling that the world of the accountants and economists is odd or suspect, but perhaps it has been enough to show at least that there is sense to be made of a distinction between the ordinary world and the economic world. The temptation to run the two worlds together is constantly present and I have tried to suggest that there is intellectual and moral point in keeping them apart. Perhaps something has been said also to sustain the belief that insisting on the priority of the ordinary world is not to be dismissed as 'folk economics', and that economics does not do better and more scientifically something that is ordinarily done less expertly, but does something else altogether. Exactly what that is, is one of the threads that have been left dangling here.

Part II

Rationality and *homo economicus*

4   The normative core of rational choice theory

RUSSELL HARDIN*

Introduction

Although it is commonly called a positive theory – to imply that it is purely descriptive and without value assumptions – rational choice theory is typically grounded in a powerful and simple value theory, from which many of its most compelling results follow. In actual applications, the word "rational" in rational choice theory is typically not a merely formal term. It is also a substantive term that refers to particular values, essentially welfare values. It may be true, as some rational choice theorists insist, that the theory could be applied to actors whose values are other than welfare and, especially, other than their own welfare. But the remarkable success of rational choice explanations turns on the surprising power they have when they are grounded almost exclusively in the actors' own welfares.

To this extent, rational choice theory is, practically, a two-fold theory that says what values govern individuals' choices and what the result of those choices will be. Often, the result is collective rather than merely individual, although rational choice explanations are strictly at the individual level and can govern individual actions outside social inter-actions as well as within such interactions. In the discussion here, however, I will focus on rational choice explanations of social-political interactions, including large group interactions.

A common complaint against rational choice theory is that it mistakes concern with self-interest for rationality. The complaint is well grounded but pointless. Rational choice theorists commonly do suppose that the

* An earlier version of this paper was presented to the political theory seminar at Yale University. I wish to thank Stephen Elkin, Kristen Monroe, James Scott, Ian Shapiro, and participants in that seminar for their comments. I also thank the Mellon and Russell Sage Foundations for generous general support.

agent's own welfare is the chief value of concern to the agent. But there is no mistake involved in such an assumption. It is rather a hypothesis than a direct finding. If it produces good predictions and explanations, it is a good hypothesis; otherwise it is a bad hypothesis. In any case, it cannot be judged a mistake merely by direct inspection of motivations. The critic should want to show not that the assumption is wrong by inspection but rather that it leads to wrong predictions and explanations.

It may be that such a theory will fail too often to be of explanatory value. In actual fact, such a theory in the hands of Bernard Mandeville, Anthony Downs, Gary Becker, and Mancur Olson seems to have swept still less successful theories from the field in various contexts. The vast literature showing that Olson gets interest groups wrong is a literature about the success of tiny fractions of people in various potential interest groups who have taken some degree of collective action. A theory that fits the overwhelming bulk of people most of the time and only fails for small fractions is so unlike any other theory in the dismal history of the social sciences that, if it were Mendel and his theory of inheritance in peas, we would think the data were phoney. That they are not phoney is best attested by the work of the critics themselves who show very low levels of contribution toward various collective provisions.

Oddly, the critics often seem to want to have their cake and eat it too. They criticize moves by many rational choice theorists to include broader concerns in individual utility functions. For example, William Riker and Peter Ordeshook include a sense of "citizen duty" in their list of "rational" motivations to vote[1] (Riker and Ordeshook 1962) and Gary Becker (1962) says the utility function can be quite catholic in its inclusions.[2] (Critics say such moves reduce rational choice theory to tautology, making it a matter of constant redefinition to fit what happens rather than a matter of prediction or explanation. But they also complain that a theory limited to self-interest is far too narrow to explain individual behavior and social outcomes.)

In any case, the power of rational choice theory has come from its clear assumption, most of the time, of a substantive value that drives individual choices. That value is often captured in the rubric "self-interest," although that is the wrong term for a value. I have an interest in having lots of money. Money is only an instrumental, not a consumption or welfare value. It is a means, not an end. Most of my interests in

---

[1] William H. Riker and Peter C. Ordeshook, "A Theory of the Calculus of Voting," *American Political Science Review* 62 (1962): 25–42.

[2] Gary S. Becker, *The Economic Approach to Human Behavior* (Chicago: University of Chicago Press 1976).

contemporary social science contexts are instrumental means, as money, power, and efficacy in voting are. The underlying value of rational choice theory is generally own welfare. This value theory gives rational choice its bite. *Without a substantive value theory, it is only conceptual, not explanatory.*

A quick survey of contemporary rational choice theory

There are two main classes of results in rational choice theory, one of which is primarily conceptual, the other of which is primarily explanatory. First, Kenneth Arrow's impossibility theorem says, in brief, that under well-specified conditions a group's interests cannot even be defined in the same terms as those that define an individual's interests. It is a fallacy of composition to speak of collective or group rationality as an analog of individual rationality.

For the second result, Downs's economic theory of democracy explained why we might get tweedle-dum and tweedle-dee candidates in competition, why voters might not know enough to vote their interests, and why many might not vote at all. Olson, in a variant of the last of Downs's points, showed why interest groups may not form at all to represent many, especially widely popular, interests and why the political interest group system has massive biases in favor of groups already organized for other purposes. Hence, it is also a fallacy of composition to suppose a group can act or be motivated to act as an individual can.

Note that Arrow's result requires no specific value theory. It follows for virtually any value theory that is a preference theory, i.e., that orders states of affairs. Downs's and Olson's results carry for any case in which we might say there is a collective benefit whose provision would benefit all the individuals in a relevant group, in which the costs of providing the collective benefit must be borne by the individuals, and in which the costs and benefits can be aggregated into net benefits. Hence, these results apply to cases in which there is a relatively clear substantive value at stake. In what follows, the concern will generally be with explanatory rational choice theory, which has generally been built on a relatively well-defined value theory.

In the sections below, I will canvass contemporary rational choice theory and then discuss a major confusion in what is at issue. I will then discuss proposals for a rational choice theory without substantive values and three non-welfarist value theories that could alternatively underlie social choice and explanation. Finally, for the problem of group, indeed, revolutionary cooperation, I will consider the chief candidate theory of politics that is not methodologically individualist: structuralist political economy. I will conclude with brief remarks on the explanatory power of the assumption of individualist welfarism.

The value theory of rational choice theory

One of the striking features of the individualist school of political economy is that it starts from a value theory: individual welfare somehow conceived, including, at its most nearly vacuous, simple preferences. This value theory may be objectionable on various grounds, sometimes including considerations of its internal consistency, but it is relatively coherent and it seems to have strong and coherent implications. When it is coupled with a modest variant of Hobbes's or any socio-biologist's psychological theory – that the first or strongest interest of the individual is the self – it leads to a remarkable blending of positive and normative conclusions. Indeed, this was the great invention of Hobbes. By putting his positive theory of human psychology together with his value theory of human welfare, he was able to devise a positive theory of government that was at once seemingly a normative theory. That is a trick many economists seem to think they turn every day.

Hobbes and then Locke insisted that politics centrally address welfare issues. Hobbes thought religious differences should be subordinated to political order, that individual citizens should, in their own interest, let their sovereign decide their religious affiliation. Locke proposed leaving religion out of politics in order to enable politics to focus on issues of property, including property in oneself. Hobbes and Locke have probably been the two most influential political philosophers in the modern western tradition. As with the best of the rational choice theorists, a chief reason for their influence and the intellectual coherence of their arguments is that they start from a particular value theory.

It may seem odd to modern positivists to say that an explanatory theory gains coherence from a value theory. But that is genuinely the story with individualist political economy. This makes sense if it is true that people are motivated by values in their choices, especially if they are motivated systematically by some set of values. Implicitly, at least, most economists and most rational choice theorists are in the tradition of Hobbes and Locke in assuming that people are so motivated. If their assumption is largely true, then rational choice theory should yield good explanatory results. Those who criticize the particular morality of the theory on the claim that people are more driven by other values should not find it objectionable *per se* to ground explanatory theory in value commitments.

What difference has economic reasoning actually made in political science? Obviously, it has contributed to major revisions in the areas that Arrow, Downs, and Olson addressed, and more recently in the study of Congressional organization, regulation, and campaign contributions. In addition, I wish to assert what may be a controversial claim: Economic reasoning has pushed us toward more closely relating normative and positive concerns. For example, it has pushed us into giving normative accounts of institutional arrangements. We assess the institutions for how well they fit our purposes. Earlier generations of social theorists made normative judgments of institutions, but they often drew their normative principles from elsewhere, not from the panoply of positive principles they used. As in Hobbes, so in current work in individualist political economy, the positive and the normative are driven by related motors: individual incentives for individual benefits. This core concern is, moreover, a powerful organizer of manifold problems and analyses across a broad front. Theory grounded in it may often falter and give seemingly wrong results, but it seldom fails to yield some kind of result.[3]

The argument here is not one of a necessary or conceptual relation between the value theory assumptions and the rational choice structure of the explanatory theory. It is, rather, a causal or explanatory claim. Practitioners of the individualist approach most often assume, with Hobbes, some version of self-interest as the goal the individual seeks to serve. Downs and Olson produce their striking results from this assumption.

But the assumption of self-interest is not necessary to the individualist approach. For example, it does not lie behind Arrow's impossibility theorem, which is arguably devastating for democratic theory.[4] Arrow's result does not depend on self-interest and could still apply even if everyone chose from purely public-spirited motivations. Imposing reasonable structures of self-interest to limit the range of plausible choices actually helps to avoid Arrow's impossibility result in specific contexts. Indeed, even a moral theorist concerned with action from non-self-interested motives may wish to start from a framework of rational choice in understanding individual moral choices. The moral theorist may even

---

[3] Some may consider that a fault, not a virtue in the approach.

[4] Kenneth J. Arrow, *Social Choice and Individual Values* (New Haven, Conn.: Yale University Press 1951; second ed. 1963). See further, Russell Hardin, "Public Choice vs. Democracy," in John W. Chapman, ed., NOMOS 32: *Majorities and Minorities* (New York: New York University Press 1990), pp. 184–203.

wish to juxtapose self-interest against other motivations. And that theorist may often be forced to conclude that self-interest is too powerful in that contest – it gives the better explanation of behavior.

This last observation suggests what is perhaps the greatest source of controversy over the explanatory and moral propriety of individualist political economy. It is not only the individualist focus, it is also the nearly universal assumption of self-interest as the major explainer of behavior that rankles. We seem to know from introspection that self-interest does not rule our lives so extensively as it rules in individualist political economy. Some academics can look within themselves and seldom find self-interest at work. Rational choice theorists seem to take special pleasure in showing, or at least in making plausibility arguments, that much of what we thought was moral or otherwise not self-interested behavior is arguably self-interested after all. Sometimes the answer to this debate is that both sides are right but in different ways. The self-interest theorists may capture much of what people do politically even in extreme contexts and the overwhelming bulk of what they do in more ordinary contexts. But individuals acting from other commitments spearhead many important activities, such as revolutionary, charitable, and ideal-regarding actions. Therefore their commitments are a very important part of explaining what happens even if they are statistically uncommon commitments.

Interests, consumptions, welfare

It is common to say that people are rational in some contexts and not in others. One might be relatively rational in considering mortgages for a home but not in considering partners for marriage. It is merely an extension of this view to suppose that in some general contexts, such as different cultures, people may be not rational even though people in other cultures might be. For example, James Scott has argued that the very conservative peasants of southeast Asia are not rational. Rather, they are profoundly risk averse and their choices are governed by a "moral economy."[5] What he means is that they are not rational in the sense of simply maximizing their production of rice. Instead of adopting seed grains that would have much higher average annual yields, they

---

[5] James C. Scott, *The Moral Economy of the Peasant: Rebellion and Subsistence in Southeast Asia* (New Haven, Conn.: Yale University Press 1976).

adopt very hardy, stable grains that will almost always produce at least enough that they will not starve.

When Scott's thesis is summarized, it sounds like a rational choice account.[6] Peasants are not interested in maximizing resources only in the sense of producing the most total food over the years or the most income from it. They want such resources, after all, only as means, not as an end. The end they want is a reasonably good life. The goodness of life depends not only on resources but also on consumptions that the resources make possible. Life with reasonable levels of consumption seems eminently preferable to a life of fluctuation between great plenty and starvation. Hence, the rational peasant might well choose Scott's risk averse policy.

Scott supposes peasants are smart but not rational in their risk aversion. One might sooner conclude that rational choice fits the conditions of scarcity, such as those of Scott's southeast Asian peasants, particularly well. It is in open-ended contexts in which available resources permit fulfillment of a wide range of values that rational choice might seem dubious. Or, at least, rational choice grounded in the narrow value of own welfare might seem dubious. I will return to this point below.

Scott's analysis is essentially Hobbesian in the following sense. Scott supposes peasants will first make sure of survival and only then go after greater wealth. Hobbes supposed we must all put order uppermost and therefore we accept government. In both cases, there is no tradeoff with the rationality of amassing greater wealth; there is merely the prior need for the *sine qua non* of survival, without which there can be no benefit from wealth. If the conditions faced by Scott's peasants are as he describes them, their risk aversion is not a matter of "moral" economy but only of rational choice.[7]

Scott speaks of "preferences which do not make sense in terms of income alone."[8] This is nothing unusual – preferences are coherently seen only over whole states of affairs, in which income is only part of what is at issue. I do not have a preference for blue. I may have a

---

[6] I will not discuss the whole of Scott's theory of his peasants, and one might suppose he has claims for putting other behaviors under the rubric moral economy. I think that all his important arguments, such as mutual insurance and reciprocity, are readily framed as directly rational, as is seemingly extreme risk aversion in the choice of seed grains as discussed here. The latter is, in any case, the most compelling part of Scott's empirical analysis.

[7] On the analogous risk aversion of the entrepreneur or manager in a market society, see Richard H. Day, Dennis J. Aigner, and Kenneth R. Smith, "Safety Margins and Profit Maximization in the Theory of the Firm," *Journal of Political Economy* 79 (1971): 1293–1301. Would anyone wish to call this the "moral economy" of the entrepreneur or manager?

[8] Scott, *Moral Economy*, p. 35.

preference for a blue shirt with certain other clothes to be worn in particular circumstances. As is presumably true of Scott and virtually everyone else as well, I similarly do not have an unrestricted preference for higher income. If higher income entails giving up my academic life or entails giving up more of my leisure time, I may not prefer it to my present income with my present lifestyle and consumption pattern. There are *no preferences* that "make sense in terms of income alone."

The issue here is a conceptually messy one at the very foundations of rational choice theory in the welfarist school. We speak, sometimes almost interchangeably, about interests, consumptions, and welfare. But these are conceptually quite different. Our interests are what put us in a position to consume and consumption typically brings welfare. I have an interest in amassing resources, but resources are of no value *per se* – I want them only in order to be able to consume. Obviously, interests and consumptions trade off with each other. If I consume some things, I must expend some of my resources. (Some social theorists argue that we should ground our normative theories in resources rather than in welfare, that certain conceptual problems in welfare make it finally an unworkable normative principle.[9] Without resolving that issue, we may all readily grant that resources are means without intrinsic value and that what gives them instrumental value is the welfare they can bring us.)

When Scott speaks of a preference for income alone, he misuses the concept of preference. I can prefer one thing to another all else equal or I can prefer one completely defined state of affairs to another.[10] I cannot simply prefer higher income – I must add what I prefer it to and I must add some rough equivalent of the phrase "all else equal." Similarly, Scott's peasants can prefer the whole state of affairs that follows from planting a highly productive but also highly fragile strain of rice to the state that follows from planting a safer but less productive strain, or vice versa. If I have either of these preferences and I act on it, then I, Scott's peasant, am rational.

The beauty of Scott's account is that, after we correct the conceptual confusions in it, the empirical case still stands its ground. Scott's analysis translates into a rich rational choice theory of peasant behavior.[11] The principal errors are evidently not in the empirical account but only in the interpretation of their economic significance.

---

[9] Amartya Sen, "Equality of What?," pp. 353–369 in Sen, *Choice, Welfare and Measurement* (Cambridge, Mass.: MIT Press 1982).

[10] Russell Hardin, "Rational Choice Theories," in Terence Ball, ed., *Idioms of Inquiry: Critique and Renewal in Political Science* (Albany, N.Y.: SUNY Press 1987), pp. 67–91.

[11] As Samuel L. Popkin argues in *The Rational Peasant: The Political Economy of Rural Society in Vietnam* (Berkeley: University of California Press 1979).

Incidentally, "moral" in this account of moral economy seems to mean no more than that, given their established practice, which is eminently in their interest, the peasants attach moral vocabulary to the practice. As do people in many other contexts as well, they deduce an "ought" from an "is."[12] Or perhaps they merely short-cut their reasoning and moralize means to the ends they value.[13]

Finally, recall the point made by some critics (especially philosophers) of rational choice that we should expect rational choice theory to fail when resources become profligate enough to allow the fulfillment of ever more diverse consumptions. At that level of resources, resources or their amassment may compete with consumption (they typically compete in the sense of trading off resources for consumptions). I may be able to gain more resources only by forgoing consumptions. Moreover, my consumptions may become much more, not less competitive, just because my indulgence of them is less constrained. Under the grim constraints of subsistence, I cannot really choose much beyond limited consumption with survival and more spectacular consumption briefly on the way to not surviving. It is not that rational choice theory becomes increasingly unstable with increasing resources, but that preference over the vast range of possibilities becomes more idiosyncratic and perhaps even less stable.

Rational choice without substantive values

There are several ways in which theorists avoid the assumption of welfarism (or any other particular substantive value) as the basis of rational choice. Two are especially instructive. In the first, it is sometimes assumed that each individual can have any values, welfarist or otherwise, and that the theory will still work, as though the theory were somehow neutral with respect to values. In the second, it is supposed that we get

---

[12] Russell Hardin, *One for All: The Logic of Group Conflict* (Princeton, N.J.: Princeton University Press 1995), pp. 60–5.

[13] In his discussion of "the moral economy of the English crowd," E. P. Thompson's central concern is with the reaction of the general populace to high prices for grain in years of short harvests. In those years, the people insist, often under threat of force, that dealers and millers not charge substantially higher prices than they would in good years. This is a "moral" concern insofar as it is an objection to profiteering from adversity. E. P. Thompson, "The Moral Economy of the English Crowd in the Eighteenth Century," *Past and Present* 50 (1971): 76–136. Thompson sometimes frames his argument as a derivation of an ought from an is – as did, no doubt, the eighteenth-century English crowd. The price in years of normal harvest becomes the morally right price.

stable results without any assumption whatever about the internal mental considerations of the actors as though the theory were purely behavioral and not implicitly cognitive.

First, consider the neutral view of values. Arrow's theorem is based on leaving it open to each individual to have any preference ordering over various states of affairs. My preferences could be ordered by an altruistic, selfish, spiteful, ideal-regarding, or any other principle. This, the most abstract form of the utility function – with any values plugged in – is a late, essentially theoretical development. Actual economic reasoning about society typically continues the traditional presumption of welfare values, the presumption that there are objective things that matter to most people. In actual reasoning, for example, it is typically assumed that people prefer more resources to fewer, more of some consumptions within a given range to fewer, reasonable survival to death, and so forth. Many applications of economic reasoning would make no sense without such assumptions, which are so much a part of second nature that they are not even explicitly stated.

Similarly, claims for the inherent neutrality of the liberal program are prima facie false or at least exaggerated. Virtually all liberals and all liberalisms share Hobbes's view of the substantive values of survival and welfare. Hence, there is real, substantive content to the values defended by liberalism, which is not an empty shell that can be filled with any values willy-nilly. Indeed, Locke, an early liberal, was particularly concerned to keep non-welfarist religious values out of politics in order to secure welfarist values. The only neutrality we might insist on is the neutrality of John Stuart Mill's skepticism in the determination of what conduces to the welfare of other individuals. One person thinks parlor games are the best way to enhance welfare at the end of the day, another thinks relaxing mindlessly before the television is the best, another thinks reading great classics is best. All may be right for themselves alone. The fact that you think television is best for you is prima facie evidence that it is best for you. I must be epistemologically neutral about which is better for you in principle and must therefore defer prima facie to your judgment unless I can find causal relations that might sway your views.

Millian skeptical neutrality is not neutrality with respect to welfare, virtue, or whatever choice of fundamental value. It is epistemological, not moral. It is neutrality with respect to judgments of what contributes to welfare for a particular individual. Some things can be shown to have systematic welfare tendencies, as health does or various resources and talents might. But any such claim for systematic tendencies is empirical, not a priori, and it can prove to be wrong in a particular momentary instance or even more generally for a particular person. Hence, these claims may still be overridden by other considerations, such as particularly grim conditions that might make life seem worse than death, or harmful causal effects of which the particular individual may be ignorant. Enjoying wine this moment may seem to me to be a good thing, but it may contribute to wrecking my life.

Although the value theory of most rational choice theory is not neutral, the theory itself is neutral with respect to substantive social problems it can address. It can address almost any problem, almost every kind of problem. It is not a theory of class conflict, state formation, revolution, or democracy. But it can be brought to bear on all of these.

Now turn to the purely behavioral view of choice – choice that is no longer rational in the usual sense, because it involves no mental suppositions about agents. Gary Becker has argued that we do not need the assumption of rational choice to get standard results in economic analysis.[14] He analyzes the demand curve on the assumption that resources are limited rather than on the usual assumption that choice is deliberately intended to maximize utility. He shows that the market demand curve is negatively sloped even if individual households are irrational in their consumption choices. Hence, Becker demonstrates that we can get market regularity from individual irregularity.

There are three, perhaps too easy, responses to this move. First, Becker himself does not follow up his claim thereafter but sensibly returns to the more common assumption of rationality. He defends this move on the compelling ground that the standard theory is so richly developed that the gains from working with it in his areas of concern far outweigh what gains might be had from attempting to create a new theory.[15]

Second, rationality that is inherently grounded in substantive values of welfare is closely related to resourcist accountings. The appeal of basing theory in resources is that, ostensibly, the theory is then fully behavioral. We need not posit mental principles for choosing. We merely lay out the resource constraints. But this apparent escape from the supposedly hidden world of the mental requires at its outset that we somehow intuit or know how the resource constraints matter. We start from the mental, we do not escape it. Becker's demonstration was not directed at the philosopher's constant concern with the mental and the behavioral but only at the understanding of large systemic patterns.

---

[14] Gary S. Becker, "Irrational Behavior and Economic Theory," pp. 153–68 in Becker, *The Economic Approach to Human Behavior* (essay first published 1962).

[15] Becker, *The Economic Approach to Human Behavior*, p. 151.

Third, in politics it is often not sensible to characterize collective choices as choices by individuals in a market. The choices are very often of collective provisions, not individual provisions. We might still expect resource constraints to affect our collective survival, just as individual resource constraints affect individual survival. But this will be a big general issue, not an issue relevant to every collective choice. If we wish to understand many particular collective choices or if we find the results of collective choice relatively stable or regular, we are likely to be driven back to assuming the individuals involved in the choices are acting rationally, not merely whimsically or incomprehensibly.

To a large extent, unless we can carry out a program such as Becker's, the difference between assuming some value theory for the actors and not assuming any is the difference between explanatory and conceptual analysis in individualist political economy. If we impute certain substantive values to the actors in our theory, we can say what behaviors or choices follow from those value commitments. If we do not, we cannot say much. Hence, we may treat rational choice theory as a strictly positive theory in the following sense. The theorist takes the values of individuals into account but the theorist need not take a value position. If a theorist seems strongly committed to the descriptive claim that all or most people share some value, one might suspect the theorist shares the value. And some rational choice theorists may seem to hold the view that self-interest is the "right" value for a person to have. But one could be completely open as to whether there are any right values while still thinking, descriptively, that some small set of values motivates a particular population in some context.

Non-welfarist value theories

Reliance on a substantive value theory is, of course, not unique to rational choice theory. Theories, both normative and explanatory, have been grounded in various non-welfarist value theories with specific substantive content. Canvassing many of these or analyzing any one of them in depth would take up far too much space for present purposes, but it is useful to consider three major traditions: contractarianism, Marxist labor theory of value, and communitarianism. All of these have been applied both to normative justification and to explanation of social results.

Contractarianism

In its explanatory mode, political contractarianism was ridiculed by Hume and it has never recovered. Hume merely pointed out what everyone knew: that no actual states seemed to have historical grounding in an act of general popular agreement or contract. Still, contractarianism, the political generalization of consent, is touted as a justificatory principle.[16] In this, it trades on the appeal of consent in ordinary personal contexts. But that appeal does not compose readily into a collective analog. The apparent moral force of contractarianism is a fallacy of composition. There might be a context in which composition from individual to collective consent would work. But modern states are not such contexts.

Hobbes clearly wanted justification. Perhaps therefore many interpreters have tried to impose a moral contractarian vision on him, as though he were arguing that because we have agreed to government we are morally obligated to stick by our agreement. His actual justification is more nearly utilitarian because it is grounded in mutual advantage. He says we are all better off to have a state and, once we have one, to avoid dissension and revolution. Mutual advantage is, of course, part of what is required for a standard contractarian argument to go through. But Hobbes did not need to take the further step of claiming that prior agreement makes obedience morally obligatory because mutual advantage was sufficient justification for his argument, as it often would be for a utilitarian justification.

Labor theory of value

Turn to the labor theory of value. The chief candidate for Marx's value theory is his labor theory of value, according to which the value of an object is a function only of the amount of labor that has gone into producing it. That value theory is conspicuously silly in general. For example, if academic journals applied that theory to the acceptance of articles for publication, the journals would deteriorate dramatically. But if that value theory fails, the Marxist argument about exploitation collapses with it. One might still think there is capitalist exploitation of

---

[16] Russell Hardin, "Contractarianism: Wistful Thinking," *Constitutional Political Economy*, 1 (1990), 35–52.

workers or first world exploitation of the third world, *but it will take a new argument grounded in a different value theory to make the case.*

Is the labor theory of value strictly normative or is it also explanatory? It would be out of character for Marx not to have treated it as explanatory. The account goes roughly as follows. Workers in some circumstances, such as the nineteenth-century industrial factory, begin to recognize their actual state through discussion of common interests. In that state, they are exploited because they get only a fraction of the labor value they contribute to the capitalist's product. As their understanding grows, they achieve class consciousness, they fully recognize their common interest as a class in opposition to another class. They are therefore then in a position to act in common for their class interest when relevant opportunities occur.

If we assert there is exploitation without grounding the claim in a value theory, such as the labor theory of value, the claim is likely to involve a naturalistic inference to a normative conclusion. We simply look at the structure of payoffs in an interaction and infer exploitation from nothing more than these facts. That would be an illegitimate and uncompelling move. Therefore, the labor theory of value or some alternative is necessary for Marxist argument, whether normative or explanatory. That is why, if the labor theory of value proves to be incoherent, then Marxist exploitation is incoherent as well – unless, again, it can be given grounding in some other value theory or normative principle.

Incidentally, it should be clear that one can reject the labor theory of value and claims of exploitation based on it and still argue for greater equality or for redistribution of resources for welfare. Indeed, exploitation *per se* is an odd notion that seems inherently to involve a naturalistic inference of a normative claim from a factual assessment. We might readily conclude that there is no exploitation but that there is grievous inequality or deprivation that merits correction. As the demand for unskilled labor falls in the United States, the permanently unemployed underclass grows. They cannot sensibly be seen as a capitalist resource, a reserve army of the proletariat available for controlling wages in the most profitable industries, although they may have that function in some service industries such as some fast-food restaurants. It is increasingly implausible to view their plight as one of exploitation. Most capitalists might be better off if there were no underclass.

Oddly, Marx's own value theory seems likely to be regressive, not progressive. For example, labor values cannot typically be expected to trump exchange or market values in a free-wheeling market. Suppose therefore that we leave it to central agencies to assign labor values in order to secure relevant incomes based in these values. These are likely to be grounded in past ways of doing things. Hence, in a period of technological transition (which is virtually always), we will tend to assign values for the manufacture of, say, cloth that derive from earlier values when there were no modern, mechanized looms. We will be Luddite. If we are, then we perversely undercut the possibilities of economic welfare for the large masses, whose poverty seemed to drive Marx's theorizing.

Communitarianism

Finally, consider an older view of what we might call cultural motivation, a view that is now articulated in communitarian thought. Communitarian argument is predominantly normative rather than explanatory. Historically, cultural motivations have been used in explaining collective action by diverse ethnic, religious, local, and national communities. In a sense, the appeal to communitarian values allows us to escape the fallacy of composition inherent in generalizations from individual to collective interest by supposing that there is no problem of composition of individual values.

Superficially, there seems to be no fallacy because every individual is supposed to want the same thing and to have the desire to contribute to achieving it. On the contribution side of the claim, however, one may still expect substantial conflict, just as in ordinary collective action contexts in which we all want the same collective provision but it is in our interest individually that others do the providing. Hence, communitarian values do not resolve the problem of composition from individual motivation to collective action. Their role is rather to admit non-welfarist values into the individual's panoply, values that are determined somehow by the group.

Some community values are merely group-level aggregations of individual-level values. For example, individuals may be expected to benefit from general economic growth in some contexts. Such welfarist values seem unlikely to be problematic for rational choice theory unless they are reified at the individual level in the form of strictly group-regarding values. Some community values, however, need not be welfarist – although it is too facile to conclude that they necessarily are not welfarist merely on the testimony of those who hold them. For example, many people may assert that the only reason to keep a promise is that it is immoral on non-welfarist grounds to break one. And yet they may generally only make promises for welfarist reasons and may typically break them for welfarist reasons.

Much of recent work on communitarian values is justificatory. The purpose of the work is to argue that communitarian values are good in some sense and that they should be honored by individuals and polities. Those who are troubled by news of atrocities and bloodshed in the name of particular community values have solid ground for complaint against too quick communitarian justification. Much of the work has been conceptual in trying to make sense of how values can get constituted at all if there is no communal basis for at least some of them.[17] So far, the "theory" is woefully underdeveloped. The relatively casual blending of Aristotelian virtues with Hegelian community commitments that stands in for communitarian value theory is too bland and unstructured to yield systematic conclusions. Worse still, the value theories of contemporary communitarians seem to share the regressive bias of the labor theory of value. Those theories elevate a form of social Luddism to the level of the good for a given community.[18]

The structuralist alternative to individual choice

Explanations grounded in these alternative value theories are still methodologically individualist. In the face of major political phenomena such as revolutions, the structuralist political economist may assert that an individualist approach is inadequate even on the accounts of individualist political economy. If the bulk of behavior would not be revolutionary and only a relatively small number of individuals make a revolution go, we cannot expect to know enough about relevant individuals to make competent predictions or even retrospective assessments of revolutions. We cannot have a theory of revolution or great social movements that depends on predicting whether a specific Lenin or Gorbachev is available to lead, and we cannot believe Leo Tolstoy's functionalist vision, at the end of *War and Peace*, that great times necessarily produce great people. We will have to look to more systematic structural considerations that finally enable the occasional revolutionary to make a difference.

One answer that the individualist theorist can give to this criticism is that the revolutions we see may be more or less accidental rather than structurally determined. Hence, the structuralist approach does no better

---

[17] Michael J. Sandel, *Liberalism and the Limits of Justice* (Cambridge: Cambridge University Press 1982).

[18] Hardin, *One for All*, chapter 7.

than the individualist. Structuralists are often uninterested in individual commitments and are willing simply to assume that relevant kinds will manifest themselves under certain conditions. They can then focus on explaining or understanding those conditions. The great strength of the individualist school is in simple generalizations about individuals, generalizations that may transform understanding even while blurring differences that seem to matter historically.

In the recent gentle revolutions of East Europe we may see seeming vindication of both individualist and structuralist arguments. For many commentators, the structural conditions of apparently declining economies seem to explain the revolutions. The accident of Gorbachev seems to many others to be the chief explanation of at least the timing of the revolutions. But individualists might further argue, as most western economists do, that the structural conditions of declining economies are eminently easily explained from individualist assumptions. The structuralist approach is therefore, at least in large part, merely shorthand for a more precise and more extensive individualist account. Moreover, individualist economists were perhaps more consistent than any other social scientists in predicting the changing conditions of the political economies of the East European nations. To trump them, structuralists would have to argue that the major condition was not economic but rather political and moral – it was the urge for democracy and openness, for national self-determination and the end of colonial domination, or whatever. Ironically, that would be an odder move in the structuralist school than in the individualist school.

Concluding remarks

If theorists of other persuasions are to take on individualist theorists on an equal footing, they too will have to accommodate their theories to a compelling value theory, which, at present levels of theoretical development of value theories, means either to accommodate to something like the individualist value theories of welfare and preference or to develop some other theory far more extensively than has yet been done. If the theory remains hollow at its core, it will be only variously of interest in its occasional insights rather than generally of interest in its overall program.

Perhaps rational choice theory has a natural tendency to develop a value theory roughly like that which drives most of it. Because it is individualist, it must be concerned with individual actions, hence, most likely, individual motivations. What motivates an individual? Typically, the desire to achieve particular ends or values, perhaps especially self-regarding ends and values, as rational choice theorists generally assume.

Rational choice theory is finally like sociobiology in the following limited sense. The most obvious sociobiological inference about human motivation is that humans seek their own interests. If they did not, they would individually reduce their chances of survival. This inference leaves open for investigation whether it could happen that group-oriented behaviors get selected. Economic reasoning about human motivation starts from the simplest self-interest assumption[19] and then turns to the same range of more complex aggregate or group-level issues. Still, in both cases, the group-level results are derived from individual interests. Even at the group-level, we would expect the individual-level result still to hold – if not always, at least very often, perhaps even predominantly often.

Much of the power of the rational choice approach may be an accident. It just happens that the welfarist value theory of economics over the past two or three centuries grew in response to theoretical and empirical attacks from vast numbers of economists and their critics. Nothing even vaguely like that has happened to any other value theory. As a result, the formal value theory of rational choice is richly articulated and supple. Anyone who wishes to oppose some other value theory to it is burdened with the virtually impossible task of first making that other theory articulate enough even to stay in debate. Worse still, at this stage in development of various theories, all others are virtually forced to deal with the formal and even the substantive value theory of rational choice if they are to address similar problems. That is to say, other theorists are likely to be forced to contribute to rational choice theory while pursuing their own preferred alternative.[20] The critics of rational choice may finally wish to weep at their complicity in its refinement.

[19] This was Hobbes's assumption long before it was a sociobiological inference.
[20] See Russell Hardin, "The Morality of Law and Economics," *Law and Philosophy* 11 (November 1992): 331–84, especially pp. 380–4.

5 The virtual reality of *homo economicus*

PHILIP PETTIT

The economic explanation of individual behaviour, even behaviour outside the traditional province of the market, projects a distinctively economic image on the minds of the agents involved. It suggests that in regard to motivation and rationality, they conform to the profile of *homo economicus*. But this suggestion, by many lights, flies in the face of common sense; it conflicts with our ordinary assumptions about how we each feel and think in most situations, certainly most non-market situations, and about how that feeling and thought manifest themselves in action. What, then, to conclude? That common sense is deeply in error on these matters? That, on the contrary, economics is in error – at least about non-market behaviour – and common sense sound? Or that some form of reconciliation is available between the two perspectives? This paper is an attempt to defend a conciliationist position.

The paper is in five sections. In the first section I describe the economic mind that is projected in economic explanation, whether explanation of market or non-market behaviour. In the second section I argue that this is not the mind that people manifest in most social settings and, in particular, that it is not the mind that common sense articulates. In the third section I show that nevertheless the economic mind may have a guaranteed place in or around the springs of human action; it may have a virtual presence in the generation of action, even action on which it does not actually impact. In the fourth section I show that where the economic mind has such a virtual presence, that is enough to license an important variety of economic explanation: the explanation of the resilience or robustness of certain patterns rather than the explanation of their emergence or continuance. And then in a short fifth section I show that this sort of explanation fits with some established ideas about the explananda of economic and social science.

1 The thesis of the economic mind

There are two sorts of assumptions that economists make about the minds of the agents with whom they are concerned. First, content-centred assumptions about the sorts of things that the agents desire: about which things they prefer and with what intensities. And, second, process-centred assumptions about the way in which those desires, those degrees of preference, issue in action.

The process-centred assumptions boil down to the assumption that people's actions serve their desires well, given their beliefs about such matters as the options available, the likely consequences of different options, and so on. There are different theories as to what it is for an action or choice to serve an agent's desires well, given the agent's beliefs: about what it is for an agent to be rational. Many economists work with relatively simple models but the family of theories available is usefully exemplified by Bayesian theories of rationality (Eells 1982). According to Bayesian theory, an action is rational just in case it maximizes the agent's expected utility.

The Bayesian idea, roughly, is that every agent has a utility function that identifies a certain degree of utility, a certain intensity of preference, for every way the world may be – every prospect – and a probability function that determines, for each option and for each prospect, the probability that the choice of that option would lead to the realization of that prospect. An action will maximize the agent's expected utility just in case it has a higher expected utility than alternative options, where we determine the expected utility of an option as follows. We take the prospects with non-zero probability associated with the option; we multiply the utility of each prospect by the fraction representing the probability of its being realized in the event of the option's being chosen; and we add those products together.

So much for the assumptions that economists make about the way desires or preferences lead to action. What now of the assumptions that they make about the content of what human beings prefer or desire? The main question here is how far economists cast human beings as ego-centric in their desires. In order to discuss it, we need some distinctions between different theses that each ascribe a certain egocentricity.

1. *Self-centredness*. This relatively weak claim says that people do what they do as a result of their own desires or utility functions. They do not act on the basis of moral belief alone; such belief issues in action, only if accompanied by a suitable desire. And they do not act just on

the basis of perceiving what other people desire; the perception that someone desires something can lead to action only in the presence of a desire to satisfy that other person.

2. *Weak non-tuism.* This is a stronger claim, in the sense that it presupposes the first but represents people as intuitively more ego-centric still. People's desires bear on how others behave and on what happens to others, so the thesis goes, but such desires are not affected by perceptions of what those agents desire, even for themselves; people's utility functions, as it is often put, are independent of one another (Gauthier 1986, 87).

3. *Strong non-tuism.* A stronger claim again: people's desires do not extend, except instrumentally, to others. Not only do people take no account of what others desire in forming their own desires in regard to others; any desires they have for what others should do, or for what should happen to others, are motivated ultimately by a desire for their own satisfaction (Gauthier 1986, 311).

4. *Self-regardingness.* A thesis that presupposes 1 but represents an alternative way of strengthening it to that represented by 2 and 3. People's non-instrumental desires may extend to others, and they may be responsive to the perceived desires of others – 2 and 3 may be false – but the more that the desires bear on their own advantage, the stronger they are; in other words, people are relatively self-regarding in their desires.

Economists almost universally accept the first, self-centredness thesis. Agents who are rational in any economically recognizable sense cannot be led to action just by moral belief or the perception of what another desires or anything of the sort; such belief or perception may affect what they do but only through first affecting what they desire. Some thinkers toy with the possibility that agents may be capable of putting themselves under the control of something other than their own desires: for example, Mark Platts (1980) when he imagines that moral belief may motivate without the presence of desire; Amartya Sen (1982, Essay 4) when he speaks of the possibility of commitment; and Frederic Schick (1984) when he canvases the notion of sociality. But economists are probably on the side of common sense in urging that all action is mediated via the desires of the agent (Pettit 1993, Chapter 1). In any case, that is what I shall assume in what follows. There is a conflict between economics and common sense, as I shall be arguing, but it does not arise in respect of this first thesis.

Do economists go beyond the rather uncontroversial form of self-centredness articulated in thesis 1? They certainly do so to the extent that certain versions of the axioms of consumer choice theory go beyond minimal requirements of rationality, self-centredness included, and imply features like the downward-sloping demand curve. But that is not the issue. The question is whether economists go beyond the postulate of self-centredness in postulating any of the more egoistic theses, 2 to 4.

Many economic theories endorse weak and strong non-tuism. They do so to the extent that various economic models assume that any good I do you is, from my point of view, an externality for which ideally I would want to extract payment: an external benefit that I would ideally want to appropriate for myself (or 'internalize') (Gauthier 1986, 87). But this seems to be a feature of particular models and not an assumption that is essentially built into the economic way of thinking. And it is a feature that affects only some of the standard results of the theories in question, not all of them (Sen 1982, 93). I am not inclined to regard it as a deep feature of economic thinking. It may have little or no presence, for example, in the application of economic thought to social life outside the market.[1]

While economics postulates self-centredness in the sense of thesis 1, then, it does not necessarily suppose that people are non-tuistic in the senses defined in theses 2 and 3. But, to come now to thesis 4, I do think that the discipline is committed to the assumption that people's self-regarding desires are generally stronger than their other-regarding ones:

---

[1] Some may say that there is a deeper reason than the frequent use of non-tuistic assumptions for thinking that economic thinking is strongly non-tuistic in nature. The deeper reason, according to these theorists, is that in holding that agents act so as to satisfy their desires, economists assume that agents act for the sake of achieving their own desire-satisfaction: that is, for the sake of attaining a certain benefit for themselves. Anthony Downs gives countenance to this line of thought when, ironically enough, he tries to explain how economists can make sense of altruism. 'There can be no simple identification of acting for one's greatest benefit with selfishness in the narrow sense because self-denying charity is often a great source of benefits to oneself. Thus our model leaves room for altruism in spite of its basic reliance upon the self-interest axiom' (Downs 1957, 37).

The line of thought in Downs's remark is confused. Accepting the economic theory of rationality may mean believing that people maximize expected utility but it does not mean believing that they act for their own greatest benefit. That a person maximizes expected utility means that they act in the way that best serves their desires, according to their beliefs, but not that they do so *for the sake of* maximum desire-satisfaction and, in that sense, *for the sake of* their greatest benefit. When I act on a desire to help an elderly person across the road, I act so as to satisfy that desire but I do not act for the sake of such satisfaction; I act for the sake of helping the elderly person. To think otherwise would be to confuse the sense in which I seek desire-satisfaction in an ordinary case like this and the sense in which I seek it when I relieve the longing for a cigarette by smoking or the yearning for a drink by going to the pub.

that in this sense people are relatively self-regarding in their desires. Whenever there is a conflict between what will satisfy me or mine and what will satisfy others, the assumption is that in general I will look for the more egocentric satisfaction. I may do so through neglecting your interests in my own efforts at self-promotion, or through helping my children at the expense of yours, or through jeopardizing a common good for the sake of personal advantage, or through taking the side of my country against that of others. The possibilities are endless. What unites them is that in each case I display a strong preference for what concerns me or mine, in particular a preference that is stronger than a countervailing preference for what concerns others.[2]

The assumption that people are relatively self-regarding in their desires shows up in the fact that economists tend only to invoke relatively self-regarding desires in their explanations and predictions. They predict that as it costs more to help others, there will be less help given to others, that as it becomes personally more difficult to contribute to a common cause – more difficult, say, to take litter to the bin – there will be a lesser level of contribution to that cause, and so on. They offer invisible-hand explanations under which we are told how some collective good is attained just on the basis of each pursuing their own advantage. And they specialize in prisoner's dilemma accounts that reveal how people come to be collectively worse off, through seeking each to get the best possible outcome for themselves.[3]

The belief that people are relatively self-regarding shows up in other

---

[2] Notice that this conception of self-interest is consistent with the recognition of a capacity on the part of ordinary agents to identify with entities beyond themselves. See Pettit 1997, Chapter 8.

[3] It may be said against this that I am focusing on purely contingent aspects of economic explanation: that there is no reason why economists should not develop their explanations on the basis of other-regarding desires as well. Perhaps fewer people will put their litter in a bin that becomes more difficult to access. But, equally, fewer people will put their litter in a bin, if it comes to be generally believed that littering is not so bad after all: say if it comes to be believed, however improbably, that littering has some good environmental side-effects. Or so any economist should be prepared to admit.

This observation shows that economists can and should recognize the relevance of relatively other-regarding desires. But it does not demonstrate that they must take those desires to be potentially just as powerful as self-regarding preferences. And the explanatory practice of economists manifests the contrary belief. The working assumption behind economic explanation is that however much people may care for others, care for a collective good, or care for some moral principle, their self-concern is likely to outweigh the effects of such care, if it comes into conflict with it. That is why it must be a miracle in the economics textbook if some aggregate or collective pattern emerges or continues when the available self-regarding reasons argue against people's doing the things that the pattern requires.

aspects of economic thought too. It may be behind the assumption of economic policy-makers and institutional designers that no proposal is plausible unless it can be shown to be 'incentive-compatible': that is, unless it can be shown that people will have self-regarding reasons for going along with what the proposal requires.[4] And it may be at the root of the Paretian or quasi-Paretian assumption of normative or welfare economics that it is uncontroversially a social benefit if things can be changed so that all preferences currently satisfied continue to be satisfied and if further preferences are satisfied as well. This assumption is plausible if the preferences envisaged are self-regarding, for only envy would seem to provide a reason for denying that it is a good if some people can get more of what they want for themselves without others getting less. But the assumption is not at all plausible if the preferences also include other-regarding preferences, as we shall see in a moment. And so the Paretian assumption manifests a further, deeper belief: that the preferences with which economics is concerned are self-regarding ones.

The Paretian assumption is not plausible – certainly not as uncontroversial as economists generally think – when other-regarding preferences are involved, for reasons to which Amartya Sen (1982, Essay 2) has directed our attention. Consider two boys, Nasty and Nice, and their preferences in regard to the distribution of two apples, Big and Small. Nasty prefers to get Big no matter who is in control of the distribution. Nice prefers to get Small if he is in control – this, because he is other-regarding and feels he should give Big away if he is in charge – but prefers to get Big, if Nasty is in control: he is only human, after all. The Paretian assumption suggests – under the natural individuation of options (Pettit 1991) – that it is better to have Nice control the distribution rather than Nasty. If we put Nice in control, then that satisfies Nasty – he gets Big – and it satisfies Nice as well: Nice's preference for having Big if Nasty is in control does not get engaged and Nice's preference for having Small – for giving Big away – if he is in control himself is satisfied. But this is clearly crazy: it means that we are punishing Nice for being nice, in particular for having other-regarding preferences; and this, while apparently attempting just to increase preference-satisfaction in an impartial manner. The lesson is that the Paretian assumption is not plausible once other-regarding preferences figure on the scene and so, if economists think that it is plausible – think

---

[4] In fairness, however, I should note that this search for incentive-compatibility could be motivated – reasonably or not – by the belief that however other-regarding most people are, policies should always be designed to be proof against more self-regarding 'knaves'. See Brennan and Buchanan 1981.

indeed that it is uncontroversial – that suggests that they only have self-regarding preferences in view.

The upshot of all this, then, is that economists present human agents as relatively self-regarding creatures who act with a view to doing as well as possible by their predominantly self-regarding desires. These desires are usually assumed to be desires for what is loosely described as economic advantage or gain: that is, roughly, for advantage or gain in the sorts of things that can be traded. But self-regarding desires, of course, may extend to other goods too and there is nothing inimical to economics in explaining patterns of behaviour by reference, say, to those non-tradable goods that consist in being well loved or well regarded (Pettit 1990; Brennan and Pettit 1993, 2000). The economic approach is tied to an assumption of relative self-regard but not to any particular view of the dimensions in which self-regard may operate.

2 The conflict with common sense

Does the picture fit? Are human beings rational centres of predominantly self-regarding concern? It would seem not. Were human agents centres of this kind, then we would expect them to find their reasons for doing things predominantly in considerations that bear on their own advantage.[5] But this isn't our common experience, or so at least I shall argue.

Consider the sorts of considerations that weigh with us, or seem to weigh with us, in a range of common-or-garden situations. We are apparently moved in our dealings with others by considerations that bear on their merits and their attractions, that highlight what is expected of us and what fair play or friendship requires, that direct attention to the good we can achieve together or the past that we share in common, and so on through a complex variety of deliberative themes. And not only are we apparently moved in this non-egocentric way. We clearly believe of one another – and take it, indeed, to be a matter of common belief – that we are generally and reliably responsive to claims that transcend and occasionally confound the calls of self-regard. That is why we feel free to

---

[5] Some might say that under the assumption that human beings are rational centres of predominantly self-regarding concern – this, in a Bayesian sense – we ought to expect that they would be, not only self-concerned, but also calculating: we ought to expect that they would think in terms of the ledger of probabilities and utilities that figure in Bayesian decision theory. I do not go along with this. Bayesian decision theory says nothing on how agents manage to maximize expected utility; it makes no commitments on the style of deliberation that agents follow. See Pettit 1991.

ask each other for favours, to ground our projects in the expectation that others will be faithful to their past commitments, and to seek counsel from others in confidence that they will present us with a more or less impartial rendering of how things stand.

Suppose that people believed that they were each as self-regarding as economists appear to assume; suppose that this was a matter of common belief amongst them. In that case we would expect much of the discourse that they carry on with one another to assume the shape of a bargaining exchange. We would expect each of them to try to persuade others to act in a certain way by convincing them that it is in their personal interest to act in that way: this, in good part, by convincing them that they, the persuaders, will match such action appropriately, having corresponding reasons of personal advantage to do so. Under the economic supposition, there would be little room for anyone to call on anyone else in the name of any motive other than self-interest.

The economic supposition may be relevant in some areas of human exchange, most saliently in areas of market behaviour. But it clearly does not apply across the broad range of human interaction. The normal mode under which people exchange with one another is closer to the model of a debate than the model of a bargain. It involves them in each presenting to the other considerations that, putatively, they both recognize as relevant and potentially persuasive. I do not call on you in the name of what is just to your personal advantage; did I do so, that could be a serious insult. I call on you in the name of your commitment to certain ideals, your membership of certain groups, your attachment to certain people. I call on you, more generally, under the assumption that like me you understand and endorse the language of loyalty and fair play, kindess and politeness, honesty and straight talking. This language often has a moral ring but the terminology and concepts involved are not confined to the traditional limits of the moral; they extend to all the terms in which our culture allows us to make sense of ourselves, to make ourselves acceptably intelligible, to each other.

One way of underlining this observation is to consider how best an ethnographer might seek to make sense of the ways in which people conduct their lives and affairs. An ethnographer that came to the shores of a society like ours – a society like one of the developed democracies – would earn the ridicule of professional colleagues if they failed to take notice of the rich moral and quasi-moral language in which we ordinary folk explain ourselves to ourselves and ourselves to one another: the language, indeed, in which we take our bearings as we launch ourselves in action. But if it is essential for the understanding of how we ordinary folk behave that account is taken of that language, then this strongly suggests that economists must be mistaken – at least they must be overlooking some aspect of human life – when they assume that we are a relatively self-regarding lot.[6]

The claim that ordinary folk are oriented towards a non-egocentric language of self-explanation and self-justification does not establish definitively, of course, that they are actually not self-regarding. We all recognize the possibilities of rationalization and deception that such a language leaves open. Still, it would surely be miraculous that that language succeeds as well as it does in defining a stable and smooth framework of expectation, if as a matter of fact people's sensibilities do not conform to its contours: if, as a matter of fact, people fall systematically short – systematically and not just occasionally short – of what it suggests may be taken for granted about them.

We are left, then, with a problem. The economic mind is that of a relatively self-regarding creature. But the mind that people display towards one another in most social settings, the mind that is articulated in common conceptions of how ordinary folk are moved, is saturated with concerns that dramatically transcend the boundaries of the self. So how, if at all, can the economic mind be reconciled with the common-or-garden mind?[7]

3 The economic mind as a virtual presence

The obvious answer for would-be conciliationists is to say that whereas ordinary folk conform in most contexts to the picture of the common

[6] We may note in passing that there is nothing surprising in the fact that our ordinary encounters with one another are articulated and shaped by a non-egocentric language. We are not just bargaining creatures who take one another's beliefs and desires as given and seek out minimal terms of cooperation. We are creatures who also try to influence what we each believe and desire, under the assumption that when obstacles do not get in the way – when there is nothing we are disposed to fault about our circumstances – then we are susceptible to the same considerations in the formation of our beliefs and desires: under the assumption, equivalently, that we are sensitive to the same norms of belief and desire formation (Pettit 1993, Chapter 2). Given that we pursue this enterprise, it is only to be expected that we should have evolved a language for framing culturally shared expectations.

[7] This problem may be dismissed by some thinkers on the ground that the literature on conditional cooperation shows how economically rational individuals may cooperate out of purely self-regarding motives (Axelrod 1984; Taylor 1987; Pettit and Sugden 1989). But that would be a mistake. This literature shows that economically rational individuals may come to behave cooperatively, not that they will come to think and talk in a cooperative way.

mind, the economic mind is still *implicitly* present in such contexts. But how to interpret this? What does it mean to say that the economic mind is implicitly present: that people are implicitly but not explicitly oriented towards the self-regarding concerns that economists privilege?

The main model of the implicit–explicit distinction is drawn from a visual analogy. It suggests that an explicit concern is something focal, something directed to the centre of a subject's field of vision, whereas an implicit concern is a concern for what lies at the edge of that field: a concern for what is peripherally rather than focally tracked. If I explicitly desire something, my desire is explicit in the sense in which I am explicitly aware of the computer screen in front of me; if I implicitly desire something, my desire is implicit in the sense in which I am – or was a moment ago – only implicitly aware of the telephone at the edge of my desk. Does this model help in explicating the idea that even if people are not always explicitly of an economic turn of mind, they are at least implicitly so?

The model certainly gives us a picture of what it might mean to say that implicitly people are economically minded. It would mean that even as people pay attention to the sorts of concerns engaged in ordinary exchanges with others, even as they keep their eyes on the needs of a friend, the job that has to be done, the requirements of fairness, they invariably conduct some peripheral scanning of what their own advantage dictates that they should do. The model does not deny the appearance of more or less other-regarding deliberation but it does debunk that appearance. It suggests that whether they are aware of it or not, those who practise other-directed deliberation indulge a more self-directed style of reflection in the shadows of the mind, on the boundaries of their attention. Gary Becker (1976, 7) comes close to endorsing this model when he writes: 'the economic approach does not assume that decision units are necessarily conscious of their own efforts to maximize or can verbalize or otherwise describe in an informative way reasons for the systematic patterns in their behaviour. Thus it is consistent with the emphasis on the subconscious in modern psychology.'

But the focal–peripheral interpretation of the claim that people are implicitly self-regarding does not make the claim seem particularly compelling. We all admit that people profess standards from which they often slip and that their slipping does usually relate to an awareness, perhaps a deeply suppressed awareness, of the costs of complying with the standards. We all admit, in other words, that weakness of will and self-deception are pretty commonplace phenomena. But what the focal–peripheral model would suggest is that the whole of human life is shot through with this sort of failure: that what we take to be a more or less occasional, more or less localized, sort of pathology actually represents the normal, healthy state of the human organism. That is a fairly outrageous claim. Most economists would probably be shocked to hear that the view of the human subject which they systematically deploy is about as novel, and about as implausible, as the picture projected in classical Freudianism.

But if we reject the focal–peripheral way of reconciling the economic and the common mind, are we forced to choose between the two pictures of the human subject? Are we forced to choose between economic science and common sense? Happily, I think not. There is a second, less familiar model of the implicit–explicit distinction that is available in the literature and it promises a different, more attractive mode of reconciliation.[8]

I call this the virtual–actual model. One area where it is sometimes deployed – though not in so many words – is in explaining the sense in which I may implicitly believe that 2 times 101 is 202, even when I have never given a thought to that particular multiplication; or, to take another example, the sense in which I may implicitly believe that Europe has more than ten million inhabitants, when I have only ever thought about the population of individual countries. I implicitly believe these things in the sense that I am so disposed – specifically, I am so familiar with elementary arithmetic or with the population figures for European countries – that even the most casual reflection is sufficient to trigger the recognition that indeed 2 times 101 is 202, indeed the population of Europe is more than ten million. I virtually believe the propositions in question – virtually, not actually – but the virtuality or potentiality in question is so close to realization that ordinary usage scarcely marks the shortfall.[9]

I propose that if we are to follow the familiar conciliationist route of describing people as economically minded, but not always in an explicit

---

[8] I explore a third model of this distinction in Pettit (1998) but it doesn't seem to have any application relevant to present concerns.

[9] The implicitness of my belief that 2 times 101 is 202 should not be confused with the implicitness of my belief, say, that for any number described in decimal notation, you get double that number by following the sort of rule that you and I apply in computing 2 times 101: a rule, as it happens, that we would probably find it hard to articulate. The implicitness of the belief in the rule does not lend itself to modelling on the virtual–actual pattern, but rather on some other analogy such as that provided by the focal–peripheral picture, because it is clear that you and I do actually believe in the rule; we do actually believe in it to the extent that we do actually rely on it. The implicitness of my belief that 2 times 101 is 202 is the implicitness of non-actuality, the implicitness of a belief that hovers on the edge of realization, not the implicitness of a belief that is realized in some sub-articulate fashion.

fashion, we should try to spell out this claim by reference to the virtual–actual model, not the focal–peripheral one. I think that it is not implausible that people are virtually self-regarding in most contexts of choice, even if they are not actually so. It is generally agreed that actual self-regard plays a great part in market and related behaviour but that it does not have the same sort of presence – if it has a presence at all – in other contexts: for example, in contexts of ordinary family or friendly interaction, in contexts of political decision, or in contexts of group behaviour. What I suggest is that in such non-market contexts self-regard may still have an important presence: it may be virtually if not actually there; it may be waiting in the wings, even if it is not actually on stage.

Here is how self-regard might have a virtual presence in such contexts. Suppose, first of all, that people are generally content in non-market contexts – we can restrict our attention to these – to let their actions be dictated by what we might call the cultural framing of the situation in which they find themselves. A friend asks for a routine level of help and, in the absence of urgent business, the agent naturally complies with the request; it would be unthinkable for someone who understands what friendship means to do anything else. There is an election in progress and, the humdrum of everyday life being what it is, the agent spontaneously makes time for going to the polls; that is manifestly the thing to do, under ordinary canons of understanding, and the thing to do without thinking about it. Someone has left a telephone message asking for a return call about some matter and the agent doesn't hesitate to ring back; even if aware that there is nothing useful they can tell the original caller, they shrink from the impoliteness, in their culture, of ignoring the call. In the pedestrian patterns of day-to-day life, the cultural framing of any situation will be absolutely salient to the ordinary agent and the ordinary agent will more or less routinely respond. Or so at least I am prepared to assume.

But that is only the first part of my supposition. Suppose, in the second place, that despite the hegemony of cultural framing in people's everyday deliberations and decisions, there are certain alarm bells that make them take thought to their own interests. People may proceed under more or less automatic, cultural pilot in most cases but at any point where a decision is liable to cost them dearly in self-regarding terms, the alarm bells ring and prompt them to consider personal advantage; and heeding considerations of personal advantage leads people, generally if not invariably, to act so as to secure that advantage: they are disposed to do the relatively more self-regarding thing.

Under these suppositions, self-regard will normally have no actual presence in dictating what people do; it will not be present in deliberation and will make no impact on decision. But it will always be virtually present in deliberation, for there are alarms which are ready to ring at any point where the agent's interests get to be possibly compromised and those alarms will call up self-regard and give it a more or less controlling deliberative presence. The agent will run under cultural pilot, provided that that pilot does not carry them into terrain that is too dangerous from a self-interested point of view. Let such terrain come into view, and the agent will quickly return to manual; they will quickly begin to count the more personal losses and benefits that are at stake in the decision on hand. This reflection may not invariably lead to self-regarding action – there is such a thing as self-sacrifice, after all – but the assumption is that it will do so fairly reliably.

If the suppositions I have described were realized, then it would be fair to say that people are implicitly self-regarding: that they implicitly conform to the image of the economic mind. The reason is that under the model of virtual self-regard, no action is performed without self-regarding consideration unless it fails to ring certain alarms: that is, unless it promises to do suitably well in self-regard terms. What it is to do suitably well may vary from individual to individual, of course, depending on their expectations as to what is feasible and depending on their self-regarding aspirations: depending on how much they want for themselves, and with what intensity. But the point is that regardless of such variations, the model of virtual self-regarding control does privilege self-regard in a manner that conforms to the image of the economic mind. Another way of putting this point is to say that under the model described, an agent will generally be moved by certain considerations only if they satisfy a certain negative, self-regarding condition: only if they do not tend to lead the agent towards a certain level of self-sacrifice. Let the considerations push the agent below the relevant self-regarding level of aspiration and the alarm bells will ring, causing the agent to rethink and probably reshape the project on hand.

The position which self-regard is given under the model of virtual self-regarding control is rather like that which it enjoys under Herbert Simon's (1978) model of satisficing as distinct from maximizing behaviour. People do pretty well in self-regarding terms, even if they do not do as well as possible. And it may even be that virtual self-regarding control enables them to do as well as possible in egocentric terms, for the absence of self-regarding calculation in most decisions represents a saving in time and trouble – these are virtues emphasized by Simon – and it may also secure other benefits: it may earn a greater degree of acceptance and affection, for example, than would a pattern of relentless calculation.

But is the model of virtual self-regarding control, in particular the scenario of the alarm bells, a plausible one? The question divides in two. First, is there any arrangement under which we can imagine that such alarms are put in place? And second, if there is, can we plausibly maintain that those alarms will reliably serve to usher self-regarding deliberation into a controlling position in the generation of behaviour?

The alarms required will have to be informational; they will have to be signals that this is the sort of situation where the agent's advantage may be compromised, if cultural framing is given its head. So are there signals available in ordinary contexts that might serve to communicate this message? Clearly, there are. Consider the fact that a decision situation is non-routine; or that it is of a kind where the agent's fingers were already burned; or that it is a situation in which the agent's peers – others who might be expected to fare about as well – do generally better than the agent; or that some conventional or other assurances as to the responses of others are lacking. Any such facts can serve as signals that the agent's personal advantage may be in especial danger. Indeed it is hard to imagine a situation where the agent's interests were likely to be compromised in significant measure by culturally framed demands – compromised in a measure that the agent would not generally tolerate – without such signals being present. Certainly it is reasonable to assume that generally there will be signals available in such situations that the agent should take care: signals to the effect that this is a situation where that framing is liable to serve the agent less well than it ordinarily does.

The other question is whether it is plausible, given the availability of signals of this kind, to postulate that the signals will generally tip agents into a self-regarding sort of deliberation: a sort of deliberation that is normally sidelined in favour of fidelity to the cultural frame. This issue is wholly an empirical matter but it is an issue on which the weight of received opinion speaks unambiguously. It has been common wisdom for at least two thousand years of thinking about politics that few are proof against temptation and few, therefore, are likely to ignore signals that their self-interest may be endangered. Human beings may be capable of reaching for the stars but, except for some romantic strands of thought, all the streams in the western tradition of thinking suggest that if there is opportunity for an individual to further their own interests, then they can generally be relied upon, sooner or later, to exploit that opportunity: all power corrupts. The main theme of the tradition is summed up in the lesson that no one can be entrusted with the ring of Gyges that Plato discusses: the ring that renders a person invisible and that makes it possible for them to serve their own interests with impunity, at whatever cost to the interests of others.

These lines of thought give support, therefore, to the picture described above. They suggest that it is very plausible to think that even where people pay no actual attention to relatively self-regarding considerations, still those considerations have a certain presence and relevance to how people behave. They are virtually present, in the sense that if the behaviour rings the alarm bells of self-interest – and there will be plenty of such bells to ring – the agent will give heed and will tend to let self-regarding considerations play a role in shaping what is done.[10]

Under the emerging picture, then, there is a sense in which people are always at least implicitly of the self-regarding cast of mind projected by economists; if they are not actually self-regarding in their mode of deliberation, they are virtually so: if self-regard does not actually occupy the pilot's seat, it is always there in the co-pilot's, ready to assume control. The picture is a rather non-idealistic representation of human beings but it is not unnecessarily bleak. It emphasizes that in the normal run, people are not calculatingly self-concerned: they articulate their lives and relationships in the currency of received values and they generally conform to the requirements of those values. Where it goes non-idealistic, it does so only in the spirit of what we might call the Gyges axiom: the principle that virtue – fidelity to the demands of the cultural frame – is fragile and generally survives only under conditions where it is not manifestly against the interests of the agent, only under conditions where the alarm bells do not ring.

There are two further points to put to those who worry about the alleged non-idealism of our picture. First, the picture leaves open the possibility that in many cases some individuals will not heed the alarms and will stick to what the culturally framed situation requires, by criteria of common values, through the thick and the thin of self-sacrifice. And, second, the picture leaves room for the Aristotelian principle that people become virtuous, become lovers of virtuous ways, through habituation in those ways. It leaves room, not just for the possibility that some people will be relatively heedless of the alarms described, but for the possibility that such heedlessness may be facilitated in increasing measure by a regime in which the alarms only rarely ring: a regime in which things are well designed and people are free, in the silence of self-regard, to develop an attachment to doing that which by the common values of the culture is what the situation requires.

---

[10] The picture of virtual self-regard may be modified by being made subject to certain boundary conditions. It might be held, for example, that the picture does not apply universally, only under certain structural arrangements: say, that it does not apply in family life, only in relations of a more public character. For related ideas see Satz and Ferejohn 1994.

4 The economic mind as an explanatory principle

We saw in the first section that the economic mind is distinctively self-regarding and in the second that it contrasts in this respect with the common mind: the mind as articulated in common ways of thinking. The last section gave us a picture under which it seems possible to reconcile these two points of view: the points of view associated respectively with economics and common sense. The common-sense viewpoint is valid to the extent that ordinary folk manage their affairs most of the time without adverting to their own interests; they are guided in their decisions by what is required of them under the cultural framing of the situations in which they find themselves. The economic viewpoint is valid to the extent that even when this is so, even when people are not explicitly self-regarding in their deliberations, still self-regard has a virtual presence; it is there, ready to affect what people do, in the event that any of the alarm bells of self-interest ring.

The question which now arises, however, is how far the merely virtual presence of self-regard is supposed to legitimate the economic explanatory enterprise: the enterprise of explaining various patterns in human affairs by reference to rational self-regard.[11] That self-regarding considerations have a virtual as distinct from an actual presence in human deliberation means that they are not actual causes of anything that the agents do. They may be standby causes of certain patterns of behaviour: they may be potential causes that would serve to sustain those patterns, did the actual causes fail. But it is not clear how anything is to be explained by reference to causes of such a would-be variety. After all, explanation is normally taken to uncover the factors operative in the production of the events and patterns to be explained; it is normally taken to require a reference to actual causal history (Lewis 1986, Essay 22).

This difficulty can be underlined by considering the explananda that economic investigation is ordinarily taken to be concerned with in the non-market area. These are, first, the emergence of certain phenomena or patterns in the past and, second, their continuation into the present and future. The explanation of the emergence of any phenomenon – say, the emergence of a norm or institution – clearly requires a reference to the

---

[11] Apart from the problem that I go on to discuss, there is an issue as to how, non-circularly, the economist is to tell the level of threat to self-interest at which an agent's alarm bells ring. I cannot discuss this problem here but would just note that it is parallel to the problem of determining an agent's aspiration level under Simon's (1978) satisficing model.

factors that were operative in bringing it into existence. And the explanation of the continuation of any phenomenon, equally clearly, requires a reference to the factors that keep it there.[12] So how could a reference to virtual self-regard serve to explain anything? In other words, how can our model of the common-cum-economic mind serve to make sense of the explanatory claims of economics, in particular of the economics of non-market behaviour: of behaviour that is motored by the perception of what situations demand, under relevant cultural frames, not by considerations of self-regard?

The answer, I suggest, is that even if virtual self-regard is of no use in explaining the emergence or continuation of any pattern of behaviour, it can be of great utility in explaining a third explanandum: the resilience of that pattern of behaviour under various shocks and disturbances.

Imagine a little set-up in which a ball rolls along a straight line – this, say, under Newton's laws of motion – but where there are little posts on either side that are designed to protect it from the influence of various possible but non-actualized forces that might cause it to change course; they are able to damp incoming forces and if such forces still have an effect – or if the ball just drifts – they are capable of restoring the ball to its original path. The posts on either side are virtual or standby causes of the ball's rolling on the straight line, not factors that have an actual effect. So can they serve any explanatory purpose? Well, they cannot explain the emergence or the continuation of the straight course of the rolling ball. But they can explain the fact – and, of course, it is a fact – that not only does the ball roll on a straight line in the actual set-up, it sticks to more or less that straight line under the various possible contingencies where perturbing forces appear and even have a temporary effect. They explain the fact, in other words, that the straight rolling is not something fragile, not something vulnerable to every turn of the wind, but rather a resilient pattern: a pattern that is robust under various contingencies and that can be relied upon to persist.

The resilience explained in this toy example may be a matter of independent experience, as when I discover by induction – and without understanding why – that the ball does keep returning to the straight line. But equally the resilience may only become salient on recognizing the explanatory power of the posts: this, in the way in which the laws that a theory explains may only become salient in the light of the

---

[12] I ignore the requirements of potential explanation – fact-defective or law-defective explanation – as that enterprise is discussed by Robert Nozick (1974). It may be interesting to know how something might have come about or might have continued to exist under a different history, or under a different regime of laws, but the interest in question is not that which motivates ordinary economic attempts at explanation.

explanatory theory itself. It does not matter which scenario obtains. In either case the simple fact is that despite their merely standby status, the posts serve to resolve an important matter of explanation. They explain, not why the pattern emerged at a certain time, nor why it continues across a certain range of times, but why it continues across a certain range of contingencies: why it is modally as distinct from temporally persistent.

The lesson of our little analogy should be clear. As a reference to the virtually efficacious posts explains the resilience with which the ball rolls on a straight line, so a reference to a merely virtual form of self-regard may explain the resilience with which people maintain certain patterns of behaviour. Imagine a given pattern of human behaviour whose continuation is actually explained by the cultural framing under which people view the relevant situations or, more prosaically, by people's sheer inertia. Suppose that that pattern of behaviour has the modal property of being extremely robust under various contingencies: say, under the contingency that some individuals peel away and offer an example of an alternative pattern. The factors that explain its actually continuing may not explain this robustness or resilience; there may be no reason why the example of mutant individuals should not display a new way of viewing the situation, for example, or should not undermine the effects of inertia. So how to explain the resilience of the pattern? Well, one possible explanation would be that as the contingencies envisaged produce a different pattern of behaviour, the alarm bells of self-interest ring – this, because of the contrast between what different individuals are doing – and the self-regarding deliberation that they prompt leads most of the mutants and would-be mutants back towards the original pattern.

The analogy with the rolling ball serves to show how in principle the model of virtual self-regard may leave room for the economic explanation of behaviour that is not actively generated by considerations of self-regard. But it may be useful to illustrate the lesson more concretely.

David Lewis's (1969) work on convention is often taken as a first-rate example of how economic explanation can do well in making sense of a phenomenon outside the traditional economic domain of the market. He invokes the fact that conventions often serve to resolve certain problems of coordination – problems of a kind that can be nicely modelled with game-theory techniques – in explanation of such conventions. But what is supposed to be explained by Lewis's narrative? Lewis is clearly not offering a historical story about the emergence of conventions. And, equally clearly, he is not telling a story about the factors that actually keep the conventions in place; he freely admits that people may not be aware of the coordination problem solved by conventional behaviour and may stick to that behaviour for any of a variety of reasons: reasons of inertia, perhaps, or reasons of principle or ideology that may have grown up around the convention in question.

The best clue to Lewis's explanatory intentions comes in a remark from a later article when he considers the significance of the fact that actually conventional behaviour is mostly produced by blind habit. 'An action may be rational, *and may be explained by the agent's beliefs and desires*, even though that action was done by habit, and the agent gave no thought to the beliefs or desires which were his reasons for action. If that habit ever ceased to serve the agent's desire's according to his beliefs, it would at once be overridden and corrected by conscious reasoning' (Lewis 1983, 181; my emphasis). This remark gives support to the view that what Lewis is explaining about convention, by his own lights, is not emergence or continuance but resilience. He implies that the servicing of the agent's – as it happens, self-regarding – desires is not the actual cause of the conventional behaviour but a standby cause: a cause that would take the place of a failing habit, so long as the behaviour remained suitable; this, in the way that he says it would displace the remaining habit at the point where the behaviour becomes unsuitable. And if the servicing of self-regard is a standby cause of this kind, then what it is best designed to explain is the resilience, where there is resilience, of the conventional behaviour.

But it is not only the Lewis explanation of conventional behaviour that lends itself to this gloss. Can we explain American slave-holding by reference to economic interests (Fogel and Engerman 1974, 4), when slave-holders articulated their duties, and conducted their business, in terms of a more or less religious ideology? Yes, to the extent that we can explain why slave-holding was a very resilient institution up to the time of the civil war; we can explain why the various mutants and emancipationists never did more than cause a temporary crisis. Can we explain the failure of people to oppose most oppressive states as a product of free-rider reasoning (North 1981, 31–2), when it is granted that they generally used other considerations to justify their acquiescence? Yes, so far as the free-riding variety of self-regarding reasoning would have been there to support non-action, to make non-action resilient, in any situation where the other, actual reasons failed to do so and alarms bells rang. Can we invoke considerations of social acceptance to explain people's abiding by certain norms, as I have tried to do elsewhere (Pettit 1990), when I freely grant that it is considerations of a much less prudential kind that keep most people faithful to such norms? Yes, we certainly can. Self-regarding considerations of social acceptance can ensure that normative fidelity is robust or resilient if they come into play whenever someone begins to deviate, or contemplate deviation, and if they serve in such cases to restore or reinforce compliance.

If it is granted that the resilience of phenomena like these is explicable by reference to virtual self-regard, I should add, then it becomes plausible that self-regard may explain something else as well. We are assuming that the day-to-day continuation of the patterns in question is explained in other terms: say, by reference to culturally established ways of thinking. But the resilience-explanation, assuming it is sound, suggests that there are likely to have been crises in the past where the virtual self-regard invoked in the resilience-explanation was actually triggered and where it had the effect of preserving the pattern under discussion. We may or may not have independent evidence of such crises but it becomes plausible to conjecture that there were some and that self-regard serves to explain the continuation of the pattern, not in day-to-day situations, but in the presence of those crises. I make this point, however, only in passing. The main claim I wish to defend is that even if self-regard serves in no way to explain emergence or continuation, still it can explain resilience.

The upshot will be clear. We can make good sense of economic explanation, even explanation of non-market behaviour, in terms of the model of virtual self-regard whereby the economic mind is reconciled with the common mind. That model recommends itself, then, on at least two grounds. It shows that the assumptions which economists make about the human mind, in particular about human motivation, can be rendered consistent with the assumptions of commonplace, everyday thinking. And it shows that so interpreted, the assumptions motivate a promising and indeed developing programme for economic explanation: and explanation, not just in the traditional areas of market behaviour, but across the social world more generally.

5 A more general view

But not only does the story that we have told show how economics, even an economics of self-regarding agents, can have something to say in explanation of ordinary social behaviour: in particular, behaviour outside the market. It does so in a way that fits the explanation to broader patterns. While the idea of explaining the resilience of a behavioural pattern – its resilience as distinct from its presence or emergence – may look suspiciously novel, it connects closely with quite familiar styles of theoretical explanation.

One is the explanation of the fitness conferred by a certain trait: the explanation that consists in showing why the trait is adaptive. That a trait confers a certain degree of fitness means that in the relevant environment the bearer has a certain propensity to survive – a certain propensity to be replicated in – a variety of more or less probable contingences.[13] Thus any explanation of fitness by reference to the adaptiveness of a trait is just like the explanations considered in the last section. Where we spoke of explaining the resilience of conventional or normative behaviour, of slave-holding or of prudence, we might just as well have spoken of explaining the fitness associated with those patterns of behaviour.

This observation keys us to the fact that the explanations we mentioned are also akin to those so-called functional explanations in sociology that attempt to explain the fitness or survival potential of certain institutions, presenting them as more or less fixed features of the society: as features fit to survive a large range of contingencies (Pettit 1996, 2000).[14] Take any institution such that whatever the reasons it obtains now, its role in private or public life means that were it to come under challenge, effects would materialize to keep it in place. The sociological explanation that points up that role and that argues for the survival potential of the institution by reference to that role parallels quite nicely the explanations considered here. One such explanation might argue for the survival potential of golf clubs by reference to the fact that golf clubs enable members to establish important business contacts; members may not be aware of this now but they would become aware of it under those pressures that might otherwise drive them away. Another such explanation might argue for the survival potential of a harsh prison regime by reference to the fact that such a regime enables politicians to satisfy the public outrage which reliably follows any heinous crime: it enables them to display the right body-language, presenting themselves as tough on crime.

But the most obvious pattern of explanation with which our story connects is equilibrium explanation. This is the explanation of a fact or pattern which does not show how it emerged or why it is present, but

---

[13] Fitness is a probabilized version of resilience under which resilience can be increased, not just through an increase in the number of contingencies guarded against, but also through an increase in the probability of the contingencies against which guards are provided.

[14] What I sketch here, of course, is a revisionist account of functional explanation in sociology: an account under which it might be better described as fitness-explanation. See Pettit 1996 for details and Pettit 2000 for a comparison between rational choice theory and functionalist explanation.

which demonstrates that the pattern is more or less inevitable, at least in a certain context, by pointing out that any ways in which it is liable to be disturbed would lead to correction. As an example Elliott Sober (1983) offers us R. A. Fisher's explanation of the 1:1 sex ratio in many species. The idea is that if a population ever departs from equal numbers of males and females, then there will be a reproductive advantage favouring parents who overproduce the minority sex and the 1:1 ratio will tend to be restored. Such an equilibrium explanation can be seen, in our terms, not as a distinctive way of explaining things – not as a distinctive *explanans* – but rather as a way of explaining a distinctive *explanandum*. That the sex ratio is in equilibrium, or that any pattern represents an equilibrium – strictly, a stable equilibrium – is a way of saying that it enjoys a particularly high degree of resilience. Being in stable equilibrium, at least for a given context, is a limit case of being resilient.

It hardly needs saying that while the notion of a stable equilibrium is variously construed, equilibrium explanation is a standard and staple practice in ordinary economics. What appears at this point, then, is that the story we told in vindication of economic explanation outside the market area vindicates it in a manner that ought to appeal to most economists. In pursuing equilibrium explanations economists show a day-to-day concern with explaining the resilience of certain patterns and not – or at least not necessarily – their emergence or persistence. Thus they ought to have no difficulty in recognizing the significance of the sorts of explanations discussed here.[15]

References

Axelrod, Robert (1984) *The Evolution of Cooperation*, New York: Basic Books.

Becker, Gary (1976) *The Economic Approach to Human Behaviour*, Chicago: University of Chicago Press.

Brennan, H. G. and J. M. Buchanan (1981) 'The Normative Purpose of Economic "Science": Rediscovery of an Eighteenth Century Method', *International Review of Law and Economics*, 1, 155–66.

Brennan, H. G. and Philip Pettit (1993) 'Hands Invisible and Intangible', *Synthese*, 94, 1993, 191–225.

(2000) 'The Hidden Economy of Esteem', *Economics and Philosophy*, 16, 77–98.

---

[15] This paper represents a further development of a theme in Pettit 1993. It overlaps in some part with the text of three lectures given at the Ecole des Hautes Etudes en Sciences Sociales, Paris and published as 'Normes et Choix Rationnels', *Reseaux*, 62, 87–112. I was greatly aided in preparing the final draft by comments received from Uskali Mäki, Raimo Tuomela, and an anonymous referee.

Downs, Anthony (1957) *An Economic Theory of Democracy* New York: Harper.

Eells, Ellery (1982) *Rational Decision and Causality*, Cambridge: Cambridge University Press.

Fogel, R. W. and S. L. Engermann (1974) *Time on the Cross: The Economics of American Negro Slavery*, Boston: Little, Brown.

Gauthier, David (1986) *Morals by Agreement*, Oxford: Oxford University Press.

Lewis, David (1969) *Convention*, Cambridge, Mass.: MIT Press.

—— (1983) *Philosophical Papers*, Vol. 1, New York: Oxford University Press.

—— (1986) *Philosophical Papers*, Vol. 2, New York: Oxford University Press.

North, Douglas (1981) *Structure and Change in Economic History*, New York: Norton.

Nozick, Robert (1974) *Anarchy, State and Utopia*, New York: Basic Books.

Pettit, Philip (1990) '*Virtus Normativa*: Rational Choice Perspectives', *Ethics*, 100, 725–55.

—— (1991) 'Decision Theory and Folk Psychology', in Susan Hurley and Michael Bacharach, eds., *Essays in the Foundations of Decision Theory*, Oxford: Blackwell, 147–75.

—— (1993) *The Common Mind: An Essay on Psychology, Society and Politics*, New York: Oxford University Press. Pb edition, with new postscript, 1996.

—— (1996) 'Functional Explanation and Virtual Selection', *British Journal for the Philosophy of Science*, 45, 1996.

—— (1997) *Republicanism: A Theory of Freedom and Government*, Oxford: Oxford University Press.

—— (1998) 'Practical Belief and Philosophical Theory', *Australasian Journal of Philosophy*, 76, 15–33.

—— (2000) 'Rational Choice, Functional Selection and Empty Black Boxes', *Journal of Economic Methodology*, 7, 33–57.

Pettit, Philip and Robert Sugden (1989) 'The Backward Induction Paradox', *Journal of Philosophy*, 86, 169–82.

Platts, Mark (1980) *Ways of Meaning*, London: Routledge.

Satz, Debra and John Ferejohn (1994) 'Rational Choice and Social Theory', *Journal of Philosophy*, 91, 71–87.

Schick, Frederic (1984) *Having Reasons: An Essay on Rationality and Sociality*, Princeton: Princeton University Press.

Sen, Amartya (1982) *Choice, Welfare and Measurement*, Oxford: Blackwell.

Simon, Herbert (1978) 'Rationality as Process and as Product of Thought', *American Economic Review*, 68, 1–16.

Sober, Elliott (1983) 'Equilibrium Explanation', *Philosophical Studies*, 43, 201–10.

Taylor, Michael (1987) *The Possibility of Cooperation*, Cambridge: Cambridge University Press.

6   Expressive rationality: is self-worth just another kind of preference?

SHAUN HARGREAVES HEAP

1   Introduction

People commonly reflect on what they do and these reflections give rise to feelings of self-worth, or sometimes the reverse when feelings of shame, guilt and embarrassment are experienced. It seems plausible to think that these feelings, or their anticipation, influence action in some way or another. Indeed, I take it for granted that, roughly speaking, people act in ways which encourage a sense of self-worth. This paper is concerned first with whether the conventional account of action as instrumentally rational offers a way of understanding such feelings and their connection to action. Action in the instrumental model is undertaken to satisfy preferences (or it conforms to a preference ordering) and it might be natural to think of self-worth as just another kind of preference which motivates people to act (or it is built in to a preference ordering). However, I argue in the next section that action which supports self-worth cannot be readily or easily subsumed within that model because self-worth cannot be reduced to some kind of preference.

Does this matter? Since no simple account of action could hope to capture exhaustively what makes people tick, it is not self-evident that the failure in this regard necessarily tells against the mainstream reliance on the instrumental model. However, in the third and fourth sections, I argue that the failure to include the reflective capacities which are responsible for the generation of self-worth in the ontology of economics does important damage to mainstream economics. In particular, it leads to an impoverished understanding of the three classic games of social and economic life: the prisoner's dilemma, the coordination and the battle of the sexes game.

My thanks go to Uskali Mäki for comments on an earlier version of this paper.

Throughout the argument, I shall be focusing on the type of *public* sense of self-worth that comes from behaviour which conforms with (or breaches) the shared standards or norms of a group. In these circumstances, the judgement about what is worthy in an action is shared by others who subscribe to the norm. So when one's action conforms (or breaches) a norm it is regarded as worthy (or shameful) for the same reasons by a group. This endows action with a symbolic dimension: the action becomes a voice to the shared reasons that find it worthy, so enabling people to say things about themselves to others who share that norm. As a result, action that is taken in support of self-worth in such conditions is often referred to as expressively rational (since the action comes to express something about the individual, see Hargreaves Heap 1989). Thus the paper is concerned with whether expressive rationality is reducible to instrumental rationality. Alternatively, as the shared standards which enable action to acquire this expressive dimension are the key to much anthropological investigation, this paper might be understood in yet a further way. It is concerned with whether the economists' rational choice model can account for what anthropologists typically find distinctive about human activity: that is, the shared meanings people attach to what they do; and if not what does economics lose through this blindness to anthropology.[1]

2 Self-worth is not simply another kind of preference nor do people get a sense of self-worth from preferences satisfaction

The conventional rational choice model of action often forgoes any explicit account of the process behind actions. It is simply action which conforms to the axioms of rational choice. This is a rather strange legacy of behaviourism in economics (e.g. see Stewart 1995) and for the reasons which make behaviourism generally difficult in social science (and because this volume is concerned with ontology), I shall treat it as a curiosity and focus on the motivational account of rational choice which is supplied when the rational choice model is pressed to account for its internal workings. This model depends on two elements: preferences over outcomes and beliefs regarding the connection between actions and

---

[1] Of course, Adam Smith in his *Theory of Moral Sentiments* made much of an individual's capacity to consider how their actions would seem to some impartial spectator. So, this paper might alternatively be viewed as study in what if anything has been lost to our understanding of economic agency by forgetting the influence of Adam Smith's impartial spectator.

outcomes. These elements together with an instrumentally rational disposition supply the ontology of a person. Thus the rational agent of rational choice theory acts having used their beliefs to calculate what action will best satisfy their preferences. The question addressed in this section is whether it is possible to make sense of action which seems to be influenced by a concern with a public sense of self-worth (or the avoidance of guilt, shame, and embarrassment) within this model of how people act. In other words, does the ontology of the rational choice model allow for what anthropologists call expressive action?

I shall consider two possible ways of accounting for expressive actions within the rational choice model. The first and perhaps obvious way is to treat self-worth as one among possibly many motives which lie behind a particular person's preferences. Thus people can be acting in support of their self-worth when they act on their preferences. The conventional theory is usefully quiet for this purpose on the source of an agent's preferences. The origin and nature of a person's preferences does not matter for the theory, so it seems perfectly possible for a desire for self-worth to be one of the motives which influences a person's preferences over outcomes. All that is required by the theory is that preferences should be well-behaved in the sense that they supply a preference ordering and that they can be taken as given. The first requirement is synonymous with rational choice theory and needs no further explanation. The second is less frequently formally stated, perhaps because it is too obvious to need saying. But it is nonetheless important because when preferences change then, at the least, a complete account of action will also require an account of preference formation. This is in part a point about the scope of the instrumental model. It does not tell the whole story in these circumstances, but this need not be especially worrying as it is often rather difficult to tell the full story. If, however, the gap is filled with an account of preference formation that makes preferences depend endogenously on action, then the damage to the instrumental model is potentially much deeper as the very sense that action flows from preferences will be undermined if the preferences themselves are formed by action.

To assess this strategy for allowing self-worth into the instrumental model of action, it is helpful to consider what is involved in the activity of reflection which gives rise to feelings of public self-worth (or their reverse). For this purpose, I distinguish two key elements in the self-reflection on action that gives rise to self-worth.

First, a sense of self-worth comes from evaluating the action and this entails comparing the action that was undertaken with others which were available. It is the comparison that gives meaning to the action which then reflects well (or otherwise) on the agent. They could have done 'x', but they did 'y' and that says something about the person. For example, it will be plain that when I invite someone for dinner and I serve a formal meal with several courses, I will be indicating to the guest that I honour the occasion in a way which is very different from the meaning I would convey by serving them baked beans on toast. My action here says something about myself in relation to my guest. On the other hand, if I am too poor to serve a formal meal, then the meaning that my guest will attach to the receipt of beans on toast would be very different. Hence what any particular action like the serving of baked beans on toast means (or says about its author) is *not* fixed: it depends on the set of available actions from which it was selected.[2]

Secondly, the generation of self-worth from the meaning attached to 'doing "x" when "y" was available' sometimes depends on a public standard or key for interpretation. For example, suppose I believe that formalities are the bane of life and should be dispensed with whenever possible. I express this commitment through my dinner menu by giving my guest beans on toast as this is what happens to be the first thing I see in my cupboard. The guest knows that I could afford a formal meal with several courses and so knows that beans are not to be interpreted as a sign of poverty. However, I shall only obtain the sense of self-worth that comes from showing, as I intend, that I am the kind of person who sets no store in formalities, when my guest also interprets the receipt of beans on toast in this way. If my guest interprets the receipt of beans on toast in a different way, as meaning, for instance, that I take the guest to be the kind of person who is not worth honouring with anything more than beans on toast, then the action no longer serves my self-esteem. Indeed quite the reverse is the case: I will have conveyed offence when I intended something quite different.

In this example a shared standard or key for interpretation is crucial for my action to generate public meanings that can then become a source of my self-worth. I am not concerned with whether this is always the case (as in anti-private language arguments), it is sufficient for my purpose that it is sometimes the case that a person's self-worth is experienced through actions which have public meanings in which the agent finds a

---

[2] In effect, this is a familiar point from linguistics and so perhaps needs no further explanation when applied to the meanings associated with actions. See Culler 1976 on how the meaning of any word depends in part in what it is not and so upon the whole set of words in a vocabulary. For instance, the precise meaning of a referential word like 'river' will depend on the full set of words available for use in connection with moving inland water: that is, whether there are words like 'stream' or 'brook' in the vocabulary.

sense of self-worth.[3] Thus I take it as a matter of fact that people's sense of worth depends sometimes on how other people perceive them and I draw the inference that people must share a language for interpreting their actions for this to be possible, as otherwise no person can reasonably expect to convey reliable messages to others through their actions.[4]

If this brief analysis of how a public sense of self-worth is constituted is accepted, then the first strategy for subsuming self-worth into the instrumental model of preference satisfaction looks shaky because the 'preferences' which reflect a sense of self-worth seem bound to become context dependent in two senses. One type of dependence relates to the set of options and the other relates to the norms or public standards for interpreting selection from any given set. An example that is commonly cited in the literature will help bring this out. Suppose a person chooses an apple when offered a choice between an apple and a banana. Now suppose they are offered the same choice again in the presence of third option, a smaller apple, the person may well now choose the banana so as to avoid the imputation of greediness, given the prevailing norm, which might come from choosing what is seen to be a 'large' apple. The choice in these circumstances depends on both the set of options and the prevailing norm (for example a different norm where the choice of a large item was interpreted as a form of enthusiasm might plausibly have generated the selection of the 'large' apple). Such context dependence is bound to be worrying for the instrumental theory of choice when the primitives of choice are apples, bananas, and their like because this dependence can be a source of apparent preference change, as in this illustration when apples are sometimes preferred to bananas and sometimes bananas are preferred to apples.

Of course it is possible to avoid the inconsistency by making the primitives more nuanced: the apple in the first choice is not the same as the 'large' apple in the second choice even though it shares the same physical characteristics. But this concedes that the preferences are

---

[3] The distinction between shame and guilt is sometimes made to turn on whether the standard is public or private. So, for those who follow this distinction, the remainder of this paper should be understood as focusing on shame rather than guilt.

[4] Although I wish to sidestep the private language argument here, it seems to me that the public sharing requirement arises for essentially the same reason. It is a simple consequence of avoiding judgements of self-worth becoming self-serving. If I am free to judge the act potentially in any way that I please then the standard and the judgement are prone to be partial in a way that will offer little psychic comfort. The sense of well-being comes precisely from the fact that the standard is independent of oneself and the public sharing of the standard is a way of achieving a measure of independence (see Taylor 1989, and on a related distinction between internal and external reasons, see Williams 1981).

not 'given' in the sense that they can change for reasons which have nothing to do with either the physical attributes of the good or the rationality of the agents. Nevertheless at first glance this need not seem such a troubling concession since agents will still be acting in a broadly maximizing fashion (the 'utility' function which is maximized is now defined not only over actions but over the set of available actions; see Sen 1994). However further reflection reveals three important problems. Firstly both the Savage and von Neumann-Morgenstern approaches to the axiomatization of this theory of rational choice under uncertainty require that the primitives of choice are defined independently of the choice set (and the states of nature; see Sugden 1991). So the existence of context dependent preferences creates a significant problem for those who hold to the axiomatic interpretation of this form of rational action (i.e. those who adopt a behaviourist approach to rational action and sidestep any account of the internal workings of agency).

Secondly such context dependence creates problems for the empirical testing of this theory of action. The trouble arises because there is always a tricky question of interpreting whether such and such an event constitutes a test in any theory and the scope of such interpretational problems increases greatly when context is allowed to affect preference in this way. The point is simple. There are rules (within a scientific community) for interpreting whether, say, an apple really is an apple for the purposes of testing the theory in question and once preferences apply not just to apples but to 'apples in their context', these rules have in effect become much looser because the grounds for claiming that an apple is not an apple have expanded from physical differences to include differences in context. Indeed, it is tempting to think that such a radical licence to individuate the circumstances of an action might undermine completely the activity of empirical testing.

Thirdly, even if these empirical problems are not regarded as a decisive objection to the instrumental theory of rational choice in these circumstances, it is nevertheless clear that the operationalization of that theory will depend on developing a theory of context which seems likely to draw, in part, on our understanding of how self-worth is publicly generated. In other words, one can preserve the instrumental account only by attaching to it the elements of a theory of expressive rationality. Whether in these circumstances it still makes sense to talk of the instrumental model may seem a matter of taste, but it may also turn on precisely how context here interacts with preference (see the earlier comments on the worry when preferences become endogenous). I do not want to beg this question now, but in what follows, so as to avoid any confusion, I shall keep the instrumental and expressive models distinct and use the instrumental model to refer to an instrumental model unadorned by any expressive embellishment.

The second, and alternative, strategy for incorporating considerations of public self-worth in the instrumental model would be to concede that self-worth is indeed, in general, something different from preference satisfaction. However, it so happens that we live in a society where people get self-worth from satisfying preferences. The satisfaction of preferences is the shared standard, so to speak. In this way the underlying model of action is unaffected by the observation that people care about self-worth because self-worth happens to come from behaving according to the postulate of rational choice. So, happily, preference satisfaction and self-worth amount to the same thing.

This strategy also suffers from problems because self-worth in this sense could never be generated by the mere activity of satisfying your preferences. That is, a person cannot, in general, value preference satisfaction and generate self-worth by being good at this activity. The reason is that while such a standard can be publicly shared, it cannot, in general, be publicly verified. It is impossible for a person to demonstrate their competence in satisfying preferences unless their preferences are publicly known (independently of action) and for genuinely personal preferences this will not be possible. Of course, one could gain a sense of self-worth from something like generating wealth (or consumption) because this is a standard which, when shared, is publicly verifiable, but wealth generation is not the same as preference satisfaction. Indeed any move towards a model of norm-driven behaviour in the form of wealth maximization (or some other publicly observable objective) rather than preference satisfaction would seem in effect to concede that self-worth rules absolutely (at least in so far as self-worth comes from behaviour which conforms to norms). In other words, self-worth would be incorporated but at the expense of the rational choice model of action altogether.

If these arguments are granted then neither of the two obvious ways of subsuming self-worth within the rational choice model seems likely to work. Of course, we might perhaps reinterpret all action as norm driven in support of self-worth instead and so solve the dilemma the other way round. But this seems unsatisfactory in the sense that most people would acknowledge that preference satisfaction captures some part of what makes us tick. Indeed, if the model of norm-driven behaviour is general-ized (that is it becomes the only account of action) then it seems liable to suffer from the mirror image of the problem encountered by generalizing the model of preference satisfaction to all forms of action. How, for example, would the generalized norm-following model account for the agent's action when norms conflict? In such circumstances it is natural to draw on some further model of individual agency to explain how choice is made (e.g. perhaps the model of preference satisfiers). In short, it seems that a concern with (a) self-worth which comes from following/breaching norms and (b) individual preferences satisfaction need to be held as two separate types of motivational influence on behaviour. The one cannot be sensibly reduced to the other whichever way the reduction is attempted.

This conclusion naturally raises the question of what the relationship is between the two types of motivation in practice. I have no general answer to this question but I do have a contribution to offer. It comes in the next two sections. I focus on two examples where an economics which is based solely on preference satisfaction fails in important respects and where the failures can be remedied through recognizing the agents' concern for self-worth.

3 The role of self-worth in economic explanations: what is lost, part I

If agents are concerned to say something about themselves through their actions and these messages projecting the agent's self-worth are to be distinguishable from simple preference satisfaction, then it will be important for the action not to be open to interpretation as possibly mere preference satisfaction. This suggests that the concern with self-worth will be at play in settings where either action is potentially under-determined by the logic of preference satisfaction or where what is entailed by preference satisfaction is quite clear and the agent chooses to act in a manner which confounds this calculation. In other words, expressive actions occur either by complementing preference satisfaction decisions when the logic of preference satisfaction is indeterminate or by overruling the clear logic of the calculating preference satisfier.

Good examples of the first type of opportunity for expressive action are provided by any interaction which when modelled solely in preference satisfaction terms has the form either of a coordination game or a battle of the sexes game or is a game which is repeated indefinitely. The key features of such games for the purpose of this argument is that they have multiple Nash equilibria. This in turn means that the agent who is guided solely by instrumental reason will not know what to do in these games.

The point is straightforward. It is commonly recognized by game theorists that an instrumentally rational agent knowing only that all agents are rational in this sense (and have common priors) and common knowledge of the game will only know that a Nash equilibrium strategy combination should be played. They will not know, however, which of the many Nash equilibria to select. In other words in such settings the model of agents as preference satisfiers fails to supply a complete account of how agents act. Since many social interactions fall into one of these three types, this would appear to be both a significant shortcoming for an economics which restricts itself to the preference satisfaction model of action and a significant opportunity for agents to use their actions to say something about their non-preference satisfying qualities.

How the concern for self-worth (in the presence of norms) might fill the explanatory gap here is unmysterious. The norm can provide so to speak a different kind of reason for action. It can single out one action where instrumental reason has no way of distinguishing between the two. Suppose the interaction is a two-person game and there are two Nash equilibria (x, x) and (y, y). To choose 'x' rather than 'y' can mean something when there is a norm in place and so agents who are concerned for their self-worth can have a reason for choosing, say, 'x' rather than 'y'. In effect the choice of 'x' says something about the agent with which they would like to identify and when they both choose 'x' in this way they reaffirm the shared value encoded in the norm (and of course they also solve the equilibrium selection problem).

It is important not to overstate this potential. This is not a general claim that expressive action plugs all these explanatory gaps because there are other ways of supplementing the rational choice model for this purpose. For example, the Nash refinement project in game theory has introduced further principles of 'rational' thought, like back and forward induction and like pay-off and risk dominance, that can help reduce the number of Nash equilibria in some games. Alternatively it is possible to appeal to the concept of salience and focal points (see Schelling 1963). Salience or focal points are coordinating schemas which just occur to agents and it would be foolish to deny their importance. For example, when Schelling asked one of his famous questions to students concerning where they would go to meet a friend in New York who like themselves did not know the meeting place, there was surprising agreement on Grand Central Station. It is difficult to imagine that any reflective process would have singled out this location. After all, the moment one begins to think about places in New York, many seem to have equal claims as a meeting spot. Instead, Grand Central must just stick out when people think of New York (or thought of New York in the 1960s, as I am reliably informed people are now more inclined to meet at the Empire State Building!).

The claim here is more restricted. It is that where both agents reflect on their action in settings with multiple Nash equilibria, then the reflection and the action take this expressive form. The reflection cannot rely on instrumental reason alone because this points only to a Nash action. So some other kind of reason (or, more loosely, reflective resource) must be at work and I offer the model of expressive reason.[5] People act in the presence of norms to say things about themselves: the actions are, so as to speak, expressive and not only instrumental.

To support this narrower claim there are examples where reflection does seem to be at work in equilibrium selection and it is easy to see how these reflections might fit the model of expressive action which I have sketched. For example when Schelling asked his students to play anonymously the equivalent of a battle of the sexes division game, they almost all opted for the 50–50 division. Salience here seems to have an obvious potential reflective base in the shared values of a liberal democracy concerning how different agents are to be treated (i.e. equally in the absence of any further reason for distinguishing between them). Likewise in disputes between people that have the structure of the battle of the sexes game (where the different Nash equilibria divide the benefits of agreement differently between the players), it is common to find in experimental settings that a norm encoding a shared theory of justice enables one of the equilibria to be selected (see Roth 1988). Thus when these players act in the presence of such a norm they express a commitment to a set of values which is a source of self-worth. Each is saying to the other that they believe in a theory of justice and in acting on this theory they enjoy a sense of self-worth.

It may be tempting to imagine that reflection of this sort is more likely in situations where the Nash equilibria differ significantly, as for instance in battle of the sexes games. Here the different Nash equilibria divide the benefits differently and so people seem likely to seek reasons for the difference whereas in a pure coordination game there is no difference between the characteristics of the equilibria and so there is no apparent need to explain why one is selected by reference to these characteristics. Serendipity ought to be enough. Indeed one might imagine that the kind of unreflective biases which are built into a habitual or routine form of decision-making select the equilibria in such circumstances without provoking much of a reflective twitch. Interestingly, however, even some important coordination games seem to involve reflection and expressive

---

[5] It is worth noting that when one agent is known to act in some unreflective manner on a bias of the Grand Central variety, then the other agent will be able to use instrumental reason alone since the other agent's bias is enough to anchor the instrumental agent's instrumental reasoning process.

action. For example consider the fashion game where people like to dress in ways which are similar to their peer group. This is a pure coordination game and yet in practice precisely because the peer group itself is formed by a web of shared beliefs those beliefs tend also to attach to the uniforms of the group (see Douglas 1978, where much action acquires symbolic content because of the interlocking webs of shared belief).

An example of the second type of opportunity for expressive action comes in interactions which when viewed from the perspective of preference satisfaction have the form of a prisoner's dilemma. In such settings action is uniquely determined by the calculation of preference satisfaction as there is a dominant strategy for each agent. As a result, there is scope for an agent to signal that they find worth in some other set of values by acting in a manner which confounds the expectation that preference satisfiers play the dominant strategy. I choose this particular example because while there are many situations where the instrumentally rational course of action is uniquely determined and so there is scope for acting in a manner which is clearly contrary to that of instrumental reason, these other settings are less likely to offer the opportunity for expressive action. The point here is that acting in a non-instrumental way is always capable of interpretation as 'irrationality'. Since expressing 'irrationality' scarcely seems a sound base for generating self-worth, it will be important for the action to be construed as worthy in some other sense even though it is irrational when judged by the lights of instrumental reason. The great virtue of the prisoner's dilemma interaction in this respect is the way that a play of the dominated cooperative strategy opens up the possibility of achieving the collectively superior outcome in the game. Thus the play of the cooperative strategy may be 'irrational', but it is not so obviously stupid as 'irrational' play is in other settings.

Again, to support this claim, there is plenty of evidence of people apparently not playing the dominated strategy in prisoner's dilemma games and it is not implausible to interpret these actions expressively. Of course, for the reason cited earlier, in many settings the action associated with preference satisfaction will not be unambiguously known as a person's preferences cannot be publicly verified, independently of action. Thus the evidence from experiments where the people are told that the structure of the interaction has the form of the prisoner's dilemma are particularly instructive; and there is considerable evidence here which shows that agents do not always play the dominant strategy. Of course, this evidence can always be interpreted as lapses from rationality rather than examples of agents applying some other sense of reason. However, it is interesting that play of the dominant strategy seems to be less likely in experiments where the partner is known and so might plausibly share a set of beliefs which would enable each of the players to interpret the message which each player is sending to the other about themselves. Moving from the laboratory, perhaps the most telling examples come from those studies where firms manage to solve the apparent prisoner's dilemma associated with expending effort by appealing to sources of 'trust' within the culture of the company (see Aoki 1990, and Casson 1991).

4 The costs of ignoring expressive reason: part II

I have argued in the previous section that the explanation of behaviour in an important class of economic interactions frequently requires that the public sense of self-worth that is generated through expressive actions be recognized as a source of motivation. Those economic theories which ignore the expressive orientation of agency suffer corresponding gaps in their explanatory canon. The damage, however, goes further than this because theory is often used not only for explanation but also for prescription.

A variety of prescriptive problems might arise when agencies are guided only by the instrumental understanding of the situation. For example the exclusively instrumental understanding may lead to a set of objectives which are different from the objectives that would guide policy when there is a more rounded view of what motivates individuals. I do not consider this problem here. Instead, I accept the objectives which come from an instrumental understanding and focus on a particular problem which can arise when a change that is introduced on the basis of an instrumental understanding of the situation also affects the expressive orientation of agents and in addition the instrumental and expressive aspects of the situation now pull in opposite directions. The result is a policy change which is less effective than had been expected and may even be counter-productive.

To make this concrete, suppose following the instrumental understanding of why people behave, it is thought desirable to encourage people to behave in some way by offering greater financial rewards to that behaviour. The problem which concerns me in this section arises when the financial encouragement also alters the expressive orientations which are at play in such a way as to undermine or offset the effects of the change in the financial rewards on behaviour. In such circumstances, the neglect of the expressive dimension actually means that the effects of the policy are not only imperfectly understood, they are liable to be smaller than expected and may even be the reverse of what was intended. Two examples will bring this out.

First consider a company that perceives its employees' effort decision solely in instrumental terms and believes there is a one-sided prisoner's dilemma which needs to be solved. The circumstances are that the worker can expend high or low effort at work. There is no way of monitoring effort, so workers are paid a flat rate. Thus the dominant strategy for a worker is perceived by the company to be low effort expenditure since in the absence of detection the worker is thought obviously to prefer to work less rather than more as no extra reward comes with effort. Perceiving this, the firm introduces a monitoring and payment system which transforms the decision over effort. Effort is monitored and a high level is financially rewarded. The dominant strategy for the worker now becomes 'making an effort' (the equivalent of the previously dominated cooperative move in the effort version of the prisoner's dilemma game). Let us further suppose that before the introduction of this new payment system there was a norm which allowed workers to express a commitment to professionalism or crafts-manship to fellow workers through working with high effort. The norm, however, went unrecognized by the firm because it perceived the situation solely through instrumental eyes and seeing only the logic of the dominant strategy of defection, it decided to introduce the new payments system.

The direct consequence of the new payment system is the undermining of the capacity to express their professionalism through high effort since this is now what is required by instrumental calculation. To 'defect' with low effort, the non-instrumental move in these new circumstances, does not provide a substitute expressive action since it seems most likely to be interpreted as 'irrational'. After all, it would seem to serve no conceivable other purpose. Thus if the norm of professionalism depends for its continuing influence on acts of instantiation, then the change in pay-ments system will undermine the norm more generally and this will have potential spillover effects for other arenas inside the company. Specific-ally there may be other dilemmas which now can only be solved through changes in the payment system and so on. The result is that resources may have to be mobilized across a range of activities inside the company to encourage cooperative play when this was actually hitherto largely generated (and costlessly) by the expressive actions of the workforce. In other words, the contractual encouragement destroys the source of trust in the relationship which hitherto generated cooperation.

This is one sketch of a worrying interplay between the instrumental and the expressive. Is it far-fetched? Perhaps, but there is much evidence to suggest that the introduction of market/contractual relations within parts of the public sector have undermined the professional ethos which had guided many employees in that sector in the UK. Of course the existence of the ethos does not demonstrate that the 'effort' problems were thereby, in large measure, previously solved. But its existence and sudden disappearance provides some support for the thought that the expressive and instrumental cannot always coexist and so the encouragement of one may come at the expense of the other.

The second possible example of this interplay at work, this time in the reverse direction, comes from the worrying emergence of persistently high levels of unemployment in many OECD countries. To illustrate this possibility, suppose initially that unemployment rises in a country above the equilibrium or natural rate as a result of a demand shock. The resulting rise in unemployment is involuntary: that is, the unemployed are willing to work at the prevailing wage or less but can find no job offers at that or a lower wage. As a result the unemployed cannot explain their unemployment in instrumental terms. It is not that they have chosen leisure. They are simply unable to find a job. Suppose also that this involuntary unemployment persists because the government takes no remedial action with respect to demand. Instead the government attacks the problem on the supply side by tightening the unemployment benefit rules (perhaps through lowering the real value of benefits or lowering the duration, etc.). This is a policy which works with an instrumental understanding of the unemployment problem because such changes increase the incentives for the unemployed to look for work. The rationale behind the policy is simple. If the incentive to look for work is increased then the unemployed should expend more effort on finding a job and increased effort should bring its own reward. The problem, of course, is that increased looking does not help the unemployed find a job when there are no extra jobs being created due to demand deficiency.

I argued before that the scope for expressive action depended on the instantiation of norms which allowed action to acquire a symbolic dimension. In this unemployment context, it is not implausible to argue the same with respect to instrumental reason. If instrumental calculation offers no remedy or is not successful in its application, then it seems likely that agents will appeal less to instrumental reason in their own psychological account of where they are and increasingly seek an expressive explanation of their position. In other words the unemployed will increasingly begin to see the state of unemployment as some form of self-expression. Of course, the creation of an expressive motivation does not just depend on this psychological desire to find a form of reason which accounts for the person's position, it depends on the existence of norms which would enable the activity of being unemployed to be interpreted expressively by others. This in turn requires instantiation: that is, other people who are unemployed. But this is, of course, precisely why a high level of unemployment is worrying because it creates the material for the instantiation of a new norm among the unemployed. Thus a high level of involuntary unemployment when it persists for long periods can be turned into a permanently high level of equilibrium unemployment as the unemployed develop a culture of unemployment.

This is but one sketch of how the phenomenon of hysteresis with respect to unemployment might arise. It turns on the competition between instrumental and expressive reason which takes place once involuntary unemployment persists and the bandwagon of an unemployment culture begins to roll. Perhaps there are better explanations or the creation of a culture of unemployment plays only a small part. Nevertheless the key mechanism here, the competition between instrumental and other forms of reason, has received considerable support in the experimental psychological literature on cognitive dissonance and cognitive evaluation theory (see Deci 1975). And in the presence of such competition there are general grounds for doubting the wisdom of prescriptions which are based exclusively on the instrumental view of agency because they will fail to take full account of the effects of a policy change (see Frey 1992 and Pettit 1995, for related arguments).

5 Conclusion

This paper has argued that the reflective capacity that agents use to generate a public sense of self-worth seems to have disappeared from the ontology of mainstream economics as a result of its reliance on the instrumental model of action. That reflective capacity is neither there explicitly and nor can it be recovered implicitly. This disappearance matters because the exercise of expressive reason, which I have associated with that capacity, can account for some of the explanatory shortcomings regarding equilibrium selection in games with multiple Nash equilibria and the failure to explain the incidence of cooperative behaviour in prisoner's dilemma games. These explanatory failings are significant and provide strong grounds for restoring the expressive orientation of agents to economics. This argument is further reinforced by the prescriptive weaknesses which may also come from overlooking the expressive motives which are sometimes at play in action.

In short, when Robert Burns wrote the following he was on to something which mainstream economics has regrettably tended to overlook:

> O wad some Pow'r the giftie gie us
> To see oursels as others see us!
> It wad frae mony a blunder free us
> And foolish notion.

References

Aoki, M. (1990) 'Towards an Economic Model of the Japanese Firm', *Journal of Economic Literature*, March, 1–27.

Casson, M. (1991) *The Economics of Business Culture*, Oxford: Clarendon Press.

Culler, J. (1976) *Sausurre*, Glasgow: Collins.

Deci, E. (1975) *Intrinsic Motivation*, New York: Plenum Press.

Douglas, M. (1978) *The World of Goods*, Harmondsworth: Penguin.

Frey, B. S. (1992) 'Tertium Datur: Pricing, Regulating and Intrinsic Motivation' *Kyklos*, 45, 161–84.

Hargreaves Heap, S. (1989) *Rationality in Economics*, Oxford: Basil Blackwell.

Pettit, P. (1995) 'Institutional Design and Rational Choice', in R. Goodin (ed.), *The Theory of Institutional Design*, Cambridge: Cambridge University Press.

Roth, A. (1988) 'Laboratory Experimentation in Economics: A Methodological Overview', *Economic Journal*, 98, 974–1031.

Schelling, T. (1963) *Strategy of Conflict*, Oxford: Oxford University Press.

Sen, A. (1994) 'The Formulation of Rational Choice', *American Economic Review, Papers and Proceedings*, 385–90.

Stewart, H. (1995) 'A Critique of Instrumental Reason in Economics', *Economics and Philosophy*, 11, 57–83.

Sugden, R. (1991) 'Rational Choice: A Survey of the Contributions from Economics and Philosophy', *Economic Journal*, July, 751–85.

Taylor, C. (1989) *Sources of the Self*, Cambridge: Cambridge University Press.

Williams, B. (1981) *Moral Luck*, Cambridge: Cambridge University Press.

7 Agent identity in economics

JOHN B. DAVIS*

1 Introduction

Many economists would agree that as a social science economics aims to explain cause-and-effect relationships in economic life, and aims to do so in close conjunction with an analysis of agency. Yet though economists constantly refer to economic agents when they speak of individuals making choices, the concept of agency itself is not sharply defined in economics. I define agency as the power to initiate and bring about events. Economic agents, then, have the power to initiate economic activity, and, together with other causal factors, such as capital, institutional arrangements, natural resources, etc., help bring about events seen as the causal effects of their actions. Choice, economists' main concern, is thus an aspect of agency in that its analysis helps us account for how economic agents act on the world. But choice needs to be understood in a wider framework of cause-and-effect explanation if economic agents are to be understood specifically as agents with powers to initiate and bring about events when making choices.

Another way of seeing economic agents as agents in a causal sense is to recognize that on this conception economic agents actually exist, and that adopting a cause-and-effect view of economic agents commits one to an ontological realism about economic agents in the sense distinguished by Mäki in his taxonomy of realisms (1992). Note that while most economists would say they are interested in actually existing economic agents, many would also allow that the logic of choice – or how agents *ought* to behave – may be evaluated apart from the question of whether there are agents whose choice behavior that logic describes (Sugden 1991,

* Thanks to Tony Lawson, Uskali Mäki, Jochen Runde, and Alex Viskovatoff – without implication – for thoughtful comments on an earlier version of this paper.

p. 752). On the view here, however, the investigation of economic agency requires one to suppose that there are economic agents with real powers to bring about events as the effects of their actions. This emphasis calls for some re-orientation of contemporary economics, since with the considerable development of axiomatic decision theory in the postwar period pursued apart from a realism about economic agents, it seems fair to say that the discipline has not focused on explaining how economic agents actually bring about events.

In the discussion that follows I begin to set out an ontological framework for an analysis of economic agents by developing stategies for investigating the *location* and *scope* of economic agency, where each of these considerations pertains to a relatively separate set of issues involved in an ontology of agents. A related way of approaching the topic of agency that has tangencies to philosophers' work on personal identity is as the investigation of the identification of economic agents or agent identity in economics. This paper consequently might also be thought to investigate how we identify or account for the identity of economic agents in terms of the location and the scope of their agency. Or, using philosophers' personal identity language, the paper investigates both how we distinguish or individuate agents – the business of locating them – and how we re-identify or track agents through change in their characteristics and surroundings – the business of determining what scope their agency possesses or sustains.

The rationale for using philosophers' thinking about personal identity to investigate agent identity in economics needs to be highlighted at the outset. In supposing economic agents actually exist, one in effect assigns oneself the task of explaining how and for how long economic agents exist. How they exist is a matter of accounting for where they are active. I label this the question of agents' location, though it will be readily seen that more is involved than simply picking out agents' site of operation, since where they are active leads us immediately to claims about the manner in which they are active and some ascription of powers to them. The question of how long agents exist concerns the durability of their powers. I label this the question of the scope of economic agency. Thus described, it will be seen that the issues of location and scope of agency are means of explaining agents' causal effectiveness. This focus is slightly different than is involved in philosophers' investigation of personal identity, since only some approaches to personal identity emphasize the effects of individuals' actions on the world. But the agent identity approach adopted in this paper shares the general realist concern personal identity theorists have regarding the persistence and distinctness of a type of real being in the world. For this reason, personal identity

theory offers insights for economics that may help develop an ontologically realist view of economic agents as having causal powers.

Mäki, in his taxonomy of realisms, distinguishes referential realism and
representational realism. Referential realism, or the semantical thesis that
the terms of language and science refer to real entities, connects in
important respects to the issue of how we locate economic agents. Our use
of language reflects our ontological commitments, and one such commitment is that the things we refer to are real entities. But to successfully refer
to real entities implies that we can ontologically distinguish or individuate
those real entities in the world. Thus we may begin to investigate the
location of agents through an analysis of our modes of reference. In
contrast, representational realism, or the semantical thesis that attributive
statements ascribe properties to real entities, has important connections
to the issue of what scope or extent of power economic agents may be said
to have. Here our ontological commitments specifically concern the
magnitude and duration of economic agency, or how long and with what
force real agents exercise their powers as agents. Thus we may begin to
investigate the scope of agency through an analysis of how economic
agents are represented in the language of economic theory.

This paper consequently attempts an analysis of the location and scope
of economic agency in terms of these two forms of realism, so as to link
ontological and semantical thinking on the subject. It postpones a veristic
realist analysis of agents (also distinguished by Mäki) on the grounds
that establishing truths about the forms of economic agency first requires
that one identify those agents whose actions have real effects in economic
life. Roughly speaking, ontology precedes epistemology. As an illustra-
tive framework, the second section of the paper begins by critically
examining the standard neoclassical view of economic agents, and
characterizes it as unsuccessful in its ability to identify economic agents.
The third section of the paper then offers an alternative, realist approach
to locating economic agents, discusses *routines* as a form of phenomena
that exhibits agency relationships, and closes with a proposed criterion
for locating agents. The fourth section turns to how we may address the
difficult topic of agency's scope, considers the point-in-time and through-
time dimensions this involves, and introduces considerations pertaining
to multiple sources of agency and changes in its structure. The paper
concludes with three brief remarks to clarify principal themes of the
discussion.

2 The neoclassical approach to locating economic agents

As an ontological issue, the location of agency concerns how we distinguish or pick out agents in economic life. To appreciate the nature of the issue, it is worth noting at the outset that this aspect of the topic of agent identity is less central to philosophers who investigate personal identity. When philosophers analyze the conditions under which individuals maintain their personal identities, they generally suppose that they know whose identity is at issue (namely, that of individual human beings), and thus rarely stop to worry about where agency is located (and whether individual human beings are indeed agents). For example, in Parfit's (1984) famous teletransporter examples regarding personal survival, he imagines what might happen to *himself* were *his* own body dematerialized and reconstituted elsewhere under various scenarios. Most economists also tend to assume that locating agents is not an issue, since they believe that individuals are automatically agents. Even when economists concern themselves with situations in which people make choices for others, mobilize others' resources, and act as others' agents, that is, in principal–agent situations, they assume there is no difficulty in locating agency, since delegated authority stems from choices previously made by autonomous individuals who are agents. But it seems fair to say that without an account of what makes an individual an independent agent in the first place – one in whom the power to affect the world exists – it is question-begging to say that individuals are even in a position to delegate authority and assign decision-making responsibility to others. Unlike philosophers in their treatment of personal identity, then, economists cannot avoid first confronting the problem of how we locate causally efficacious agents preparatory to a full analysis of the scope and extent of their powers as distinguishable agents.

Note first, then, that when we use language to refer to things, we suppose that we can locate and distinguish the things we refer to. If one uses the term "chair" referentially, this implies one can pick out an object thought to be a chair, and distinguish it from other pieces of furniture. This suggests we ought to look at how economic theories make reference to the things they name. But before doing so, we ought to first ask ourselves what conception of reference a theory involves, since it is well possible a theory employs a view of reference that does not help us to pick out the sorts of things we are interested in ontologically identifying. For example, it might be my theory of reference that "whatever my friends call a 'dog' does indeed pick out real dogs in the world," where that they also refer to people they dislike as dogs tells us that my theory of reference does not enable me to consistently pick out real dogs. Of course these friends do refer when they use the term "dog," but because their use of the term is often metaphorical, they do not thereby help us to disinguish and locate real dogs. Here my theory of reference is inappropriate to the task at hand. And since our project here is not to investigate the rhetorical use of language, but to pursue the ontological project behind referential realism, we ought similarly to ask whether our economic theories employ theories of reference that will allow us to locate and distinguish real economic agents.

Let us distinguish two philosophical approaches to reference for constative utterances, the early analytic Fregean theory dating from the turn of the century (Frege 1892; Russell 1905), and the more recent causal theory associated with scientific realism (Kripke 1971; Putnam 1970, 1973). The Fregean theory explains the meaning of a name (common noun or proper name) in terms of its intention, or in terms of that conjunction of properties analytically true of the name. As Putnam characterizes it,

On the traditional view, the meaning of say, "lemon," is given by specifying a conjunction of *properties*. For each of these properties, the statement "lemons have the property P" is an analytic truth; and if P1, P2, . . ., Pn are all of the properties in the conjunction, then "anything with all of the properties P1, . . ., Pn is a lemon" is likewise an analytic truth. (1970, p. 51)

The theory then supposes that the intension of a name determines its extension, where a name's extension is that to which it refers – or more simply that meaning determines reference. The theory is neo-Kantian in that the logical structure of language (rather than as for Kant the psychological structure of the mind) determines what can be picked out and said about things in the world. But this is problematic, since it essentially renders the idea of a world independent of thought empty (as Kant did the notion of things-in-themselves), creates ambiguities between the act of judging and that which is judged, and generates paradoxes of meaning variance across conceptual structures *à la* Kuhn.

On the causal theory, in contrast, it is argued that names come to refer in a quite different manner. Things are, as it were, "baptized" at some historical point in time, and then generally retain their original names through causal chains of events linking the inaugural naming to later language-users, despite modifications in meaning and the way names are understood. On this theory reference is accounted for in terms of our causal interactions with things in the world and among us, and presupposes that we can ontologically distinguish real entities from one another. Unlike the neo-Kantian approach, that is, things in the world are first supposed to be distinguishable and re-identifiable through change, and this conditions the way in which we use language to refer to them. Put differently, reference is not established in an *a priori* manner by picking out things to which definitions should apply, but rather in an *a posteriori* manner by affixing names to the things we distinguish.

In Davis (1989), I argued that neoclassical economic theory in its axiomatic form employs a Fregean approach to reference, and that, because the Fregean approach does not provide an adequate account of reference, axiomatic neoclassical economic theory thereby fails to distinguish and pick out real economic agents in the world. Neoclassical economic theory relies on the Fregean theory of reference, essentially because it distinguishes and defines distinct economic agents in terms their different preference sets. Of course it is not analytically true that particular individuals have the particular preferences they do, but it is analytically true that any given individual is defined in terms of his or her *own* preferences. Our language sometimes obscures this point, because it allows us to say two individuals may "have" the same preferences. However, the theory clearly holds that two individuals may not have the same preferences in the sense of one doing the other's preferring. Preferring, as a propositional attitude, always implicates the particular individual doing the preferring, and is thus inseparable from that individual. Understood in this way, the theory holds that distinguishing two individuals is analytically equivalent to distinguishing two sets of own preferences.

How, then, does reference actually fail on this view? In Davis (1995), I argued that using an individual's *own* preferences to distinguish that individual presupposes the very individual those preferences are meant to distinguish. If a set of preferences picks out an individual, they must be that individual's preferences and not someone else's preferences. But if we have already picked out the individual to whom a set of preferences belongs in order to call these preferences that individual's own preferences, we cannot then use those preferences to pick out that individual.[1] Neoclassical theory thus involves itself in a circularity in its implicit account of individual and agent identity, arguably causing it to employ the ad hoc assumption that preferences are exogenous to foreclose critical evaluation of its individualist project. For our purposes, however, the conclusion that is of chief interest here is that the theory is unable to

---

[1] An early antecedent to this argument is Bishop Butler's charge that Locke's view, that individual identity depends on memory and states of consciousness, was circular. Butler argued that memory presupposes rather than explains personal identity. Hume, whose critique of the idea of the self is better known, essentially followed Butler in this argument (see Noonan 1989).

locate real economic agents in the world. Its claim that individuals are agents, that is, is not supported by an understanding of reference that gives us a means of actually distinguishing individuals as real economic agents.

It thus follows that neoclassical theory lacks a way of systematically distinguishing between agents who are single individuals and agents made up of groups of individuals. Gary Becker's family decision-making analysis is a good example (1976). Husbands' preferences are taken to represent wives' and other family members' preferences, thus substituting the preferences of a single individual for a group of individuals. But because own preferences cannot pick out individuals, this account cannot distinguish (as feminists have continually argued) the case of a husband acting on his own preferences in the name of the family from the case of a husband acting on some sort of truly shared family preferences. Subsequent intra-family bargaining models have attempted to get around Becker's difficulty by assuming that husbands and wives are both independent agents whose negotiations create shared preferences for the family as a joint agent. But this similarly begs the question of whether husbands and wives are independent agents in the first place. In comparison to Becker's analysis that cannot determine whether husbands are single agents or representatives of group agents, the bargaining approach cannot determine whether individual agents constitute a group agent or a pre-existing group agent enfranchises individual agents.

But that neoclassical theory cannot credibly distinguish between agents who are single individuals and agents made up of groups of individuals, implies that it fails to locate agency in the world. And, failing in this first step, it cannot proceed to investigate the issues surrounding determination of the scope of agency, where that concerns the duration and magnitude with which distinguishable economic agents exercise their powers. Indeed in Davis (1995), it was also argued that even were we to suppose individuals are distinguishable economic agents (or locate agency in individuals), neoclassicism's dynamical analysis of human capital accumulation precludes its re-identifying them as distinct agents through change. Specifically, since on time allocation models (Becker 1965) certain of an individual's preferences are enhanced in significance by past accumulations of human capital, human capital accumulations indirectly contribute to the constitution of an individual's identity over time. But that we accumulate particular human capital stocks is partly a function of the price system and thus the decisions and preferences of others. This indirect influence of other individuals' preferences on any given individual disrupts neoclassicism's attempt to distinguish individuals in terms of their own preferences, making their re-identification through change problematic. And lacking an ability to track individuals through change, the theory has few resources to explain the scope of agency in terms of its magnitude and duration.

What this discussion of neoclassical theory is meant to demonstrate is that addressing the problems involved in explaining agency requires that a theory be formulated so as to take ontological commitments seriously. One cannot, then, simply assume individuals are always and everywhere agents, because one's ideological predilections encourage one to think this must be the case. Rather, given this intellectual predisposition, one needs to establish when and how individuals are able to act as agents. Neoclassical theory, to be fair, is hardly alone in its limited success in this regard, since similar sorts of arguments could be developed to show how methodologically collectivist theories fail to refer to distinguishable and re-identifiable group economic agents. In the section that follows an attempt is made to describe how one might go about locating economic agents through an analysis that places ontological realism in the foreground.

3 A realist approach to locating economic agents

How should we proceed if our first task is to explain how economic agents are distinguished from one another? The circularity problem associated with the Fregean approach to reference arises when one attempts to distinguish agents using an *a priori*, definitional criterion, primarily motivated by theoretical concerns (as the neoclassical preference criterion is motivated by the desire to apply the theory of instrumental rationality to all economic agents). Suppose, however, one were rather to attempt distinguishing economic agents in an *a posteriori* manner where this involved making explicit use of the causal theory of reference. In this instance, theory is built up around an inherited set of ontological commitments, namely, that such-and-such sorts of things exist in the world, which we are able to refer to by developing our theories around past namings (or "baptisms") meant to pick out and distinguish these real entities. Theory from this perspective follows rather than precedes reference, and accordingly allows different theories to share objects of reference, and so avoid the problem of meaning variance.

It will naturally be said in response to this suggestion that premising a set of ontological commitments itself involves some theory, and that it is illusory to think one can postpone theorization until one has agreed on

what one is referring to. This is certainly correct in that there is indeed a
theorization implicit in one's ontological claims, but I will put this
difficulty aside here by assuming that the sort of implicit theorizing we
imagine attaches to many of our ontological commitments is extra-
theoretical in the sense of not belonging to any particular theory
developed by an identifiable collection of professional theorists. Different
economic theories, for example, can refer to "markets" as real entities,
but in doing so they adopt a very basic conception not reducible to any
one group's theorization of markets. Specifically, markets involve exchange, the items exchanged are valued, traders in markets have different
interests, some form of property relationship is implied, etc. Loosely, we
might say that rather than presuppose implicit theorizations, the use of
terms such as "markets" signals widely held beliefs we may understand
as constituting collections of "social facts." Following Gilbert (1989) we
may characterize social facts as facts in the eyes of reasonably informed
individuals in society, where their ordinary understanding of these facts
contributes a conceptual element separate from the further interpretative
contribution that comes of more systematic analysis in social science
theory. The prior element of understanding contributed by society both
underlies social facts' status and acceptance as facts in society, and serves
as a conceptual penumbra about these facts that assists their further
analysis in more formal social science investigation. An *a posteriori* social
science approach, then, attempts to anchor investigation in what the
social world takes as given, rather than in a series of deductions made
from theories constructed around views of a subject matter's essential
requirements.[2]

From this perspective, we may suppose, first, that analysis of the set of
social facts relevant to agency begins with attention to evidence regarding
how economic agents themselves understand the distribution and scope
of agency in the economy. Presumably agents of any sort must rely on
some understanding of agency in order to act as agents. Here the causal
theory of reference comes into play in that an acknowledged set of social
facts would naturally include facts about how historically we have come
to pick out and refer to agents. On the causal theory, reference depends
on historical namings or "baptisms" and subsequent chains of connection as names evolve, change, and are modified. Economic agents, then,
rely on this information in acting as agents just as they rely on various
other ordinary social facts.

Second, our investigation of those social facts relevant to agency

---

[2] The approach here also distances itself from the traditional empiricist project of beginning
with scientists' collections of observation statements.

requires we also recognize that, because economics in its mission as causal social science aims to characterize economic life in terms of relatively enduring relationships, the evidence regarding agency relevant to our interests in economics concerns what we may observe in persistent patterns of economic activity. Clearly we do not expect to learn much about agency from evidence about episodic phenomena. These two points together imply that the social facts which underlie an analysis of agency in economics are those recognized by the economy's agents in connection with recurring patterns of activity investigated in science. It seems uncontroversial to add, thirdly, that these recurring patterns of activity involve intentional behavior in situations of social interaction. Intentional behavior, of course, is our principal concern in investigating economic agency, while social interaction allows our scope to include relations between individual agents, between group agents, and between individual and group agents.

Following the lead of Nelson and Winter (1982), then, I propose that these relatively enduring patterns economists wish to investigate be initially described as routines or as routinized behavior. I define routines in economic life and elsewhere as organized collections of rules and procedures that guide behavior in regularly encountered circumstances. Routines help individuals recognize domains of activity in which they may act. Routines do not themselves have causal powers, but rather create a framework in social settings that permits the assignment of agency to individuals who act.[3] Central in this regard is the normative force possesed by the rules and conventions that make up routines. Rules and conventions tell us what we ought to do when we participate in a given routine. Thus an individual who abides by a routine becomes an agent in accepting the normative force of the rules and conventions characteristic of that routine.[4]

Other units of social analysis might be proposed, but there are important advantages to focusing on routines in an analysis of agency. First, since routines may be investigated for both individuals and groups, an examination of routines *per se* is not likely to bias our analysis at the outset toward either individualist or collectivist interpretations of the location of agency. Indeed both individual and group responsibilities are often recognizable in the duties that many routines imply. Second, because routines tend to be relatively self-contained social practices, they

[3] Obviously some routines are personal and carried out mostly apart from other individuals. The discussion here focuses on those routines that involve social interaction.
[4] I do not wish to suggest that agency does not exist outside of the context of routines. Routines, however, provide a valuable framework in which agency may be explained in economic life.

appear more susceptible to analysis than many other more complex forms of behavior. More complex behavioral settings can indeed plausibly be argued to combine routines, so that these "institutional" environments are explained in terms of routines as their elements. Third, routines are an ordinary feature of the social world, and as such their common-sense description does not require immediate introduction of elaborate theoretical constructs. In fact, almost anyone can both describe a variety of routines in which people engage, and on prompting cite a number of facts relevant to the scope and location of agency that these routines imply.

For example, in economic life, say in the context of business firm routines, many can describe routines employees regularly observe, and analyze this evidence to produce an initial set of facts regarding the location of agency in business firms. What sort of analysis we initially attempt of course depends upon what cause-and-effect questions immediately concern us. Suppose we are interested in how a firm's organization causes it to address new business, and we find that a firm's routine is that customer orders to purchase goods are sent sequentially to the billing and shipping departments. That the group agent made up of the shipping department does not act before the group agent made up of the billing department locates agency at different points and different times in the firm with respect to new orders. If we also learn that departmental subroutines require that new business be processed by teams of individuals in each department, we might further conclude that agency rests with departments rather than individuals. Alternatively, if in each department the routine adopted requires that the first available individual take sole responsibility for new business until it is concluded, we might say that individuals act as agents, but that their agency is rotating and recurrent, rather than continuous, where this is a matter of numbers of individuals in a department, volume of business, time needed per order, etc. Or, a department might include a routine for trouble-shooting unexpected problems that is always delegated to the same individual. This sort of case clearly would contrast with the revolving responsibility type of routine in which individuals act in the name of their department.

Note that these simple examples treat routines as if they were isolated from one another. However, routines clearly occupy places in larger patterns of behavior and/or complex organizations, and how these larger patterns of behavior and organizations are structured generally plays an important role in determining which routines are exercised and which ones go unexercised. Thus a trouble-shooter type agent in one department of a business firm who has a particular set of duties as a representative of that department might well find that he or she has prior duties according to a set of firm routines that transcend department routines. Clearly then, analyzing the interconnections and hierarchical relationships between routines in this fashion would be a step toward a more general theory of action for business firms and other sorts of organizations. But it still seems reasonable to suppose that routines remain the building blocks for an analysis of economic agency, since whether or not a given routine is exercised does not alter the power of individuals to initiate sequences of events on the basis of that routine. That is, if individuals acting in connection with routines are plausibly described as the source of events, we may comfortably speak of the action in which organizations engage in a derivative manner, prepared to provide an analysis of how the organization structures action in terms of its assignment of responsibilities to individuals and collections of individuals through their embedding in routines.

The shorthand claim that routines can be plausibly described as event-generating may be reinforced by attention to what individuals involved in routines tend to believe individuates particular routines as distinct forms of activity. Note again, then, that an important dimension of routines is that the rules and procedures they involve typically possess an element of obligatoriness. Following a routine means one *ought* to follow certain rules and adopt certain procedures in the circumstances in which the routine applies. Putting aside whether we understand this as substantively or procedurally rational, one way of capturing the normative force routines possess is to think of routines as depending upon systems of mutually reinforcing expectations held by the individuals who participate in them. Routines may then be thought to be forms of conventional behavior in which agents act interdependently in such a manner that each recognizes rules and practices in routines have normative force. Thomas Schelling, David Lewis, and Robert Sudgen have contributed to an explanation of conventions as spontaneously emerging equilibrium solutions to coordination problems in interdependent decision-making contexts. However, we cannot follow them too closely in their game-theory formulation of conventional behavior if we want to explain agency by analyzing the social facts routines imply, since their approach assumes individuals are instrumentally rational or rational in Bayesian terms, and we have seen that this presupposes that individuals are already characterizable as independent agents. Since our *a posteriori* method is meant to avoid the circularity and question-begging regarding agency inherent in the neoclassical approach, our seeing the rule-governed routines as systems of mutually reinforcing expectations must allow that, though individuals may not always have the status of agents, they may nonetheless have mutually reinforcing beliefs about expected behavior.

What, then, does treating routines as forms of conventional behavior based on mutually reinforcing expectations contribute to our understanding of agency? In a simple two-individual case, mutual expectations regarding one individual's entitlement or responsibility to act as an agent may be described as follows: individual x expects to do A, individual y expects individual x to do A, individual x expects individual y to expect individual x to do A, and so on potentially to higher order expectations. What we see here is that in determining entitlement or responsibility to act, expectations such as these confer agency status by recording the judgments of the individuals involved. Since our method treats social facts as widely recognized phenomena, treating routines as forms of conventional behavior based on mutually reinforcing expectations implicitly provides us with a criterion by which agents may be located and distinguished from one another. Abstracting out this location criterion, we may thus say that *in the context of a given routine, an independent agent is that individual or group of individuals that expects to act as an agent, is expected by others to act as an agent, believes others have the relevant expectation, is thought to have this belief by others, and so on.*[5]

4 Addressing the scope of agency

The issue of the *scope* of economic agency concerns the magnitude and duration of the powers that distinguishable economic agents may be represented to realistically exercise as causal agents. Here there are affinities to the philosophers' topic of personal identity, since philosophers often imagine situations in which an individual suffers an impairment in his or her power to act, and then ask whether that individual's identity is sustained. For example, an individual might lose consciousness for an extended period of time. Does this person remain himself or herself during this period? Or an individual might be transported into some unfamiliar setting in which his or her chief skills and views fail to apply. Must this individual become a new person? In economics, however, the parallel topic of agent identity necessarily approaches the magnitude and duration of agent powers from a somewhat different perspective. Recall that philosophers interested in personal identity are typically concerned with the fate of some already distinguished individual. But economists cannot presuppose who or what an economy's

---

[5] I put aside the question of what sort of regress is involved here. See Mongin and Walliser (1988) for a discussion of when infinite regressions are problematic and when not. In general, not all infinite regressions need be paradoxical.

agents are if they intend to actually explain agency. Nor for that matter should economists follow philosophers of personal identity in supposing that economic agents (when distinguished) are likely candidates for survival through change in time and/or circumstances. Whereas philosophers hope to demonstrate personal identity is sustained through a variety of changes, or at least say under what conditions this may be the case, in economic life organizational and behavioral developments often erase the space occupied by particular routines together with the agency relations they imply. Consequently, just as we cannot presuppose that in economics we are automatically concerned with certain types of agents, for example, individuals or classes in the methodological individualist and collectivist traditions, so neither can we assume that certain types of agents automatically retain the status of being agents across different spheres of activity and through processes of change.

Explaining the magnitude and duration, or strength and permanence, of particular forms of economic agency accordingly requires that we place boundaries on distinguishable agency relations both at a *point in time* and also *through time*. At a point in time, the magnitude or strength of an agent's powers are a matter of how far-reaching the effects of an agent's actions are. For example, if in a business firm a team of individuals has responsibility for a set of cross-department activities, say, with respect to firm internal audit procedures, the influence of this team-agent's actions may in certain circumstances outweigh the actions taken by departmental agents. Conversely the scope of the latter's activities at any point in time would be partly defined by scope the team-agent's activities possessed. Regarding an agent's powers through time, that is, their duration or permanence, we need to be able to say when a given instance of agency ceases to operate, and when another emerges. Again using the business firm as a type of organization, we might in this instance look for changes that ended reliance on some routines while creating the occasion for others. Technological change affecting information storage surely would provide examples of this kind. Activities and routines made obsolete by the appearance of new ones mark off the boundaries of agency relations through time.

These remarks, however, only provide an initial outline of the dimensions involved in explicating the scope of economic agency relations, since they ignore the complexity of most real-world cause-and-effect relationships. Following J. S. Mill, contemporary philosophers of economics (Cartwright 1983, 1989; Lawson 1989; Hausman 1992; Mäki 1994)[6] have

---

[6] I ignore here the differences between these individuals regarding interpretation of *ceteris paribus* clauses.

begun to sort out this complexity by distinguishing (i) between an agent's having a power to act in principle and that agent's actions possessing distinguishable effects in the presence or absence of overlapping and/or countervailing sources of action, and (ii) between an agent's actually exercising a capacity to act and not exercising that capacity, for whatever reason. Thus in terms of our *point-in-time* example above regarding the magnitude of an agent's powers, it could be found in terms of dimension (i) that a team-agent responsible for firm audit procedures has routine authority over individual departments, but that individuals within a number of departments routinely delay providing the relevant data (a case of countervailing power). Alternatively, rather than engage in delaying actions, individuals within some departments could be found to expedite firm audit routines (a case of overlapping power). Both of these cases might further be complicated along dimension (ii) were individuals in some departments able to engage in delaying actions, but did not do so (a case of an unexercised countervailing power), or were individuals in some departments able to engage in expediting actions, but did not do so (a case of unexercised overlapping power). Parallel cases concerning agency relationships *through time* might also be imagined.

These additional characteristics of real-world cause-and-effect relationships clearly make the analysis of the scope of agency relations more difficult, but attention to them seems only to reinforce the importance of first sorting out simple agency relationships before looking at the interrelationships between them. Ontologically, that is, investigation of the basic concepts of agent identity involving location and scope precedes investigation of their manifestations in complex cause-and-effect phenomena. This claim may seem at odds with the social facts approach taken here, since it could be argued that ordinary individuals' appraisal of routine behavior is recorded in terms of the manifestations or observed effects of agency relations rather than in terms of their originating sources. Against this, the position taken above is that ordinary individuals understand routines in terms of responsibilities to act, where having responsibility is an element of being an agent. Thus ordinary thinking regularly operates in simple ontological terms even though this more philosophical language is typically unfamiliar to most people. In contrast, what ordinary thinking is not particularly good at is moving from recognition of basic relationships of responsibility and agency to an analysis of complex agency patterns, both on account of the fact that ontological matters are rarely enunciated in ordinary thinking, and because of the inherent difficulties involved in working out representationally adequate, ontologically unified accounts of cross-cutting, multidimensional agency interrelationships.

What the analysis here generally calls for, then, is the examination of structures of routinized behavior in various domains of economic activity within which it appears possible to distinguish decentralized responsibilities for action on the part of different sorts of economic agents. The business firm as a type of organization naturally lends itself to a variety of examples, and the method illustrated in the examples above would equally apply to the analysis of agency in the family, government, and other distinguishable domains in which routines are commonly noted. But our emphasis on routines as relatively enduring, and the relative enduringness of these traditional domains of interest, should not be thought to imply that the agency relations we may ascertain to lie behind routines by this method constitute permanent causal elements for economics as a social science. That is, in addition to the complexity we encounter in terms of multiple sources of causality, complexity also enters our analysis on account of the evolution of structures of routinized behavior. This evolution, it seems fair to say, comes about because economic agents' actions are both conditioned by the frameworks in which they operate, and simultaneously condition or bring about change in those frameworks themselves. Suppose we were to treat economic evolution as a multi-mechanism process with both selection and adaptive learning and also as a multi-level process with individuals and groups of individuals acting as agents (Vromen 1995, p. 213). Then explaining the scope and location of agency would require our considering the relative success of different types of routines empowering different types of agents in different types of environments. That evolution may well transform the forms which agency assumes, however, only demonstrates the importance of having a method for explaining its location and scope.

5 Three concluding remarks

(1) The discussion of agent identity here has proceeded as if one might investigate the location and individuation of agents apart from treatment of the scope of their powers as causal agents. There is modest justification for this in that the causal theory of reference adopted above allows us to communicate about things in the world without agreeing upon theories about these things. In practice, however, conventional location of responsibility to act according to systems of mutually reinforcing expectations quickly introduces scope of agency considerations into talk about who or what an economy's agents are. Being able to say where responsibility to act lies typically involves being able to say something

about what that responsibility involves. At the same time, because action often possesses considerable unintended effects, analysis of the scope of agency goes beyond what our location criterion involves. Those party to a convention cannot anticipate all that assignment of responsibility for action implies, particularly where an agent's actions have transformative effects upon the structure of routinized behavior itself.

(2) A theme emphasized in the discussion here is that there is an important difference between the way philosophers approach the problem of personal identity and the way economists need to approach the problem of agent identity. My view is that if economists were to begin to investigate agent identity they would tend to do so along the lines of the problem of personal identity. The worst perpetrators of this misconsception are neoclassical economists who generally assume that all individuals are agents (and that households and firms, when acting as agents, are resolvable into collections of individuals). But traditional institutionalists and Marxists have made comparable mistakes by substituting their collective agents into the neoclassical equation. In both cases, normative reasoning about preferred social subjects displaces ontological reasoning about causal power and cause-and-effect relationships. Economists, however, need to examine the way the world works if they are to explain it. Indeed, policy goals regarding the well-being of different types of agents may only be promoted with an adequate understanding of the economic process.

(3) This paper began with reference to two methodological traditions in economics regarding agency: methodological individualism and methodological collectivism. The argument of this paper should have made clear that these orientations are both ontologically naïve. Their being so is in part a matter of historical forces alluded to in the remark above. No one would deny that individuals and classes have been defended as economic agents, because doing so has suited different social thinkers' world views. Nonetheless, agency as a domain of analysis is susceptible to careful examination. That it has not received it seems due in part to a failure of philosophers and methodologists of economics to focus on ontological issues. Recently, the topic of causality has begun to receive some attention (e.g. Hoover 1990). The hope this paper concludes with is that this interest will be further extended to investigation of the agents that initiate cause-and-effect sequences.

References

Becker, G. (1965) "A Theory of the Allocation of Time," *Economic Journal*, 65, 493–517.

(1976) *The Economic Approach to Human Behavior*, Chicago: University of Chicago Press.

Cartwright, N. (1983) *How the Laws of Physics Lie*, Oxford: Clarendon Press.

(1989) *Nature's Capacities and their Measurement*, Oxford: Clarendon Press.

Davis, J. (1989) "Axiomatic General Equilibrium Theory and Referentiality," *Journal of Post Keynesian Economics*, 11 (3), 424–38.

(1995). "Personal Identity and Standard Economic Theory," *Journal of Economic Methodology*, 2 (1), 35–52.

Frege, G. (1892) "Über Sinn und Bedeutung," *Zeitscrift für Philosophie und philosophische Kritik*, 100, 25–50. English translation, "On Sense and Reference," *Philosophical Writings*, ed. P. Geach and M. Black, Oxford: Blackwell, 1952.

Gilbert, M. (1989) *On Social Facts*, London: Routledge.

Hausman, D. (1992) *The Inexact and Separate Science of Economics*, Cambridge: Cambridge University Press.

Hoover, K. (1990) "The Logic of Causal Inference," *Economics and Philosophy*, 6 (2), 207–34.

Kripke, S. (1971) "Identity and Necessity," in *Identity and Individuation*, ed. M. Munitz, New York: New York University Press, 135–64.

Lawson, T. (1989) "Abstraction, Tendencies and Stylised Facts: A Realist Approach to Economic Analysis," *Cambridge Journal of Economics*, 13, 55–78.

Mäki, U. (1992). "Friedman and Realism," *Research in the History of Economic Thought and Methodology*, 10, 1–36.

(1994). "Isolation, Idealization and Truth in Economics," in *Idealization VI: Idealization in Economics*, ed. B. Hamminga and N. De Marchi, Amsterdam and Atlanta. Rodolpi.

Mongin, P. and B. Walliser (1988) "Infinite Regressions in the Optimizing Theory of Decision," in *Risk, Decision and Rationality*, ed. R. Munier, Dordrecht: Reidel.

Nelson, R. and S. Winter (1982) *An Evolutionary Theory of Economic Change*, Cambridge, MA: Harvard University Press.

Noonan, H. (1989) *Personal Identity*, London: Routledge.

Parfit, Derek (1984) *Reasons and Persons*, Oxford: Clarendon Press.

Putnam, H. (1970) "Is Semantics Possible?", in *Language, Belief, and Metaphysics*, ed. H. Kiefer and M. Munitz, Albany: State University of New York Press, 50–63.

(1973) "Meaning and Reference," *Journal of Philosophy*, pp. 699–711.

Russell, B. (1905) "On Denoting," *Mind*, reprinted in *Logic and Knowledge*, London: Allen and Unwin, 1958.

Sugden, Robert (1991) "Rational Choice: A Survey of Contributions from Economics and Philosophy," *Economic Journal*, 101 (407), 751–85.

Vromen, J. (1995) *Economic Evolution*. London: Routledge.

8 Chances and choices: notes on probability and belief in economic theory

JOCHEN RUNDE[1]

A recurring point of contention in rational choice theory is the legitimacy or otherwise of assuming that decision-makers choose as if they were guided by precise numerical probabilities of the consequences of their actions. Economists, broadly speaking, fall into two groups on this issue. One holds that beliefs can only be taken to correspond to point probabilities in situations that approximate games of chance or where numerical probabilities can be assigned to events on the basis of a knowledge of relative frequencies. The other holds that beliefs should be treated *as* point probabilities, entering economics via decision theory and emerging as the parameters of consistent choice. I shall call these the traditional and the Bayesian view respectively.

An important feature of the Bayesian view is that it makes it possible to apply rational choice theory even in situations in which there are no obvious 'objective' probabilities. This feature has contributed enormously to its popularity in economic theory and, until quite recently, to the steady decline of the distinction between risk and uncertainty that tends to accompany the traditional view (between situations in which agents' beliefs about random outcomes are, or are based on, point probabilities and situations in which they are not). In fact, even now the dominance of the Bayesian view is such that some of its more prominent proponents feel justified in declaring the distinction a 'sterile one' (e.g. Hirshleifer and Riley 1992, p. 10). Yet there have always been some who have continued to insist on the importance of uncertainty as distinct from risk in economic analysis, particularly in the more heterodox strands of the discipline. And, over the last ten years or so, a

[1] I am grateful to Chuck McCann, Tony Lawson, Uskali Mäki, members of Gay Meek's M.Phil seminar on Philosophical Issues in Economics (Cambridge) and three anonymous referees for comments on earlier versions of this paper.

similar view has begun to emerge in the mainstream literature in economics and decision theory (Kelsey and Quiggin 1992). The purpose of this paper is to examine this 'dissident' view, focusing on some of the ontological presuppositions that inform the traditional and the Bayesian positions.

I begin in the first section with a sketch of the traditional view. The representatives I have chosen are Knight (1921) and Keynes (1973a), partly because they are routinely cited in connection with the risk/uncertainty distinction in economics and partly because they provide philosophically sophisticated statements of two prominent versions of the chance-based interpretation of numerical probability. One of my aims in this section is to show why it is legitimate to speak about Knightian or Keynesian uncertainty in the same breath,[2] despite the differences in the foundations of their respective theories. The second section outlines the Bayesian model and attempts to account for its popularity in modern economics. Finally, the third section assesses the Bayesian model in its descriptive capacity as a representation of the economic actor and examines the ontological shift in some recent generalizations of the Bayesian model on Knightian or Keynesian lines.

1 Chances

Situations of chance, in what follows, are defined as ones in which a numerical probability may be assigned to some B on the basis of the number of times it is instantiated in a class of otherwise homogeneous A's. The central metaphysical presupposition of the chance-based approach to probability, then, is the homogeneity or sameness of the members of the classes on which it is based. I shall argue that the two theories of numerical probability advanced by both Knight and Keynes are at one on this point. This will allow us to derive a general criterion for the traditional 'Knightian' or 'Keynesian' distinction between risk and uncertainty.

---

[2] For example, Anand (1993), Curley and Yates (1989), Epstein and Wang (1994), Fishburn (1993), Hodgson (1997), Hogarth (1987), Kelsey and Quiggin (1992).

Knight

Knight's (1921) *Risk, Uncertainty and Profit* is best remembered for distinguishing between uncertainties that take the form of 'a known chance' (risks) and 'true' uncertainties that do not. But his position is in fact more subtle than this simple dichotomy might imply. For as he presents it, there exists a gradation of uncertainties running through the following three types of 'probability situation': *a priori* probability, statistical probability and 'estimates' (Knight 1921, pp. 224–5). As there are some problems with Knight's own presentation, I shall use the following slightly reformulated version of his three categories:[3]

1. *A priori* probability. The ideal case in which numerical probabilities can be computed on general principles, namely where they are assigned to equally probable, exhaustive and mutually exclusive possible outcomes such as the six sides of a perfect die. Given a list of such possibilities $x_1, x_2,...,x_n$, the probability of any one of them $p(x_i) = 1/n$. If m of the x's are also y's, then $p(y) = m/n$.
2. Statistical probability. Situations in which frequencies are derived on the basis of an 'empirical classification of instances [trials]' rather than from abstract possibilities. The statistical probability r of some outcome y is simply the proportion or relative frequency of a reference class of empirically tabulated x's that are also y's. This might be written $p_x(y) = r$.
3. Estimates. Situations in which *a priori* probabilities cannot be determined or in which there are not enough trials sufficiently 'like' to form a reference class against which frequencies can be determined.

The first two of these probability situations fall into the category of risk, in Knight's terminology, the third into the category of uncertainty: whereas it is possible to assign numerical probabilities to events on the basis of a calculation of the 'chances' in the first two cases (risk), it is not possible to do so in the third (uncertainty). The assignment of numerical probabilities in situations of risk, according to Knight, is always based on the assumption that 'the unknown causes in a case will distribute themselves according to the law of indifference among the different

---

[3] The discussion of chance-based interpretations of probability in the previous version of this paper published in the *Monist* was badly corrupted by the fact that I had originally failed to notice these problems (now discussed in detail in Runde 1998). The present version of this section supersedes the original entirely.

instances [trials]' (p. 219), where this 'law' is an expression of the metaphysical indeterminism of the world (p. 222). In the case of *a priori* probability the trials are by hypothesis completely homogeneous except for 'really indeterminate factors' (although the key assumption in the calculation of *a priori* probabilities is of course the equiprobability of outcomes, rather than the homogeneity of trials). In the case of statistical probability it is generally not possible to ensure that all but these factors have been eliminated to arrive at a grouping of absolutely homogeneous trials.[4] Even so, where probabilities are assigned on the basis of statistical frequencies it is necessary to assume that the differences between trials 'not subject to measurement or elimination are in fact indifferent' (p. 221). A judgement of the probability of some event x on the basis of a knowledge of a statistical frequency, according to Knight, therefore presupposes that there is no probabilistically relevant difference between the trial that may produce x on the one hand, and each of the class of trials that forms the basis on which the statistical frequency was determined on the other.

Keynes

Keynes's *Treatise on Probability* is a huge work that touches on issues far wider than can be summarized here. At its core, however, is the idea that probability should be analysed as a relation of partial entailment between the conclusion of an argument h and some set of evidential premises e. These relations are presented as logical entities, the apprehension of which warrants some rational degree of belief in h intermediate between certainty or maximum probability on the one hand (where h is a logical consequence of e) and impossibility or minimum probability on the other (where h stands in a contradictory relation with e). Relations of partial implication are written $h_1 | e_1$ (read 'h_1 relative to e_1') and, in modern terms, the theory may be described as one that builds on binary comparisons of the form $h_1/e_1 \geq^* h_2/e_2$ (the symbol $\geq^*$ denotes the relation 'is at least as probable as' and the relations $=^*$ and $>^*$ are then defined in the normal way for 'is as probable as' and 'is more probable than'). It is important to recognize that Keynes's probability relations form only a partially ordered set, that is, that in many cases it may not be

---

[4] Knight acknowledges that the classification of trials will involve the exercise of judgement: 'it is always possible to form classes if the bars are let down and a loose enough interpretation of similarity is accepted' (p. 227).

possible to say that one proposition, relative to the evidence, is more probable than, less probable than, or as probable as, another (Kyburg 1995).

Keynes's ontology of logical probability relations is probably the most characteristic and controversial feature of his theory.[5] Yet he has remarkably little to say about the probability relation itself, which he presents as primitive not analysable in terms of simpler ideas. What he does do is develop a formal logic of comparative or qualitative probability, much of which is devoted to conditions under which further comparisons of probability relations can be derived from comparisons already given. But he also shows how, under special circumstances, numerically definite probabilities may be derived from qualitative comparisons of probability relations. The special circumstances are that the relevant situation must be such as to allow the legitimate application of the principle of indifference.

The principle of indifference, that 'there must be no known reason for preferring one of a set of alternatives to any other', provides a criterion by which alternative hypotheses may be judged as equiprobable. Keynes's formalization of this criterion turns on the notion of the *relevance* of differences in the evidence bearing on each of a pair of alternatives. As the logic of relevance can be quite complex I shall mention only Keynes's 'simple' definition: e_1 is irrelevant to h/e if h/e & $e_1 =^* h/e$; e_1 is then relevant to h/e if it is not irrelevant. Keynes uses this definition to spell out the principle of indifference. The basic idea is that the evidence must be symmetrical with respect to each of the alternatives, that there must be no relevant evidence bearing on any one alternative that does not bear equally on all of the others. The procedure Keynes has in mind thus involves determining what parts of the evidence are relevant to each alternative hypothesis by a series of judgements of relevance. Then, if this evidence is of the same form for each of the alternatives, the principle authorizes a judgement of equiprobability, that is, that $h_i/e =^* h_j/e$, for all i, j.

Keynes goes on to elaborate a second requirement for the legitimate application of the principle of indifference, namely that the relevant alternatives be 'ultimate' or indivisible. This is to ensure that the instances to which probabilities are to be assigned are not capable of being split into sub-alternatives of the same form. This condition is

---

[5] The major thrust of Ramsey's (1926) famous critique of the *Treatise* is to question the existence of the logical probability relations posited by Keynes. I have argued elsewhere that Keynes's subsequent concession on this point does not disturb his logic of comparative probability, which does not depend on any particular theory of partial beliefs and how they may arise (Runde, 1994a).

necessary to avoid the classic paradoxes to which naïve applications of the principle of indifference fall prey.[6] Then, if the list of equiprobable and indivisible alternatives h_1/e, h_2/e, ... h_n/e is exhaustive (and they are mutually exclusive) the conditions necessary to arrive at numerically definite probabilities within the framework of comparative probability are met.[7] Let $H = h_1/e$ & h_2/e & ... & h_m/e ($0 < m < n$). The (Keynesian version of classical or *a priori*) probability of H is then $p(H/e) = m/n$.

Clearly the conditions necessary to assign probabilities in this way are likely to be restricted largely to games of chance. Like Knight, however, Keynes also suggests that it may sometimes be possible to assign numerical probabilities on the basis of relative frequencies. The version of the frequency theory sketched in chapter 8 of the *Treatise*, presented as a special case of his own theory in terms of relations between sets of propositions, also makes heavy use of judgements of relevance and indifference. As relative frequencies are truth-frequencies relative to some reference class, the problem for the frequency theorist is to find the appropriate reference class. Keynes (1973a, p. 113) defines the reference class as the class of propositions of which everything that is relevant in the circumstances is known to be true of the proposition to which the probability is to be assigned. The determination of a numerical probability of some proposition on the basis of a relative frequency may then be sketched as follows. Suppose we want to determine the probability of proposition y knowing that of a class of n x's, m are also y's. The x's satisfy the requirements of a reference class, on Keynes's theory, if (i) our relevant knowledge about each member of that class is symmetrical with our relevant knowledge about the next member, and (ii) our relevant knowledge about each member of that class is symmetrical with our relevant knowledge about y. If such a class can be found, according to Keynes, a numerical probability may be assigned to a proposition on the

---

[6] One famous example concerns the probability of some book being red in the absence of any evidence to the contrary. A naïve application of the principle of indifference would lead to equal probabilities being assigned to the probability of a book being red and being not-red. But the same rule could equally well be applied to the hypothesis that the book is black or that it is blue, leading to the contradictory situation in which there are three mutually exclusive hypotheses each as probable as not.

[7] It is possible to distinguish between two categories of 'Keynesian' uncertainty within the framework of comparative probability. The first consists of the cases in which it is not possible to determine numerical probabilities but it remains possible to make qualitative comparisons of relations of partial implication. The second category consists of cases in which it is not possible even to compare relations of partial implication, either because they are not comparable, or simply because they do not exist or, if they do, are not known.

basis of its truth-frequency within that reference class. In the present case $p_x(y) = m/n$.

Comparison

The two types of theory of probability advanced by Knight and Keynes are usually classified as opposites. Knightian statistical probability is often given as a variant of what Hacking (1975) calls aleatory probability, for example, whereas Keynes's 'logical' approach is generally regarded as a variant of epistemic probability. The difference is that whereas aleatory probabilities are regarded as a (measurable) property of the external world, epistemic probabilities are regarded as a property of the way in which we think about the external world. This dichotomy is reflected in the way that Keynes writes of the probabilities of propositions (about outcomes or events) rather than of outcomes or events themselves, and in the different ways in which Knight and Keynes think of the concept of indifference. Whereas Knight's references to indifference concern gaps in the causal determination of reality, Keynes's concern gaps in our knowledge of the causal determination of reality.[8]

Yet as will already have become clear, Knight and Keynes have remarkably similar views about the situations in which it is possible to determine numerically definite probabilities. Both of them tend to think of numerical probabilities as deriving from chance-based setups and both of their accounts therefore presuppose the existence of classes of equiprobable, exhaustive and mutually exclusive outcomes or alternatives (in the case of *a priori* probability) or reference classes of more or less homogeneous 'instances' or trials on the basis of which statistical frequencies can be determined. There are also similarities at the epistemological level, not least in that their claims about the 'objectivity' of

---

[8] For example, Knight writes: 'We do not merely feel that we know no reason why the coin shall fall heads or tails; we know in a positive sense that there *is no reason*, and only under this condition do we make the probability judgement with any confidence. And furthermore, as already argued, it appears that only on condition that there is no reason would the results of experience confirm the judgement, as they do. The entire science of probability in the mathematical sense is based on the dogmatic assumption that the ultimate alternatives are really *equally probable*, which seems to the writer to mean real indeterminateness' (p. 222). Keynes, in contrast, is concerned with the absence of *knowledge* of reasons for regarding one alternative as more probable than another. Whereas Knight is quite explicit about his belief in the real indeterminacy of the universe, Keynes is more circumspect, leaning towards a determinist view, but ultimately declaring agnosticism on the matter (Keynes 1973a, pp. 311–38).

probabilities (or judgements of probability) are far weaker than is commonly supposed. We have seen that Knight is fully alive to the fact that judgements regarding the homogeneity of instances are agent-relative, and Keynes describes his formulation of the principle of indifference as 'displaying its necessary dependence upon judgements of relevance and so bringing out the hidden element of direct judgement or intuition, which it has always involved' (Keynes 1973a, p. 69).[9] The main difference here is that Keynes attempts to formalize judgements of 'likeness' by giving explicit epistemic criteria for judgements of (ir)relevance and, accordingly, indifference.

Modern proponents of the traditional chance-based interpretation of probability in economics tend to be somewhat less explicit on the issues considered in this section than are Knight and Keynes. But the ontological presuppositions are much the same, namely that there exist identifiable classes of more or less homogeneous trials that are in reasonable agreement with the mathematical concept of independently repeated events (e.g. Bewley 1986; Davidson 1988; Hicks 1979; Lawson 1988; Lucas 1981).[10] Situations of risk, and leaving aside the special case in which it is possible to determine numerical probabilities on an *a priori* basis, are ones in which there exist identifiable classes of more or less homogeneous trials on the basis of which frequencies can be determined. Situations of uncertainty are ones in which such classes do not exist or, if they do, cannot be identified.

---

[9] Keynes in fact sometimes goes out of his way to ensure that his theory is not interpreted as placing *too* much emphasis on the subjectivity of individual judgements (see 1973a, p. 56). His famous 1937 QJE passage on uncertainty, moreover, suggests that, like Knight, he too sometimes thinks in terms of a gradation of uncertainties depending on the degree of homogeneity of the members of the class of 'instances' relative to which frequencies are determined: 'By "uncertain" knowledge, let me explain. I do not mean merely to distinguish what is known for certain from what is only probable. The game of roulette is not subject, in this sense, to uncertainty; nor is the prospect of a Victory bond being drawn. Or again, the expectation of life is only slightly uncertain. Even the weather is only moderately uncertain. The sense in which I am using the term is that in which the prospect of a European war is uncertain, or the price of copper and rate of interest twenty years hence, or the obsolescence of a new invention, or the position of private wealth owners in the social system in 1970. About these matters there is no scientific basis to form any calculable probability whatever' (Keynes 1973b, pp. 113–14).

[10] Commenting on the rational expectations hypothesis, for example, Lucas (1981, pp. 223–4) remarks that it will not 'be applicable in situations in which one cannot guess which, if any, observable frequencies are relevant: situations which Knight called "uncertainty." It will *most* likely be useful in situations in which the probabilities of interest concern a fairly well defined recurrent event, situations of "risk" in Knight's terminology.'

2 Choices

On the Bayesian view the probability of a proposition or event is interpreted simply as the strength of the actor's personal belief in that proposition or event.[11] It is often argued that the strength of personal beliefs is a causal property of those beliefs, reflected in the extent to which actors are prepared to act on them (Ramsey 1926, p. 71), and which may be measured by examining choice behaviour in betting situations. Suppose we wish to find the actor's subjective probability of some proposition h, $p(h)$. Bayesians propose that this can be done by finding the lowest value P_* that the actor would be prepared to exchange for a gamble that pays S if h is true and nothing if h is false.[12] Two assumptions are crucial here. First, the value P_* is assumed to exist. Second, and as the second formulation below suggests, P_* must leave the actor exactly indifferent between accepting the gamble and refusing it. Given that the actor is an expected utility maximizer, his or her declaration of indifference between P_* on the one hand and S if h, 0 if $\neg h$ on the other, is then often written as:

$$P_* = p(h)S + (1 - p(h))(0)$$

or,

$$p(h)(S - P_*) + (1 - p(h))(- P_*) = 0$$

This gives a real-valued probability $p(h) = P_*/S$.

It is not hard to explain the appeal of this approach in economic theory. First, it is extremely simple and based on what is widely regarded as no more than a systematic and analytically tractable expression of the common-sense idea that people's actions issue from their desires and their beliefs (in conjunction with the old and equally venerable idea that actions should be evaluated in terms of the expected

---

[11] Ramsey (1926), de Finetti (1964), and Savage (1954) (readers interested in the differences between the different versions of the Bayesian model should consult Fishburn 1981 or Kreps 1988).

[12] P and S are assumed to be (numerically definite) utility values rather than amounts of money. I have adopted the (Ramseyan) approach of taking utility as primitive to keep things as simple as possible. Savage (1954), the author economists most frequently appeal to in justifying their use of subjective probabilities, defines probabilities in a more general way in terms of preferences over 'acts' (the concept of a consequence is primitive in Savage's theory and every mapping from the set of possible 'states of the world' into the set of possible consequences constitutes an act). Ramsey's and Savage's systems are nevertheless quite similar in their implications, and the noted difference will not affect the argument at the level of abstraction pursued here.

utility of their consequences). Second, since it is possible to bet on just about any decidable proposition or event, the Bayesian interpretation of probability brings a large class of cases within the compass of the probability calculus that could not be on chance-based interpretations. This then makes it possible to argue that the traditional distinction between risk and uncertainty becomes redundant. And third, the theory appears quite modest in ontology insofar as it avoids making claims about observer-independent probabilities (hence de Finetti's famous remark that 'Probability does not exist'). In particular, it does not presuppose the existence of classes of repeated events and is often praised for making it possible to model beliefs without getting immersed in deep questions about the connection between actors' beliefs and 'reality' (Lucas 1981, p. 223).

But the feature of the Bayesian interpretation of probability that might appeal most to many economists is the contention that it is a *condition of rationality* that an actor's subjective degrees of belief be related so as to conform to the axioms of the probability calculus. This contention is supported by the so-called Dutch Book argument, that an actor whose beliefs do not meet this requirement could be induced to accept a sequence of bets that would result in a sure loss whatever the outcome of the events bet upon. It is at this point, however, that the theory's modesty about mind-independent probabilities begins to be offset by the rather stringent prerequisites of its own. For in order for the Dutch Book argument to go through it is necessary, not only that actors must evaluate options in terms of the mathematical expectation of the value of their consequences and that they must *always* be prepared to act (bet) on their beliefs, but also that they be prepared to bet *against* the hypothesis in question at the least odds that characterize their degrees of belief (Kyburg 1978). In the above example this would mean that the actor would also have to agree to accept a payment of P^* in exchange for a gamble that involves a *loss* of S if h is true and nothing otherwise, such that $P_*/S = -P^*/ -S = p(h)$.[13] I shall assume that this condition is met for the moment and return to when it is not later on.

An example may be useful to illustrate how a Dutch Book may occur.[14] Suppose that there are two mutually exclusive hypotheses h and k, and that the actor is prepared to exchange up to the following values to take the following gambles:

---

[13] This condition is implied by the expression $P_* = p(h)S + (1-p(h))(0)$, but not by a declaration of indifference between P_* on the one hand and S if h, 0 if h on the other (see below).

[14] Adapted from Schick (1986).

	h is true	*k* is true	neither *h* or *k* is true
(1)	win $S - p(h)S$	lose $p(h)S$	lose $p(h)S$
(2)	lose $p(k)S$	win $S - p(k)S$	lose $p(k)S$
(3)	lose $S - p(h$ or $k)S$	lose $S - p(h$ or $k)S$	win $p(h$ or $k)S$

Fig. 1

(1) $p(h)S$ to receive S if h, 0 if $\neg h$

(2) $p(k)S$ to receive S if k, 0 if $\neg k$

and to demand at least

(3) $p(h$ or $k)S$ in exchange for having to give up S if (h or k), 0 if $\neg (h$ or k).

Suppose also that someone accepts these gambles at the stated odds and that the probabilities implicit in (1), (2) and (3) above are such that $p(h) + p(k) - p(h$ or $k) < 0$. These 'probabilities' violate the probability axioms which require that $p(h) + p(k) = p(h$ or $k)$ for mutually exclusive events. It can be shown that the actor has entered into a Dutch Book.

To see this consider the possible outcomes. There are three: h is true, k is true, or neither, leaving the three scenarios in Fig. 1. The actor's degrees of belief are 'incoherent' because he or she will incur a sure loss whichever of the three possible eventualities obtains. For example, if h turns out true the actor will gain $S + p(h$ or $k)S$ *and pay or lose* $p(h)S + p(k)S + S$. Since $p(h)S + p(k)S < p(h$ or $k)S$, the net gain will be less than zero. The same will be the case if h is true or (h or k) is true. Such losses will be avoided only if probabilities are assigned such that $p(h) + p(k) = p(h$ or $k)$. Economists count the idea that actors whose beliefs violate the axioms of probability are open to economically self-destructive behaviour as a strong argument in favour of the Bayesian view. The argument is analogous to the money pump argument used to justify transitive preferences.

I have emphasized the Dutch Book argument to highlight some of what the claim that actors' choices reveal their subjective probabilities entails. In particular, the existence of numerically definite subjective probabilities seems to presuppose both that actors have real-valued degrees of belief at the back of their minds and that they are prepared to bet *for and against* every uncertain hypothesis at the *same* least odds that correspond to these degrees of belief. This is equivalent, in terms of the

Bayesian framework, to their being able to identify sure consequences P_* that are *exactly* equal in value to mathematical expectation of a pair or random consequences (S and 0), where the value of the mathematical expectation of the random consequences depends on beliefs that the whole procedure is aimed at quantifying.

3 Choices and chances

Introspection and experience suggest that these requirements, that actors have real-valued degrees of belief and that they are always willing to take bets at all the odds that correspond to these degrees of belief, are seldom met. This may be no objection to the Bayesian view in its normative capacity, when it is used as a means of checking and improving the consistency of one's decisions. Indeed, it may even be a possible justification for it.[15] But this is not the way it is typically used in economic theory, where it tends to be thought of as a *representation* of behaviour that is approximated in the behaviour that economists study (e.g. Kreps 1988, p. 6). And in this descriptive capacity, the generality the theory achieves in virtue of its ontological modesty about 'objective' probabilities is only achieved at the price of having to live with rather immodest metaphysical claims about the extent to which actors have, are in touch with, and are prepared to act on, what are assumed to be quantifiable values and beliefs. Of course, I am taking a very literal reading of the theory here, and the noted immodesty may be no particular cause for embarrassment on instrumentalist or other non-realist interpretations of economic theory.[16] Nevertheless, and notwithstanding the argument that it is sufficient justification for the theory that only those who behave 'as-if' on the basis of economically sound reasoning will survive in a competitive environment (Alchian 1950; Friedman 1953), many economists do seem to believe that any predictive power that formal decision theory may have has to come from a *real* tendency human actors have to deliberate and act in accordance with its prescriptions (e.g. Sugden 1991).

That said, there are two well-known challenges to the Bayesian commitment to real-valued beliefs which, as they involve what seem to be systematic violations of the theory, are no less problematic on its

---

[15] Of course there are also those who reject the normative interpretation of the Bayesian model (e.g. Anand 1993).

[16] Indeed, as Uskali Mäki (private correspondence) notes, ontological immodesty may encourage instrumentalist interpretations.

$ in k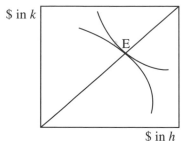

$ in k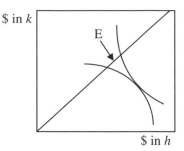

$ in h

$ in h

Fig. 2

instrumentalist than on its realist interpretations. The first of these challenges is that if people were in fact rational Bayesians, and if it were true they often have very different beliefs, then we should observe considerably more betting behaviour than we in fact do. For it is an implication of the Bayesian view that rational actors whose beliefs differ will always enter into bets with one another. This can shown diagramatically. Suppose there are two individuals 1 and 2 who are uncertain about two mutually exclusive events h and k. Each of them is endowed with an initial amount of money c that is independent of which of the two events obtains. This situation may be depicted in terms of a square Edgeworth box, where the amount of money received in event h is measured on the horizontal axis and the amount of money received in event k is measured on the vertical axis. Let E be the initial endowment and suppose that the two individuals are risk averse, that is, that their indifference curves are convex to the origin.[17] Then consider the following scenarios in Fig. 2.

The absolute slope of the indifference curves is equal to $p(h)/p(k)$ at all points on the 45° line.[18] In the first figure the two actors share the same subjective probabilities $p_1(h)/p_1(k) = p_2(h)/p_2(k)$. Indifference curve tan-

---

[17] As expected utility maximizers, the actors' objective functions have the form $U = p(h)u(c_h) + p(k)u(c_k)$, where $p(h)$ and $p(k)$ are the probabilities of h and k and $u(c_h)$ and $u(c_k)$ are the utilities of the amounts of money received in events h and k respectively. The objective function describes a locus of combinations of c_h and c_k which are equally preferred, and there is one such 'indifference curve' for every value of U (with expected utility increasing away from the origin). Indifference curves that are convex to the origin are termed risk averse because they reflect a preference for less rather more variation in the amounts of money contingent on each event.

[18] The slope of the indifference curves (the marginal rate of substitution of money contingent on each event) is obtained by total differentiation:

$dU = p(h)u'(c_h)dc_h + p(k)u'(c_k)dc_k = 0$. Rearranged, this expression gives:

$$\frac{dc_k}{dc_h} = -\frac{p(h)u'(c_h)}{p(k)u'(c_k)}$$

As $c_h = c_k$ on the 45° line, it follows that the slope of the indifference curves on that line must be equal to $p(h)/p(k)$.

	Red	Black	Yellow
	30	60	
I	$100	$0	$0
II	$0	$100	$0
III	$100	$0	$100
IV	$0	$100	$100

Fig. 3

gency (equilibrium) accordingly occurs at E on the diagonal and they will not take opposite sides of a bet. In the second figure, however, the actors' probabilities differ $(p_1(h)/p_1(k) > p_2(h)/p_2(k))$ and their indifference curves are not tangential at E on the diagonal. Here the actors will increase their utility by betting, that is, by trading in contingent claims to a point off the diagonal. The question which proponents of the Bayesian view must answer, then, is why there seems to be so much less betting behaviour than there seem to be differences in opinion. Why do people tend to shun bets even though they disagree?

The second challenge to the Bayesian interpretation of probability is provided by the well-known counter-examples given by Ellsberg (1961). One of these involves two urns, Urn I known to contain 100 balls *each of which* may be either black or red, and Urn II known to contain exactly 50 black balls and 50 red balls. The actor wins a prize of $100 in the event of correctly predicting the colour of the next ball drawn. I shall write R_I for a bet on a red ball from Urn I, B_{II} for a bet on a black ball from Urn II, etc. Most people profess indifference between R_I and B_I and R_{II} and B_{II} respectively, implying that $p(R_I) = p(B_I) = p(R_{II}) = p(B_{II})$. When offered a choice between R_I and R_{II} (B_I and B_{II}), however, most display a preference for betting on Urn II. The trouble is that this implies that $p(R_{II}) > p(R_I)$ and $P(B_{II}) > p(B_I)$, contradicting the previous choices.

A second example involves an urn known to contain 30 red balls and 60 balls, each of which may be either black or yellow. The actor is given a choice between options I and II, and then between options III and IV below, the prize depending on the colour drawn, as in Fig. 3.

It turns out that most people prefer I over II and IV over III. Again there is a contradiction as these preferences imply that $p(R) > p(B)$ and $p(B) > p(R)$ respectively. The conclusion, in both this and the previous example, is that there is no unique additive probability distribution consistent with the observed pattern of choices maximizing the expected value of some utility function.

The absence of widespread betting and the aversion to 'vague' probabilities illustrated by the Ellsberg examples suggest that most people do not or do not act 'as if' they assign point probabilities to the outcome of all events. Proponents of the Bayesian view tend to respond in two ways. One is to admit that there may be plausible psychological reasons for the noted behaviour, but that these ultimately constitute failures of rationality. In other words, the strategy is to fall back on the normative justification of the theory. For example, Hirshleifer and Riley (1992, p. 34) write:

The dissident literature claims that the discrepancies revealed by these results [such as the Ellsberg experiments] refute the economist's standard assumption of rationality, or at least the expected utility hypothesis as a specific implication of that assumption. We reject this interpretation. A much more parsimonious explanation, in our opinion, is that this evidence merely illustrates certain limitations of the human mind as a computer. It is possible to fool the brain by the way a question is posed, just as optical illusions may be arranged to fool the eye. Discovering and classifying such mental illusions are fruitful activities for psychologists, but these paradoxes are of relatively little significance for economists.

The second response is to interpret a reluctance to bet and the Ellsberg choices as rational responses to the possibility of asymmetric information, that is, that actors may shun bets or discount 'vague' probabilities because of a suspicion that the person offering the bet knows something they do not (Hirshleifer and Riley 1992, p. 36, n. 12; Morris 1993). Clearly this may be a possibility in some cases, although, as Morris (1993, p. 27) admits, decision-makers tend to display an aversion to 'vague' probabilities even when strategic considerations are ruled out.

An alternative possibility is to accept the consequences of the apparent fact that the central prediction of the Bayesian model in its descriptive capacity, that people's choices are or are 'as if' they are informed by real-valued subjective probabilities, is, in general, false. Before moving on to this possibility, however, I should like to return briefly to Knight (1921, p. 219) and Keynes (1973a, p. 82), who *would* both recommend assigning equal probabilities to the contents of the first of the 'ambiguous' urns described above. But this should not be construed as an argument in favour of the Bayesian view. According to Keynes's decision theory it is rational to prefer to be guided by probabilities determined on the basis of greater evidential 'weight', the amount or completeness, in some sense, of the relevant evidence on which a judgement of probability is based. The evidential weight in favour of assigning probability of 1/2 each to red and black is greater in the case of urn I than urn II, for example, thus providing a rationale for the observed choices. Keynes (1973c, p. 148) later suggests a link between weight and confidence, distinguishing between the 'best estimates we can make of probabilities and the confidence which we make them' (p. 240). Knight (1921, p. 227) makes a similar point, arguing that the action that issues from an opinion depends as much on the confidence in, as on the favourableness of, that opinion. The distinction between a judgement of probability and the confidence with which it is made has no place in the world of a committed Bayesian because it drives a wedge into the link between choice and degrees of belief on which it is founded.[19]

Choice under uncertainty and economic theory

The foregoing arguments should not be taken to suggest that our choices are not informed by the strength of our beliefs, merely that our beliefs tend to be much more vague and partial than the Bayesian model implies. We often seem to be able to at least grade possible choice-outcomes in terms of probability, if only roughly, and these gradations often seem to be useful in guiding our choices. A Bayesian might express this in the following terms. Suppose the actor is not prepared to commit to definite values of P_* and P^* such that $p(h) = P_*/S = -P^*/-S$. He or she may nevertheless be prepared to accept a bet on h at odds sufficiently favourable and to accept a bet against h at odds sufficiently favourable (shunning bets either way at any odds in between). In other words, the actor may be prepared to give up any value below P_* in order to receive S if h is true (and nothing otherwise) and be prepared to accept any value above P^* in return for having to give up S if h is true (and nothing otherwise), where $P_* < P^*$. Beliefs would thus take the form of intervals,

[19] As Knight emphasizes this distinction, I would resist recent interpretations that suggest that he 'implicitly accepted the modern view that by modelling individuals as able to choose consistently among unknown outcomes, we in effect represent them as always having subjective probabilities' (LeRoy and Singell 1987, p. 398; see also Langlois and Cosgel 1993, p. 460; Lawson 1998, p. 51). It is true that Bayesians sometimes argue that they can accommodate this distinction (e.g. Hirshleifer and Riley 1992, pp. 10–11, 175–7), the idea being that actors' confidence in their probabilities is reflected in the incentive they have to postpone choice until they can update their 'vague' (but numerically definite) priors in the light of new information. The problem, however, is that this proposal undermines the Bayesian account of where priors are supposed to come from. If actors' probabilities are supposed to be reflected in their propensity to choose and act on them, how then are priors to be established when they prefer not to do so?

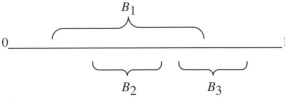

Fig. 4

the lower and upper bounds of which would be given by $p_*(h) = P_*/S$ and $p^*(h) = -P^*/ -S$ respectively. These intervals may overlap, giving rise to situations that might look like those in Fig. 4.

As B_3 dominates B_2 it is possible to argue that B_3 is unambiguously more probable than B_2. But it is not possible to arrive at an unambiguous ranking of B_2 and B_1 in terms of probability, or, for that matter, of B_3 and B_1 (the possibility of non-comparability that Keynes is so insistent on). The above schema provides a possible expression of the situation in which people are reluctant to bet both ways at the same odds on some event, is immune to Dutch Books (see Kelsey 1994, pp. 436–7) and provides a way of thinking about the Ellsberg examples. In the case of the urn containing 30 red balls and 60 balls in an indeterminate proportion of black and yellow, for instance, the statistical probability of red is 1/3 and the probability of black (yellow) is anywhere in the interval [0, 2/3]. On this 'multiple prior' approach to the problem, no colour is unambiguously more or less probable than, or as probable as, any of the others, and it is hard to see how those who resist committing themselves to a unique probability distribution, as the Bayesian view requires, should be regarded as irrational. It follows, on this line of reasoning, that no option unambiguously dominates (or is indifferent to) any of the others in expected utility terms. Determinacy can only be ensured by introducing additional decision rules, the most popular of which seems to be a maximin criterion.[20]

But what if indeterminacy were retained? This possibility, almost

---

[20] See Gärdenfors and Sahlin (1982), Gilboa and Schmeidler (1989, 1993), Kyburg (1990, pp. 237–8), Levi (1986, pp. 128–40) and, for some recent applications and discussions of the multiple prior approach in economic theory, Bewley (1986), Epstein and Wang (1994), Kelsey (1993, 1994), Kelsey and Quiggin (1992), and Gilboa and Schmeidler (1993). An alternative approach to 'Knightian' uncertainty replaces the Bayesian prior with a non-additive measure or capacity (Gilboa 1987; Schmeidler 1989). The underlying idea here is that people discount 'ambiguous' probabilities: by assigning probabilities of 1/3 to red and 1/4 each to black and yellow in the second of the Ellsberg examples, for instance, the paradox is resolved. But as this approach remains committed to real-valued degrees of belief (although these will no longer conform to the standard probability axioms), it is to this extent open to the same objections that I have been raising against

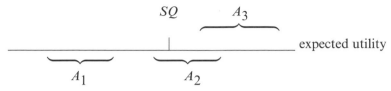

Fig. 5.

unheard of in economic theory, is explored in an imaginative paper by Bewley (1986). Bewley generalizes the Bayesian model by dropping completeness and introduces a privileged 'status quo' (*SQ*) position amongst the set of available options.[21] Beliefs are represented as convex sets of classical probability distributions, generating intervals of probabilities similar to those depicted above. The decision rule is that an option is preferred to another if and only if it yields a higher expected utility with respect to every distribution in that interval. (If beliefs correspond to intervals, of course, then so will the expected utility – the 'non-numerical mathematical expectation' (Keynes 1973a, p. 344) – associated with each option.) The 'status quo' is retained unless there is an option which dominates it in the sense just described. To illustrate, consider the expected utility intervals associated with three possible actions A_1, A_2 and A_3 (Fig. 5). *SQ* and A_2 (A_2 and A_3) are not comparable, but *SQ* dominates A_1, and A_2 and A_3 both dominate A_1. A_3 will be the preferred option as it is the only one that unambiguously dominates *SQ* (note that the fact that A_3 dominates the status quo whereas A_2 does not restores comparability between A_2 and A_3).

Now I would not want to go to great lengths to defend Bewley's particular formalism. His decision rule is extremely conservative, for example, and the implicit claim that people have sets of probability distributions at the back of their minds, while perhaps reasonable in cases such as Ellsberg's urns, seems no less dubious as a general claim than claiming that their beliefs are point-valued. Bewley's approach, and the multiple prior approach more generally, nevertheless marks two significant shifts from the ontology of orthodox Bayesianism. In the first place, it drops the metaphysics of real-valued degrees of belief and thereby rehabilitates the distinction between risk and uncertainty. Second, it goes some distance towards loosening the connection between

the Bayesian model. For some recent economic applications, see Dow and Werlang (1992a, 1992b, 1994).

[21] Completeness is the requirement that for every pair of options x and y, the decision-maker either prefers x to y, prefers y to x, or is indifferent between them. Completeness rules out non-comparability of options.

degrees of belief and dispositions to act on which the Bayesian approach is founded. This makes it possible to express the situation in which people respond to uncertainty by refraining from making a choice and taking an action (in Bewley's framework an option is not taken unless acceptance, which always involves a departure from one's existing circumstances, is preferred to rejection). Not only does all of this seem to accord with what we know about ourselves, it also appears to be consistent with a range of economic phenomena that seem resistant to standard Bayesian analysis: the tendency for bid (buyer) prices for insurance against uncertain contingencies to be systematically less than asking (selling) prices, even if the insured event results in losses to the bidder and not to seller; the adoption of conventions in the face of uncertainty, such as the practice of 'going on' as before except in so far as there are definite reasons to expect a change (Keynes 1973c); rule-following, habits and behavioural routines (Cyert and March 1992; Hodgson 1997; Vanberg 1994); the incompleteness, rigidity and long-term nature of wage contracts (Mukerji 1998; Williamson 1985); and that more liquid assets are often preferred to less liquid assets that dominate them in return (Runde 1994b).

4 Conclusion

Proponents of what I have called the traditional view tend to resist assuming that actors are guided by sharp numerical probabilities save for the situations in which they have knowledge of (the relevant) chances. The ontological basis for the traditional 'Knightian' or 'Keynesian' distinction between risk and uncertainty, on this view, turns on the absence or otherwise of classes of equiprobable (exclusive and exhaustive) outcomes in the case of *a priori* probabilities, or classes of homogeneous trials or suitably defined reference classes in the case statistical frequencies. Situations of uncertainty arise where such classes do not exist or, at least, cannot be identified.

The 'betting' interpretation of probability associated with the Bayesian view provides an ingenious means of transforming decision-making under uncertainty, in the traditional sense, to decision-making under risk. For this reason, and because denying the existence of subjective probabilities is widely perceived as coming uncomfortably close to denying that actors are able to make consistent choices over gambles, it continues to serve as the dominant theory of probability and belief in modern economic theory. Yet the generality and simplicity the Bayesian approach achieves in virtue of avoiding claims about the existence of 'objective' probabilities (or probability relations) should not be allowed to distract from the strength of its own ontological presuppositions. I have focused on two of these, that actors have real-valued degrees of belief and that they are always willing to take bets at all odds that correspond to these degrees of belief. These presuppositions are highly implausible on descriptive grounds and, I have suggested, overly demanding requirements even on the theory's normative interpretations. Economic choices are generally not informed by a knowledge of chances or their Bayesian surrogates. The epistemological concerns that motivated so much of the economic theorizing of Knight and of Keynes are as relevant as they ever were.

References

Alchian, A. A. (1950) 'Uncertainty, Evolution and Economic Theory', *Journal of Political Economy*, 58, 211–21.

Anand, P. (1993) *Foundations of Rational Choice Under Risk*, Oxford University Press.

Bewley, T. (1986) 'Knightian Decision Theory: Part 1', Cowles Foundation Discussion Paper, no. 807.

Curley, S. P. and J. F. Yates (1989) 'An Empirical Evaluation of Descriptive Models of Ambiguity Reactions in Choice Situations', *Journal of Mathematical Psychology*, 33, 397–427.

Cyert, R. M. and J. G. March (1992) *A Behavioural Theory of the Firm*, 2nd edition, Oxford: Blackwell.

Davidson, P. (1988) 'A Technical Definition of Uncertainty and the Long-Run Non-neutrality of Money', *Cambridge Journal of Economics*, 12, 329–37.

de Finetti, B. (1964) 'Foresight: Its Logical Laws, Its Subjective Sources', in H. E. Kyburg and H. E. Smokler (eds.), *Studies in Subjective Probability*, New York: John Wiley, 93–158.

Dow, J. and S. R. Werlang (1992a) 'Excess Volatility of Stock Prices and Knightian Uncertainty', *European Economic Review*, 36, 631–8.

    (1992b) 'Uncertainty Aversion, Risk Aversion and the Optimal Choice of Portfolio', *Econometrica*, 60, 197–204.

    (1994) 'Nash Equilibrium under Knightian Uncertainty: Breaking Down Backward Induction', *Journal of Economic Theory*, 64, 305–24.

Ellsberg, D. (1961) 'Risk, Ambiguity and the Savage Axioms', *Quarterly Journal of Economics*, 75, 643–69.

Epstein, L. G. and T. Wang (1994) 'Intertemporal Asset Pricing Under Knightian Uncertainty', *Econometrica*, 62, 283–322.

Fishburn, P. C. (1981) 'Subjective Expected Utility: A Review of Normative Theories', *Theory and Decision*, 13, 139–99.

(1993) 'The Axioms and Algebra of Ambiguity', *Theory and Decision*, 34, 119–37.

Friedman, M. (1953) 'The Methodology of Positive Economics', in *Essays in Positive Economics*, Chicago: Chicago University Press, 3–43.

Gärdenfors, P. and N. E. Sahlin (1982) 'Unreliable Probabilities, Risk Taking and Decision Making', *Synthese*, 53, 361–86.

Gilboa, I. (1987) 'Expected Utility Theory with Purely Subjective Non-Additive Probabilities', *Journal of Mathematical Economics*, 16, 65–88.

Gilboa, I. and D. Schmeidler (1989) 'Maximin Expected Utility with a Non-Unique Prior', *Journal of Mathematical Economics*, 18, 141–53.

(1989) 'Updating Ambiguous Beliefs', *Journal of Economic Theory*, 59, 33–49.

Hacking, I. (1975) *The Emergence of Probability*, Cambridge: Cambridge University Press.

Hicks, J. R. (1979) *Causality in Economics*, Oxford: Basil Blackwell.

Hirshleifer, J. and J. G. Riley (1992) *The Analytics of Uncertainty and Information*, Cambridge: Cambridge University Press.

Hodgson, G. (1997) 'The Ubiquity of Habits and Rules', *Cambridge Journal of Economics*, 21, 663–84.

Hogarth, R. M. (1987) 'Decision Making Under Ambiguity', in R. M. Hogarth and M. W. Reder (eds.), *Rational Choice: The Contrast Between Economics and Psychology*, Chicago: Chicago University Press, 41–67.

Kelsey, D. (1993) 'Choice Under Partial Uncertainty', *International Economic Review*, 34, 297–308.

(1994) 'Maxmin Expected Utility and Weight of Evidence', *Oxford Economic Papers*, 46, 425–44.

Kelsey, D. and J. Quiggin (1992) 'Theories of Choice Under Ignorance and Uncertainty', *Journal of Economic Surveys*, 6, 133–53.

Keynes, J. M. (1973a) *A Treatise on Probability. The Collected Writings of John Maynard Keynes*, vol. 8, London: Macmillan.

(1973b) 'The General Theory and After: Part II Defence and Development', *The Collected Writings of John Maynard Keynes*, vol. 14, London: Macmillan.

(1973c) 'The General Theory', *The Collected Writings of John Maynard Keynes*, vol. 7. London: Macmillan.

Knight, F. H. (1921) *Risk, Uncertainty and Profit*, Chicago: University of Chicago Press.

Kreps, D. M. (1988) *Notes on the Theory of Choice*, Boulder: Westview.

Kyburg, H. E. (1978) 'Subjective Probability: Criticisms, Reflections, and Problems', *Journal of Philosophical Logic*, 7, 157–80.

(1990) *Science and Reason*, New York: Oxford University Press.

(1995) 'Keynes as a Philosopher', *History of Political Economy*, 27, 7–32.

Langlois, R. N. and M. M. Cosgel (1993) 'Frank Knight on Risk, Uncertainty and the Firm: A New Interpretation', *Economic Enquiry*, 31, 456–65.

Lawson, T. (1988) 'Probability and Uncertainty in Economic Analysis', *Journal of Post Keynesian Economics*, 11, 38–65.

LeRoy, S. F. and L. D. Singell (1987) 'Knight on Risk and Uncertainty', *Journal of Political Economy*, 95, 394–406.

Levi, I. (1986) 'The Paradoxes of Allais and Ellsberg', *Economics and Philosophy*, 2, 23–53.

Lucas, R. E. (1981) *Studies in Business Cycle Theory*, Cambridge, MA: MIT Press.

Morris, S. (1993) 'Risk, Uncertainty, and Hidden Information', CARESS Working Paper, 93–10.

Mukerji, S. (1998) 'Ambiguity Aversion and Incompleteness of Contractual Form', *American Economic Review*, 88, 1207–31.

Ramsey, F. P. (1926) 'Truth and Probability', in D. H. Mellor (1978) *Foundations: Essays in Philosophy, Logic, Mathematics and Economics*, London: Routledge & Kegan Paul, 60–100.

Runde, J. H. (1994a) 'Keynes After Ramsey: In Defence of *A Treatise on Probability*', *Studies in History and Philosophy of Science*, 25, 97–121.

(1994b) 'Keynesian Uncertainty and Liquidity Preference', *Cambridge Journal of Economics*, 18, 129–44.

(1998) 'Clarifying Frank Knight's Discussion of the Meaning of Risk and Uncertainty', *Cambridge Journal of Economics*, 22, 539–46.

Savage, L. J. (1954) *The Foundations of Statistics*, New York: John Wiley.

Schick, F. (1986) 'Dutch Bookies and Money Pumps', *Journal of Philosophy*, 83, 12–119.

Schmeidler, D. (1989) 'Subjective Probability and Expected Utility Without Additivity', *Econometrica*, 57, 571–87.

Sugden, R. (1991) 'Rational Choice: A Survey of Contributions from Economics and Philosophy', *Economic Journal*, 101, 751–85.

Vanberg, V. J. (1994) *Rules and Choice in Economics*, London: Routledge.

Williamson, O. E. (1985) *The Economic Institutions of Capitalism*, New York: Free Press.

Part III

Micro, macro, and markets

9   Essences and markets

JOHN O'NEILL

Socialists and liberals have engaged in a long-standing debate in political philosophy about the desirability of markets. Those debates have focused on a series of questions about the market: the kind of moral character it fosters, its tendency to enhance or diminish human welfare, the distribution of goods it promotes, its relationship to political democracy and freedom, its compatibility with socialist goals, and so on. Recently, the very possibility of this debate has been questioned. The whole tradition of argument about the market is rejected on the grounds that it assumes an "essentialist" view of the market.[1] Both defenders of the market and its traditional socialist critics assume that it is possible to talk of "the market." They assume that different markets share some essential nature such that one can engage in a general discussion of the relation of the market to moral character, welfare, justice, freedom, democracy, and so on. However, the argument goes, that essentialist assumption should be rejected. The standard arguments between defenders and critics of the market rest on a mistake.

"Essences and Markets" by John O'Neill, *The Monist*, vol. 78. no. 3, pp. 258–275. Copyright © 1995. THE MONIST, La Salle, Illinois 61301.
[1] For typical examples of such attacks on market essentialism see B. Hindess, *Freedom, Equality, and the Market* (London: Tavistock, 1987), pp. 147–58, T. Cutler, "Social Theory and Social Policy," *Economy and Society*, 17 (1988), 251–71; J. Tomlinson, *The Unequal Struggle? British Socialism and Capitalist Enterprise* (London: Methuen, 1982), ch. 7, and "Market Socialism," in B. Hindess (ed.), *Reactions to the Right* (London; Routledge, 1990). The anti-essentialism about markets of Hindess and Cutler has its roots in a general anti-essentialism that appears in their earlier work: see for example the criticism of Hilferding for his essentialism in A. Cutler, B. Hindess, P. Hirst, and A. Hussain, *Marx's "Capital" and Capitalism Today* (London: Routledge and Kegan Paul, 1977). p. 69. Another influential anti-essentialist "post-Marxist" text which includes specific criticism of essentialism about the economy is E. Laclau and C. Moufe, *Hegemony and Socialist Strategy: Towards a Radical Democratic Politics* (London: Verso, 1985), pp. 75–85 and passim.

This rejection of the existence of any essence to "the market" has clear appeal in an intellectual world dominated by a variety of positions that employ that most empty of prefixes "post." Thus, the rejection of market essentialism is attractive to those "post-Marxists" and "post-liberals" who assume that the market is an achievement which the recent demise of "actually existing socialism" shows that we can now look beyond: the debate over the relation between socialism and the market is one that we can put behind us since it depended on the assumption that the market has certain essential properties which render it incompatible with socialism. In the "post-Marxist" and "post-liberal" world, the debate moves onto new territory concerning the proper institutional framework in which markets can operate.[2] Amongst "post-modernists" the term "essentialist" is used as a term of abuse: we live in a world without essences, one in which Heraclitus is proclaimed a hero. Essentialism is rejected variously for being incompatible with the recognition of "difference," for entailing a reduction of social categories to non-social natural categories; it is taken also to be philosophically naïve, having been effectively demolished by Wittgenstein. The post-modern moves against essentialism are most frequently employed in discussions of gender. However, the same moves can and have been made in debates in political economy and appear in particular in discussions of "market essentialism."

My aim in this paper is to defend the questions about the market that have been traditional to political philosophy against these recent anti-essentialist arguments. I argue that *if* essentialism is presupposed by these questions, the debate is none the worse for it.[3] Neither liberal defenders of the market nor its socialist critics are in error in making essentialist assumptions. Much of the recent criticism of essentialism is founded on a caricature which is defended by nobody. In the first section I draw a more accurate picture of the essentialist position by looking back at the work of the founder of essentialism, Aristotle, and outlining something of his influence. The second section shows that, properly characterized, the essentialist position is immune to the recent anti-essentialist wave of arguments that the various positions that are "post" this or that have offered. However, to reject those arguments is not to render essentialist claims about the market immune from criticism. I conclude by briefly outlining what a defensible and empirically grounded criticism of essentialist assumptions about the market would need to look like.

---

[2] I criticize this line of argument in J. O'Neill "Essentialism and the Market," *Philosophical Forum*, 26 (1994).

[3] I leave aside here the issue as to whether essentialism is necessarily presupposed in the traditional debate. As I note in section 2.D, many of the questions that the traditional debate assumes may survive the failure of an essentialist approach to markets.

1 Aristotle, essences, and markets

The distinction between an entity's essential and accidental properties, the ascription of essences to social institutions, and the use of essentialist assumptions in discussion of the market, can all be traced back to the work of Aristotle. His work provides a paradigmatic example of an essentialist position.

A Essence and accident [4]

The essential properties of an entity of a particular kind are those properties of the object that it must have if it is to be an object of that kind. Accidental properties of an entity of a particular kind are those properties it has, but could lack and still be an entity of that kind. To take a standard example from the modern natural sciences, consider what it is for a substance to be copper. There are properties an entity must have if it is to be a specimen of copper, e.g., ductility, malleability, fusibility, electrical conductivity, atomic number 29, and so on. There are other properties possessed by some or all samples of copper that they could lack and still be copper. Thus, for example, it may be this lump of copper is a doorstop. It is a property it could lack and still be copper. It may be that all copper comes in lumps smaller than that of the Taj Mahal. However, that property, if it is true of all lumps of copper, is not one that they must have. It is possible, given the nature of copper, for them to come in sizes greater than that.

A few standard observations about essences thus defined:

1. Essence precedes investigation and requires investigation. The essential properties of objects are properties that we discover that they have by investigation, not by simply looking at them or by looking in a dictionary. The electrical conductivity of copper and its specific atomic number are properties that we once did not know copper possessed and that we now know that it does. The essence of an object precedes its discovery. The appearance of an object does not reveal to us directly its essence.

2. Many essential properties of objects are dispositional properties that are only actualized in certain circumstances. Thus ductility, malleability, fusibility, and electrical conductivity are all clearly dispositional properties

---

[4] Aristotle, *Topics*, Book I.

– capacities and powers that particular samples of copper have, which they exhibit in certain conditions. To discover those properties requires that those conditions be realized. A sample of copper may never exhibit the powers and capacities that it possesses. That this is the case is one reason why the discovery of the essences of natural objects involves experimental investigation: powers can be discovered by setting up those conditions in which they are exhibited.

3. Some of the essential properties of objects are dependent upon others and part of the purpose of scientific investigation is to discover those dependencies: it is the atomic structure of copper that explains its ductility, malleability, fusibility, and electrical conductivity.[5] However, the dependent-essential properties of objects are no less real than those that are explanatorily prior to them. To explain is not to explain away.

B Essence and development

Aristotle's biological and social writings contain a second and distinct set of teleological claims about essences that need to be distinguished from the basic claims just made. Aristotle asserts that an entity's essence can be revealed in the pattern of its development, that is, that there is a normal developmental sequence to an entity of some kind which represents an unfolding of the essential nature of that entity, such that the final "mature" stage of the normal developmental sequence exhibits most clearly the essential nature of the entity. Entities that exhibit such developmental sequences include both biological beings and social institutions. Consider, for example, his account of the development of the *polis* from the earlier associations of household and village:

[The *polis*] is the end or consummation to which those associations move, and the "nature" of things consists in their end or consummation; for what a thing is when its growth is completed we call the nature of that thing, whether it be a man or a horse or a family . . .[6]

Aristotle here treats the development of both individual organisms – humans and horses – and of social institutions – families and political communities – as exhibiting in the same way a development from

[5] In the language of Locke, the atomic structure of copper is its real essence, the explanatorily dependent properties, its nominal essence (J. Locke, *Essay Concerning Human Understanding*, III, 3). See also Aristotle's distinction between "real" and "nominal" definitions in *Posterior Analytics*, Book II.

[6] Aristotle, *Politics*, I.ii, trans., E. Barker (Oxford: Clarendon Press, 1950).

immature to mature states. The developmental pattern exhibits the unfolding of the essential nature of a being of that species, that development that would occur if not interrupted by some external accident. For both organisms and institutions the essential nature of an object is exhibited in its mature stage since at that stage all the potential powers of that kind of being are fully developed.

C Essences and markets

Aristotle uses both the general essence/accident distinction and the more particular teleological account of essences to describe the market as a social institution. To characterize those properties of the market which it possesses in virtue of the kind of economic institution it is, as against accidental features of this or that market. Aristotle starts by considering the features of the market that distinguish it from non-market economic institutions, specifically the household. He proceeds thus in virtue of his taxonomic approach to the characterization of an essence which he inherits from his biology: a sentence characterizing an essence of an entity of a particular kind standardly has the form of a noun phrase indicating a genus modified by an adjectival phrase that expresses the differentiae,[7] the properties that are peculiar to that kind.[8] The market is defined as a mode of acquisition (genus) which considers objects for exchange and which knows no limits to the accumulation of wealth (differentiae).

In the *Politics* Aristotle distinguishes between two forms of acquisition, the economic and the chrematistic: the former is characteristic of the household,[9] the latter is characteristic of the market. The two modes of acquisition are correlative with two possible uses that articles of property

---

[7] In the *Metaphysics* the definition of the essence of a species is reduced to just one differentiating property (*Metaphysics*, VII 12 and VIII 6). However, in the *De Partibus Animalium* he claims that "no single differentia . . . can possibly express the essence of a species," and defends, rather, definition through clusters of differentiae (*De Partibus Animalium* I. 2–3).

[8] See *Topics*, Book I, 4–6 and Book VI. The procedure of defining the nature of a being of a particular kind through consideration of what is peculiar to it is not always felicitous – what is peculiar to entities of a certain kind is not co-extensive with that which is characteristic of their nature.

[9] The household here needs to be understood as a unit of both production and consumption, and not, as it is in the modern world, only as a unit of consumption: in the classical world commerce operated at the margins of the household. On the central place of household in the ancient economy and the marginal role of commerce see G. St. Croix, *The Class Struggle in the Ancient World* (London: Duckworth, 1981), ch. III, iv.

can have: the first a use which is "peculiar and proper" to the object –
say of a sandal, to be worn – the second a use as an item to be exchanged
with others.[10] Economic acquisition, that of the household, considers
acquisition only with respect to the object's primary use, as an object
that satisfies a need. Objects thus employed constitute, for Aristotle, the
real components of wealth and, in opposition to Solon, Aristotle asserts
that this wealth has bounds: "the amount of household property which
suffices for a good life is not unlimited."[11] The second form of acquisition, the chrematistic,[12] is concerned with the accumulation of the means
of exchange in the market: "It is the characteristics of this second form
which lead to the opinion that there is no limit to wealth and property."[13]
This form of wealth-making is often confused with the first, but the two
are distinct, and constitutive of quite different institutions. While there is
a limit to the accumulation of natural goods in the household, namely
the needs they satisfy, there is no limit to the acquisition of the means of
exchange: "There is no limit to the end it seeks; and the end it seeks is
wealth of the sort we have mentioned [i.e., wealth in the form of currency]
and the mere acquisition of money."[14]

The development of the second art of acquisition, the chrematistic, is
presented by Aristotle as the outcome of a natural developmental
sequence leading to market institutions. The market begins in simple
exchange, barter, in which "things which are useful are exchanged
themselves, and go directly, for similar useful things," which in turn
develops into exchange through the medium of money, which in turn
gives rise to the new and distinctive art of acquisition:

When, in this way, a currency had once been instituted there next arose, from the
necessary process of exchange [i.e., exchange between commodities with money
serving merely as a measure], the other form of the art of acquisition which
consists in retail trade [conducted for profit] . . . The result has been the
emergence of the view that the art of acquisition is specially concerned with
currency. . .[15]

The chrematistic art of acquisition, because it involves acquisition of
objects not for their "proper and peculiar" properties, is, for Aristotle,
"unnatural" for humans, and hence to be held in check. It needs to be

[10] Aristotle, *Politics*, Book I, ch. 8, 1256b 27ff, p. 26.
[11] Aristotle, *Politics*, 1236b 31.
[12] The use of the term "chrematistic" I outline here is that which Aristotle employs most
widely in the *Politics*. Aristotle does however sometimes use it in a more neutral sense:
for an account of the different uses see Barker in Aristotle, *Politics*, pp. 226–7.
[13] Aristotle, *Politics*, 1256b 40ff, p. 27.
[14] Aristotle, *Politics*, I. ix 1257b 28ff, p. 31.
[15] Aristotle, *Politics*, I. ix.

held in check, however, because it is the normal developmental outcome of exchange.

The essential nature of market exchange is revealed for Aristotle in its developed "unnatural" form. In this final state the dispositional properties of markets are exhibited. The most significant of these for Aristotle is the particular moral character it tends to produce: Aristotle's political theory is by and large concerned with the tendency of different social and political institutions to issue in different virtues and vices. The market, where its development is unchecked, tends to issue not in the virtues constitutive of a flourishing human life, but in the vice of *pleonexia*, the disposition to want more than is proper.

D Aristotelian essentialism: distinctions and influences

Aristotle's essentialism is a complex of claims that are logically independent of one another. One might accept his basic distinction between the essential and accidental properties of an object without accepting the further teleological specification of essences in terms of normal patterns of development. Indeed it is worth noting that the example of essentialist descriptions of copper I used in section A does not conform to the Aristotelian teleological model. Likewise one might accept essentialism in its basic form without accepting his particular taxonomic approach to the specification of essences. Again, it is possible to adopt an essentialist position in either its basic form or its teleological elaboration for entities in the natural world, but to reject it for the social world. One might accept essentialism about social institutions generally and markets in particular, but reject the teleological elaboration of essentialism that Aristotle offers. The options open to the "essentialist" are much more varied and complex than recent anti-essentialist caricatures of the position allow.

The picture of Aristotle's influence on subsequent essentialist thought about social institutions in general and the market in particular is similarly complex. Both Aristotle's essentialism and his discussion of the market have had a large influence on philosophical and economic thought. Aristotelian essentialism, as far as description of the natural world is concerned, has had a long-standing influence and indeed has recently undergone something of a revival.[16] In the social realm it is

[16] See, for example, D. Wiggins, *Sameness and Substance* (Oxford: Blackwell, 1980), H. Putnam, *Philosophical Papers*, vol. 1 (Cambridge: Cambridge University Press, 1975), and S. Kripke, *Naming and Necessity* (Oxford: Blackwell, 1972). In the philosophy of

possible to find theorists, most notably Hegel and Marx, who self-consciously defend Aristotle's essentialism in its full teleological form.[17] Aristotle's discussion of the market has also exercised a large influence on subsequent economic thought.[18] In some theorists both philosophical and economic influences converge. The most notable example of such a thinker is Marx, whose work exhibits the influence of Aristotle's basic distinction between essence and accident, his teleological specification of essences, and his more particular discussion of the market and its specific mode of acquisition.[19]

However, Aristotle's influence in economics has often been independent of any explicit or self-conscious appeal to his essentialist premises. Moreover, where essentialist reconstructions of later economics is possible, they often require the rejection of Aristotle's teleological specification of essences. Consider for example the work of Karl Polanyi whose work owes an explicit debt to Aristotle's discussion of the household and market. Aristotle's contrast between household and market is taken by Polanyi to provide the key to the analysis of the development of modern market society: Aristotle's "famous distinction of householding proper and money-making . . . was probably the most prophetic pointer ever made in the realm of the social sciences; it is certainly still the best analysis we possess."[20] The development of modern market society, the story of Polanyi's *The Great Transformation*, is a story of the escape of the economy from the social and ethical limits that constrained it in pre-modern societies: Aristotle's greatness lies in his anticipating the consequences of this disembedding of the economy from constraining institutions.[21] However, Polanyi employs Aristotle's account of modes of acquisition without self-conscious reference to his essentialist presupposi-

science the work of Harré has been particularly influential in reviving essentialism, although Locke's essentialism is often the immediate influence. See R. Harré and E. Madden,*Causal Powers* (Oxford: Blackwell, 1977).

[17] For an excellent discussion see S. Meikle, *Essentialism in the Thought of Karl Marx* (London: Duckworth, 1985).

[18] On Aristotle's influence in ecological economics see J. Martinez-Alier, *Ecological Economics* (Oxford: Blackwell, 1987). See also J. O'Neill, *Ecology, Policy and Politics: Human Well-Being and the Natural World* (London, Routledge, 1993), ch. 10 and "Polity, Economy, Neutrality," *Political Studies*, forthcoming.

[19] For a further elaboration of Marx's essentialism and its debt to Aristotle see S. Meikle, *Essentialism in the Thought of Karl Marx* (London: Duckworth, 1985), especially ch. 3. See also A. Wood, *Karl Marx* (London: Routledge and Kegan Paul, 1981), part 5, and J. O'Neill, "Essentialism and the Market," *Philosophical Forum*, 26 (1994).

[20] Polanyi, *The Great Transformation*, pp. 53–4; cf. Polanyi "Aristotle Discovers the Economy", in *Primitive, Archaic and Modern Economies* (Boston, MA: Beacon Press, 1957).

[21] K. Polanyi, *The Great Transformation* (Boston, MA: Beacon Press, 1957), p. 54.

tions. Moreover, Polanyi's arguments are clearly inconsistent with Aristotle's specific teleological account of the development of market exchange: a central thesis of *The Great Transformation* is that there is no natural developmental sequence in the development of the modern market economy.[22] While, as I show below, Polanyi's work is best interpreted in essentialist terms, it is in terms of Aristotle's basic essentialism without its teleological turn.

Aristotelian essentialism in a non-teleological form also provides the best philosophical foundation of much in the Austrian tradition of economics.[23] However, some of the theorists in that tradition, most notably Hayek, have a complex relation to the Aristotelian tradition. Hayek is strongly opposed to the tradition of criticism of the market represented by Aristotle and his socialist successors such as Marx and Polanyi. He is aware of the Aristotelian heritage of modern socialism and deeply critical of it.[24] However, Hayek does take over and rework the Aristotelian distinction between household and market. The distinction between them is reinterpreted not as that between economic and chrematistic arts of acquisition, but as that between economic and catallactic social orders. The account of the economic order is built on the household. However, its distinguishing feature is now understood to be the deliberate subordination of means to a shared set of ends.[25] The market is not in the proper sense of the term an economy, since "its activities are not governed by a single scale or hierarchy of ends."[26] The market rather consists of a network of economies, of households and enterprises, each with its own ends, each having to adjust and coordinate its activities with others through exchange, but together ungoverned by any order of ends. The market order is governed only by abstract rules of property and contract. An order of that kind Hayek refers to as a catallaxy.[27]

At the level of his philosophical presuppositions the relation is still

---

[22] See especially Polanyi, *The Great Transformation*, ch. 5.

[23] On the relation between Austrian economics and Aristotelian essentialism see B. Smith, "Austrian Economics and Austrian Philosophy", pp. 2–5 in W. Grassl and B. Smith (eds.), *Austrian Economics* (London: Croom Helm, 1986) and "Aristotle, Menger and Mises: An Essay in the Metaphysics of Economics", in B. Caldwell, *Carl Menger and His Legacy in Economics* (Durham, NC: Duke University Press, 1990). For an essentialist reading of Austrian economics see U. Mäki, "Mengerian Economics in Realist Perspective", in B. Caldwell, *Carl Menger and His Legacy in Economics* (Durham, NC: Duke University Press, 1990) and "Scientific Realism and Austrian Explanation," *Review of Political Economy*, 2.3 (1990), 310–44.

[24] See, for example, Hayek, *The Fatal Conceit* (London: Routledge, 1988), pp. 45–8.

[25] F. Hayek, *Law, Legislation and Liberty*, vol. 2 (London: Routledge and Kegan Paul, 1976) p. 107.

[26] Ibid., p. 108.   [27] Ibid., p. 109.

more complex. Hayek's economic thought has been presented as essentialist by some of his recent anti-essentialist critics, for example Hindess.[28] Others, notably Gray, have given a strong anti-essentialist reading to Hayek's own methodological claims about his work.[29] My own view is that, whatever Hayek's own philosophical conception of his work, his writing is best understood in realist and essentialist terms.[30] For example, Hayek's claim that the market is a catallactic order is best interpreted as a putative discovery about the *nature* of the market order and likewise his rejection of the claim that the market order is an economy is best understood as a criticism of a misconception about its nature.[31] In the following I will assume that the charge of essentialism made against Hayek by his critics is one that can be made out. However, against these critics, I argue this is a virtue of his work, not a vice.

In the rest of the paper I defend essentialism about markets against recent criticism. In doing so I consider only the claim that the market has an essential nature. I will bracket any critical discussion of the claims made by Aristotle and Marx that the essential nature of the market is revealed in a developmental sequence. I do so because they are not relevant to the question of whether or not the traditional debates of political philosophy about the market rest on a mistake. While the debates may assume essentialism about the market, they do not normally depend on any assumption about the normal developmental sequence of the market.

2 In defence of essentialism

A How not to talk about essences

Criticism of essentialism often begins with quite misleading characterizations of what is meant by "essence." Consider for example the criticism of market essentialism offered by Hindess against both defenders of free markets such as Hayek, and socialist critics of the market such as Marx:

[28] B. Hindess, *Freedom, Equality, and the Market* (London: Tavistock, 1987), ch. 9.
[29] Gray offers a Kantian reading of Hayek's position which is set against the "Aristotelian method of seeking essences or natures of things"; J. Gray, *Hayek on Liberty* (Oxford: Blackwell, 1984), p. 6. For criticism of Gray see M. Peacock, "Hayek, Realism and Spontaneous Order," *Journal of the Theory of Social Behaviour*, 23 (1993), 249–64.
[30] Gray himself acknowledges that this is possible. J Gray, *Hayek on Liberty*, p. 117.
[31] Ibid., pp. 112ff.

These various positions arrive at their assessments of the market in rather different ways, but they nevertheless share an essentialization of the market and the problems that this generates for social analysis. To write of essentialism in this context is to say that the market is analyzed in terms of an essence or inner principle which produces necessary effects by the mere fact of its presence.[32]

The criticism relies on a caricature of what it is to say that an entity has an essence, and it results in an account of essentialism about the market that neither liberal proponents of markets nor socialist critics hold. In using the language of essences one is not, as Hindess claims, describing inner principles that produce "necessary effects" by the mere fact of their presence. Rather, one is concerned with the nature and explanation of the capacities and powers of objects to produce certain effects. The liberal and socialist theorists that Hindess criticizes claim that the market has certain dispositional properties – to facilitate the accumulation of capital without limit, to foster vices, say that of pleonexia, or virtues, such as those of the autonomous character, to determine a particular price for a commodity, and so on – and are concerned to explain these. It does not follow that these dispositions are always exhibited. That Hindess wrongly characterizes essentialism undermines his more substantial criticisms of market essentialism. The criticisms are aimed at positions that nobody holds.

B The institutional contexts of the market

At the centre of Hindess's substantial criticism of market essentialism is the claim that markets do not and could not exist in an institutional vacuum. Markets appear in a variety of institutional contexts. In elaborating this claim Hindess makes two points – that markets presuppose other institutions, and that markets operate in different institutional contexts. Both points can and should be accepted. Neither, however, entails the falsity of essentialism.

In criticizing Hayek's essentialism, Hindess accuses him of inconsistency in also holding that market institutions presuppose non-market institutions.

[I]n parts of *The Constitution of Liberty* (especially Ch. 4, "Freedom, Reason and Tradition") he suggests that the effective workings of the market depend on the presence of the appropriate traditions and moral codes. But in spite of that

---

[32] B. Hindess, *Freedom, Equality, and the Market*, p. 149.

recognition his anti-planning polemic achieves its superficial appearance of plausibility by essentializing "the market."[33]

Hayek's recognition that market transactions presuppose a set of prior non-market institutions sets him against pure contractarian versions of liberalism which hold that all relations could be modelled on contract. However, Hayek is guilty of no logical inconsistency in combining non-contractarianism about markets with essentialism. That a particular kind of object or institution can exist only given particular conditions is quite irrelevant as to whether the object or institution has essential properties. That there are institutional preconditions of markets does not entail that markets lack essential powers. Hayek's claim that the market has institutional prerequisites is quite consistent, for example, with the claim that it is essentially a catallactic order that reduces coercion and thereby cultivates human freedom.

Hindess's second point is that markets operate in different institutional contexts:

what is shared by all markets is little more than the fact that something is marketed in them. Otherwise they are highly differentiated. Markets always operate under specific institutional conditions, which can vary considerably from one case to another. What is meant by institutional conditions in this context are: the market actors (large corporations, government departments, small businesses, producer and retail co-operatives, private individuals, etc.) and the resources made available to them; legislative regulation and other forms of administrative and political controls; customary and other informal constraints on acceptable behaviour; linkages with and spillovers into other markets engaging different actors and controls.[34]

That markets operate under a number of distinct institutional conditions and have different effects given these conditions is uncontentious. However, it does not follow that essentialism about markets is false or that the *only* general statement one can make about markets is that "something is marketed in them."

Two initial general points are in order here. First there is nothing in essentialism that disallows variation in the properties of different instances of some kind of entity: the distinction between accidental and essential properties serves in part to distinguish what is of the nature of a thing and what varies. Second, that the essential properties of markets might be exhibited only in certain institutional conditions does not entail that they are not present nor that reference to them might not feature in the explanations of the behaviour of markets.

An essentialist account of the market can allow that there exist a

---

[33] Ibid., p. 159.   [34] Ibid., p. 150.

variety of accidental features of specific market relations in particular institutional contexts. These conditions will often entail that the powers of markets are not exhibited. There may exist constraints that "inhibit" the exercise of those powers. Consider Polanyi's use of the concept of chrematistic acquisition to specify the nature of market economies. It is only in modern conditions, in which the market is "disembedded," that the potentialities of a market economy based on the principle of the unrestrained acquisition of wealth without limit are fully exhibited. In saying that the market is disembedded in modern capitalism Polanyi is not claiming that markets here exist without any institutional context. He recognizes that it was the product of and still relies upon a particular political and legal framework.[35] When Polanyi refers to the disembedding of the market he is referring to the disappearance of legal and customary regulatory constraints on the working of the market. In these conditions the potentialities of markets become visible. However, those potentialities existed within markets in their embedded state. The relation between markets and surrounding institutional contexts was one of tension. It was this tension to which Aristotle was responding in making his distinction between household and money-making. Reference to those potentialities appears in Polanyi's explanation of the collapse of the Speenhamland Law which prevented a free market in labor.[36]

The co-existence of non-market relations alongside market relations between agents might also entail that the market does not exhibit its essential properties. For example, it might be the case that, as Hegel claims, market relations are essentially impersonal, and this might be taken to be a virtue or vice of markets. However, the impersonality of market relations might often not be exhibited in virtue of other personal ties between particular actors. Ties of kin, particular historical loyalties between members of a community, and so on, might mean that market transactions within a small village community do not exhibit the impersonality of those of the city. The defender of the claim that markets are essentially impersonal might still quite properly argue that the personal bonds are accidental features of those specific market transactions: as the surrounding accidental ties are eroded, markets tend to impersonality.

That essentialism about the market is compatible with acceptance of the existence of variation in markets in different institutional conditions also undermines a criticism of essentialism, popular in postmodern literature. The term "essentialist" has, in postmodernist circles, become a term of abuse. The major reason for this anti-essentialism is the

---

[35] Polanyi, *The Great Transformation*, p. 139.
[36] Ibid., ch. 7.

assumption that essentialism is incompatible with difference. Postmodernists claim to celebrate difference and diversity and to say that a certain class of entities has an essential nature that they all share is taken to entail a denial of difference. In the postmodern thesaurus the term "essence" appears in the same list as "uniformity" and "homogeneity." Similarly, the assumption that essentialism is incompatible with difference underlies the rejection of essentialism about markets. It is assumed that to talk of there being an essential nature of markets involves a denial of the possibility of differences between distinct markets. That assumption is false for the reasons outlined. Essentialism is quite compatible with the recognition of variation. That a number of entities share some common nature is quite consistent with the existence of differences between them.

There is, however, a partial concession that needs to be made to the anti-essentialist about markets. There is certainly a danger associated with essentialism of taking properties of one particular variant of a species of being to be essential properties of all. Thus, for example, there feminists criticize essentialism, it is often the way that culturally specific attributes and relations are taken to be shared by all women that is the object of criticism. Likewise it is a mistake to assume specific accidental properties of a particular market order, say that in Western Europe or the United States, to be essential properties of all markets. However, the defensibility of specific essentialist claims needs to be distinguished from the defensibility of essentialism. That some essentialist theorists make false claims does not entail the falsity of essentialism.

C Social meaning and essence

Thus far I have outlined the essentialist position by way of parallels between the use of the language of essences to describe natural objects and its use in social theory. There are dangers in parallels between essentialist claims about human beings and social institutions, and essentialist claims about natural objects, which invite criticism of essentialism in social theory. Thus another common reason why some feminists are critical of any essentialist account of the nature of women is that it is assumed that it entails biological reductionism and a commitment to a purely biological explanation of gender differences and power relations. If this is the case then the anti-essentialist criticism would be well-founded. However, essentialism need not involve any such failure to recognize the differences in the nature of the objects of the human sciences and those of the natural sciences. More specifically, the essentialist can accept that institutions like markets are not natural objects: in particular, essentialism is consistent with the claim that social objects are constituted by relationships and acts which have social meanings whereas natural objects are not. Consider, for example, the account offered by Hegel, a strong essentialist in the Aristotelian tradition, of the essential differences between the contractual market sphere of civil society on the one hand and the family on the other. Hegel claims that "marriage, so far as its essential basis is concerned is not a contractual relation."[37] The relationship of marriage partners is such that one's identity is partially constituted by that relationship. In contrast, contracts are essentially between persons considered as "self-subsistent persons," whose identity is independent of the contractual relation. Whatever might be said for or against Hegel's position, his arguments are based on differences in the social meanings of different relationships and acts. Contractual relations and personal relations are essentially different in virtue of the meanings constitutive of them. In this respect at least, the essential natures of social objects are different from those of natural objects. However, the essentialist need have no difficulty in recognizing that the objects of the human sciences do have such distinct properties.

D Wittgenstein, games, and family resemblance

Another major source of inspiration for the rejection of essentialism, including that about the market, is Wittgenstein's well known criticism of the "craving for generality":

There is . . . the tendency to look for something in common to all the entities which we commonly subsume under a general term. – We are inclined to think that there must be something in common to all games, say, and that this common property is the justification for applying the general term "game" to the various games; whereas games form a *family* the members of which have family likenesses.[38]

I have no argument at all with Wittgenstein's argument here. However, I do not believe that it undermines essentialism. It is quite true that there is no reason to assume that there *must* be something in common to all entities that fall under a general term which justifies the application of

---

[37] Hegel, *Philosophy of Right* (T. Knox trans.) (Oxford: Oxford University Press, 1967), 163R.

[38] L. Wittgenstein, *Blue Book* (Oxford: Blackwell, 1960), p. 17; see also *Philosophical Investigations* (Oxford: Blackwell, 1958), paragraphs 66 and 67.

the term. However, no general conclusion follows from that about the truth of essentialism. The scientific endeavour to specify and explain the nature of copper or certain species of animal or plant is not ruled out by Wittgenstein's argument. The proper conclusion that follows from Wittgenstein's discussion is that one cannot assume in advance that there is some set of essential properties shared by all entities that fall under some concept, not that no essential properties exist. Turning to markets, it is quite possible that different markets, like games, may turn out to share only some family resemblances. It does not follow that the attempt to discover essential properties is a mistake. It does mean that one may be unsuccessful. In the end it is a matter of empirical investigation.

Two further points need to be added. First, Wittgenstein's conclusion is quite independent of the nominalist thesis that the only thing in common between all entities that fall under a general term X is that they are called X, such that, in principle, we could extend the reference of term to whatever we like. The entities that fall under a term do share family resemblances – "a complicated network of similarities overlapping and crisscrossing: sometimes overall similarities, sometimes similarities in detail."[39] Those similarities are real – there does exist a network of properties that thread together entities that fall under a term. If it is the case that markets are, like games, united only by a set of family likenesses, those likenesses are real.

Secondly, this existence of real family resemblances is sufficient for the intelligibility of many of the traditional questions asked about markets in political philosophy. For example questions like "What effects do markets have on the moral character?" like the question "What effects does engagement in games have on the moral character?" make perfect sense even in the absence of any single essential property shared by all markets or all games. Likewise it makes sense to investigate the reasons for blocking markets in certain goods – votes, bodily parts, blood and so on – just as it makes sense to ask of games whether it is appropriate to play them at a funeral. The existence of a family network of real resemblances will suffice for such traditional questions raised in political philosophy.

E How to criticize market essentialism

Wittgenstein's argument does highlight the openness of essentialist claims to empirical criticism. It is important to distinguish between

---

[39] Wittgenstein, *Philosophical Investigations*, paragraph 66.

arguments aimed quite generally against essentialism and specific empirical arguments against an essentialist claim about some set of entities that fall under a general term. My criticism in this paper is entirely of those arguments aimed quite generally against essentialism. That general anti-essentialist arguments fail does not show that there must be some form of market essentialism that is true. There may be good empirical evidence specifically aimed only against essentialism about markets. It may be that markets do not share any essential characteristics, and hence that no essentialist theorist will get it right.

This last point can be developed in essentialist terms. It may be that in exploring the differences between markets, what looked like one species is in fact many. Dore opens a paper on "What Makes the Japanese Different?" as follows:

Sheep come in all shapes and sizes. So do goats. In fact some sheep look like goats, and vice versa. But as biological systems they are distinct; they won't interbreed. Shoats and geep don't exist. Are capitalisms like that? Is it true that there are different types of capitalism, and that the differences between them are systematic. . . . ?[40]

Superficially similar beings can turn out to be essentially different. It might be the case that, as Dore suggests, superficially similar economic orders turn out to have quite different natures. The differences are systematic. Those claims are not only consistent with essentialism about social orders, they assume an essentialist programme. What is denied is the more specific essentialist claims about the market. If it is right, some of the essentialist claims made about *the* market would turn out to be false, and theorists like Marx, Polanyi, and Hayek would have failed to distinguish essentially different social orders. Whether this is the case is in the end a question of empirical investigation. However, such empirical criticism of market essentialism is not to be confused with those founded on a general rejection of the language of essences. My main purpose in this paper has been to clear the ground for proper discussion of essentialist claims about the market by weeding out recent growths of anti-essentialist scrub.[41]

---

[40] R. Dore, "What Makes the Japanese Different?" in C. Crouch and D. Marquand (eds.), *Ethics and Markets* (Oxford: Blackwell, 1993) , p. 66.

[41] My thanks to Russell Keat, Uskali Mäki, Mark Peacock, Andrew Sayer, and Barry Smith for their comments on earlier versions of this chapter. I owe a special debt of gratitude to the late Mary Farmer with whom I had several conversations on the issues discussed here.

10   The metaphysics of microeconomics

ALEX ROSENBERG

The study of economics has been a going concern among philosophers for the better part of twenty years without very many people even noticing that economics has a metaphysics. Indeed, among economists the term "metaphysical" is probably an epithet of opprobrium, employed to suggest that a claim is untestable or otherwise without cognitive significance. Philosophers of economics will admit to the existence of an epistemology of economics – the study of the nature, extent, and justification of economic knowledge. But even this is controversial among some economists.[1] The notion that economics might have a metaphysics as well as an epistemology will be scoffed at by those economists doubtful about the enterprise of the philosophy of economics altogether. Nevertheless, philosophers of economics should have no trouble identifying a metaphysics in some of the theoretical commitments of economics.

Or at least philosophers who have adopted a Quinean view of metaphysics as continuous with physics – and science generally, will have no trouble finding metaphysical compartments of economic theory. To see why, recall the Quinean teaching that there is no well-founded distinction between necessarily true propositions, true in virtue of meaning alone – analytic truths, and contingent statements, true in virtue of content – synthetic truths. Nor do scientific claims meet experience for tests one at a time; rather they meet experience in units no smaller than entire theories. Accordingly, the difference between sets of metaphysical statements and sets of empirical ones cannot be a matter of kind, say testable versus non-testable, or necessary versus contingent; instead

"The Metaphysics of Microeconomics" by Alex Rosenberg, *The Monist*, vol. 78, no. 3, pp. 352–67. Copyright © 1995. THE MONIST, La Salle, Illinois 61301.

[1] Cf. Donald McCloskey, *The Rhetoric of Economics* (Madison, WI: University of Wisconsin Press, 1985), who rejects epistemology as a standard on which to assess economics.

the difference is at most one of degree. The difference between metaphysics and theory is one of generality and abstractness, and where metaphysics begins and theory leaves off turns out often to be arbitrary.[2] For this reason there is no really adequate and illuminating definition of metaphysics to be found in philosophy.

It is not surprising that sometimes research programs in the sciences are driven by commitments which might as well be deemed metaphysical as theoretical: determinism, reductionism, atomism. The role of metaphysics in directing research programs will be even more prominent in the empirically underdeveloped and non-experimental sciences. In the social and behavioral sciences there are fewer hard experimental or observational findings to guide theorizing; the need for some direction in theorizing can only be filled by appeal to very abstract and general constraints often derived from other disciplines via philosophy – epistemology, metaphysics, or their amalgam in the philosophy of science. Thus, many research programs in psychology and sociology have been inspired by metaphysical dicta variously inspired by understandings and misunderstandings of everything from Darwinian evolution to Heisenbergian uncertainty. So it is with a good deal of economic theory. Important features of the theory are determined by metaphysical commitments both borrowed and invented.[3] Among empirically well-developed disciplines – the physical sciences, in particular – metaphysical disputes are rare because they have already been settled by the success of some basic theories and the failure of others: controversies surround the significance of experimental data, and the competition among theories to account for these data.

Interestingly, in all the other social sciences, debates about methodology and epistemology bulk larger, and it is the absence of much agreement on what the data are that leads social scientists often to be guided by metaphysics. Economics, especially neoclassical microeconomics, like physical science, is almost entirely free of such debates. But this does not show that there is among economists agreement about what constitutes the data and what the data show. Rather, it betokens a substantially greater agreement about metaphysics among economists than in other social disciplines.

Metaphysics *sans phrase* is sometimes defined as the study of the

---

[2] See W. V. O. Quine, *From a Logical Point of View* (Cambridge, MA: Harvard University Press, 1953).

[3] I argue for this view at some length in Alex Rosenberg, "Methodology, Theory and the Philosophy of Science," *Pacific Philosophical Quarterly*, 66 (1985), 377–93, and Alex Rosenberg, "Normative Naturalism and the Role of Philosophy," *Philosophy of Science*, 57 (1990), 34–43.

ultimate constituents of reality – what fundamental kinds of things there are, and how the differing things in this world and out of it can be shown to be examples of these basic kinds. *Mutatis mutandis* the metaphysics of a discipline is therefore the basic set of kinds or types of entities countenanced by the established theory or theories of the discipline. Microeconomics is the traditional theoretical core of the discipline of economics, a widely known body of concepts, generalizations, and analytical strategies shared by almost all academic economists. It is the similarity across textbooks of economics, compared to the vast diversity among the textbooks of other social sciences that reveals the metaphysical homogeneity of the discipline.

The metaphysics of economics is in part the study of the basic kinds over which the theory quantifies – that is what sorts of things the truth of the theory commits us to. But, there is potentially something more to the metaphysics of economics. For, it may be that economists are not fully committed to the existence of entities of the sort the theory's truth requires. If so, the metaphysics of econom*ists* seems to come into conflict with the metaphysics of econom*ics*, for we need to distinguish what economic theories state from what economists who use them believe. This inconsistency between economists' beliefs and their favorite theories may be tolerable to some economists, as inconsistencies seem tolerable in other disciplines, like physics.[4] But inconsistency will not sit well with philosophers, and for that matter with others interested in whether to believe economists or their theories. Of course, to some economists, metaphysical inconsistency is just as unacceptable as any other kind, and for the same reason: at least one of the inconsistent propositions must be false, and false beliefs are to be expunged.

In this paper I attempt to identify some components of the metaphysics of microeconomics, and to explore the interpretations of the theory economists often provide because of their discomfort with the metaphysical commitment of their theory. Even independent of the Quinean conception of metaphysics, there appear to be significant metaphysical assumptions behind well-known methodological strictures of economic theory. For example, conventional welfare economics subscribe to a clear-cut distinction between facts and values, between normative claims which cannot be empirically adjudicated and factual claims which can be. If pressed to defend this orthodoxy the defender will begin with epistemological considerations which suggest that we cannot test moral prescriptions, but eventually the defender needs to seek a metaphysical

---

[4] Consider for example wave/particle duality, renormalization in quantum electromagnetism, or attitudes towards Bell's inequality.

basis for this claim, one which explains why there are no moral facts, or what it is about their character that unsuits them for accommodation by economic theory. There are, of course, philosophical theories that economics could help itself to for such a task,[5] but the task is clearly a metaphysical one.

Relatedly, economic theory needs a metaphysical argument for its rejection of interpersonal comparability of preferences. It is easy, of course, to maintain a dignified silence when faced with the demand to justify the claim that normative matters cannot be adjudicated beyond the satisfaction of a criterion of Pareto optimality among incomparable personal preferences. But without a fundamental argument – a metaphysical one – the rejection of interpersonal comparisons of preference will face repeated rejection, and microeconomic theory will continue to be threatened with rejection for ideological motives. Or again, consider the resolute refusal of microeconomic theory to accommodate a distinction between wants and needs. Such a distinction is obvious outside economics, and seems to have a reasonable foundation in biology, psychology, and common sense. But economics is blind to the wants/needs distinction largely because there seems no way to accommodate the distinction while preserving the character of the theory of consumer choice. Here too philosophers have entered where economists have declined to tread.[6]

As with other cases, the economist's defense of these claims may be stigmatized as metaphysical to the extent that it is not empirical. Economists will be criticized for continuing to embrace a fact/value distinction, or the interpersonal incomparability of preferences, or the assimilation of wants to needs as matters of metaphysical commitment. Some defenders of economic theory's legitimacy in the absence of empirical confirmation have implicitly embraced this metaphysical defense, especially writers on economic methodology who have adopted Lakatos's notion of a scientific research program.[7] They have identified a "theoretical hard core" of claims beyond the reach of empirical test which are in effect metaphysical commitments beyond empirical challenge.[8]

[5] For example, J. L. Mackie, *Ethics: Inventing Right and Wrong* (New York: Penguin Books, 1977).

[6] See David Braybrooke, *Meeting Needs* (Princeton, NJ: Princeton University Press, 1987).

[7] Imre Lakatos, "The Methodology of Scientific Research Programs," in *Philosophical Papers*, vol. 1, pp. 1–74 (Cambridge: Cambridge University Press, 1978).

[8] For the best example of this strategy see E. Roy Weintraub, *General Equilibrium Analysis: Studies in Appraisal* (Cambridge: Cambridge University Press, 1985).

Change, stability, and equilibrium

The explanatory role of equilibrium – general and partial – in economic theory must rest primarily on its metaphysical attractions. General equilibrium theorizing derives the existence of a unique stable equilibrium of supply and demand in every market for every good from the present into the infinite future from the preferences of individual agents and their current endowment of goods (given some further assumptions such as certainty, the absence of increasing returns to scale, infinite divisibilities, an infinite number of agents, etc.). Much economic theorizing involves attempts to vary the assumptions of a general equilibrium model and determine whether the equilibrium is still derivable. For example, economists seek to know whether a general equilibrium exists if we surrender assumptions about returns to scale, certainty about the future, the number of consumers, the privacy of goods, the imposition of various governmental policies, etc. Less demanding in its assumptions is the approach of partial equilibrium, which examines how changes in one market can move its equilibria in supply and demand from one point to another, on the assumption that the change will not significantly influence prices on any other market.

It is pretty clear to most people that general equilibrium does not characterize any real market, not even as a first approximation, and that partial equilibrium is at best the exception to the rule of economic processes. So, why the attachment of economic theory to such equilibrium-approaches. A sociological and historical approach like Mirowski's will find the sources of this attachment to equilibrium in the nineteenth-century envy of physical theory, and the conscious aping of its theoretical structure by Walras and others.[9] But this analysis *cum* critique fails to do intellectual justice to economic theory, and fails to recognize the important metaphysical commitment that explanations in physics and economics share.

In both physics and economics, and for that matter evolutionary biology, the object of theory is to explain changes: displacement or motion in physics, diversification and evolution in biology, exchange of commodities in economics. But, how are such changes best explained? Plato famously held that no sort of change can be explained. Therefore Plato forswore natural science and causal inquiry.[10] Newtonian me-

---

[9] See Philip Mirowski, *More Heat than Light* (Cambridge: Cambridge University Press, 1989).

[10] See, for instance, *The Phaedo*.

chanics provides one of the most powerful approaches to the explanation of changes. For Newtonian mechanics shows us that what we view as change is really rest – the absence of change. What we take to be change – the motion of the planets around the sun for example – is actually an equilibrium in a closed system conserving total energy. The solar system's behavior reflects the absence of interfering forces, stasis, changelessness. By showing that what we identity as change is in reality the result of the constancy of more profound forces, and by showing how the system returns to a new equilibrium when new forces intervene, Newtonian mechanics provides a deeply satisfying, perhaps the most deeply satisfying explanation for apparent change. Similarly, contemporary evolutionary theory explains diversity of flora and fauna as the result of changes in gene ratios caused by interfering forces – mutation, migration, drift, and environmental change, all of which disturb an equilibrium. The result is evolutionary adaptation as organisms interact with one another and with the environment over generations in the diirection of a new adaptational equilibrium. Nature selects among random variants those more well adapted to local environments – where the local environment means not just a place in space and time, but also competing organisms, and for that matter other adaptations of the organisms evolving. The ceaseless variation of the biosphere is in fact either merely cyclical variation that masks the constancy of gene ratios or the result of persistent movement in the direction of local optimal equilibrium solutions to adaptational problems. Here too, change is explained by showing that beneath it is changelessness or else movement back towards a changeless state.

The commitment to equilibrium explanations in these disciplines is deep enough to be metaphysical. Even in the succession of theories in physics, from Newtonian mechanics to the special and general theories of relativity, and to quantum electro- and chromodynamics, equilibrium strategies of explanation have been preserved.

So too in economics. There seems little that is constant in economic activity as we observe it. How to bring explanatory illumination to this buzzing, blooming confusion? The apparently ceaseless change that characterizes economic activity would be most powerfully and most satisfyingly explained if we could show that beneath the appearance of change was the reality of changelessness, or at least that the actuality of change was but a ceaseless readjustment back towards states that would be changeless once attained. General equilibrium theory shows that a constant total quantity of goods is exchanged in trade in such a way as more nearly to satisfy a set of constant preference functions, and that once the trades are made, in the absence of interfering forces, nothing more of economic interest will happen. Moreover, economists hope to show that the continual interference of exogenous shocks that characterize a real market simply produces decentralized responses the net effect of which is always to move the market back towards unique, stable, and changeless equilibria. If economists find it difficult to free themselves from the commitment to equilibrium explanations, the reason is not hard really to understand. When it comes to explaining change there are few more appealing stratagems than reducing change to stasis. The commitment to equilibrium explanation is metaphysically if not empirically as well grounded in economics as it is in physics or biology. The trouble is that the appeal to equilibrium is not well-founded in economic data the way it is in evolutionary or mechanical dynamics. Whence the decidedly metaphysical – that is, non-empirical – commitment to its theoretical centrality.

Methodological individualism

Perhaps the most widely recognized metaphysical commitment of economics is to some version of a doctrine of methodological individualism: roughly the proposition that the behavior of economic systems, economies, markets, industries, firms, unions, and other collective entities are to be explained by appeal only to the behaviors of their parts. Some version of this thesis stands behind the methodological dictum that economic phenomena of whatever level – the individual trade, the firm, the industry, the whole economy – are ultimately to be explained adequately by showing that they are the exclusive effects of the sum of the behaviors of individual economic agents – consumers, producers, firms, etc. The methodological dictum is evident outside of microeconomics in the widespread demand that macro-theories be provided at least eventually with complete microfoundations. Within microeconomics, the very existence of a theory without microfoundations is impossible: all microeconomic analysis begins with individual agents responding to boundary conditions and then aggregates these responses to determine a market effect.

The individualism of microeconomic theory is resolute, and has had remarkable explanatory pay-off. Perhaps most striking is the unwillingness of economists to surrender their commitment to individualism in the face of apparently recalcitrant phenomena dealt with in game theory and the theory of public goods. Public goods – like police protection – are ones which cannot be provided to some consumers without being provided to others. Thus individuals have an incentive to decline to pay for them in the hope that others will do so, and thus provide a commodity to non-players for nothing. Since all individuals are capable of thus reasoning, in many cases we should not expect public goods to be provided. However, it is obvious that many such goods are provided. It would be easy to explain the provision of public goods simply by appealing to group-preferences and the coercion of individuals by the group to pay for the good.

But such explanations are *ad hoc*, and many of them are undermined by the insight that rational agents all have an incentive to free-ride on group preferences, thus leading to undersupply or serious enforcement problems we do not in fact observe. Much of the advance in our understanding of public goods and of the social and political institutions which they often constitute is the result of a commitment to individualism which refuses to countenance such irreducible group entities, and seeks instead conditions that made the provision of public goods really individually rational.

The resolute reductionism of microeconomics has been extolled as one of its important strengths, akin to the atomism of successful physical theories like the kinetic theory of gases. Elsewhere in social science, and especially in some parts of sociology, under Durkheim's influence, holism continues to hold sway.

There have been endless discussions of what exactly a commitment to individualism consists in. As with other disputes in the philosophy of science which began as linguistic, this one started out as the question whether social or other sorts of "wholes" and their properties could be defined exhaustively by appeal to individuals and their properties. But like the other disputes, the problem of holism versus individualism has been transformed over time from a definitional problem into an explanatory one.[11] It is now the question of whether adequate fundamental explanation of all phenomena adverts only to individuals and their properties. While the original dispute might have been settled by the provision of suitable definitions, such definitions were not forthcoming. The current version of the dispute may eventually be settled by the advance of theory in the social sciences. But since theory has not advanced far enough to settle the matter one way or another, the continued dispute about holism versus individualism has become metaphysical.

---

[11] See, for instance, the work of Jon Elster, especially *Nuts and Bolts for Social Science* (Cambridge: Cambridge University Press, 1988), and *Explaining Technical Change* (Cambridge: Cambridge University Press, 1983).

Philosophers, economists and others are reduced to providing *a priori* considerations – mainly in the form of rhetorical questions and *tu quoque* arguments for and against individualism. Perhaps the best argument for individualism is the observation that if there were no individuals there would be no institutions, coupled with the rhetorical question of where does the remainder come from, if institutions are more than the sum of the individuals who participate in them? Holists will reply that on the one hand they are not committed to the existence of a mysterious substance above and beyond individuals that together with them constitutes social whole. Rather, the interaction of individuals brings into existence higher-level properties of social institutions which explain other features of institutions without themselves being explainable by simple aggregation from the properties of their component individuals.

Though philosophy may keep this metaphysical dispute alive, it can never settle it. Only advances in empirical theory or decisions about the scope of economics can do so. Should a theory whose axioms quantify only over individuals, their expectations and preferences come to be deemed adequate in its explanation of some body of aggregate economic phenomena then of course individualism will be vindicated. Alternatively, should economists decide to restrict their study only to such institutions as can be explained by appeal to the behavior of individuals only, individualism in economics will have been vindicated by the device of a question-begging restriction on economics' scope. Until such time, individualism will remain a metaphysical commitment widely shared by economists.

Intentionality

Meanwhile, not only does the development of microeconomics reflect a commitment to individual human behavior as its fundamental explanatory factor. It also endorses a conception of the causes of human behavior which involves taking sides on issues of the gravest metaphysical import in western philosophy: the nature of mind. For economic theory treats human behavior as choice and identifies the causal variables in determining behavior as expectations and preferences.

Expectations and preferences are cognates for beliefs and desires. Thus, microeconomic theory is committed to explaining individual behavior – choice – as the effect of the joint interaction of beliefs and desires. Microeconomic theory makes very strong claims about preferences, and traditionally has operated under very unrealistic assumptions about the accuracy and completeness of expectations.

The standard assumptions of the theory of consumer choice include the claim that the agent can rank all commodities or other alternatives in a weak transitive order, that the agent can identify all those alternatives that are attainable for choices given the agent's resources, and that the agent will always choose the attainable alternative that ranks highest. In other words, the theory is committed to treating economic agents as goal-directed systems that instantiate intentional states. But unlike ordinary humans, economic agents are omniscient both about their own preference orders, their budget constraints, and the attainable set of outcomes. It is this omniscience that obscures the intentional character of the expectations and preferences which drive economic choice. Intentional states – beliefs and desires – are referentially opaque and not truth-functional: the substitution of co-referential terms and co-extensive predicates in statements describing them can convert such statements from true descriptions of what people want and believe to false ones describing neither their wants nor beliefs. Thus, for example, Lois Lane may believe that Clark Kent is cowardly, but disbelieve that Superman is pusillanimous, even though the names "Clark Kent" and "Superman" are co-referring, and the predicates "cowardly" and "pusillanimous" are co-extensive. So much is well-known.

But when agents are omniscient, and perfectly rational in the economist's sense – their preference orders are complete, continuous, and transitive – their set of beliefs will be closed under substitution of coextensive terms, as will their wants. Complete information and transitivity of preferences make it difficult to see immediately that expectations and preferences are the intentional variables to which common sense adverts under the names "belief" and "desire."

To the extent that economists view their discipline as methodologically allied with the natural sciences, it is committed to a naturalistic metaphysics for intentional states – that is to the view that intentional states determine choice in accordance with causal laws we can discover. Thus, on their most obvious interpretation, as generalizations about the causes of individual behavior, the fundamental assumptions of microeconomic theory attribute the same psychological processes to all economic agents, and explain differences among agents as the effects of different preferences and expectations. What is metaphysical here – in the classical, philosophical sense of the term – is the commitment to causal interaction between the mind and the body on the basis of causal laws. Assuming the falsity of dualism, this commitment is tantamount to a strong type-type materialist identity theory of the relation between brain states and mental states.

There is another reason to identify these psychological commitments of microeconomic theory as metaphysical – in a potentially derogatory sense. It is well known that there is a long-term tradition of indifference by economists to findings and theories in psychology – even favorable ones – which might bear on the truth, falsity, or tenability of these commitments about the causes of individual human action. To the extent a substantive commitment is recalcitrant to countervailing empirical evidence, it would be a pardonable positivist criticism to call the commitment "merely metaphysical."

There are reasons well known in the philosophy of psychology to be pessimistic about prospects for uncovering any such psychological laws of the sort economists need in any case. And this makes for what is perhaps the deepest metaphysical mystery of microeconomic theory: the conjunction of explanatory individualism and indifference to the truth of its claims about individual psychology makes for a metaphysical problem of major proportions for microeconomics. If the basic explanatory categories of economics are individual expectations and preferences and yet economists have little interest in the further question of whether their claims about preferences and expectations are reasonable, approximately correct empirical hypotheses, then questions must arise about the cognitive status of economics. To the extent that methodology has metaphysical ramifications, answers to these questions must have importance for anyone interested in the metaphysics of microeconomics.

One traditional way in which economists have responded to this problem is simply to adopt a crude behaviorism about choice, an interpretation of the axioms of the theory known as "revealed preference." Another, more radical approach is to reject any interest in or commitment to individual choice behavior as a subject for economics. This stratagem completely deprives economics of commitment to methodological individualism. But this is a small price to pay for the freedom from any need to defend the truth of the theory's assumptions. Still a third, more traditional approach is to treat the theory as an idealization without ontological commitments as to what there is.

Behaviorist relief from metaphysics?

Ever since Paul Samuelson discovered operationalism (or was it B. F. Skinner he discovered?) many economists have argued that their theory makes no claims about the psychological processes that determine choice. This at any rate seems the simplest account of how "revealed preference theory" got started. Samuelson (and Houthekker)[12] realized that if preferences and expectations could between them determine choice, then holding expectations constant, we could read preferences off of choices. By offering an agent many pairs of commodities and allowing the agent to select the object preferred in each case, a map of the agent's preferences could be constructed, provided only the agent's choices honored the assumption of weak transitivity: for every pair of commodities a, b, either a is preferred to b or vice versa or the agent is perfectly indifferent between a and b. From a map so constructed additional intermediate choices can be predicted. If all we need for the theory of consumer choice is that actual choices be transitive, then we can remain agnostic about the causes of these choices; we need not embrace extravagant claims about the psychological structure of tastes and preferences. And, of course, by suitable employment of the von Neumann-Morgenstern theory of uncertainty we can extend our behaviorism about preferences to a behaviorism about expectations as well: they will turn out to be choices made as probabilities vary while preference-behavior remains constant.

For a time this sort of behaviorism was popular among economists who thought twice about the apparent falsehood of their theory of consumer choice as a psychological theory. Revealed preference theory also comports with the commitment to methodological individualism. Both may be justified on the epistemic ground that all we ever see are individual economic agents; we can directly observe neither aggregates of them nor the "insides" of any one of them.

The trouble with revealed preference theory is, of course, the trouble with behaviorism in psychology and positivism in epistemology. Behavior can only reveal preference if preference causes behavior. If preference is just a synonym for behavior that satisfies intertemporal transivity then not only is behavior often not preference – say, whenever what the non-behaviorist calls tastes change – but the economist must forswear the explanation of individual choice behavior. Moreover, by declining to commit itself to the causes of behavior – "internal" expectations and preferences – the economist surrenders the aim of explaining why consumers and producers make the choices they do. Additionally, they are committed to interpreting their own theory in a way that fails to take its metaphysics seriously.

Defined as the science which studies how scarce resources are distribu-

[12] Paul Samuelson, *Foundations of Economic Analysis* (Cambridge, MA: M.I.T. Press, 1947); Hendrick S. Houthakker, "Revaled Preference in the Utility Function," *Economica*, n.s., 17 (1950): 159–74.

ted and ought efficiently to be distributed, economics has long been committed to explaining individual choice, and of course, to explainin aggregate economic data by showing that they are the consequences of such choice. The only reason to surrender this goal is the realization that it is unattainable. Here the distinction between the commitment of economics and of economists becomes crucial. The theory makes a claim which the theorists either ignore, or reinterpret. Economists have not so much admitted that explaining individual choice is unattainable as they have pretended that it never was a goal of theirs. Instead, many economists have claimed that the goal of theory is simply to systematize the data of markets, industries, and whole economies. For these purposes it is convenient to couch their theory in the form of assumptions ostensibly about the preferences and expectations of individuals, but such claims are not to be taken seriously. Rather, following Friedman,[13] they are to be understood as merely heuristic devices, convenient fictions whose justification consists only in their success in systematizing aggregate data. Assume for the nonce that the theory of consumer behavior and the theory of the firm actually do systematize aggregate data about supply and demand in the market for consumer goods and factors of production. Then the question immediately arises why these two theories successfully systematize observations. It would be quite convenient for economists if they could help themselves to an instrumentalist approach to theories, which eschews metaphysical issues – like whether the theory is true or false. According to such an approach, the question of why a theory is empirically adequate is an epistemically impertinent question which no scientist is obliged to answer. Any attempt to answer it is an excursus into metaphysics most pejoratively construed. On this view the most plausible answer to the question of why a theory is empirically adequate – the claim that it is approximately true – is a groundless excursion into metaphysics since no empirical data are available to warrant the truth of its claims about unobserved underlying mechanisms. Regardless of the plausibility of this doctrine in the interpretation of, say, quantum mechanics, it seems remarkably unavailing in any defense of microeconomic theory. Quarks are observationally inaccessible, and for this reason, instrumentalists have some epistemic basis for skepticism about the truth – approximate or otherwise – of the ontological claims of quantum physics. However, economic agents – consumers, producers, firms, etc. are hardly beyond our observational powers. Accordingly, the question remains: assuming a set of claims about consumers and

[13] Milton Friedman, "The Methodology of Positive Economics," in *Essays in Positive Economics* (Chicago: Chicago University Press, 1953).

producers does systematize aggregate data, what explains this fact? If the answer is the approximate truth of the claims about consumers and producers, then there seems little reason beyond a commitment to an overstrict empiricism to deny that the theory makes claims about individual action as well as claims about the market.

But of course, we know that the claims of the theory of consumer behavior and the theory of the firm are factually false and not even approximately correct for the vast range of choices people actually make over time in the real world. What is even more important, the claim that the theories of consumer choice and the theory of the firm actually do systematize aggregate data is, to say the least, highly controversial. And between them these two facts about the empirical bearing of economic theory make for the gravest of metaphysical problems: for they raise the question of what economic theory is about, and what sort of an enterprise it constitutes.

A theory which systematizes observations on the basis of assumptions we know to be factually false is not by itself problematical. Newtonian mechanics provides a fine example of such a theory. The theory embodies a large number of idealizations and abstractions – from frictionless planes to point masses – about whose non-existence there seems to be no question. But the approximation of physical objects and processes to these abstractions is close enough to make the theory which employs them predictively unproblematical. The theory raises some metaphysical problems just because it is on the one hand empirically adequate and on the other metaphysically bootless. But while the problems the theory raises are metaphysical, it raises fewer epistemological problems, just because of its empirical adequacy.

A separate science?

In wrestling with what is essentially the same question of reconciling economics' appeal to a set of generalizations about individual choice with the predictive weakness of economic theory, Daniel Hausman has argued that economists are committed to the existence of a "separate science."[14] Though he does not say so, this is I think the fundamental metaphysical commitment of economists.

Every attempt to establish a science reflects a commitment to "sepa-

[14] Daniel Hausman, *The Inexact and Separate Science of Economics* (Cambridge: Cambridge University Press, 1992), p. 222.

rateness," that is, to the existence of a small number of tractable independent variables that explain a significant range of the data which is the discipline's explananda. Successful sciences are those in which the commitment to separateness has been vindicated, not by metaphysical considerations, but by empirical successes. Economics still awaits the unambiguous vindication of its separateness by this success. The long period in which it has remained committed to separateness in the absence of empirical success is a testimony to the strength of its metaphysical commitments.

11 Ontological commitments of evolutionary economics

JACK VROMEN

1 Introduction

Any attempt at offering a discussion of 'an ontology of evolutionary economics' is immediately fraught with difficulties. First, evolutionary economics is proliferating so rapidly that any attempt runs the danger of being obsolete before it is published (see, for example, Hodgson 1997). Second, at present evolutionary economics does not constitute an unequivocally defined school or movement. It rather covers many different approaches and standpoints (see, for example, Langlois and Everett 1994 and Nelson 1995). And, finally, even if we confine our attention to a few clearly circumscribed branches within evolutionary economics and forget about the rest, it is not at all clear what exactly we are looking for if we want to focus on their ontologies (or ontological commitments).[1] Given these difficulties some preliminary remarks are in order.

'Evolutionary economics' in this paper comprises two distinct branches: Nelson and Winter's evolutionary theory and evolutionary game theory. This already involves a choice that will affront many self-confessed proponents of evolutionary economics. To many Nelson and Winter's evolutionary theory (let alone evolutionary game theory) is already too close to neoclassical economics to be called 'evolutionary economics' at all. Such proponents of evolutionary economics typically plea for a radical break with equilibrium theorizing and stress phenomena like nonlinear and self-organizing systems (see, for example, Day and Chen 1993) and endogenously created novelty and – consequently – the open-endedness of economic evolutionary processes (see,

---

[1] For a study of ontological commitments of evolutionary economics with a focus quite different from mine, see, e.g., Herrmann-Pillath (1996).

for example, Saviotti and Metcalfe 1991). If this is what evolutionary economics is all about, then this paper does not address evolutionary economics at all. My justification for concentrating on the two branches mentioned above is that they both clearly associate themselves with evolutionary theorizing and that they both attract much attention in the economics profession.

What then could the ontology of these two branches of evolutionary economics possibly be? As a first attempt we could loosely follow a Quinean strategy of identifying the ontological commitments of the theories that are formulated within these branches: what entities must exist, and what properties must they have for the theories in question to be true? But following this strategy is not unproblematic. It has been observed by some that it may be one of the peculiarities of economics that what is stated explicitly in economic theories need not coincide with what their advocates – the economists – believe to be true of the economy (see, for example, Caldwell 1992, 1994; Rosenberg 2001). Rosenberg argues that if economists as a matter of fact do entertain beliefs about the actual economy different from what their theories explicitly state, then we should distinguish between the metaphysical commitments of economists and the metaphysical commitments of economics (Rosenberg 2001, pp. 176, 186). Apparently Rosenberg believes it is possible to identify the metaphysical commitments of economics without looking at beliefs of the economists using its theories, simply by taking the theories at face value. By contrast, I shall argue that in identifying the metaphysical (or rather ontological) commitments of economics the beliefs of economists using its theories should be taken into account. If the beliefs of economists do not match with what their theories express (or rather appear to express), then we should investigate why they nevertheless cling to their theories. Only after this investigation we can tell what ontological commitments are involved in their theories.

The paper is organized as follows. I start with a discussion of Rosenberg's views on the ontological presuppositions of neoclassical economics. I then turn to the so-called selection arguments put forward by Alchian and Friedman. The selection arguments, it will be argued, do not only foreshadow subsequent theoretical developments in the two branches of evolutionary economics mentioned above, but also reveal ontological commitments of at least some neoclassical economists that give rise to a reinterpretation of neoclassical economics. Next the basic tenets of Nelson and Winter's evolutionary theory and evolutionary game theory will be discussed. The paper concludes with some final reflections on the differences in ontology between the various versions of neoclassical economics and of evolutionary economics.

2 Prelude

My main reasons for taking Rosenberg's work as a starting point are the following. First, Rosenberg has done some pioneering and provocative work on the metaphysics and ontology of neoclassical microeconomics (for a critical reaction, see, for example, Ross 1995). The second reason is that Rosenberg has recently published several papers on the very same exemplars of evolutionary arguments and theorizing that I address in this paper (see Rosenberg 1992b, 2001). Since Rosenberg is an acknowledged expert in the philosophy of biology, the views that he expresses in these papers cannot be left unaddressed. Let us have a closer look then at what Rosenberg has to say on both subjects – first, the metaphysics and ontology of neoclassical microeconomics and, second, the exemplars of evolutionary arguments and theorizing in economics.

As has been observed also by other commentators, Rosenberg's criticism of neoclassical microeconomics proceeds from the presupposition that neoclassical microeconomics tries to explain individual behaviour as the effect of the joint interaction of beliefs and desires (see, for example, Rosenberg 2001, p. 182). To be more precise, Rosenberg identifies expectations and preferences as '. . . cognates for beliefs and desires' (ibid.) in neoclassical economics as the causal variables determining human behaviour. It will turn out to be expedient to split up Rosenberg's presupposition about neoclassical economics (*NE*) in two parts:

(NE_{1R}) among other things, neoclassical microeconomics purports to explain the behaviour of individual human agents;

(NE_{2R}) neoclassical microeconomics pinpoints preferences and expectations as the two (interacting) causal determinants of the behaviour of individual human agents.[2]

Rosenberg's criticism of neoclassical economics mainly focuses on (NE_{2R}). According to Rosenberg, it is (NE_{2R}) that makes neoclassical microeconomics of a piece with folk psychology. And the problem with folk psychology, Rosenberg argues, is that it does not allow for improvements in prediction beyond the predictive powers that are reflected in our

---

[2] Henceforth propositions with subscript 1 refer to the tasks or goals that some type (or school) of economic theory is said to pursue. Propositions with subscript 2 denote what some type (or school) of economic theory is said to take to be the actual causal determinants of individual behaviour (i.e., behaviour of individual agents).

everyday projections of people's actions. In Rosenberg's view the key concepts of folk psychology – desire and belief – do not denote natural kinds; they do not cut the world at its joints.

What is curious, however, is that Rosenberg himself expresses some doubts as to whether (NE_{2R}) is really representative of neoclassical microeconomics. Rosenberg refers to revealed preference theory and von Neumann-Morgenstern cardinal utility theory as self-conscious attempts to purge neoclassical microeconomics from its affiliation with folk psychology (Rosenberg 2001, pp. 184–6). As Rosenberg himself observes, adherence to these theories allows neoclassical economists to remain agnostic about the causes or determinants of individual human behaviour. Yet Rosenberg does not take the acceptance of these theories by neoclassical economists to be indicating that there may be something wrong with (NE_{2R}). He does not seriously consider the possibility that the popularity of these theories among neoclassical economists calls for a reinterpretation of neoclassical microeconomics, or at least for a qualification of (NE_{2R}).[3] No, for Rosenberg (NE_{2R}) captures an invariant essential of the neoclassical programme. Given this fixation of the neoclassical programme, revealed preference theory and von Neumann-Morgenstern cardinal utility theory cannot appear to Rosenberg other than as ingenious attempts of neoclassical economists to sidestep the vexing problems inherent in the neoclassical programme.

Rosenberg argues that these attempts fail. An instance of individual human behaviour can only be explained in terms of the preferences and expectations that are identified in revealed preference theory and von Neumann-Morgenstern cardinal utility theory, he argues, if this instance is really caused by these preferences and expectations (see Rosenberg 2001, pp. 184–6). Here (NE_{1R}) comes in. Rosenberg's argument here clearly presupposes that individual human behaviour is an *explanandum* of neoclassical microeconomics. But, again, it is noteworthy that Rosenberg himself casts doubt on the truth of this presupposition.[4] Rosenberg appears to be aware of remarks of neoclassical economists such as Friedman, stating that the behavioural assumptions are not meant to explain individual behaviour, but to systematize aggregate data (of industries, markets and whole economies; Rosenberg 2001, p. 186). As in the case of (NE_{2R}), this acknowledgement does not seem to affect Rosenberg's understanding of neoclassical economics. Rosenberg does

---

[3] If we are to believe Binmore (1994), then nowadays all neoclassical economists embrace revealed preference theory and von Neumann-Morgenstern cardinal utility theory (and have thus left the old 'Benthamite', folk psychological interpretation behind).

[4] And so do Kincaid (2001) and Ross (2001), for example.

not call (NE_{1R}) into question. Again, what he does instead is to argue that this escape route does not bring neoclassical economists relief either. For, Rosenberg asks himself, how could theories of individual behaviour systematize aggregate data without being at least approximately true (Rosenberg 2001, pp. 186–7)?[5]

At this point Rosenberg brings in a new element. The problems with explaining individual behaviour in terms of preferences and expectations are not just of a metaphysical kind (the problem that preferences and expectations are not natural kinds), Rosenberg argues, but also of an empirical kind: '. . . we know that the claims of the theory of consumer behaviour and the theory of the firm are factually false and not even approximately correct for the vast range of choices people actually make over time in the real world' (Rosenberg 2001, p. 187). Now this seems to be in need of some further clarification. On the basis of the above discussion, one could expect that Rosenberg believes that preferences and expectations (as cognates for desires and beliefs) should play no role in explanations of individual behaviour. After all, in Rosenberg's view its dedication to these folk psychological derivates prevents neoclassical economics from achieving major improvements in predictive power. Given that in Rosenberg's mind neoclassical economics is bound to explain individual behaviour (even if it is mainly interested in systematising aggregate data), it seems to follow that economists are well-advised to dispense with preferences and expectations altogether (and thus to abandon the neoclassical programme).

This is not the conclusion that Rosenberg draws, however. Rosenberg seems to hold the view that consumers and producers do have desires and beliefs and that these mental states are consequential for the actions that consumers and producers undertake. What is more, he argues that desires and beliefs are indispensable in explaining individual behaviour (see Rosenberg 1992a, p. 151). What Rosenberg takes to be false in the theories of the firm and of consumer behaviour are rather the *additional* claims made in the theories that consumers and producers have the best possible beliefs (rational expectations) and that they choose the best possible action given their desires (preferences) and their beliefs. In other words, Rosenberg takes it to be beyond doubt that real consumers and producers are less rational than the ones that are portrayed in the neoclassical theories of consumer behaviour and of the firm (see, for example, Rosenberg 1992a, p. 116).

---

[5] See also Rosenberg (1992a), p. 129, where he argues that it is improbable that predictive improvements at the aggregate level can exceed predictive improvements at the individual level.

Thus it must be concluded, I think, that in Rosenberg's eyes the situation for economics is quite hopeless. According to Rosenberg, economics is wedded to explain individual behaviour. As we have seen, he thinks that economics is committed to this even if its sole purpose were to be to systematize aggregate data. Furthermore, Rosenberg holds that explaining individual behaviour necessarily invokes desires and beliefs. Hence, the affinity between economics and folk psychology is not incidental but fundamental and inescapable. Maybe economic theories could be made more realistic by relaxing their rationality assumptions. But the hope of achieving real predictive improvements beyond our everyday capacity to predict is forlorn, Rosenberg believes, because preferences and beliefs do not denote natural kinds. Is Rosenberg committed to the view then that economics is destined never to attain scientific respectability?

3 Neoclassical economics and the selection arguments

Rosenberg (1992b) regards the selection arguments put forward by Friedman (1953) and Alchian (1950) as just another desperate attempt to defend neoclassical economics.[6] Rosenberg contends that the selection arguments are attractive to neoclassical economists because they appear to offer a way out of the acknowledged empirical inadequacy of the theories of consumer and firm behaviour. Friedman's and Alchian's arguments hold out the promise, Rosenberg argues, that the neoclassical claim about firm behaviour can be vindicated even though it is granted that not all firms are rationally informed profit-maximizers. But, again, Rosenberg argues that the hope is forlorn; this line of defence is also bound to fail.

There certainly are several things to be said in favour of Rosenberg's treatment of the selection arguments. Rosenberg is right that selection arguments did pop up in economics in order to defend neoclassical economics. And they were indeed devised to get around the problem of the apparent falsity of the neoclassical theory of the firm. These merits notwithstanding, my main problem with Rosenberg's treatment of the selection arguments is again that he views them as mere *ad hoc* escape manoeuvres. Rosenberg simply refuses to consider the possibility seriously that the selection arguments reveal more than just the wish of neoclassical economists to evade difficult problems with their theories.

[6] See also Rosenberg (1992a), pp. 183–93, and Rosenberg (1994).

By contrast, I do not want to rule out the possibility in advance that by studying the selection arguments carefully we can learn something about neoclassical economics itself. To be more precise, I shall examine the possibility that the arguments reveal beliefs of (at least some) neoclassical economists about the workings of competitive markets; beliefs that cast a different light on the nature of their theoretical enterprise than Rosenberg does. But before I can come to that I first have to put the selection arguments in their historical context.

In the 1930s and 1940s the empirical adequacy of the neoclassical assumption of profit maximization was challenged from within the economics profession, notably by the Oxford Research Group in the UK and by Lester in the USA.[7] In the ensuing marginalism controversy these so-called antimarginalists held that the neoclassical (marginalist) theory of the firm had to be discarded. Questionnaires and subsequent interviews clearly pointed out, the antimarginalists claimed, that entrepreneurs do not base their decisions on the type of marginalist deliberations that neoclassical theory ascribes to them. What they found instead was that entrepreneurs typically use rules of thumb, such as the 'full cost' pricing rule in setting their prices. The antimarginalists took these results to be ample evidence that the neoclassical theory of the firm was unrealistic. They concluded from this that this neoclassical theory was to be rejected.

The neoclassical theory of the firm was defended by Machlup (1946). Machlup's main strategy was to show that the answers to the questionnaires given by the entrepreneurs can be rephrased in terms of the marginalist principles underlying the neoclassical theory of the firm. What Machlup pointed out in particular was that behaviour that is routinized rule-following from the (first person's) point of view of the entrepreneurs themselves, can be interpreted as maximizing behaviour from a (third person's) theorist's point of view. For this purpose Machlup drew an analogy with an experienced automobile driver. When making the decision whether or not to overtake a truck that is proceeding ahead of her at slower speed, Machlup argues, an experienced automobile driver typically 'sizes-up' the relevant factors in a routine way. Yet if we want to develop a 'theory of overtaking', Machlup contends, we would have to break the decision down into its factors and to state how changes in any of the factors would affect the driver's actions. The message is clear: the antimarginalists may well be right that just as with the experienced driver's behaviour most of the behaviour of entrepreneurs is routinized. But they are wrong in concluding from this that a

---

[7] See Vromen (1995) for a detailed discussion.

theoretical account of entrepreneurial behaviour in terms of conscious deliberations and calculations is incorrect. Machlup seems to be convinced even that an '*explanation* of an action must often include steps of reasoning which the acting individual himself does not *consciously* perform (because the action has become routine)' (Machlup 1946, p. 535).

Alchian's classic (1950) paper was prompted by Alchian's feeling that both the antimarginalist criticisms and Machlup's defence were misguided.[8] In Alchian's view, both the antimarginalists and Machlup proceed from the mistaken assumption that the neoclassical theory of the firm is meant to be a theory of the behaviour of individual firms. They both confuse 'axioms' with 'theorems', Alchian argues: the axioms of the neoclassical theory of the firm pertain to the behaviour of firms, but its theorems are about aggregate industry (or market) behaviour. To be more precise, the theorems of neoclassical economics are generic or pattern predictions about changes in aggregate industry variables. A paradigmatic example is the pattern prediction that, *ceteris paribus*, the aggregate capital/labour ratio in an industry increases if (real) wage rates rise (see Alchian 1950, p. 17; see also Lester 1946, p. 65).

Now what Alchian wants to point out is that even if the antimarginalists were right that individual firms do not behave as stated in the neoclassical axioms, neoclassical pattern predictions still hold.[9] Or, to use Alchian's own terms, even if the axioms are false, they can nevertheless be used to derive the neoclassical theorems. The axioms still are useful tools for analysing industry behaviour, Alchian argues, because 'market selection' is going on: 'impersonal market forces' see to it that firms in the industry that happen to make positive profits grow at the expense of firms that happen to suffer losses. In the paradigmatic example mentioned above, after (real) wage rates have risen those firms in the industry will have a higher probability of survival that have relatively lower costs because of their relatively higher capital/labour ratio. As a consequence, the average capital/labour ratio in the industry increases.

Roughly the same idea can be found in Friedman (1953). Friedman also argues that even if the antimarginalists' empirical findings were to be taken seriously, the neoclassical theory of the firm can be maintained because there are processes of 'natural selection' going on in markets that

---

[8] See Alchian in Zerbe (1982), p. 149.

[9] Alchian does not argue that we can *a priori* know that the neoclassical theorems hold in all cases. In each and every case the theorems have to be tested empirically. But he seems to be quite confident that, whatever the results of these tests, the neoclassical axioms can be retained as a useful starting point in analysing industry behaviour.

lead to the same results as the ones predicted by the neoclassical theory. At first the relevant passages in Friedman (1953) might suggest that Friedman defends the neoclassical theory as a theory about the behaviour of individual firms. For he argues that unless the behaviour of firms approximates behaviour that is consistent with the assumption of profit maximization (or the 'maximization-of-returns hypothesis' as Friedman prefers to call it), the firms will not remain in business for long (p. 22). Friedman claims that the assumption of profit maximization appropriately summarizes the conditions for survival.[10] But from the remainder of the paper (and from other papers written by Friedman) it becomes clear that Friedman just like Alchian takes the neoclassical theory of the firm to be a theory of aggregate industry behaviour (see also Hammond 1991).

In the same passage, Friedman remarks that the argumentative support thus given to the maximization-of-assumptions hypothesis is in part similar to the argumentative support that Savage and he have given for the expert billiard player hypothesis.[11] The expert billiard player hypothesis states that before making his shots, an expert billiard player makes lightning calculations and solves a set of mathematical equations, resulting in the identification of the uniquely best shot. Friedman and Savage (1948) bet that this hypothesis yields excellent predictions about the expert billiard player's behaviour even though presumably no expert billiard player really goes through these calculations. Expert billiard players are likely to rely on their skill and experience when playing the game instead of executing complicated calculations.

Friedman and Savage's discussion of the expert billiard player hypothesis is reminiscent of Machlup's experienced automobile driver analogy. Like Machlup, Friedman and Savage want to illustrate the point that the question whether a hypothesis is descriptively unrealistic of the decision processes individuals go through is irrelevant when assessing the usefulness of the hypothesis. The assessment of the usefulness of the hypothesis should be based on other grounds.[12] And acceptance of a hypothesis does not mean commitment to the belief that the hypothesis is descriptively realistic. The hypothesis that Friedman and Savage (1948, p. 281) develop and defend in the paper is based on von Neumann-Morgenstern

---

[10] In Vromen (1995), I call this Friedman's intermediate claim, stressing that his ultimate claim is much more akin to Alchian's claim. Related to this, I also argue there that 'conditions' are to be understood as sufficient and not as necessary conditions.

[11] Friedman himself speaks of 'evidence' instead of 'argumentative support'. See Vromen (1995), pp. 29–34, for a detailed discussion.

[12] Of course, the ground that Friedman and Savage think is to be decisive – whether the hypothesis yields accurate predictions – is different from Machlup's.

cardinal utility theory and is meant to rationalize observable behaviour by attributing utility functions to individuals. No claim is made that individuals really have these functions in their minds nor that they actually are engaged in attempts at maximization. The claim is only that they behave *as if* they actually maximized the functions.

What characterization could we give of the type of neoclassical economics that Alchian and Friedman are defending with their selection arguments? First, it seems that Rosenberg's presupposition (NE_{1R}) has to be replaced by something like:

> ($NE_{1A\&F}$) neoclassical economics purports to predict industry behaviour.[13]

Furthermore, it seems that especially Friedman prefers to remain agnostic about the 'immediate determinants' of consumer and producer behaviour. This suggests that Rosenberg's (NE_{2R}) has to give way to something like:

> ($NE_{2A\&F}$) neoclassical economics does not pinpoint any specific mental states of individual agents (and, indeed, does not pinpoint any causes) as the actual determinants of their behaviour.[14]

Thus what makes Alchian and Friedman feel confident that neoclassical economics is on the right track in predicting industry behaviour is not their belief that individuals are actually conducting the calculations that neoclassical economists are ascribing to them. What is behind their confidence is rather their belief that 'impersonal market forces' lead to the very same tendencies in industry behaviour that would accrue if individuals were to do literally what neoclassical economists ascribe to them. We can unpack this belief as follows:[15]

> ($NE_{3A\&F}$) 'market selection' is a dominant force in shaping industry behaviour

and

---

[13] Later on, Machlup (1967) also subscribes to this view.

[14] Clark (1997) and Satz and Ferejohn (1994) make the similar point that neoclassical economics (and rational choice theory in general) need not, and indeed should not, be understood as entailing specific claims about individual psychology.

[15] Henceforth, propositions with subscript 3 refer to the forces (or mechanisms or causes) that some type (or school) of economic theory is said to believe to be *the* forces shaping industry (or market) behaviour. Propositions with subscript 4 relate to the implications at the industry or market level that some type (or school) of economic theory is said to associate with the workings of these forces.

$(NE_{4A\&F})$ 'market selection' produces the same tendencies in industry behaviour as fully informed and fully rational firms would do.[16]

In his comments on the selection arguments, it does not seem to dawn on Rosenberg that (NE_{1R}) and (NE_{2R}) are called into question. Rosenberg is only concerned with showing that selection arguments do not give comfort to neoclassical economics *as he interprets it*: as a theory about individual behaviour. In particular, Rosenberg does not show any awareness that if the selection arguments are taken seriously, they imply both $(NE_{1A\&F})$, that the neoclassical theory of the firm is about industry behaviour, and $(NE_{2A\&F})$ $(NE_{3A\&F})$ and $(NE_{4A\&F})$, that the tendencies that the neoclassical theory predicts at this aggregate level are not supposed to be brought about by rationally informed maximizing firms, but by 'market selection'.[17] He fails to see that $(NE_{3A\&F})$ and $(NE_{4A\&F})$ together provide an answer to his question: '. . . assuming a set of claims about consumers and producers does systematize aggregate data, what explains this fact?' (Rosenberg 2001, pp. 186–7).

4 Nelson and Winter's evolutionary theory

No other book is so much referred to in 'evolutionary economics' as Nelson and Winter's *An Evolutionary Theory of Economic Change* (1982). It has become *the* classic in evolutionary economics. Although not all proponents of evolutionary economics agree with everything in Nelson and Winter's book, it still is the main reference point and a major source of inspiration. In this section I want to point out that in turn Nelson and Winter have been inspired by Alchian's and Friedman's selection arguments. Much of what Nelson and Winter are doing in their book can be understood as a further elaboration and examination of what was already advanced in the selection arguments.

---

[16] To repeat, Alchian and Friedman do not hold that we can know *a priori* that the neoclassical tendencies hold. Whereas testing of the neoclassical assumptions (or 'axioms' as Alchian calls them) is misguided, Alchian and Friedman contend, testing of its implications (or 'theorems' as Alchian calls them) remains necessary.

[17] Rosenberg himself does not seem to reject the idea that there is something like 'natural selection' going on in competitive markets out of hand. But what he does reject out of hand is that such an idea underlies the acceptance of neoclassical theory by at least some economists.

Rosenberg on Nelson and Winter

But let us first have a look on what Rosenberg (1994) has to say on Nelson and Winter's evolutionary theory. According to Rosenberg, Nelson and Winter are inspired by Darwinian evolutionary theory in biology. Indeed, his comments on their theoretical endeavour is based on the presupposition that Nelson and Winter aim 'to show how economic processes instantiate Darwinian natural selection' (Rosenberg 1994, p. 404). Rosenberg argues that Nelson and Winter's attempt fails to develop an economic theory that is strictly analogous to Darwinian evolutionary theory. In his view Nelson and Winter's attempt is likely to surrender to Lamarckism. As in Lamarckism almost everything is possible ('anything can evolve into anything by any means', p. 405), Rosenberg argues, this would shed no special light on economic processes. Rosenberg then develops the outlines of what could be a fully-fledged Darwinian theory in economics. He winds up with something like a Simon and Cyert and March type of organization theory that, as he contends, only few economists are prepared to accept.

It is hard to avoid the impression that Rosenberg's comments are based on a cursory reading of Nelson and Winter's book. Let it suffice to quote the following passage from Nelson and Winter's book at length:

[Relatedly,] our theory is unabashedly Lamarckian: it contemplates both the 'inheritance' of acquired characteristics and the timely appearance of variation under the stimulus of adversity.

We emphatically disavow any intention to pursue biological analogies for their own sake, or even for the sake of progress toward an abstract, higher-level evolutionary theory that would incorporate a range of existing theories. We are pleased to exploit any idea from biology that seems helpful in the understanding of economic problems, but we are equally prepared to pass over anything that seems awkward, or to modify accepted biological theories radically in the interest of getting better *economic* theory (witness our espousal of Lamarckianism). (Nelson and Winter 1982, p. 11)

Two things are made immediately clear in this passage. First, in contrast to what Rosenberg asserts, Nelson and Winter are not looking for an economic evolutionary theory that is strictly analogous to Darwinian evolutionary theory in biology. They are looking for 'better economic theory', using only those insights and parts of biological theories that are conducive to this theoretical purpose. Second, and again contrary to what Rosenberg claims, Nelson and Winter do not surrender to Lamarckism. They wholeheartedly embrace Lamarckism right from the start, because they think it provides a better starting point for 'better economic theory' than Darwinism. The only valuable idea in Rosenberg's comments is, I think, that as such the notion of Lamarckism does not tell us very much about the 'nuts and bolts' of economic processes. The obvious conclusion to draw from this idea, I venture, would be to study Nelson and Winter's 'Lamarckian' economic theory in a more detailed and careful way. This is not what Rosenberg does, however. In this section I shall redress this omission. Ironically, the upshot of my discussion will be that a Simon and Cyert and March type of organization theory that Rosenberg thinks would be a promising candidate for an unadulterated Darwinian economic theory precisely provides the key to the understanding of the alleged 'Lamarckian' element in Nelson and Winter's economic theory.

Nelson and Winter's evolutionary theory as an explication of 'appreciative' orthodox theory

Nelson and Winter call the selection arguments of Friedman and especially Alchian 'direct intellectual antecedents' of their own book (p. 41). In particular, what they take over from these arguments is the *ex post* viewpoint: when there is uncertainty, the success or failure of an action cannot be determined *ex ante*. Success or failure can only be ascertained *ex post* then, after the action has passed the 'market test'. But whereas the *modus operandi* of market selection remained somewhat implicit in the selection arguments, Nelson and Winter endeavour to make it explicit. Market selection favours firms that make positive profits over those that make negative profits (suffer losses), they argue, because making positive profits means acquiring additional means that the firms then can use to expand, whereas suffering losses means diminishing means and, hence, compulsory contracting. In their models, the shifts in market shares that may follow from this are called *selection effects*.[18]

Nelson and Winter believe that this idea of market selection reveals a genuine insight into how markets actually function. They subscribe to the view that 'natural selection' is an important force in moulding market and industry behaviour. Nelson and Winter also agree with Alchian *cum suis* that this view, though it is most of the time not made explicit anymore, has always been with economic theory. Indeed, they argue that

[18] With this interpretation Nelson and Winter elaborate upon Becker's (1962) interpretation of (and adherence to) the selection arguments. In Becker's view, the selection arguments show that just like households, firms face 'budget constraints'.

the central place given to the force of market selection in their evolutionary theory is consonant with the emphasis put on notions like competition, competitive pressure and competitive forces in orthodox economic theory (p. 32). And like orthodox economic theory, Nelson and Winter contend, the focus of evolutionary economic theory is on analysis of the larger systems (like industries and markets) and not on the individual actors (like firms or the individual stakeholders of firms; p. 51): 'our theory is a theory about market processes' (p. 41).[19]

It is here that Nelson and Winter's distinction between formal and appreciative theory becomes relevant (pp. 9, 32–3, and 46–8; see also Nelson 1995, pp. 50–3).[20] Formal theory is characterized by heroic abstractions. It selects a few variables, mechanisms or relationships, formalizes them and traces their consequences. Tractability and elegance of models (mostly, but not necessarily mathematical models) are valued highly in formal theory. Formal theory is developed, refined and modified in theoretical and foundational research. Appreciative theory, on the other hand, is used mostly in applied and policy-oriented research. Appreciative theory refers to a way of looking at phenomena, or a framework of appreciation that a group of theorists share with one another (p. 46). The intuitions (p. 33) and beliefs (see Nelson 1995, p. 50) of theorists about the phenomena they are studying are reflected in their appreciative theory.

With its characteristic commitments to the assumptions of individual maximizing behaviour and aggregate equilibrium behaviour formal orthodox economic theory lives up to the demands of delivering rigorous, tractable and elegant models. These models are used to conduct static and comparative static analysis. According to Nelson and Winter appreciative orthodox economic theory entertains the very same complex and 'messy' notions and ideas that are put centre stage in their own evolutionary theory: evolution, change, dynamic processes, adaptation, learning and search (see also Nelson 1995, p. 49). It is clear that these biology-oriented notions do not fit readily with formal orthodox theory's assumptions.

Orthodox economists do not seem to be very bothered about this tension. Why not? One reason is provided by the selection arguments.

[19] See for similar views, Mayr (1982) – in the realm of biology – and Metcalfe (1989) – in the realm of economics.

[20] Although I believe that this distinction is suggestive and (at least potentially) contains valuable insights, I can only agree with Nelson and Winter (1982, p. 9) that their treatment leaves a lot wanting. Many different features seem to be lumped together in these notions. In what follows I shall concentrate on those features that seem to be relevant for the purposes at hand.

The selection arguments attempt to reconcile formal and appreciative orthodox theory. They do so by arguing that the central claims of formal orthodox theory are backed up by appreciative orthodox theory. This attempt at a reconciliation presupposes that formal orthodox theory is not taken at face value. Indeed, the proponents of the selection arguments urge us to reinterpret the claims of formal orthodox theory considerably. The neoclassical theory of the firm, they tell us, is not about individual firm behaviour but about aggregate industry behaviour. The neoclassical theory does not claim that individual firms actually solve the maximization problems that it ascribes to them. It is said to claim at most that the behaviour of firms surviving market selection coincides with that of hypothesized firms solving the maximization problems. Neither does the theory claim that industries are in equilibrium all of the time. What is claimed is that industries tend to move in the direction of equilibria.

This has consequences for our attempts to identify the ontological commitments of economic theory. For if we reinterpret economic theory along the lines outlined above, economic theory is not ontologically committed to grant the existence of mental states being the 'immediate causal determinants' of individual behaviour. Or, to put it in the terms proposed by Nelson and Winter, for formal orthodox theory to be true the behaviour of individual agents need not be caused by their mental states. What orthodox theory is ontologically committed to is captured in its appreciative theory: the existence of market selection which is held to be causally responsible for industry behaviour. Thus interpreted, it is not so much certain properties attributed to individual agents as certain properties attributed to (competitive) markets that are believed to be crucial in orthodox theory.

This still leaves us with a question. If orthodox economists really believe that what is actually going on in economies is quite something different from what is expressed in their formal theories, why then do they cling to their formal theory? Why do not they formalize their beliefs and intuitions as they are revealed in their appreciative theory and present *that* theory as their theory? According to Nelson and Winter, orthodox economists' reasons for refusing to go this way have changed over time. Marshall's primary reason for developing formal static orthodox theory further, instead of trying to provide the ground work for a truly dynamic evolutionary theory (even though he famously saw the 'Mecca' of economics lying in 'economic biology'), seems to have been that at that time no techniques were available to build tractable dynamic models. But now, Nelson and Winter contend, with all kinds of techniques at their disposal to build such models, the resistance among orthodox economists must be explained in terms of their predilection for simple and elegant models.

If Nelson and Winter are right in this (and I think there is much to say in favour of it), then it is primarily aesthetic and not ontological reasons that prevent orthodox economists from leaving their formal theory. This all the more supports the idea that the ontological commitments of orthodox economic theory cannot be read off directly from its formal theory. Its appreciative theory should also be taken into account.

In Nelson and Winter's view, appreciative orthodox theory coincides to a large extent with their own appreciative evolutionary theory. They see the main difference between orthodox theory and their own evolutionary theory lying in their respective formal theories. Orthodox economists apparently take their belief that their formal theory and their appreciative theory are reconcilable with one another (joined with their aesthetic predilection) to be a sufficient reason to cling to their formal theory. By contrast, Nelson and Winter insist on it that the core ideas in appreciative theory should be reflected in their formal theory by explicitly modelling them. Borrowing Mäki's (1994) terminology, orthodox appreciative theorists are methodological instrumentalists in this respect – they accept a (formal) theory despite the fact that they do not take the causal mechanisms that are described in the theory to be literally true – while Nelson and Winter are methodological realists – they believe that a theory is only acceptable if it specifies the causal mechanisms that are thought to be actually operating in reality. In this, Nelson and Winter follow a suggestion made by Koopmans about the role that 'natural selection' plays in Alchian's and Friedman's arguments: 'if this is the basis for our belief in profit maximization, then we should postulate that basis itself and not the profit maximization which it implies in certain circumstances' (Koopmans 1957, pp. 140–1).

Further ontological commitments of Nelson and Winter's evolutionary theory

'Market selection' is modelled explicitly by Nelson and Winter. One of the objectives they pursue with this is to examine systematically under what conditions evolutionary processes governed by 'market selection' produce neoclassical results.[21] In other words, they do not believe

---

[21] In fact, many different models appear in Nelson and Winter's book that serve many different purposes. One of these purposes, that has been taken up later also by Dosi et al. (1988), is to account for technical innovation and change.

($NE_{4A\&F}$) offhand. In fact, from Winter (1964) onwards especially Winter has gone at great length to demonstrate in a rigorous formal way that 'market selection' produces neoclassical results only under quite restrictive conditions.[22] From Winter (1964) also stems the assumption that firms follow fixed, rigid behavioural rules. Winter seems to have introduced this assumption merely to be able to derive definite results from his model. But in Nelson and Winter's (1982) evolutionary theory this assumption is assigned the same grounding status as the assumption that there is 'market selection' going on.

In Nelson and Winter's view, understanding firm behaviour means identifying the routines that firms follow. Most of the informal discussions in their book are devoted to bring home this view. Nelson and Winter develop their notion of routine at the firm level in analogy with the notion of skills at the level of individual persons. They argue that 'routine' closely resembles Polanyi's notion of tacit knowledge and Ryle's notion of 'know how'. Routines are enabling and restricting at one and the same time – they both determine what firms can and cannot do. Nelson and Winter contrast their view of firms displaying (quasi-) *automatic* routine behaviour with what is stated in formal orthodox theory: firms are engaged in conscious and deliberate choice. They stress in particular that in their view firms are not able to respond in the prompt and flexible way to environmental changes that formal orthodox theory envisages. A firm's extant routines severely restrict the firm's opportunities to change its behaviour in response to environmental changes. If changes in a firm's behaviour are possible at all, they at the very least take time.

Nelson and Winter argue that they are much closer to orthodox appreciative theory also in this respect. They take Machlup's experienced automobile driver and Friedman's (and Savage's) expert billiard player to illustrate that Machlup and Friedman also hold that much of actual behaviour is routine behaviour.[23] Nelson and Winter's catch phrase 'routines as genes' clearly indicate that Nelson and Winter believe that routines instruct firm behaviour in much the same way as the genes of an individual organism instruct its behaviour.

Still another important element of Nelson and Winter's evolutionary theory has to be mentioned. As already alluded to above, Nelson and

---

[22] In some cases (when dealing with comparative statics and growth theory), however, Nelson and Winter demand from their own models that they are able to reproduce neoclassical results.

[23] In the previous section we have seen, however, that Friedman does not seem to be wedded to any particular view on the 'immediate determinants' of firm behaviour.

Winter do not hold that routine firm behaviour necessarily implies firm behaviour that is completely unresponsive to changing circumstances. In the first place, a routine may be conditional in the sense that the routine specifies different lines of behaviour under different conditions. Changes in firm behaviour that result from such conditional routines when conditions change are placed under the rubric of '*along-the-rule effects*' in some of Nelson and Winter's models. And, second, Nelson and Winter assume that if, for whatever reason, the prevailing routines of firms cease to yield satisfactory results, firms engage in search activities for better routines. Changes in firm behaviour resulting from such search efforts are called '*search effects*' by Nelson and Winter.

'*Lamarckianism*' in Nelson and Winter's theory?

Here we encounter a supposedly Lamarckian element in Nelson and Winter's evolutionary theory: the timely appearance of variation under the stimulus of adversity. New routines are likely to enter the industry if the old ones do not work well any more. And if the new routines turn out to do reasonably well, Nelson and Winter do not only assume that the firms who have first found the routines stick to them, but also that they will be imitated by other firms in the industry. The new routines can thus spread over the population. This supposedly stands for the second Lamarckian element in Nelson and Winter's theory: the 'inheritance' (or better transmission) of acquired characteristics. Given the ambiguities that surround the use of the notion Lamarckism, however, what does putting this label of Lamarckism on Nelson and Winter's theory add to our understanding of their theory?[24] Nothing, I venture.[25] It is more instructive to follow Nelson and Winter's own modelling efforts in treating 'search effects' separate from selection effects and along-the-rule effects.

Nelson and Winter assume that Simon's notion of satisficing provides

---

[24] There seem to be more strict and more loose interpretations of Lamarckism around. Hull (1982), for example, adopts the strict interpretation that Lamarckism is committed to the claim that changes in phenotype cause changes in genotypes.

[25] Note that my problem with the label Lamarckism is quite different from Rosenberg's. Rosenberg's problem seems to be that because Nelson and Winter revert to Lamarckism, their evolutionary theory lacks definite economic meaning. In contrast, my problem is that without putting the label of Lamarckism on it Nelson and Winter's theory already has definite economic meaning (if you take the trouble of looking carefully at it), and that using the label is more likely to create confusion than clarification.

the key to the understanding of the processes in which search effects are produced. Firms are assumed to engage in search only if their extant routines yield profits that lie below some aspiration level. Search terminates as soon as some new routine is found that leads to profits exceeding the aspiration level.[26] At first it may seem that Nelson and Winter run into trouble here: how is the assumption that firms are engaged in satisficing behaviour – that seems to be clearly conscious and deliberate goal-directed behaviour – to be reconciled with Nelson and Winter's basic contention that firm behaviour is (quasi-) automatic routine behaviour? Nelson and Winter's way out of this is to assume first that engaging in search behaviour need not imply that conscious decisions are made. Whether firms engage in search behaviour or not may itself be routine-guided: dissatisfactory results may 'trigger' search behaviour in an (quasi-) automatic way. And, second, Nelson and Winter argue that search behaviour itself is also routine behaviour; search behaviour is assumed to be guided by second-order search routines. In this they follow Cyert and March (1963) and, again, Simon with his notions of procedural rationality and selective search.[27] These are precisely the authors who and the key ideas which Rosenberg recommends to Nelson and Winter for making their theory a genuinely Darwinian evolutionary theory!

We are now in the position to complete our picture of the basic explanatory structure of Nelson and Winter's economic evolutionary theory. The main purpose that Nelson and Winter ascribe to evolutionary economics (*EE*) can be formulated as follows:

> ($EE_{1N\&W}$) Economic evolutionary theory purports to explain changes in aggregate industry behaviour.

As the actual determinants of firm behaviour are routines in Nelson and Winter's view, we can state for a start:

> ($EE_{2N\&W}$) Economic evolutionary theory takes firm behaviour to be (quasi-) automatically instructed by their rigid routines.

To repeat, it is important to see that ($EE_{2N\&W}$) can account for changes in firm behaviour. Rigid routine following by firms can nevertheless lead to changes in their behaviour. It can do so in two different ways.

---

[26] To be fair, it must be added that Simon's notion of satisficing also allows for adjusting aspiration levels in an upward or downward direction.

[27] Indeed, it has been noted by Simon himself that the kind of learning that his notions of procedural rationality and selective search imply closely resemble Darwinian natural selection (see Simon 1983, p. 40).

First firms may have relatively sophisticated conditional routines that may lead them to change their behaviour when conditions change (Nelson and Winter's 'along-the-rule effects'). And, in the second place, among the routines that firms have are routines that may trigger search behaviour (depending on the actual results obtained) and search routines that guide their search behaviour. Thus Nelson and Winter's 'search effects' may come about. Needless to say, both along-the-rule effects and search effects result in changes in firm behaviour that in turn can bring about changes in industry behaviour.

Finally, Nelson and Winter believe that 'market selection' can produce 'selection effects' that also bring about changes in industry behaviour. Thus we have:

> ($EE_{3N\&W}$)   Economic evolutionary theory takes 'market selec-
> tion' to be a dominant force in bringing about
> changes in industry behaviour.

Note the similarity between ($NE_{3A\&F}$) and ($EE_{3N\&W}$). Whether 'market selection' produces changes in industry behaviour depends on the 'materials' it works on. In Nelson and Winter's theory the 'materials' are provided by the firms' routines. 'Selection effects' will obtain only if there is variety (or diversity) in routines. Now Nelson and Winter assume that routines of firms are firm-specific. Routines are assumed to differ from firm to firm. This assumption is not only instigated by their belief that real-to-life firms actually are different in their operating procedures, but also by their belief that it is wrong, methodologically speaking, to assume from the outset that one and only one type of firm exists (or can exist). In particular, they think that it is wrong to premise a standard of performance that is independent of the characteristics of firms (p. 94). The 'representative firm' should not be assumed to exist from the outset. If it exists at all it cannot be anything but the end product of evolutionary processes.

We can capture the facts, first, that Nelson and Winter take routines to be firm-specific, and, second, that routines do not only comprise (first-order) operating procedures, but also (second-order) search routines, by replacing ($EE_{2N\&W}$) by:

> ($EE_{2N\&W'}$)   Economic evolutionary theory takes the behaviour
> of each and every firm in the industry to be
> instructed by its own specific set of routines.
> Among these firm-specific routines are routines that
> determine under what conditions the firm in ques-
> tion engages in search behaviour and (second-

order) search routines that guide the firm's search activities.[28]

We can complete our picture of Nelson and Winter's evolutionary theory by adding a fourth characteristic stating that orthodox (neoclassical) industry results are not reproduced by Nelson and Winter's evolutionary theory under all conceivable conditions:

$(EE_{4N\&W})$ 'market selection', working on routine-following firms, produces the same tendencies in industry behaviour as fully informed and fully rational firms would do only under particular conditions.

5 Evolutionary game theory

In his discussion of the relation between economics and evolutionary biology, Rosenberg asserts that 'the terms of the trade are always in the direction from economics to biology and not vice versa' (Rosenberg 1994, p. 385). Rosenberg apparently believes that biology never had a significant impact on economic theorizing. This is in line with Rosenberg's general point that economics is quite different from evolutionary biology.

What Rosenberg seems to overlook here is that his own assertion about economics exporting ideas to biology implies that ideas stemming from economics later on have been taken on board in biology. This seems to run counter to his general point that economics and evolutionary biology share next to nothing with each other. Indeed, Rosenberg himself refers to Malthus and to the Scottish moral philosophers (such as Hume and Smith) who paved the way for Darwin to develop his notion of natural selection. Apparently, then, Rosenberg acknowledges that there have been rudimentary ideas of 'natural selection' around in 'classical economics'. The only way for Rosenberg to reconcile his assertion and his general point seems to be to hold that these ideas that once were present in classical economics disappeared from economics in its transition to neoclassical economics. In section 3 I have argued that these ideas did not vanish completely from economics. In this section I argue that Rosenberg's assertion by itself is questionable as well. For it overlooks that recently a significant transfer

---

[28] This does not mean that Nelson and Winter take search behaviour to be an altogether deterministic affair. Their models of search behaviour also contain stochastic elements.

of ideas from evolutionary biology to economics has been taking place: the adoption (and transformation, as we shall see) of evolutionary game theory by economists.

Evolutionary game theory: some preliminaries

Evolutionary game theory has been developed by biologists. Path-breaking work in this field has been done especially by John Maynard Smith. Maynard Smith and his collaborators tried to accommodate traditional game theory, as pioneered by von Neumann and Morgenstern (1944) and made more accessible by Luce and Raiffa (1957), in such a way that it would be suited to analyse animal contests. It is important to note that the type of game theory Maynard Smith developed is radically different from the traditional type of game theory. The traditional type of game theory focuses on the question what ideally rational players would (or should) do in situations where the payoffs of the behaviour of players do not only depend on their own behaviour, but also on the behaviour of others. The players are assumed to have common knowledge of the preferences of all players. Under this assumption of complete transparency of the game to all players, in the traditional type of (noncooperative) game theory fully rational players are typically assumed to be able to reason their ways immediately to a Nash equilibrium.

Evolutionary game theory differs from this by removing the assumptions of ideal (or unbounded, or omniscient) rationality and common knowledge. It is assumed instead that if individual players converge on a Nash equilibrium at all, they can do so only after having gone through some laborious and time-consuming evolutionary process. In the crudest biological version of evolutionary game theory, individual players are taken to be organisms that are genetically programmed to follow certain behavioural strategies. The individual 'players' are assumed to have no choice at all. Whether they like it or not, they are predisposed to play a certain strategy. As the individuals are assumed to pass on their genes to their offspring (in the simplest models it is assumed that reproduction is asexual), their descendants are assumed to be programmed to play the same strategy.

Constancy in the behavioural predispositions of individual organisms, however, does not necessarily imply that change is absent also at the level of the population. For the crucial assumption is that the force of natural selection impinges on the individuals. Natural selection can produce differential reproduction. The fitter individuals are assumed to produce more offspring than the less fit ones, so that the frequencies (proportions) of the genes of the former in the population's gene pool increase at the expense of the frequencies of the latter. Thus we can say that in this crudest form of evolutionary game theory changes at the population level are explained by natural selection working on a variety of individuals that are assumed to be unchanging in the relevant (genetic) respect.

Maynard Smith introduced the notion of an Evolutionarily Stable Strategy (ESS) as the appropriate concept of a stable equilibrium in this setting (see Maynard Smith 1982). The basic idea is that if all individuals in a population have converged on playing an ESS (they all play ESS), then no mutant strategy (a strategy that is slightly different from the ESS) can have a higher fitness than the ESS. Thus, if a mutant strategy happens to enter a population in which all other individuals play ESS,[29] it will be wiped out by the force of natural selection. Hence the situation of all individuals playing the ESS will be restored. Evolutionary game theoretic analyses in terms of ESS's are static analyses, for such analyses do not account for the processes of change that might lead populations to converge on ESS's. Such dynamic processes were first explicitly modelled in Taylor and Jonker (1978). The *replicator dynamics* (also sometimes called 'Malthusian dynamics' or the 'replicator equation') that Taylor and Jonker formulated captures the simple idea that the population's average fitness is the threshold value that determines whether the population share of some strategy increases or decreases. If the fitness of playing some strategy exceeds the population's average fitness, then the proportion of players in the population playing the strategy increases; if it is below the population's average fitness, then the proportion decreases.

In most of the applications of evolutionary game theory in economic contexts, the crudest biological interpretation of evolutionary game theory is repudiated. In particular, the idea that the behaviour of individuals is fully determined by pre-established programs is abandoned. Economic agents, it is maintained, are less dumb and more sophisticated than the animals that figure in the crudest biological interpretations. It is typically assumed that individuals are capable of learning and imitating other successful individuals. What these less crude

---

[29] An important assumption here is that the population is very large, so that the chance of two mutants meeting each other is negligible (compared to the chance of a mutant meeting an individual playing the ESS). Another important assumption is that pairs of individuals are drawn randomly from the population to play the game (there is no 'selective play').

interpretations have in common with the cruder ones, however, is that the reasoning and calculating skills of individuals are less developed and less sophisticated than the ones that rational choice theory ascribes to them. In the more refined interpretations, individuals are not assumed to be farsighted and omniscient, or 'unboundedly' rational, but myopic and boundedly rational only (see, for example, Mailath 1992). Furthermore, although it is not assumed in the more refined interpretations that the behaviour of individuals is completely preprogrammed genetically, it is still assumed that the learning and imitation behaviour is programmed in some sense (see, for example, Weibull 1995, chapters 4 and 5). Learning and imitation behaviour, it is assumed, are governed by fixed decision rules. It is sometimes argued that in social and cultural evolution, memes, the term that Dawkins (1976) coined to designate the units of 'replication' in imitation, take the place of genes (see, for example, Binmore 1994).

Whence the attractiveness of evolutionary game theory?

The crucial behavioural assumption in evolutionary game theory that the behaviour of individuals is programmed clearly parallels Nelson and Winter's contention that routines 'as genes' instruct the behaviour of firms. Of course, a difference is that the elementary behavioural units in Nelson and Winter's evolutionary theory are firms, and not individuals (their constituent parts) as in evolutionary game theory. But the basic explanatory structure seems to be the same: change at an aggregate level of analysis is explained by evolutionary forces working on programmed elementary behavioural units.

It is questionable, however, whether evolutionary game theorists are in general as committed to the belief that human persons really display (pre)programmed behaviour as Nelson and Winter are to the belief that firms really follow routines (quasi-) automatically. Most evolutionary game theorists do not seem to be committed to the view that human persons are computing machines or finite automata of some sort or another.[30] What they are primarily interested in, it seems, is in the properties or the 'behaviour' of some hypothesized theoretical system. The fact that many evolutionary game theorists typically investigate properties of different systems with differently programmed behavioural

[30] See, e.g., Binmore and Samuelson (1992), p. 279, for two different interpretations of the analysis of computing machines and finite automata in game theory.

units already suggests that they are not claiming that any of their models adequately (or truly) represents the 'real world' that we inhabit. They are 'fleshing out' the system-level implications of certain behavioural assumptions, leaving aside the issue what behavioural assumption is most realistic. Their theoretical endeavours are directed at finding answers to questions like: what would happen at the system level if the individuals involved were programmed in such and such ways?

Sometimes it seems that game theorists in economics resort to evolutionary game theory in order to overcome difficulties with conventional noncooperative game theory (see Binmore 1995 and Rizvi 1997). The key solution concept in conventional noncooperative game theory is, as we have seen, that of a Nash equilibrium. One major difficulty, however, is that it is not at all clear why ideally rational players would or should converge on a Nash equilibrium. A second difficulty is that many games typically have several Nash equilibria. This gives rise to the 'equilibrium selection problem': in the case of multiple equilibria, which equilibrium is to be selected on what grounds? So many different refinements of the Nash equilibrium concept have been proposed to solve this problem in conventional game theory, that in the end almost any Nash equilibrium could be justified in terms of one refinement or another.

In this problem setting, evolutionary game theory provides an attractive way out. Evolutionary game theory holds out the promise to solve both difficulties. So far, this hope does not seem to be forlorn. Systems that behave according to the replicator dynamics turn out to have only (symmetric) Nash equilibria as stable stationary points. Evolutionary game theory can also solve the equilibrium selection problem. In evolutionary game theory, the equilibrium selected is a function of the equilibrating process by means of which it is arrived at. And the equilibrating process in turn may not only depend on the replicator dynamics by which it is governed, but also on the initial situation from which the process starts. This means that 'details' of equilibrating processes, their historical 'contingencies' and 'accidents', must be taken into account.[31] Much of what is currently going on in evolutionary game theory seems to concentrate on the issue whether the results that are derived from replicator dynamics are invariant under perturbations of the details in the specification of the dynamics.

On the other hand, at least to some the attractiveness of evolutionary game theory does not stem entirely from its potential to solve problems

---

[31] 'History matters' one could say; evolutionary game theory can be used to illustrate 'path dependent' processes and 'lock-in' effects.

'internal' to game theory. What is appealing in evolutionary game theory to some is that it dispenses with the 'grotesque' exaggerations of the rationality of players that characterize conventional game theory. Evolutionary game theory, it is thought here, can tell us more about the ways people actually play games than conventional game theory (see, for example, Sugden 1986, p. 16). This feature of evolutionary game theory seems to be important especially for those who want to make use of game theory to explain real-to-life phenomena. A fascinating example of the latter is provided by attempts to use game theory in order to shed more light on 'the spontaneous evolution' of conventions, institutions and norms. These evolutionary game theorists are not interested in the properties of hypothesized theoretical systems for their own sake, but in how the insights gained in investigating these properties can enhance our understanding of how prevailing conventions, institutions and norms in society have (or, to put it more carefully could have) evolved.

'Theoretical' and 'applied' evolutionary game theory

Binmore, Kirman and Tani (1993) make some useful distinctions that nicely bring out the differences in theoretical interests within the field of evolutionary game theory. Binmore et al. do not only distinguish between theoretical work and applied work in game theory, but also between five general purposes for which game-theoretic models may be designed: prediction, explanation, investigation, description, and prescription. The first distinction relates to types of issues game theorists address. When game theorists analyse properties of game-theoretic models (which is also called 'gamesters looking in' by Binmore et al., p. 3), they are engaged in theoretical work. Applied work is done when game theorists use their analyses to address 'phenomena out there' ('gamesters looking out'). Binmore et al. argue that in principle each of the five general purposes mentioned above can be aimed at both in theoretical and in applied work. This leaves us with ten different types of game-theoretic analyses.

   In the present context of discussing the ontological commitment of evolutionary game theory our attention can be confined, I think, to only two of them: *theoretical* work (also sometimes called 'pure' or 'foundational' work) devoted to the *investigation* (or 'exploration') of the properties of theoretical systems, and *applied* work directed to the *explanation* (or 'explication') of the spontaneous evolution of conventions, institutions and norms. Examples of work falling within the former category are Hansen and Samuelson (1988), Schaffer (1989), and Weibull (1994). They all examine the conditions that are to be met for evolutionary processes to result in a situation in which all agents behave *as if* they were fully rational. Within the latter category fall for example Sugden (1986) and Binmore and Samuelson (1994). Of course, there are also borderline cases such as Young (1993) containing both elements of theoretical investigation and applications to study the spontaneous evolution of conventions.

We can summarize the work done in the first category of theoretical evolutionary game theory (*tegt*) as follows:

(EE_{1tegt}) Theoretical evolutionary game theory investigates properties of hypothesized systems (it explores models of population behaviour in particular);

(EE_{2tegt}) Theoretical evolutionary game theory represents individuals as programmed computing machines (and as finite automata in particular).

Theoretical evolutionary game theory typically investigates whether different models, populated by computing machines with different degrees of sophistication, have different properties. The fact that 'individuals' with different degrees of sophistication are often considered by the same game theorist indicates that theoretical evolutionary game theory as such is not committed to any particular view on the essential properties of real-to-life individuals. In particular, evolutionary game theorists engaged in theoretical work do not seem to claim that individuals *are* finite automata.

Applied evolutionary game theory (*aegt*), on the other hand, seems to be committed to a particular view on the essential properties of individuals. In its attempts to explain how conventions and institutions evolved spontaneously applied game theory does seem to involve a particular view on the causal role that individuals play in such processes of spontaneous evolution. After all, how can such game-theoretic accounts claim to provide an explanation of such processes if they get the role that individuals play wrong? Things turn out to be a little bit more complicated, however. As Binmore et al. point out, applied game theory does not straightforwardly claim to explain how conventions and institutions *de facto* evolve spontaneously. It rather gives 'possible stylized explanations of how things might have come about' (Binmore et al. 1993, p. 5). Applied evolutionary game theory does not claim that the actual ways in which conventions, institutions and norms came about correspond precisely to the dynamic processes that it specifies. It only shows that it is possible or logically coherent to entertain the view that they emerged spontaneously out of the interactions of boundedly rational individuals (p. 6).[32]

I take it that this last statement does not imply that applied evolutionary game theorists leave open the possibility that real individuals are 'unboundedly' (perfectly) rational after all. What they leave open is the possibility that the essential properties of individuals do not exactly match the properties that are ascribed to them in their models. Real individuals may be different from how their models portray them. The rationality of real individuals may be either more or less bounded than that of the individuals populating their models. What applied evolutionary game theorists do not question, however, is that the rationality of real individuals falls short of being perfect. Furthermore, real individuals may be quite unlike the mechanical (machine-like) rule followers in their evolutionary game-theoretic models. Like theoretical evolutionary game theory, applied evolutionary game theory is not committed to the view that there is no volition, consciousness, deliberation, and ratiocination involved on the part of the individuals.

Evolutionary game theory as such is committed to the assumption that individuals are boundedly rational (in some sense, and to some degree). This assumption, together with the claim that the behaviour of boundedly rational individuals can be represented theoretically in terms of mechanical rule following, can be found in theoretical and applied evolutionary game theory. But game theorists engaged in theoretical evolutionary game theory do not seem to be wedded to the view that individuals really are boundedly rational. They simply want to explore what follows from the assumption that individuals are boundedly rational. By contrast, although game theorists engaged in applied game theory do not claim that real individuals are boundedly rational exactly to the degree as they are depicted in their models, they do seem to hold that real individuals are boundedly rational.

Thus we have:

(EE_{1aegt}) Applied evolutionary game theory gives possible stylized explanations of the spontaneous evolution of conventions, institutions and norms;

(EE_{2aegt}) Applied evolutionary game theory holds that individuals are boundedly rational (their imitating and –

---

[32] Binmore et al. argue that the main intellectual achievement of such applications of game theory is one of liberation: it provides a first step to break out from fixed preconceptions that imprison our thoughts (one such preconception being that conventions and institutions can only come about by conscious design).

trial-and-error type of – learning behaviour can be described in terms of rule following).

6 Further reflections on evolutionary economics' ontological commitments

Now that we have had a closer look at Nelson and Winter's evolutionary theory and evolutionary game theory, we can delineate general tenets in their ontologies and compare these with those in neoclassical economics. In the previous section we already started with delineating shared tenets in the ontologies of Nelson and Winter's evolutionary theory and evolutionary game theory by noting that in both theories the elementary behavioural units (firms and individual agents respectively) are taken to display programmed behaviour. We qualified this observation by arguing that whereas Nelson and Winter really seem to believe that routines instruct firm behaviour in much the same way as genes programme the behaviour of organisms ($EE_{2N\&W}$), evolutionary game theorists only want to go as far as to assume that individuals behave *as if* they were programmed (EE_{2tegt}, EE_{2aegt}).

Indeed, I argued that evolutionary game theorists can coherently entertain the view that individuals act purposefully and choose consciously. Nelson and Winter put quite some effort in challenging this view. They contrast their notion of quasi-automatic routine behaviour with that of flexible, deliberate choice. At the same time they also acknowledge, however, that flexible, deliberate choice can be described in terms of rule following. It is demonstrated by Nelson and Winter themselves that optimizing behaviour can be translated into rule-governed behaviour (Nelson and Winter 1982, p. 150). This is the reverse manoeuvre of the one that Machlup (1946) made to defend neoclassical economics: rule-following behaviour can be redescribed and thus theoretically accounted for in terms of optimal behaviour.

This once again shows that the ontological commitments of economic theories cannot be read off directly from how individual agents and the system in which they are operating are depicted in theory. Some economic theory may either suggest that individual agents are taken to act consciously and deliberately, whereas its defenders believe that much individual behaviour is displayed in a mindless, automatic routine way, as in Machlup's case. Or, conversely, an economic theory may suggest that individual agents are believed to behave as a machine, whereas its practitioners may believe that individual agents act consciously and deliberately, as in the case of evolutionary game theory.

Thus evolutionary game theorists do not necessarily subscribe to Nelson and Winter's view that individual behaviour is routine most of the time. Ontologically speaking, however, they do have several beliefs about individual agents and their essential properties in common with Nelson and Winter. There is first of all the recognition that individual agents are only boundedly rational. The capabilities of individual agents to foresee future contingencies, to gather and process information, and to calculate best responses are severely restricted. The possibility that the behaviour of boundedly rational agents equals that of hypothesized unboundedly, perfectly rational agents cannot be foreclosed *a priori*. But Nelson and Winter and evolutionary game theorists concur in the view that (pure luck aside) boundedly rational agents can at most be expected to display such behaviour after having gone through laborious and time-consuming evolutionary process. And indeed both types of evolutionary economists agree that it is one of the tasks of evolutionary economics to find out under what conditions this can be expected to happen.

This brings us to a second point. Individual agents and their essential properties are seen as products of the past. Another way of putting this is to say that the operating characteristics of individual agents are believed to exhibit some degree of *inertia*. The past casts a lasting shadow over the present and future in that past occurrences and processes severely restrict the opportunities of individual agents to adapt to new environmental circumstances. Individual agents are unable to shape their operating characteristics *ex nihilo* (or *de novo*). It is likewise considered to be impossible that individual agents revise their operating characteristics overnight.

Besides this feature of inertia there is a third related point on which both proponents of evolutionary economics seem to concur. The operating characteristics of individual agents are considered to be agent-specific. Individual agents are believed to differ in their operating characteristics. This can be called the feature of *heterogeneity*.[33] What characterizes a particular agent is his or her set of routines or programmes. Indeed, one could say that agents are identified by their routines. As Binmore (1992, p. 414) puts it, in evolutionary game theory programmes must be seen as substitutes for players. This feature marks a clear break with economic theorizing in terms of representative agents. Again there is no presumption that after having gone through an evolutionary process different agents having different characteristics cannot wind up having the same representative characteristics. But there is no presumption to the opposite effect

---

[33] This element of heterogeneity is also stressed in present-day computational economics (see, e.g., Vriendiggs).

either. Whether homogenized representative agents will be ultimately produced in evolutionary processes is precisely one of the questions that both types of evolutionary economics investigate.[34]

So far we have been discussing mainly beliefs of evolutionary economists about essential properties of individual agents (be it firms or individual human beings). But in Nelson and Winter's evolutionary theory a crucial role is played also by beliefs about essential properties of the system (or regime) in which agents are operating. Competitive markets are believed to exert selection pressure on individual agents. The root idea behind this is that individual agents have to compete for scarce resources. Scarcity here does not so much refer to a predicament necessitating (intra-)individual choice as to an inevitable inter-individual conflict of interests. All individuals are dependent for their scale of operation (if not for their survival) on the amount of resources that they manage to acquire. And the resources that the one is able to acquire are subtracted from the remaining stock of resources that are left to others to compete for.

This idea of a putative ubiquitous 'brute fact of life' should not be confused with that of a competitive market, however. If competition for scarce resources is seen as belonging to the 'natural order', the competitive market is best viewed as one 'social order' among others that can be chosen to organize it.[35] There are some (following Hayek, for example) who prefer to view the competitive market as a social order that evolved spontaneously rather than by fiat or by concerted action. But even they do not deny that a choice can be made to replace the competitive market by other market forms or by various forms of planning.[36] Moreover, it has been observed by many that safeguards have to be installed and enforced in order to prevent the competitive market from 'naturally' transforming into a monopoly.[37]

---

[34] To some (e.g. Witt 1993, Foss 1994, and Hodgson 1997) it is one of the defining characteristics of evolutionary economics that processes of economic evolution are not only assumed to start with already existing variety, but also to constantly engender novelty and, hence, new variety. In my account of Nelson and Winter's evolutionary theory and evolutionary game theory this characteristic is not put centre stage, although it is to some extent captured in $(EE_{2N\&W}')$, (EE_{2tegt}), and (EE_{2aegt}).

[35] Cf. Hirshleifer's distinction between 'natural economy' and 'political economy' (Hirshleifer 1987). This also explains why 'market selection' is more properly called a social than a natural mechanism. See, e.g., Mäki (1990).

[36] This is not so say that society is malleable to our liking. Attempts to replace competitive markets may fail (or may not lead to the goal intended). And, of course, in the eyes of Hayekians any attempt to do so is regrettable.

[37] If some firm consistently outcompetes other firms in the market (and its emerging monopoly position is not endangered by new entrants), then of course the market ceases

The fact that market form can be altered by a decree issued by some collective agent or by concerted action of individual agents does not imply that market participants can subvert the regime of the competitive market. Indeed it can be said to belong to the essence of competitive markets that market participants lack the power to do so. In competitive markets firms are prohibited to act in concerted or orchestrated ways and, hence, are for example unable to inaugurate barriers to new entrants.

Nelson and Winter's idea that firms in competitive markets are exposed to selection pressure finds its counterpart in evolutionary game theory in the idea of external environments imposing selection pressure on individuals. Types that are relatively well adapted to the environment spread in the population at the expense of types that are relatively poorly adapted. Here the properties of the prevailing environment determine to a great extent what types come to dominate the population. One may be intuitively led to think of a *natural* environment here. But if there is frequency-dependent selection, the properties of the *social* environment can be said to have an impact on the selection process as well. In frequency-dependent selection, as in the paradigmatic Hawk-Dove game, the adaptedness of the types depends on the prevailing frequency (or proportion) of the types in the population. Instead of saying that the natural and social environment jointly (co-)determine the evolutionary process here, one could also say that the evolutionary process does not only depend on properties of the prevailing natural environment but also on properties of the prevailing population.

Once again individuals are believed to be subject to pressure that they cannot control. Individuals are believed to be unable to withstand the pressure, let alone to overrule or nullify it. The rules of the game are believed to be as 'inert' (or fixed) as the operating characteristics of the players. Unlike the natural environment the social environment can change in processes of frequency-dependent selection. But this does not mean that the rules of the game are alterable as well. On the contrary, if there are changes in the social environment, they unfold according to fixed, pre-established rules of the game.

In sum, then, the ontological commitments of Nelson and Winter's evolutionary theory and those of evolutionary game theory overlap to a considerable degree. Both species of evolutionary economics can be said to refer crucially to a natural and social environment exerting selection pressure on individual agents. Although the social environment is not taken to be immutable, it is believed to be beyond the reach of individual

to be competitive. Among others, late-nineteenth-century American economists have stressed this possibility of 'self-annihilation' of competition.

agents to change it. Furthermore, as to the properties of the individual agents themselves, both species of evolutionary economics concur on the view that individual agents are boundedly rational, that their essential operating characteristics exhibit inertia and that they differ (or, at the very least, can differ) among different individual agents. Where the two species differ is in their view on the immediate determinants of individual behaviour. While Nelson and Winter hold that individual agents follow rules in an unthinking machine-like way most of the time, evolutionary game theory only goes so far as to claim that the behaviour of individual agents can be represented theoretically in terms of rule-following behaviour.

References

Alchian, Armen A. (1950) 'Uncertainty, Evolution, and Economic Theory', *Journal of Political Economy*, 58: 211–21.

Becker, Gary (1962) 'Irrational Behavior and Economic Theory', *Journal of Political Economy*, 70: 1–13.

Binmore, Ken (1992) *Fun and Games. A Text on Game Theory*, Lexington, Mass.: D. C. Heath and Company.

(1994) *Playing Fair. Game Theory and the Social Contract (Part I)*. Cambridge, Mass.: MIT Press.

(1995) 'Foreword' to Weibull (1995), pp. ix–xi.

Binmore, Ken, Alan Kirman and Piero Tani (1993) 'Introduction: Famous Gamesters', pp. 1–25 in Ken Binmore, Alan Kirman and Piero Tani (eds.), *Frontiers of Game Theory*, Cambridge, Mass.: MIT Press.

Binmore, Ken and Larry Samuelson (1992) 'Evolutionary Stability in Repeated Games Played by Finite Automata', *Journal of Economic Theory*, 57: 278–305.

(1994) 'An Economist's Perspective on the Evolution of Norms', *Journal of Institutional and Theoretical Economics*, 150: 45–63.

Caldwell, Bruce J. (1992) 'Commentary' on Alan Nelson's 'Human Molecules', pp. 135–49 in Neil de Marchi (ed.), *Post-Popperian Methodology of Economics*, Boston, Dordrecht, etc.: Kluwer Academic Publishers.

(1994) 'Two Proposals for the Recovery of Economic Practice', pp. 137–53 in Roger E. Backhouse (ed.), *New Directions in Economic Methodology*, London: Routledge.

Clark, Andy (1997) 'Economic Reason: the Interplay of Individual Learning and External Structure', pp. 269–90 in J. D. Drobak and J. V. C. Nye (eds.), *The Frontiers of the New Institutional Economics*, San Diego: Academic Press.

Cyert, Richard M. and James G. March (1963) *A Behavioral Theory of the Firm*, Englewood Cliffs, New Jersey: Prentice Hall.

Dawkins, Richard (1976) *The Selfish Gene*, Oxford: Oxford University Press.

Day, Richard H. and Ping Chen (1993) *Nonlinear Dynamics and Evolutionary Economics*, New York, Oxford: Oxford University Press.

Dosi, G., C. Freeman, R. Nelson, G. Silverberg, and L. Soete (eds.) (1988) *Technical Change and Economic Theory*, London: Pinter.

Foss, Nicolai (1994) 'Realism and Evolutionary Economics', *Journal of Social and Evolutionary Systems*, 17: 21–40.

Friedman, Milton (1953) 'The Methodology of Positive Economics' in *Essays in Positive Economics*, Chicago: University of Chicago Press.

Friedman, Milton and Leonard Savage (1948) 'The Utility Analysis of Choices Involving Risk', *Journal of Political Economy*, 56: 279–304.

Hammond, J. Daniel (1991) 'Early Drafts of Friedman's Methodology Essay', paper presented at the Annual Meeting of the History of Economics Society, June.

Hansen, R. G. and W. F. Samuelson (1988) 'Evolution in Economic Games', *Journal of Economic Behavior and Organization*, 10: 107–38.

Hayek, Friedrich von (1948) 'The Meaning of Competition' in *Individualism and Economic Order*, Chicago: University of Chicago Press.

    (1968) 'Competition as a Discovery Procedure', reprinted as pp. 254–65 in *New Studies in Philosophy, Politics and Economics and the History of Ideas*, London: Routledge & Kegan Paul.

Herrmann-Pillath, Carsten (1996) 'On the Ontological Foundations of Evolutionary Economics' (mimeo, paper presented at the Second Workshop on Evolutionary Economics, University of Witten-Herdecke, 25–27 October 1996).

Hirshleifer, Jack (1987) 'Natural Economy Versus Political Economy', in *Economic Behaviour in Adversity*, Sussex: Wheatsheaf Books, pp. 169–93.

Hodgson, Geoffrey M. (1997) 'Economics and Evolution and the Evolution of Economics', pp. 9–40 in Jan Reijnders (ed.), *Economics and Evolution*, Aldershot: Edward Elgar.

Hull, David L. (1982) 'The Naked Meme', pp. 273–327 in H. C. Plotkin (ed.), *Learning, Development and Culture*, New York: John Wiley & Sons.

Kincaid, Harold (2001) 'The Empirical Presuppositions of Metaphysical Explanations in Economics', this volume, pp. 15–31.

Koopmans, Tjalling (1957) *Three Essays on the State of Economic Science*, New York: McGraw-Hill.

Langlois, Richard N. and Michael J. Everett (1994) 'What is Evolutionary Economics?' pp. 11–47 in Lars Magnusson (ed.), *Evolutionary and Neo-Schumpeterian Approaches to Economics*, Boston, Dordrecht, etc.: Kluwer Academic Publishers.

Lester, R. A. (1946) 'Shortcomings of Marginal Analysis for Wage-employment Problems', *American Economic Review*, 36: 63–82.

Luce, R. D. and Howard Raiffa (1957) *Games and Decisions*, New York: Dover.

Machlup, Fritz (1946) 'Marginal Analysis and Empirical Research', *American Economic Review*, 36: 519–54.

(1967) 'Theories of the Firm: Marginalist, Behavioral, Managerial', *American Economic Review*, 57: 1–33.

Mailath, George J. (1992) 'Introduction: Symposium on Evolutionary Game Theory', *Journal of Economic Theory*, 57: 259–77.

Mäki, Uskali (1990) 'Scientific Realism and Austrian Explanation', *Review of Political Economy*, 2: 310–44.

(1994) 'Isolation, Idealisation and Truth in Economics', in Bert Hamminga and Neil de Marchi (eds.), *Idealisation IV: Idealisation in Economics*, Amsterdam, Atlanta, Georgia: Rodopi.

Maynard Smith, John (1982) *Evolution and the Theory of Games*, Cambridge: Cambridge University Press.

Mayr, Ernst (1982) *The Growth of Biological Thought*, Cambridge, Mass.: Harvard University Press.

Metcalfe, Stanley (1989) 'Evolution and Economic Change', in A. Silberston (ed.), *Technology and Economic Progress*, Basingstoke, Hampshire: Macmillan Press.

Morgan, Mary S. (1995) 'Evolutionary Metaphors in Explanations of American Industrial Competition', pp. 311–37 in Sabine Maasen, Everett Mendelsohn and Peter Weingart (eds.), *Biology as Society, Society as Biology: Metaphors*, Dordrecht/Boston: Kluwer Academic Publishers.

Nelson, Richard (1995) 'Recent Evolutionary Theorizing about Economic Change', *Journal of Economic Literature*, 39: 48–90.

Nelson, Richard and Sidney Winter (1982) *An Evolutionary Theory of Economic Change*, Cambridge, Mass.: The Belknap Press of Harvard University Press.

Rizvi, A. (1997) 'The Evolution of Game Theory' (paper presented at Erasmus *EIPE* Seminar, 17 December 1997).

Rosenberg, Alex (1992a) *Economics – Mathematical Politics or Science of Diminishing Returns?*, Chicago: University of Chicago Press.

(1992b) 'Neo-classical Economics and Evolutionary Theory: Strange Bedfellows?', *PSA*: 174–83.

(1994) 'Does Evolutionary Theory Give Comfort or Inspiration to Economics?' pp. 384–407 in Ph. Mirowski (ed.), *Natural Images in Economics*, Cambridge: Cambridge University Press.

(2001) 'The Metaphysics of Microeconomics', this volume, pp. 174–88.

Ross, Don (1995) 'Real Patterns and the Ontological Foundations of Micro-Economics', *Economics and Philosophy*, 11: 113–36.

Satz, Debra and John Ferejohn (1994) 'Rational Choice and Social Theory', *Journal of Philosophy*, 91: 71–87.

Saviotti, P. Paolo and J. Stanley Metcalfe (1991) 'Present Developments and Trends in Evolutionary Economics', pp. 1–30 in P. Paolo Saviotti and J. Stanley Metcalfe (eds.), *Evolutionary Theories of Economic and Technological Change*, Chur, Reading, etc.: Harwood Academic Publishers.

Schaffer, Marc E. (1989) 'Are Profit-maximizers the Best Survivors?', *Journal of Economic Behavior*, 11: 29–45.

Simon, Herbert A. (1983) *Reason in Human Affairs*, Oxford: Basil Blackwell.

Sugden, Robert (1986) *The Economics of Rights, Co-operation and Welfare*, Oxford: Basil Blackwell.

Taylor, P. and L. Jonker (1978) 'Evolutionarily Stable Strategies and Game Dynamics', *Mathematical Biosciences*, 40: 145–56.

Van Damme, Eric (1994) 'Evolutionary Game Theory', *European Economic Review*, 38: 847–58.

Von Neumann, John and Oskar Morgenstern (1944) *Theories of Games and Economic Behavior*, Princeton: Princeton University Press.

Vriend, Nicholaas (1995) 'Self-organisation of Markets: An Example of a Computational Approach', *Computational Economics*, 8: 205–31.

Vromen, Jack J. (1995) *Economic Evolution. An Inquiry into the Foundations of New Institutional Economics*, London: Routledge.

Weibull, Jürgen W. (1994) 'The "As If" Approach to Game Theory: Three Positive Results and Four Obstacles', *European Economic Review*, 38: 868–81.

(1995) *Evolutionary Game Theory*, Cambridge, Mass.: MIT Press.

Winter, Sidney (1964) 'Economic "Natural Selection" and the Theory of the Firm', *Yale Economic Essays*, 4: 225–72.

Witt, Ulrich (1993) 'Evolutionary Economics: Some Principles' pp. 1–16 in Ulrich Witt (ed.), *Evolution in Markets and Institutions*, Berlin: Springer Verlag.

Young, Peyton (1993) 'The Evolution of Conventions', *Econometrica*, 61: 57–84.

Zerbe, R. O. Jr. (ed.), (1982) *Research in Law and Economics*, 4, Greenwich, Conn.: JAI Press Inc.

12   Is macroeconomics for real?

KEVIN D. HOOVER*

> All are keeping a sharp look-out in front, but none suspects that
> the danger may be creeping up from behind. This shows how
> real the island was.
>
> J. M. Barrie, *Peter Pan*

Children are often thought to be peculiarly honest – witness the story of
"The Emperor's New Clothes." My title comes from a group of my
academic children: first-year graduate students. I teach a mandatory class
in macroeconomic theory to graduate students in both an economics
department and an agricultural economics department. The students in
agricultural economics are typically more interested in crop patterns or
natural resources – relentlessly microeconomic topics – than in unemployment, GDP growth, or interest rates. Each year at least one student,
who I assume comes from the agricultural economics department, writes
on the anonymous class evaluation something like this: "If macroeconomics were real economics – which it is not! – this would have been a
good class." What is one to say to the honest and piercing doubts of an
academic child?

The idea that macroeconomics stands in need of a microfoundational
base is a commonplace among economists. I shall argue that what
motivates this belief are principally ontological concerns, naïvely, but
pointedly expressed, in my students' questions about the reality of
macroeconomics. I shall argue that ontological reduction of macroeconomics to microeconomics is untenable. Thus, while the program of
microfoundations may illuminate macroeconomics in various ways, it
cannot succeed in its goal of replacing macroeconomics.

* I am grateful to Uskali Mäki and Thomas Mayer for valuable comments on the first
version of this paper, and to D. Wade Hands for some pointers on the literature on
supervenience. This research was supported under National Science Foundation grant
No. 9311930.

To begin at the beginning, it might help to define the key terms. "Macroeconomics" is sometimes thought to be the economics of broad aggregates, and "microeconomics" the economics of individual economic actions. Although he did not use the terms "microeconomics" and "macroeconomics," John Maynard Keynes (1936, pp. 292–3) drew a related distinction: microeconomics is the theory of the individual industry or firm; macroeconomics is the theory of output and employment as a whole. As Maarten Janssen (1993, ch. 1) shows, these alternative definitions cut in somewhat different ways. They are, however, similar enough for present purposes, since any quantification of output and employment *as a whole*, is bound to involve broad aggregates. Macroeconomics is thus that area of economics that treats of GDP, unemployment, interest rates, the flow of financial resources, exchange rates, and so forth.

Uskali Mäki (1996) offers a careful discussion of realism in relation to economics that might help to define the term "real" in the title. Mäki distinguishes between ontological realism, which raises questions about what there is, and semantic realism, which raises questions about the connection between language and what there is. Semantic realism can be analyzed further, but the central claim of this essay is ontological: *macroeconomic aggregates exist*. More precisely, and again using Mäki's terminology, I will argue that macroeconomic aggregates exist *externally* (i.e., independently of any *individual* human mind) and *objectively* (i.e., unconstituted by the representations of macroeconomic theory). This claim, if it can be sustained, undermines one of the central rationales for the program of microfoundations for macroeconomics that since at least the mid-1940s has dominated thinking among economists.

1 The program of microfoundations

Before this century, the most common definition of economics was epitomized by Alfred Marshall (1920, p. 1): "[A] study of mankind in the ordinary business of life; [economics] examines that part of individual and social action which is most closely connected with the attainment and with the use of the material requisites of well-being." This definition, which is reasonably hospitable to macroeconomics, has now largely been supplanted by that of Lionel Robbins (1935, p. 16): "Economics is the science which studies human behaviour as a relationship between ends and scarce means which have alternative uses." On Robbins's definition, economics must be fundamentally about the individual.

Modern macroeconomics developed in the wake of Keynes's *General Theory of Employment Interest and Money* (1936). Typical elements of Keynes's analysis were the consumption function, which related aggregate consumption to aggregate national income, the investment function, which related aggregate investment to the general rate of interest, and the liquidity preference function, which related the aggregate stock of money to aggregate national income and the general rate of interest. It is easy to understand that in a profession committed to Robbins's definition of economics, such aggregate relationships were at best rather unappealing way-stations on the path to an individualist economics. The program of microfoundations, as it has developed over the past fifty years, aims to explain all macroeconomic properties of the economy – *in principle*, at least – by reference to the behavior of rational economic actors such as postulated by microeconomics.[1]

Approval of the program of microfoundations is almost universal among economists. Those economists who have reflected on the matter at all deeply typically associate microfoundations with methodological individualism (e.g., Janssen 1993, pp. 26–9 *passim*; Boland 1979, chs. 2 and 5).[2] Blaug (1992, p. 44) defines *methodological individualism* as the principle that ". . . asserts that explanations of social, political, or economic phenomena can only be regarded as adequate if they run in terms of the beliefs, attitudes, and decisions of individuals."

Methodological individualism is a doctrine about explanation. Despite lip-service to it, it is not widely practiced by economists. The reason is what I have elsewhere labeled the "Cournot problem" after its lucid, early formulation by Augustine Cournot (1838/1927, p. 127), the nineteenth-century mathematician and economist: there are too many individuals (firms and consumers) and too many goods to be handled by direct modeling.[3] Mark Blaug (1992, p. 46) observes that few explanations of macroeconomic phenomena have been successfully reduced to their microfoundations, so that insistence on microfoundations would eliminate explanations of macroeconomic phenomena *tout court*. Even Lucas (1987, pp. 107–8), an important advocate of the program of microfoundations, holds up only the *hope* of the elimination of distinction between microeconomics and macroeconomics.

The commitment of economists to methodological individualism is

---

[1] See Weintraub (1979) and Janssen (1993) for general discussions of microfoundations for macroeconomics.

[2] I must be careful not to leave a false impression: both Janssen and Boland are critics of the program of microfoundations.

[3] Hoover (1988, p. 135). Also see Hoover (1988, ch. 9, esp. section 2; ch. 10, pp. 241–4); Friedman (1955).

thus not grounded in successful applications. Rather it appears to be based on an instinctive belief in *ontological individualism*: the doctrine that all that exists fundamentally for the economy are individual economic actors. Lucas and his fellow new classical economists have promoted representative-agent models, a class of models in which the mathematical methods of microeconomic optimal choice are applied to a single individual who takes national income as his budget constraint and whose choices are taken to represent the aggregate choices of the economy, because they appear to achieve the reduction of macro-economics to microeconomics as required by the program of microfoundations for macroeconomics. A. P. Kirman (1992) severely criticizes the representative-agent model, not because it aspires to methodological individualism, but because it fails to fulfill the necessary conditions for perfect aggregation, so that the representative agent in the models fails to represent actual individuals successfully. Methodological individualism remains the goal. Similarly, David Levy (1985) argues that complete methodological individualism is impossible, because, given imperfect information, individual economic actors must make reference to collec-tive entitites as part of their own decision-making processes. Neverthe-less, Levy (1985, p. 107) writes: "These collectives have no real existence but are simply the product of theories." While defending macro-economics against the strong claims of the program of microfoundations, Blaug (1992, p. 45) nevertheless writes: "ontological individualism is trivially true."

It is important to understand that there are some senses in which neither the methodological nor the ontological individualist denies the existences of aggregates, collectives, or wholes. No one denies that GDP calculations can be made and reported, or even that GDP may have some locally stable relationship to unemployment or average interest rates or some other aggregate. Similarly, no one denies the existence of social organizations such as governments or firms (in the sense that talk of governments and firms conveys meaning). What is typically denied is that such aggregates or organizations are among the fundamental units from which economic reality is constructed.

Hayek (1979, ch. 4) argues that such entities are secondary, and that the role of a social science is "compositive" – that is, that it must explain these entities as arising from the fundamental individual components.[4] Hayek (1979, ch. 6) denies that the wholes that social science explains

---

[4] While not denying that aggregates such as GDP or the general price level can be calculated, Mises (1949/1966, p. 217) goes further than Hayek in arguing that they are quite devoid of meaning (also see Lachmann 1976, p. 96).

through compositive methods are subject to scientific laws. He holds up the attempt to connect them through laws as an example of Whitehead's "fallacy of misplaced concreteness." He writes: "the wholes about which we speak exist only if, and to the extent to which, the theory is correct which we have formed about the connection of the parts which they imply, and which we can explicitly state only in the form of a model built from those relationships" (Hayek 1979, p. 98). Hayek thus argues that aggregates exist, but derivatively rather than fundamentally, and that in Mäki's terminology they do not exist objectively (i.e., unconstituted by the representations of theory).[5] Still, even Hayek does not endorse practicable methodological individualism, stressing the importance of a reduction to microfoundations *in principle* and himself citing the Cournot problem (Hayek 1979, pp. 74–5, esp. fn. 8).

2 Is macroeconomics ontologically problematic?

One might concede the main point of the last section – namely, that the drive for microfoundations is driven by ontological individualism – yet not believe that any interesting metaphysical issue is involved, because the ontology of economics is too well understood by common sense to pose any serious puzzle. Mäki (1996, p. 434), for example, contrasts *folk economics* with *scientific economics*, arguing that scientific economics merely presents modifications of the " 'ontic furniture' of the general folk views of 'man' and society." He lists some types of possible modifications: selection, abstraction, idealization, exaggeration, projection, aggregation. But he maintains that none of these modifications or combinations thereof "accomplishes a major departure from the ontic furniture of the ordinary realm. No new *kinds* of entities or properties are introduced" (Mäki 1996, p. 435). Mäki illustrates his point with a discussion of the business firm in standard neoclassical analysis, and concludes "that folk economics and neoclassical economics have real business firms as their shared referent even though they represent these firms differently."

Mäki's case for the "ontological commonsense realism" of economics in which the ontic furniture poses no special challenges to the under-

---

[5] The terminology of "fundamental" or "derivative" existence is fraught with difficulties. It is beyond my purpose to try to sort such matters out here. It is enough for the point at hand, however, to note that Hayek does not believe that economic aggregates can be causes in their own rights. They might serve as some sort of shorthand, but he argues that there is always an adequate causal mechanism independent of that shorthand.

standing is more persuasive for some parts of economics than others. I want to argue that for some important macroeconomic aggregates, it is not particularly cogent, and that some such aggregates do not share a referent with folk notions. The case can be illustrated with reference to the related notions of "real GDP" (or "real income" or "real output," these terms being used almost interchangeably) and the "general price level."

On any interpretation, macroeconomics takes a larger view of the economy and deals with aggregates, which are, in turn, constructed from characteristics of individual economic actors. It is helpful to distinguish two types of aggregates.

First are what we might call *natural* aggregates: simple sums or averages. Examples of natural aggregates are the level of total employment or the average rate of interest on six-month commercial paper. I call these natural aggregates because they are measured in the same units (i.e., they have the same dimensionality) as the individual components that they comprise and, therefore, preserve a close analogy with those individual components. Employment, for instance, is measured by the number of workers or the number of man/hours at both the level of a single individual and in aggregate. The rate of interest on a bond and the average rate of interest on a group of similar maturity bonds are both expressed as a percentage yield per unit time.

A second type of aggregate, what we might call *synthetic* aggregates, are important for macroeconomics. I call these synthetic because they are fabricated out of components in a way that alters the structure of the components, so that they are dimensionally distinct from the components and so that there is no close analogy (despite their sometimes sharing a common name) with the components. The nature of the synthesis is well illustrated by the general price level. The notion of a general price level aims to capture a pre-scientific insight: "a dollar just ain't what it used to be!"; "when I was a lad a penny would buy what a quarter does these days." To capture this insight, one would like to have some notion of the average level of prices. A simple average will not of course work: (10¢/orange + 20¢/apple + $27,948/Volvo stationwagon)/3 does not convey any useful information. One cannot add apples and Volvos, as they say.

It might be argued that any sort of an average is altogether the wrong way to start. What is really wanted is an estimate of the price of money itself, and not the average price of goods. The price of money would, like the price of oranges, be a single number. The general price level could be defined to be its inverse ($1/p_m$). Since relative prices of goods change because of changes in the conditions of demand and supply, there would be, at best, a rough proportionality between individual prices and the general price level. Indeed, it would permit one to isolate which changes in individual prices were the result of "real" factors and which of monetary factors.

This approach, however, does not do justice to the pre-scientific insight, for it does not provide us with a concept or a measurement of prices that is independent of highly particular and highly inadequate theoretical models. To see this consider, how one would actually determine the value of p_m. One might, for instance, write down a complete Walrasian general equilibrium model in which commodities were expressed in natural quantities, prices in terms of money, and all assets denominated in money were valued using p_m. Aside from the impracticality of formulating and solving such a model for an actual economy (the Cournot problem again), it is well-known that p_m might not be determinable in such a model, or if it is, might not be unique (Hahn 1965; Samuelson and Sato 1984; see Hoover 1988, ch. 5, section 1 for a simple exposition). The essence of the problem is that the real quantity of money (i.e., the useful services that it provides), unlike the real quantities of apples or Volvos, depends fundamentally on the price of other goods. In adjusting the prices of various goods, including money, unique convergence may not be possible, because each time prices adjust to remove an excess demand or supply, the quantity of money changes – possibly in a discontinuous manner – which can increase rather than diminish some of the excess demands or supplies.

This problem in the foundations of monetary theory has yet to be satisfactorily resolved. But what if it had been? It would tie the notion of the general price level extremely closely to a particular theoretical analysis. The measurement of p_m would be "derived" rather than fundamental (see Ellis 1966, ch. 8). The pre-scientific notion is not tied to such a derivation. That would not pose any special problem if the general price level derived in this way correlated closely with numerous other theoretical methods of deriving it, which in turn correlated reasonably with the pre-scientific sense of a general rise in prices.[6] Temperature provides an example of what is wanted (Ellis 1966, ch. 6). The notion of hotter and colder is pre-scientific. The first attempts to provide quantification relied on some presuppositions – e.g., the linearity of the expansion of the various fluids used in thermometers – but were not tied to particular theories. Temperature measures can now be derived from particular theoretical understandings – e.g., from the kinetic theory of

---

[6] Avogadro's number, for example, can be computed to take the same value from numerous theoretically independent methods (see the discussion in Hacking 1983, pp. 54–5).

gases. Such derived measures show considerable consilience with the pre-scientific notions of hotter and colder and with the atheoretical measurement systems. They permit the extension of temperature scales beyond ordinary experience – e.g., to the measurement of the temperature of the sun – but retain their independence from particular theories because of the consilience of measurements derived from different theoretical starting points. In contrast, the measurement of the general price level remains at the atheoretical stage in which the makers of price index numbers, Laspeyres, Paasche, and Fisher, are the economists' Fahrenheit and Celsius.

The point of raising these difficulties in measuring the general price level is not that the existence of aggregates is tied to their measurement. Rather it is that the difficulties in measuring them help to expose what problematic entities they are, and undermine the appeal of seeing them as close analogues of their components (particular prices, particular goods, and so forth). The disanalogies can be made clearer through a more detailed examination of the general price level.

The fundamental insight of the index number is that one can avoid some of the dimensional nonsense of averaging disparate prices by averaging percentage rates of change instead. A simple average, however, does not capture the commonsense feeling for the degree of price change. A change in the price of gasoline should count for more than, say, a change in the price of caviar in measuring the change in the general price level. How to weight various price changes turns out to have an irreducible degree of arbitrariness.

In general the percentage change in the general price level, indicated as p (where p is the logarithm of the general price level), is related to the individual underlying prices as

$$\Delta p = f(\Delta p_1, \Delta p_2, \ldots, \Delta p_n),\tag{1}$$

where p_j is the price of good j for $j = 1, 2, \ldots n$. Now, the properties that theoretically restrict the functional form of f(.) are very weak:

1. if $\forall j\ \Delta p_j \gtrless 0$, then $\Delta p \gtrless 0$.
2. $\Delta p \leq \max\{\Delta p_1, \Delta p_2, \ldots, \Delta p_n,\}$.
3. $\Delta p \geq \min\{\Delta p_1, \Delta p_2, \ldots, \Delta p_n,\}$.

Conditions 2 and 3 together imply an obvious corollary:

4. if $\Delta p_1 = \Delta p_2 = \ldots = \Delta p_n$, then $\Delta p = \Delta p_j$ for any j.

Condition 1 says that if each price increases (decreases) the general price level must itself increase (decrease), and that the general price level cannot change if no individual price changes. Conditions 2 and 3 say that the general price level cannot increase by more than the largest nor decrease by less than the smallest individual price change. Condition 2 says that if every individual price changes equiproportionally, so must the general price level. An infinite number of functions fulfill these conditions, and the range of consistent changes in the general price level, given a fixed set of underlying price changes is wide. In practice, price indices are generally linear

$$\Delta p = \sum_{j=1}^{m} w_j \, \Delta p_j, \text{ where } \sum_{j=1}^{m} w_j = 1. \tag{2}$$

For $m < n$, this formulation recognizes the practical fact that price indices are based on samples of selected goods. The weights w_j in these indices are chosen in practice to capture the pre-scientific sense of the amount of a price rise. Two common weighting schemes with rationales in microeconomic consumer theory are the Laspeyres index, which chooses the weights to reflect the share of each good in base period consumption, so that the general price level effectively measures the changing cost of a fixed bundle of goods, and the Paasche index, which chooses weights to reflect the share of each good in current period consumption, so that some compensation is made for substitution from relatively more expensive to relatively cheaper goods in the face of changes in relative prices.

Neither index is "correct"; there are an infinite number of indices lying between the two; and economists have from time to time argued the case for other indices with different weighting schemes [7] The non-uniqueness of the price index is important for the point of this essay. It is a fundamental property. A price index is an attempt to quantify the pre-scientific insight that the value of money changes. The different admissible price indices are not, however, approximations to some true underlying general price level. The general price level is in some fundamental sense non-scalar, although there is no currently acceptable scientific refinement that captures that fact.[8] No similar indefiniteness attaches to any of the prices of the underlying individual goods.

The change in the general price level, p, may be integrated over time to generate a price level ($p_{t+n} = \int_t^{t+n} \Delta p \, dt = p'_{t+n} + c$). The constant of integration (c) permits us to choose an arbitrary base usually $P_t = 1$ or

---

[7] Generally one expects the Laspeyres index to be greater than the Paasche index, but this can be guaranteed only if certain regularity conditions are imposed on preferences that may not always hold for individual agents.

[8] This may be an area in which the theory of fuzzy sets would be helpful. The use of scalar indices may account for some portion of the apparently irreducible randomness in estimated macroeconomic relations.

$P_t = 100$, where $P = \exp(p)$, for some desired base period t (other base values are less common, but not unknown). P differs from the particular price of, say, a Volvo, not just in its intrinsic indefiniteness, but also in its dimensions. The dimensions of the price of a Volvo are dollars/Volvo; the dimensions of P are period-t dollars/base-period dollars. The dimensions of P are not the dimensions of the price of any good. They appear to be the inverse dimensions of the price of money, taking base-period money to be the numeraire. Given the indefiniteness of the price index, however, it is evident that the price of money is unlike the price of other goods, and represents a substantial departure from pre-theoretic notions of price. The price index is used to normalize the price of particular goods, thereby to decompose individual price changes into a common or general element and a "real" or relative (to the index) element. That this operation is not obvious to common sense will be evident to anyone who has taught elementary economics or read policy analysis by non-economists.

Real GDP is another important example of a synthetic aggregate. Considered as national income, nominal GDP adds up the incomes of each individual in the economy and is an obvious extension of the accounting framework for business or personal income. In a major innovation in economic analysis, the national accounting framework since the 1930s establishes the three-way identity between the sum of all incomes, the value-added in production, and the value of all final goods and services. That these other methods of computing GDP have obvious commonsense analogues is less clear. If final goods (i.e., goods that are not inputs into other production processes) are indicated by Q_j, then nominal GDP is

$$Y^N = \sum_{j=1}^{n} P_j Q_j \qquad j = 1, 2, \ldots n. \tag{3}$$

The dimension of income is dollars/unit time. Money provides the common unit that is essential if disparate goods are to be added.

If some or all of the prices of individual goods increase, it is obvious that nominal GDP could increase without any of the individual quantities changing. In the utilitarian framework that underlies economics this is an undesirable characteristic, because the measure of income has changed without the underlying utility, which is assumed to be generated by the quantities of the goods themselves, changing. It is clearly desirable to correct for changing prices. The usual way to do this is to compute real GDP as

$$Y^R = Y^N / P. \tag{4}$$

Real GDP is often treated as the analogue of an individual good. It does not, however, have the dimensions of a real good. Rather its dimension is base-period dollars (not dollars/unit good). Real GDP is a derivative measurement. One gets a different measurement for it for every different admissible price index. It inherits the fundamental fuzziness of the general price level.

The analogy of real GDP to an individual good is suggested to some by the possibility of perfect aggregation. If, for example, relative prices are constant (i.e., p_j/p_k is constant for all j and k), then $\sum_{j=1}^{n} P_{j,t}Q_{j,t}$ (where the t in the subscript indicates the base time period t) can be normalized by choosing the units for the $Q_{j,t}$s so that each $P_{j,t} = 1$. Then nominal GDP at time n can be written

$$\sum_{j=1}^{n} P_{j,t+n}Q_{j,t+n} = P_{t+n}\sum_{j=1}^{n} Q_{j,t+n}. \tag{5}$$

In this case, conditions 1 to 4 above insure that P is unique. Some conclude therefore that in this limited case, one can treat the summation in the right-hand side of equation (5) as a natural aggregate quantity analogous to an individual quantity. The conditions for constant relative prices are almost certainly never fulfilled, but even if they were the summation is not analogous to an individual quantity. The general price level P in (5) still has the dimension period-n dollars/period-t (i.e., base period) dollars. To sum heterogeneous goods, they must still be converted to a common denominator, and in this case, the summation still has the dimensions of period-t dollars. This would be more perspicacious if (5) were written as

$$\sum_{j=1}^{n} P_{j,t+n}Q_{j,t+n} = P_{t+n}\sum_{j=1}^{n} 1_{j,t+n}Q_{j,t+n}, \tag{6}$$

where the subscripted numeral 1 is a place holder for the dimensional conversion.

The general price level and real GDP are the most important aggregates in macroeconomics. There are many others. Each mixes the characteristics of simple and synthetic aggregates to different degrees. Average interest rates were cited above as an example of a simple aggregate, but when averaging is across nonhomogeneous maturities and risk classes, interest rates too are complicated by the fundamental problems of index numbers. Aggregation of employment across skill or quality levels faces similar considerations. There are other derivative quantities as well. The real rate of interest is defined to be the market interest rate less the percentage change in the general level of prices (Δp). Like real GDP, the real rate of interest inherits the fundamental fuzziness of the general price level.

The history of quantitative economics demonstrates that even the use of simple averages represented a difficult conceptual leap. On the best interpretation what is accepted to common sense is relative. To treat synthetic aggregates as mere extensions of commonsense notions appears in comparison to make a category mistake. Despite their deceptively related names, there is no simple analogy between the general price level and individual prices or between quantities of individual goods and real GDP.

3 The supervenience of macroeconomics on microeconomics

Synthetic aggregates, at least, are not direct extensions of folk ontology. It is clear, however, that, if their independent reality is to be demonstrated in a sense more fundamental than that one can always calculate them according to some algorithm, we must first show that such aggregates cannot be reduced to properties of individual economic actors. Aggregates are in fact calculated; they clearly do not exist in a separate Platonic realm; and ontological individualism has immediate appeal, because we all have first-hand experience as economic actors. Any account of the autonomy or nonreducibility of macroeconomic aggregates must account, therefore, for the relationship of the individual to the aggregate.

Macroeconomic aggregates I believe *supervene* upon microeconomic reality. What this means is that even though macroeconomics cannot be reduced to microeconomics, if two parallel worlds possessed exactly the same configuration of microeconomic or individual economic elements, they would also possess exactly the same configuration of macroeconomic elements. It is not the case, however, that the same configuration of macroeconomic elements implies the same configuration of microeconomic elements.

Biology provides analogies and disanalogies for economics. Alexander Rosenberg (1985, ch. 4, section 8, ch. 6, section 3, *passim*) applies the notion of supervenience to the relationship of functional biology (macro) to molecular biology (micro). To take one example, hemoglobin is an element in functional explanations of the operations of the cardio-pulmonary and circulatory systems of higher animals (Rosenberg 1985, ch. 4, section 2). At the molecular level, hemoglobin is not a single chemical, but a family of chemicals. To be hemoglobin at the macro level, a molecule must possess nine particular proteins at critical junctures in the molecular structure. Across different species the approximately 140 remaining proteins that the hemoglobin molecule comprises vary considerably. Similarly, Rosenberg argues that Mendelian genetics supervenes on a molecular base. Mendelian genetics uses a conceptual scheme that is not easily mapped onto molecular features, but nevertheless identical molecular configurations produce identical genetic behavior.

The notion of supervenience was initially suggested in the philosophy of mind as a method of retaining the dependence of the mental on the physical, while at the same time denying psychophysical laws (see Kim 1978, p. 153). Rosenberg draws on the analysis of Jaegwon Kim (1978). For Kim, supervenience is a relationship between two distinct realms of properties (or relations). Consider I_j, which is a conjuction of properties in the micro realm in which every one of the properties or its complement form one of the conjuncts.[9] Each I_j is then a complete characterization of a possible micro state, and the disjunction of every I_j defines every possible micro state. Consider the A_j, constructed *mutatis mutandis* for the macro state. A family of macro properties is supervenient on a family of micro properties when any objects which share the same micro properties necessarily share the same macro properties. Kim (1978, pp. 152–3) shows that one can derive the following relationship:

$$I_1 \vee I_2 \vee \ldots \vee I_n \to A_k, \text{ for any } A_k, \tag{7}$$

where the I_h, $h = 1, 2, \ldots, n$, are a subset of the I_j.[10] Of relation (7), Kim (1978, p. 153) says: "I don't see how such generalizations could fail to be lawlike."

Using Kim's analysis, Rosenberg argues against the autonomy of Mendelian genetics. The conceptual scheme of Mendelian genetics (the macro level) does not map easily into the conceptual scheme of molecular biology (the micro level). Mendelian genetics permits explanation of phenomena not easily explainable directly from the molecular level. However, Mendelian genetics fails to account for some phenomena within its scope. Rosenberg argues that Mendelian genetics supervenes on molecular biology, and that molecular biology is the more scientifically advanced, more fundamental and autonomous theory. Mendelian genetics is reducible in principle (that is the upshot of Kim's analysis in

---

[9] The account of Kim's analysis here omits most of the technical details (these are also reproduced in Rosenberg 1985, pp. 113–16), and changes his notation. The identification of the distinct realms of properties as "micro" and "macro" is my addition – literally *ad hoc* – and does not significantly affect Kim's analysis.

[10] Kim goes on to show that in some cases the implication in (7) can be strengthened to a biconditional.

(7) above), but it retains heuristic power, because something like the Cournot problem prevents the practicable application of molecular biology to some phenomena in which Mendelian genetics is relatively successful.

Can a similar argument be applied to economics? I do not think so. Rosenberg (1992, p. 129) himself has argued that the intentional character of microeconomics limits its scientific development: microeconomic "theory's prediction and explanation of the choices of individuals [cannot] exceed the precision and accuracy of commonsense explanations and predictions with which we have all been familiar since prehistory." In fact, macroeconomic explanation and prediction is not only often better, but may have more scope for improvability. An electric supplier could not say when Mary Smith will switch on her oven, but it may know pretty precisely how many kilowatts it must supply at a given time, based on an aggregate analysis of past behavior. Insurance companies know that whether an individual is, say, a smoker or obese matters probabilitistically to his chances of dying. But the company would go broke trying to predict individuals' precise dates of death.[11]

It is important to remember that it is not macroeconomic theory that supervenes on microeconomic theory, but macroeconomic reality that supervenes on microeconomic reality. The disabilities of microeconomic theory thus prove, at most, that there can be no automatic presumption that microeconomics is more basic, because more successful, and that macroeconomics is merely heuristic. The critical relationship is the reducibility in principle suggested by (7) above. To begin to undermine reducibility in the case of macroeconomics, it helps to note a crucial disanalogy with biology. Reduction appeals to biologists because it removes scientifically suspect teleological explanation common in evolutionary biology and other functional accounts. The aim of reduction in economics, however, is precisely the opposite: macroeconomics appears mechanical and dehumanized, and the point of the program of micro-foundations is reintroduce human decision-making as an explanatory element. The point is to recover intentionality.

Kim's analysis posits two levels of properties that are (semantically at least) distinct and then investigates how they must be related if one set is supervenient on the other. Intentionality at the microeconomic level undermines the distinctness of microeconomic properties from macroeconomic properties. Levy's argument (see section 1 above) that individual economic actors will invariably make reference to social wholes and aggregates is even more fundamental than he imagines. In evaluating

---

[11] Both these examples are repeated verbatim from Hoover (1995a).

the future individuals must form expectations about real prices and real quantities. Independently of the uncertainty of the future, the Cournot problem implies that it is impracticable to solve good-by-good, price-by-price, period-by-period planning problems in all their fine detail. The best that one is practically able to do is to work with aggregates. The information on which these are based is fundamentally monetary. Economic actors must use estimates and expectations of the general price level and real interest rates to form any practical assessment of their situations.

Hayek (1979, p. 62) writes:

> in the social sciences it is necessary to draw a distinction between those ideas which are *constitutive* of the phenomena we want to explain and the ideas which either we ourselves or the very people whose actions we have to explain may have formed *about* these phenomena and which are not the cause of, but theories about, the social structures.

What Levy's argument demonstrates is that Hayek is mistaken, that how people theorize about the economy *is* constitutive of macroeconomic phenomena.[12] Since people cannot theorize about certain sorts of phenomena without appealing to macroeconomic categories – that are not themselves reducible to microeconomic categories – the Cournot problem introduces analytical constraints, not only in practice, but in principle as well. The distinctiveness of the properties at the microeconomic and macroeconomic levels is breached, undermining Kim's analysis, because complete characterizations of the microeconomic must include characterizations of the macroeconomic on the part of individual agents.

To challenge the applicability to economics of the reductionism in principle, implicit in Kim's analysis and in Rosenberg's application of it to biology, does not challenge the notion that macroeconomics supervenes on microeconomics. Kim's analysis is epistemological: it argues that there must be laws that would permit us to draw connections between the micro and macro levels. The point here is ontological: even though macroeconomics cannot be reduced to microeconomics as the program of microfoundations suggests, the elements of macroeconomics could not exist without the substrate of microeconomic individuals.

---

[12] In contrast to Hayek, his fellow Austrian-school economist Mises (1943, p. 252) argues that knowledge of economic theory can prevent the mistaken investments that fuel the business cycle.

4 Two arguments for the reality of macroeconomics

So far we have argued that the ontological status of macroeconomic entities is problematic in the sense that, like other entities posited by scientific theories, they are not part of our commonsense ontic furniture. Furthermore, the nature of the relationship through which the elements of macroeconomics supervene on the elements of microeconomics precludes direct reduction of the macroeconomic to the microeconomic, even in principle. If macroeconomic entities exist, they cannot be said therefore to exist only derivatively, despite their supervenience on microeconomic entities. It remains to argue directly for the existence of macroeconomic entities.

The first argument is based on the argument from manipulability championed by Ian Hacking (1983, esp. pp. 22–4): "If you can spray them, then they are real." Hacking argues that convincing evidence of the reality of the electron is found in experiments aimed at detecting the existence of free quarks, in which niobium balls are charged by "spraying" them with electrons. The general point is that an entity defined by a scientific theory has real existence when procedures that are best understood as using the entity referred to by the theory as a tool to manipulate other parts of the world, such as in laboratory experiments. I take this argument to be related to the "no-miracles" argument for the reality of scientific entities.[13] The best explanation of why theories are predictively successful, including successfully predicting the consequences of using them to design experimental or engineering manipulations of the world is that the entities posited by them in fact exist – anything else would be an inexplicable miracle.

It is common to denigrate the empirical success of economics (see e.g., Rosenberg 1992, pp. 18, 56, 112, 238, *passim*). It is true that economics does not have the precision of physics or chemistry, although it is less clearly inferior to meteorology, geology, climatology, and parts of biology – to name just a few of the less exact, but nevertheless scientific disciplines. The reputation of economics for predicting poorly arises partly because people seek unconditional forecasts ("what will happen tomorrow?") while economic theories typically predict only conditionally

[13] Mäki (1996, section 6) argues that the no-miracles argument and other arguments from manipulability cannot be successfully applied to economics, even if they apply to physical sciences. (There may, of course, be other arguments – and Mäki supplies some – for existential beliefs about economic entities.) The essence of my position is that *macro*economics shares characteristics with physical sciences that microeconomics *may* not.

("tomorrow X will happen if Y happens"). Quantified economic relations are at best locally stable: the precise estimate of the price elasticity of demand for Volvos changes with changes in the range of alternative brands and models, with changes in the proportion of academics to the total population, and with changes in other background conditions. Nevertheless, qualitatively stable relations are well established: e.g., demand curves slope down (i.e., when the price of Volvos rises, sales of Volvos fall). And there is often enough local stability that useful quantitative assessments are possible. Can irreducible macroeconomic aggregates be manipulated as well?

The answer seems to be clearly yes. Consider the following example. Almost every macroeconomic theory predicts that sufficiently large expansions of government expenditure will change (probably increase) nominal GDP and the general level of prices.[14] Different theories differ in their precise understanding of the mechanisms. Similarly, no macroeconomic theory disputes the ability of the Federal Reserve to use its ability to supply or remove reserves from the banking system to set the level of the Federal funds rate (the rate at which one commerical bank borrows from another overnight). The empirical evidence in support of these propositions is also overwhelming. Now consider two irreducibly macroeconomic aggregate entities: the real rate of interest (i.e., the market rate of interest less the percentage change in the aggregate price level (p)) and the yield curve (an aggregate relation portrayed as a graph of market interest rates against time to maturity of the associated bonds). Both the real rate of interest and the yield curve are synthetic aggregates and both are entities with causal powers in some economic theories. Every macroeconomic theory that I know predicts that actions that increase the general price level or the Federal funds rate will shift the yield curve upwards in the short-run. And, at least if the changes are unanticipated, increases in the general price level will reduce the level of the real interest rate. The empirical evidence for these effects is overwhelming, and indeed are easily confirmed by anyone willing to read the *Wall Street Journal* regularly for a month. Just like the electron, some macroeconomic aggregates not only can be controlled, but can be used to manipulate other macroeconomic aggregates.

The second argument is related to the first. Nowak (1980) and others

---

[14] The caveat "almost" and the ambiguity over the direction both hinge on the financial market. If the interest elasticity of money demand were zero (empirically a false supposition), there would be no change in prices; if the substitution effect on money demand induced by an increase in government bonds financing an increase in government expenditure were large enough (again unlikely), the price level could fall.

have argued that the principal method of constructing scientific theories is *idealization*. Nowak's (1980, p. 29) paradigm idealization statement is:

> If $G(x)$ and $p_1(x) = 0$ and . . . $p_{k-1} = 0$ and $p_k = 0$ then
> $F(x) = f_k(H_1(x), \ldots, H_n(x))$ $\qquad$ (8)

where H_i ($i = 1, \ldots, n$) denote *primary factors* and the p_j ($j = 1, \ldots, k$) denote *secondary factors*. An idealized theory is one which picks out the primary factors by setting the secondary factors to extreme values: zero or, represented here, without loss of generality, as $p_j = 0$.

Were $G(x)$ a known and exhaustively complete theory of the phenomenon within its explanatory range such that one could accurately specify each of the secondary factors that were set aside, then the distinction between primary and secondary factors would in fact be be unclear, because our complete knowledge of $G(x)$ would allow us for example to replace (8) with

> If $G(x)$ and $H_1(x) = 0$ and . . . $H_{n-1} = 0$ and $H_n = 0$ then
> $F(x) = f_n(p_1(x), \ldots, p_k(x))$. $\qquad$ (9)

In the case of either (8) or (9), releasing the idealizing conditions ($p_k = 0$ or $H_i = 0$) allows us to recover the complete theory, $G(x)$. Idealization has been reduced to a fancy name for an arbitrary selection of *ceteris paribus* conditions or to a formal nesting relationship for theories.

Hoover (1994) argues that in an empirical context, the method of idealization has power only if we recognize that not all of the idealizing conditions can be explicitly stated. The claim to distinguish between primary and secondary factors is then a claim that the primary factors are the *essence* of the matter. Idealized theories thus aim to identify, isolate and relate the real essences or causally effective capacities of economic reality.[15] The success of such an idealized theory then amounts to an ontological claim for its primary factors.

That Keynesian macrocecononomics could be cast as an idealization that employs macroeconomic aggregates essentially is beyond doubt. The

---

[15] Cartwright (1983, 1989) argues for realism with respect to causal capacities, but for an instrumentalist interpretation of scientific laws. Laws are either literally false ("the laws of physics lie" – to quote the title of Cartwright's (1983) earlier book) or are merely *phenomenal* – i.e., atheoretic regularities. Hoover (1994a) argues that if idealized models represent essences, then phenomenal laws are necessary bridges to take the place of those secondary factors that cannot in fact be identified explicitly. Mäki (1992) argues that Nowak conflates idealization with *isolation*, which comprises idealization, omission, and other techniques. To apply Mäki's account we would have to say that the omission of secondary factors amounts to a claim that retained primary factors are the essence of the matter.

major competitor to Keynesian macroeconomics today, new classical macroeconomics, trades on an explicitly microfoundational approach. There is, however, less here than meets the eye. The currently most popular new classical macroeconomic theory is embodied in the real-business-cycle model (see Hoover 1995b and forthcoming). The proponents of this representative-agent model would like it to be interpreted as an idealization from a complete Walrasian general equilibrium model of the economy in which distributional issues are idealized out of the model so that what remains is a one-agent, one-good, one-price representation of the economy. This would work if the Walrasian model (the analogue for $G(x)$ in Nowak's schema) were both true and known in detail. At least the second condition is false, which undermines the evidential basis for the first condition.

Empirically, far from isolating a microeconomic core, real-business-cycle models, as with other representative-agent models, use macroeconomic aggregates for their testing and estimation. Thus, to the degree that such models are successful in explaining empirical phenomena, they point to the ontological centrality of macroeconomic and not microeconomic entities. The appeal to the methods of microeconomics does not in this case amount to the successful implementation of the program of microfoundations, for they are but the simulacrum of microeconomics. The relationship between models that are microeconomic in form and their macroeconomic empirical implementation is metaphorical. The nature of metaphorical connection deserves futher exploration. It is enough for the present purpose to understand that, at the empirical level, even the new classical representative-agent models are fundamentally macroeconomic in content.

5 The contingency of economic reality

Unless one is committed to a certain kind of apriorism, then what we judge to be real depends on experience, on the nature of our theorizing, and the success of our scientific and everyday practices. The best guess of a scientist in 1789 would have been that phlogiston was real, although most scientists would today say that it is not. The point is not that reality is constituted by our theorizing: for a realist it is not only the case that phlogiston is not real today, but that it *was* not real in 1789. The point is rather that our knowing whether or not something is real is a scientific fact like other scientific facts, which are established by argument and evidence, and about which we may be mistaken. There is, therefore, no timeless, certain answer to the question in the title of this paper. What I have sought to show in this essay is that the nature of microeconomics and macroeconomics – as they are currently practiced – undermines the prospects for a reduction of macroeconomics to microeconomics. Both microeconomics and macroeconomics must refer to irreducible macroeconomic entities. These macroeconomic entities occupy ontologically independent places in economic theory. To the degree that such theories are empirically successful, the best account of these macroeconomic entities is that they are real.

References

Blaug, Mark (1992) *The Methodology of Economics: Or How Economists Explain*, 2nd edition, Cambridge: Cambridge University Press.

Boland, Lawrence (1979) *The Foundations of Economic Method*, London: George Allen and Unwin.

Cartwright, N. (1983) *How the Laws of Physics Lie*, Oxford: Clarendon Press.

(1989) *Nature's Capacities and Their Measurement*, Oxford: Clarendon Press.

Cournot, Augustin (1838/1927) *Researches into the Mathematical Principles of the Theory of Wealth*, Nathaniel T. Bacon (trans.), New York: Macmillan.

Ellis, Brian (1966) *Basic Concepts of Measurement*, Cambridge: Cambridge University Press.

Friedman, Milton (1955) "Leon Walras and His Economic System: A Review Article," *American Economic Review*, 45(5): 900–9.

Hacking, Ian (1983) *Representing and Intervening: Introductory Topics in the Philosophy of the Natural Sciences*, Cambridge: Cambridge University Press.

Hahn, Frank H (1965) "On Some Problems of Proving the Existence of Equilibrium in a Monetary Economy," in Frank H. Hahn and F. P. R. Brechling (eds.), *The Theory of Interest Rates*, London: Macmillan.

Hayek, Friedrich von (1979) *The Counter-revolution of Science: Studies in the Abuse of Reason*, Indianapolis: Liberty Press.

Hoover, Kevin D. (1988) *The New-classical Macroeconomics: A Skeptical Inquiry*, Oxford: Blackwell.

(1994) "Six Queries About Idealization in an Empirical Context," *Poznan Studies in the Philosophy of Science and the Humanities*, 38: 43–53.

(1995a) "Why Does Methodology Matter for Economics? A Review Article," *Economic Journal*, 105: 715–34.

(1995b) "Facts and Artifacts: Calibration and the Empirical Assessment of Real Business Cycle Models," *Oxford Economic Papers*, 47: 24–44.

(forthcoming) "Quantitative Evaluation of Idealized Models in the New Classical Macroeconomics," in Nancy Cartwright and Martin Jones (eds.), *Correcting the Model. Poznan Studies in the Philosophy of Science and the Humanities*, Amsterdam: Rodopi.

Janssen, Maarten (1993) *Microfoundations: A Critical Inquiry*, London: Routledge.

Keynes, John Maynard (1936) *The General Theory of Employment Interest and Money*, London: Macmillan.

Kim, Jaegwon (1978) "Supervenience and Nomological Incommensurables," *American Philosophical Quarterly*, 15(2): 149–56.

Kirman, A. P. (1992) "Whom or What Does the Representative Agent Represent?" *Journal of Economic Perspectives*, 6(2): 117–36.

Lachmann, Ludwig (1976) "On the Central Concept of Austrian Economics: Market Process," in Edwin G. Dolan (ed.), *The Foundations of Austrian Economics*, Kansas City, MO: Sheed and Ward.

Levy, David M. (1985) "The Impossibility of a Complete Methodological Individualist: Reduction When Knowledge is Imperfect," *Economics and Philosophy*, 1(1): 101–8.

Lucas, Robert E., Jr (1987) *Models of Business Cycles*, Oxford: Blackwell.

Mäki, Uskali (1992) "On the Method of Isolation in Economics," *Poznan Studies in the Philosophy of Science and the Humanities*, 25: 289–310.

—— (1996) "Scientific Realism and Some Peculiarities of Economics," in R. S. Cohen et al. (eds.), *Realism and Anti-Realism in the Philosophy of Science*, Boston Studies in the Philosophy of Science, Vol. 169, Dordrecht: Kluwer, pp. 425–45.

Marshall, A. (1920) *Principles of Economics: An Introductory Volume*, 8th edn, London: Macmillan.

Mises, Ludwig von (1943) " 'Elastic Expectations' and the Austrian Theory of the Trade Cycle," *Economica*, ns 10(3): 251–2.

—— (1949/1966) *Human Action: A Treatise on Economics*, 3rd edn, Chicago: Henry Regnery.

Nowak, L. (1980) *The Structure of Idealization: Towards a Systematic Interpretation of the Marxian Idea of Science*, Dordrecht: Reidel.

Robbins, L. (1935) *An Essay on the Nature and Significance of Economic Science*, London: Macmillan.

Rosenberg, Alexander (1985) *The Structure of Biology*, Cambridge: Cambridge University Press.

—— (1992). *Economics: Mathematical Politics or Science of Diminishing Returns?* Chicago and London: Chicago University Press.

Samuelson, Paul A. and Ryuzo Sato (1984) "Unattainability of Integrability and Definiteness Conditions in the General Case of Demand for Money and Goods," *American Economic Review*, 74(4): 588–604.

Weintraub, E. Roy (1979) *Microfoundations. The Compatability of Microeconomics and Macroeconomics*, Cambridge: Cambridge University Press.

13 The possibility of economic objectivity

DON ROSS AND FRED BENNETT

Among philosophers of science, the phrase 'positive economics' is apt, these days, to produce snickers. Economists tend to be less embarrassed by the term – Lipsey and Crystal, after all, use the phrase as the title of their bestselling introductory text – but only slightly. In a 1994 paper, Samuel Weston defends the utility of a positive/normative distinction in economics, but in a strikingly tepid way. He concedes the impossibility of 'a purely positive, that is, value-free or ethically neutral economics' (p. 5), but argues, following Machlup (1969), that economists should preserve the concept of *relative* normativity in order to encourage self-consciousness about the more overtly ideological influences on their theories and policy recommendations. For Weston, the positive/normative distinction is based on purely pragmatic considerations, and is to be drawn *despite* the fact that it has no sound epistemological or ontological basis. This sort of defence of the distinction has polemical import only against the most extreme denial of the possibility of objectivity. Such extreme denial, like most forms of philosophical scepticism, must be motivated on the basis of highly general epistemological theses. Engaging it, therefore, is unlikely to turn on any issues that arise from within the practice of economics, or of any other special science. This is illustrated by Weston's own argument, much of which could be applied with only minor amendments to any science that suggests practical advice – which is to say, to any science at all.

In the following discussion, we wish to provide a much stronger defence of the possibility of positive economics, from a perspective that sees the challenges to economic objectivity as arising from, and needing to be answered with regard to, particular problems that arise within economics. This does not mean that broad philosophical issues are to be bypassed. Indeed, some quite general problems, properly called 'metaphysical,' will be the focus of much of our attention. Furthermore, we expect that our defence of positive economics, if successful, could serve as a model for a defence of the possibility of objectivity in a number of other sciences. However, our argument will not be a reply to general epistemological scepticism, because we take that position to be unanswerable – and uninteresting, just because neither the thesis itself nor any attempted refutations of it depend on knowing anything specific about the sciences to which it is meant to be applied. If general epistemological scepticism is true, then inquiry should simply stop; but since we could never be sure that scepticism is true, we are best off continuing to pursue scientific inquiry on the assumption that it is not. This answer will not suffice, however, against less sweeping sceptical theses advanced on the basis of problems arising within specific sciences. Among recent critics, Rosenberg (1991) and Dupré (1993) have advanced precisely such theses concerning economics.

Weston's paper will serve as a useful foil for getting the discussion started. He considers four grounds for supposing that value-free economics is impossible. First, there is the fact that all scientific activity presupposes that truth-seeking is valuable activity in the first place, even in circumstances where this activity threatens to undermine other valued ends and pursuits. Second, because economics arises from recognition of the fact of scarcity, economic theory is almost always directly relevant to questions of distribution, and these questions are, in turn, among the most fundamental issues of political and moral debate. Third, certain assumptions of value are built into sciences by virtue of the fact that their central terms are irremediably infected with value-leaden connotations. This is particularly true in economics, which inherited much of its basic vocabulary from utilitarian and proto-utilitarian political philosophy.[1] Fourth, economists justify much of their activity by reference to the policy advice that they are expected to give; and since there is no such thing as a distributively neutral economic policy, any research directed towards producing policy includes a normative element.

Let us consider the extent to which these four problems genuinely undermine the possibility of positive economics. The first and the third are of least interest, since they are not based on distinctive aspects of economics, and can be applied with equal justification to any science.

---

[1] 'Utility', which is arguably the single most fundamental concept of contemporary economics, is the best example of a term which has passed into the discipline through political philosophy, undergoing several substantial changes in meaning over the course of this history (see LaCasse and Ross 1991; Ross 1999). Weston, citing Myrdal (1954, 1958), gives as examples of value-leaden terms 'economic integration', 'productivity', 'equilibrium', 'balance', and 'adjustment'. The point of calling such terms 'value-leaden' should be evident: 'adjustments' are naturally assumed to be for the better, and to call something 'productive' or 'balanced' is implicity to offer approval of it.

This may not seem immediately to be true of the third complaint, which directs our attention to the fact that economics, unlike most sciences, takes as fundamental many terms which have overtly normative uses outside of their technical context. Notice, however, that given Weston's conception of the pragmatic point of the positive/normative distinction, this should make *relative* objectivity *easier* to achieve in economics than in other sciences. If the terminology used in, say, biology, is infected with assumptions of value to which its users are socially conditioned to be blind (as feminist critics such as Harding (1986) have charged), then, on Weston's reading, this should leave them epistemically worse off than economists, who can scarcely be similarly unaware of the normative relevance of concepts derived from moral philosophy. Among those who attack scientific objectivity on the basis of some version or near relative of the Sapir-Whorf hypothesis, almost none imagines that any science could be rendered objective by being purged of normative terms, since they hold such purging to be impossible. The best one can do, according to such views, is maximize self-awareness of the normative assumptions built into and reinforced by one's language. Therefore, it is hard to imagine why we should think that the use in economics of overtly normative terms constitutes a *special* challenge to its objectivity.

Weston's second and fourth problems do seem to direct our attention to distinctive aspects of economics. The two problems are closely related. Indeed, they may be seen as expressions of a single, slightly more general problem: to what extent does the individuation of an economic domain in the first place result from concerns with distributional fairness (or the lack of it) and the need for policies that regulate and influence distribution? If one believes that there would be no domain for economics in the absence of certain normative interests, then one is likely to suppose that economists' selection of problems as meriting their attention will reflect those interests, especially where it is expected that study of a problem will eventuate in policy recommendations. Here, indeed, is a fundamental challenge to objectivity. To say that a particular aspect of the world is *imposed* on it from an interest-driven perspective, rather than *discovered*, seems conceptually equivalent to saying that the aspect in question is not an objective feature of the world.

In preparing this issue for examination, we must proceed carefully with the distinction between imposition and discovery. Saying that something would not be an objective feature of the world if it were accessible only from an interest-driven perspective is not equivalent to claiming that in order to be objective, a feature would have to be evident to investigators who cared about nothing in particular. Such investigators appear to be impossible, since investigation must be motivated and organized by some set of interests or other. This point warns us against taking the question before us as an historical one. It is quite plausible to think that had our environment never presented people with scarcity, it would never have occurred to anyone that there might be such things as economic generalizations. But if this were the sceptic's point, then it would fail, after all, to tell in any special way against economics. There would likely be no science of geology if we were intelligent clouds of dust particles living in open space.[2] If the sceptic's concern is to offer an interesting basis for suspicion about the *possibility* of positive economics, then she must identify objectivity with perspective-independence *in principle*. What does 'perspective-independence in principle' mean? Suppose that we identify C as the set of cognizers whose perceptual capacities and neural complexity (biological or artificial) permits recognition of the patterns in data that would be generalized over by the set of scientific theories 'in the limit' (i.e., the set of scientific theories that would be accepted if science were finished. The idea goes back at least to Pearce; for a clear refinement of the notion, see Friedman (1979).) A science fails to describe a set of objective features in the world, the sceptic might then say, if its domain *could not* be consistently individuated from outside the perspective of some set of cognizers smaller than C. Interpreting the sceptic this way does not, at least prima facie, saddle her with an unreasonably heavy burden of argument, to judge from the sorts of positions on questions of fundamental ontology that have been popular among philosophers. Reductionists, in the venerable sense of Oppenheim and Putnam (1958), should be comfortable with this conception of objectivity, since such a conception seems to be a necessary part of the motivation for reductionism in the first place. As for those – the majority these days – who are non-reductionists about the special sciences, most are functionalists of one sort or another. Though a functionalist about the objects of quantification of a given special science S denies the reducibility of S on epistemic grounds, most functionalists seek to preserve the variety of objectivity defined above for S by endorsing one sort or another of supervenience hypothesis (see Kim 1989; Marras 1993) about the properties featuring in S's generalizations. The discussions in Savellos and Yalçin (1995) reveal an array of competing notions about what supervenience precisely amounts to, but we need not concern ourselves with their differences here; the point, for now, is that all supervenience hypotheses are motivated by the concern that a given putatively autonomous special science inherits in-principle objectivity from a specifiable

---

[2] The counterfactual here seems to us a bit *less* implausible than the idea that intelligence could arise in the absence of the selection pressures produced by scarcity.

relation of either causal (though accidental) or nomic co-variance between the properties it recognizes and those recognized at a base level with respect to which in-principle objectivity is already presumed. It might be objected that appeals to supervenience are in fact motivated, as was Oppenheim and Putnam's sketch of reduction, by reference to concern with the unity of science, rather than with objectivity. However, the physicalism presumed by both projects is itself best motivated by the conviction that if anything exists objectively, it is physical properties and objects. Furthermore, functionalists of the sort who are most interested in supervenience generally believe that unification of the sciences is an unlikely or impossible ambition in any case. In general, then, most attempts to show that the objects featured in the domain of some special science are not part of objective reality generally appeal, at least implicity, to the idea that they neither reduce to nor supervene upon any types of objects which the sceptic does take to be real. (The objects with respect to which this sort of debate has been loudest among philosophers are, over the past couple of decades, the propositional attitude concepts used in the generalizations of psychology.)

The foregoing remarks might suggest the following conclusion where economics is concerned. To show that economics tracks objectively existing objects or processes, one would have to show that the properties in terms of which these objects or processes are individuated either reduce to or supervene upon other properties whose objective existence is less contentious. Note that the base properties need not be physical; if microeconomic properties ultimately reduce to or supervene upon physical properties, they presumably do so by way of psychological properties. Now, of these two possibilities, reduction or supervenience, only one actually seems to be a live option. If one *presumes* that economics tracks an objective domain, than few sciences offer more compelling instances of the problems with reductionism. To borrow an example from Fodor (1974), it seems inconceivable that the economic type 'monetary exchange' could turn out to be coextensive – let alone *nomically* coextensive, as required by reductionism – with any physical, or, for that matter, psychological type. The same can be said of virtually all of the types to which macroeconomic generalizations, and axioms in microeconomic theories, make reference. The objectivity of economics thus appears to be straightforwardly incompatible with reductionism. This, in turn, leaves us with a nicely sharp central question: does the objectivity of economics depend on the claim that economic properties supervene on physical or (more plausibly) psychological properties?

Many philosophers hold views that would lead them to answer 'yes' to this question. This seems, for example, to be an essential part of the basis for the scepticism about the possibility of economic objectivity expressed by Dupré (1993). Economics, according to Dupré (1993, p. 260), is contaminated from the beginning by normative assumptions because the types to which it seeks to assign properties – unemployment being his example – are invented rather than discovered, in the sense that the typology is imposed on the world by economists, rather than found in it, as a result of ideological or more narrowly political motivations. Dupré's second claim does not derive from a review of case studies in macro-economics. Rather, it is an application of a book-length metaphysical argument to the effect that nothing like unemployment *could* be discovered. A crucial part of this argument is a case against the claim that special sciences such as economics are (as it were) 'metaphysically legitimated' by appeals to supervenience hypotheses (pp. 96–8). I will not review Dupré's particular criticism of the plausibility of establishing supervenience claims, because I find it unpersuasive. However, I am in agreement with him, and with Kim (1989), that supervenience is less an alternative to reduction than a refinement of it. More importantly, philosophers have not yet provided an adequate formulation of the claimed asymmetry of the supervenience relation (i.e., the assumption that mental properties should depend on physical properties in some way, but that physical properties should not, in general, depend on mental properties) (Marras 1993). The fact that we can therefore not yet be said to fully understand the concept is good grounds for hoping that the possibility of economic objectivity does not *depend* on our being able to show that economic properties are supervenient. Finally, and most decisively, attempting to ground economic objectivity in the claim that economic properties supervene on psychological ones would commit us to a cure worse than the disease. Since the fundamental axioms of microeconomic theory are, famously, utterly unrealistic as generalizations about individual behaviour and motivational structures, commitment to seeking a supervenience base for microeconomics in psychology would entail destroying microeconomics in order to save it. And where else could one even *imagine* looking for a supervenience base for micro-economics?

The view that objectivity in special sciences requires supervenience rests, we contend, on a failure to appreciate that reduction and super-venience do not constitute an exclusive disjunction of routes to objectivity. In earlier work (Ross 1995; Ross and LaCasse 1995), one of us has argued, with direct reference to economic examples, that economics should be viewed as studying what Dennett (1991) has called 'real patterns'. We do not have space to reiterate that argument here. What we wish mainly to do in the present discussion is to provide a fuller account than Dennett has done of the sense in which real patterns exist objectively.[3] This will enable us to articulate the most reasonable sense in which economic objectivity is possible and to explain why philosophers have so frequently supposed that it is not possible. We will then offer some examples of economic patterns which seem to us to be undeniably real in the sense that we will defend.

Dennett's 'Real Patterns' is his mature response to the charge, levelled from many quarters over the years, that his view on the ontology of intentional states such as beliefs is a form of instrumentalism. Specifically, Dennett holds that intentional states are *ascribed* to certain sorts of systems – intentional systems – in the course of explaining and predicting their behaviour. Since intentional states are thus attributed properties of whole systems according to Dennett, his view contradicts the most common sort of realism about beliefs and desires, according to which they are either nomically coextensive with, or supervene upon, particular neural states or disjunctions of neural states. To many, this has appeared to involve him in a denial of realism about intentional states altogether; they seem to emerge as at best idealizations, like frictionless planes, or at worst mere fictions whose invention serves predictive purposes, rather as epicycles do in Ptolemaic astronomy. Dennett's early denials of this charge (e.g., Dennett 1979) usually seemed unconvincing, and the reason for this, we can now see, is that he in fact *cannot* accommodate his view of intentional states to any of the traditional varieties of realism. What is needed is a *non*-traditional variety of realism, and this Dennett duly sets out to provide in 'Real Patterns'.

Before beginning the account of real patterns, it is worth drawing attention to the similarity between the polemical situation that called forth Dennett's paper and the controversy over the status of economics with which we are concerned here. From the time of his earliest work, Dennett has talked of intentional properties as emerging when the intentional *stance* is assumed towards a system whose behaviour exhibits too much differential sensitivity to its environment to permit it be tracked at the level of physical causes and effects. It is this reference to stances, more than anything else, that has made the charge of instrumentalism against Dennett appear inescapable. He seems to be admitting, from the outset, that intentional states exist only under a certain *perspective* that can be taken towards ethological phenomena. Now, the charge against economic objectivity advanced by Dupré and others, and

---

[3] The full presentation of the relationship between our extension of Dennett's view and Dennett's own self-interpretation will appear in Ross (2000) and in Dennett's (2000) reply.

accepted by Weston, is essentially similar: that the objects of economics also emerge only under a certain perspective, in this case one that is motivated by a set of socio-political values. In effect, the entire discipline of economics is accused of resting on instrumentalism. This accusation gains credence from the fact that many economists, following Friedman (1953), have explicitly endorsed instrumentalism as an account of their methodology, failing, apparently, to recognize that this move entails a surrender of their ambition to be engaged in positive science. In light of this, it is clearly worthwhile asking whether Dennett's way out of his dilemma can also serve as the basis for a defence of positive economics. We contend that it can.

We will now reconstruct Dennett's idea of a real pattern. The word 'reconstruct' should be emphasized here. Dennett provides a host of examples to demonstrate the utility of granting existence to patterns of a certain sort, but he does not provide explicit criteria for the reality of a pattern. These must be arrived at by induction on his examples, and on the basis of his remarks about the conditions under which reference to a pattern is necessary in order to track some data. We will work from the idea of a pattern in general, and then inquire as to what properties a pattern must have if it is not to be shaved away by Occam's razor. Patterns, let us say, are organizations of data from perspectives, where the structural relations among the data that a pattern recognizes are sufficiently stable over time to permit some process or processes to be tracked from the relevant perspective. Patterns so defined come cheap; the world teems with them. This is not sufficient reason in itself, however, for denying reality to them. In deciding whether we *should* regard a given pattern as real, the crucial question, as noted above, is this: is it something that is imposed, on the data, or is it more accurately viewed as being discovered in the data? In the case of some patterns – for example, the grand 'cycles' in human affairs that certain sorts of historians are disposed to construct, or macroeconomic cycles of the kind exemplified by 'Kondratiev waves' – scepticism (which is maintained by the majority of historians in the first case, and by the majority of economists in the second) rests largely on intuitions to the effect that the patterns are imposed on the data rather than discovered in it.[4] Is this intuition reliable? Consider the second example. Kondratiev waves are fishy scientific objects because they are a function of a periodicity choice that is arbitrary. We know, as matters of mathematical fact, both that an infinite number of periodicities are available for the organization of data

---

[4] As noted above, this is the position maintained by Dupré (1993) with respect to *all* of the objects of economics.

in a series, and that, given this infinity, regularities will appear in some of them even if the series is generated by a chaotic physical process. To predict a regularity given a previously untested periodicity and then find it there is epistemically impressive; but to merely report discovered regularities is not, and does not in itself justify the construction of theories to explain them. Notice, however, how natural it is here to speak of 'mere *discoveries*'. Our intuitions are correct in their judgement that something is 'imposed' on the data by long-wave theory, but it is not the waves themselves that are imposed. After all, once one has chosen the periodicity and the variables of measurement, the question of the shape of the curve through the data is a factual one. Kondratiev waves *are* 'in' the data and are *not* imposed on them; what is imposed is the assumption that tracking these waves is of epistemic significance.

If these reflections lead us to admit the reality of patterns, however, then we appear to be stuck with an infinite number of real objects. This does not represent a direct violation of Occam's principle. That principle – or, at least, the version of it that is a justified part of scientific rationality – does not concern the number of entities that we hold there to be; rather, it concerns the need for limits on recognizing the existence of particular posited entities. (In its most modest version, it is simply the acknowledgement that any ontological principle that excludes *nothing* is worthless.) The Kondratiev wave through the data to the present time is not posited but found. However, part of what is implied in saying that the discovery is without epistemic significance is that we have no good reason to suppose that the pattern will continue through the next period in the series. In this respect, the wave violates projectibility requirements on the objects of scientific generalizations.[5] This was always true of it, despite the fact someone using it to predict the future before the most recently completed period would have been fortuitously right. Here, finally, is a reason for denying reality to the pattern, and holding it to be a mere artifact: there is not, and never has been, a perspective from which the pattern is stable.

At least two notions employed in the above analysis require clarification: we must say what we mean by 'projectibility', and explain our appeal to 'perspectives'. Let us begin with projectibility. We are persuaded by the arguments of Cartwright (1983) that sciences do not produce true nomic generalizations; we thus cannot define projectibility

---

[5] Of course, we do not wish to have to say that only patterns that continue to be instantiated were ever real. Projectibility to a next unanalysed case in some logically structured sequence of cases is the relevant necessary (though not, as we shall see, sufficient) condition here.

in terms of laws. Cartwright (1989) has also argued, drawing on a rich analysis of the history of econometrics, that the generalizations implicit in privileging some curves through data over others are parasitic on the identification of causal relations holding among particulars; generalizations are then summary approximations of the quantitative causal propensities of particulars that have been arranged into types. This helps us to refine our diagnosis of what is wrong with 'long-wave' theories in macroeconomics: they report mere correlations, unjustified by any suggestions, let alone evidence, as to what causal relations among particulars might explain the observed correlations in question. Note, however, that following Cartwright in denying that the generalizations produced by sciences are laws does not entail the conclusion that arriving at generalizations is not an important goal of sciences. Furthermore, it does not eliminate the significance of projectibility. We will discuss the appropriate range of the projectibility requirement in the course of explaining our reference to perspectives. As far as the notion itself is concerned, we shall simply say this: a generalization is projectible just in case our discoveries of causal relations ground confidence in, and help to explain, the prediction that it will apply approximately to a (not necessarily infinite) run of future or counterfactual cases in which the relevant causal relations obtain.

We now expand on our reference to the role of perspectives in identifying real patterns. To 'track a real pattern' is simply to recover, in some encoding, the information instantiated in the pattern. Information must flow through channels between sources and receivers; hence, a perspective is simply the receiving end of an informational channel, that is, any point along the channel where noise (i.e., increased entropy) has not so degraded the information at the source that it has ceased to be recoverable. Where any scientific generalizations are concerned, the scope of existence claims must be wider than the actual world, since we do not want to restrict existence to patterns that contingently *occupied* perspectives have tracked or could track. On the other hand, the set of logically possible perspectives is too wide, since this will lead to a reality criterion that will exclude almost nothing. Let us say instead that what is relevant is the set of *physically possible* perspectives; put more precisely, the set of perspectives available in the possible worlds that are nearby according to physics. This is a very large set, to be sure, but it is not infinite, since it is restricted by physical limitations on information flow. There is, for example, no perspective from which an occupant can track events occurring outside its light-cone, nor a perspective from which an occupant can track patterns whose processing at speeds near that of light would require computational resources of unbounded size. Nor can information flow across singularities on the time-like dimension (e.g., the Big Bang) or a space-like dimension (e.g., black holes).

We are now ready to state a necessary condition on the reality of a pattern: if a pattern is real, then it must be recoverable from at least one physically possible perspective. This condition is clearly not sufficient, however. It fails to exclude Hegelian historical patterns or Kondratiev waves,[6] or such artifacts as the arbitrary conjunction of two stable patterns. Occam's principle *does* forbid our granting reality to patterns that are epistemically redundant. Therefore, we add a second necessary condition (which also incorporates our deflationary understanding of projectibility), this one partly based on a direct suggestion of Dennett's: if a pattern is real, then it must encode information about at least one other type of structure S where that encoding is more efficient, in information-theoretic terms, than the bit-map encoding of S, and where for at least one of the physically possible perspectives under which the pattern is projectible, there exists an aspect of S which cannot be tracked unless the encoding is recovered from the perspective in question. The two necessary conditions just stated are, we maintain, jointly sufficient for the reality of a pattern.

It should be clear that patterns defined according to the above criteria need not supervene on any 'lower-level' objects or sets of objects. Indeed, the very idea of 'levels' is undermined by identifying existence with pattern-reality. Since any informational encoding more efficient than a bit-map encoding involves compression at the receiving end of the channel, it is possible to recover various *aspects* – that is, a multiplicity of patterns   from any set of brute events that are reliably connected by causal relations. Thus a given set of events may be simultaneously tracked, to equally essential but different epistemic purposes, from a perspective that picks out (e.g.) psychological types as real patterns and a perspective that picks out economic types as real patterns. We may thus speak of 'an economic perspective' *without* implying that that perspective could be voluntarily discarded without loss of objective knowledge once an actual perceiver comes to occupy it. Nor does reference to 'sets of events' presume ultimate ontological bedrock; sets of events are themselves individuated as real patterns from some other perspective, perhaps

---

[6] We should make clear that, as naturalists, we do not presume that the reality of these patterns, or any others that are suggested, should be rejected on a priori grounds. We have already discussed our basis for suspicion about Kondratiev waves above. As for Hegelian historical patterns, the grounds for insisting that an ontological principle must sanction their exclusion are empirical: Hegel's data were notoriously selective, interpreted through the lens of a highly idiosyncratic metaphysics, and cannot be said to have stood the test of predictive success.

physics. The Dennettian view, as we have enlarged and interpreted it, is consistent with the primacy of physics in just the sense, we would argue, that the actual practice of science incorporates materialism: all sciences save mathematics and logic confine their attention to the class of physically possible worlds, and physics is the science that defines this class. This is why special sciences may not violate the generalizations of the physics contemporary with them, but no symmetrical limitation holds in the other direction.

We hope that the motivation for referring to the patterns satisfying the Dennettian criteria as 'real' is now clear: nothing subjective enters into determining which patterns meet the criteria. What else could possibly motivate a denial of reality to such patterns other than intuitions about physicalistic reductionism? But these intuitions are just what is at stake. They are called into question precisely by the fact that they render it deucedly hard to account for the patterns of explanation and theory development in special sciences such as psychology and economics. Naturalists should not require sciences to respect a priori philosophical preconceptions such as reductionism; the burden of argument must lie with the philosophical critics of scientific practice. Thus against both reductionists and those, like Dupré, who push particular sciences into defensive corners by assuming that only reduction or supervenience can legitimate them, it is sufficient to merely produce a viable alternative. The ontological view that we have derived from Dennett's suggestions, we contend, constitutes such an alternative.

While the above considerations seem to us to establish a very strong presumption in favour of the *possibility* of positive economics, one naturally wants to add something that suggests the *actuality* of positive economics. Only very timid claims can rest everything on burden-of-proof arguments. So what is needed are some motivations for believing that at least many objects of economics are real patterns. In other work (Ross 1994; Ross and LaCasse 1995), one of us has provided detailed examples of real patterns identified by microeconomics. Here, we will present what seem to us to be some real patterns which require organization of data in terms of macroeconomic patterns.

Could someone be said to be in good epistemic touch with the world if they could not track the type 'currency'? Perhaps it will be objected that currency is plausibly supervenient. But on what disjunction of physical tokens might currency *futures* supervene? What about the patterns that relate unemployment levels, inflation rates and the currency supply? Which tokens could even be *proposed* as possibly fleshing out their supervenience base? Of course, we do not suppose that we can get far in persuasion by means of rhetorical questions. We will thus revisit the problems with supervenience accounts after reviewing our examples. Their point is to suggest patterns that seem to have a deeply robust reality, based on the fact that near-certain disappointment awaits any economic manager who fails for long to track them, and that independent worldly pressures will force them to the attention of anyone whose personal values incline him to discount them, as Mr Chernomyrdin in Russia discovered during his time as Prime Minister, and as the tempermentally Marxist-inclined ANC government of South Africa has recognized since assuming power. Appeal to such cases will likely strike many readers as being suspiciously reminiscent of the sorts of 'no free lunch' aphorisms tossed glibly about by fiscally conservative politicians and in corporate boardrooms. The illustrations are not taken to establish our philosophical point *by themselves*, however. We should not coyly pretend that we are not sympathetic with many of the common aphorisms. But the aphorisms are typically uttered in a context of philosophical naïveté. If someone says that 'there is no free lunch', do they mean that there are no free lunches as a function of someone's or some instituional complex's policy preferences, or that there could not be free lunches as a matter of objective fact? Clearly, the ahporisms are often used in both senses. Our illustrations below are of patterns which plausibly exist independently of anyone's policy decisions. Having already presented, in the discussion above, a philosophical perspective under which the existence of such *types of* patterns can be maintained non-mysteriously, we now defend the existence of some *particular* patterns by applying a strategy familiar in the literature on scientific realism. It is excellent evidence that something is real if attempts to pretend that it isn't consistently lead to frustration, and if this 'kicking back' by the world occurs through a small set of causal mechanisms of which a comfortable level of theoretical understanding is available. It is highly relevant to our case for their independent reality that these patterns are not artifacts of a world whose distributional structures were designed according to a particular ideology; that is, macroeconomic patterns were not brought into being by economists. Finally, these are cases of patterns which, if *not* tracked, would leave us epistemically impoverished with respect to our disinterested understanding of the world. To reiterate an example one of us (Ross 1994) has discussed elsewhere, and with respect to which little or nothing of normative policy-relevance is at stake, one cannot understand important features of civilizations, such as ancient Greece and Rome, that themselves lacked the economic perspective unless one brings those economic patterns to bear on one's analysis of them. Without the economic perspective, for example, we would miss the contribution to the collapse of the Roman Empire made by the ruinous inflation that was caused by the continuous wage-extortion of the legions.

We shall, then, consider some examples of macroeconomic patterns whose reality is suggested by the fact that policy-makers, in pursuit of normatively based goals with respect to distributional fairness or other political considerations, must work *around* them, being unable – by virtue of their objective reality – to wish or legislate them away. We have deliberately chosen examples whose reality is controversial, in the sense that governments trying to acknowledge them must overcome pressures from publics or sectors that do *not* acknowledge their reality. Frequently, of course, governments have either failed to overcome these pressures, have themselves been victims of subjectivist fallacies, or perhaps have been fully aware of the reality of the patterns, but have felt obliged by social concerns to pursue policies which, to those with different normative agendas, make governments *appear* to be ignorant of economic reality. Clearly, however, some governments have simply denied economic reality. When Victor Geraschenko became Chair of Russia's Central Bank in 1992, he declared on television that 'It's impossible to apply economic theory to Russia' (Rosett 1993). As Hoover (1995, p. 732) says of this remark:

it rightly strikes most economists of widely differing political persuasions as absurd: whatever theory of the relationship of central bank behavior to hyper-inflation that they subscribe to, they think it applies as surely to Russia as to the United States, Germany or Papua New Guinea. Even Marx, who would place his economic analysis at the service of a particular political philosophy, does not see the truth of his analysis as depending on the truth of that philosophy.[7]

For reasons to be explained at the end of the paper, which result from the current state of macroeconomic theory, we will not be able to name the patterns whose existence is suggested by the non-malleability of macroeconomic forces for which we will be arguing. Our point, however, is that the goal of macroeconomic science should be to identify the patterns responsible for this non-malleability.

The failure of political leaders either to accept, or, in other cases, to act in the light of, the reality of macroeconomic patterns or changes in existing patterns has not been uncommon in diverse sorts of political systems. A commonly cited example is the response (or lack thereof) of fiscal policies throughout the world to changes which occurred in the international economy subsequent to the rapid rise in energy prices in 1973. N. Roulini and J. D. Sachs (1989) reviewed the fiscal performance of the major OECD countries in the fifteen years following the energy

---

[7] We are grateful to an anonymous referee for bringing this example to our attention.

shock and concluded that political considerations had been allowed to determine the economic response: 'We suggest that in several countries the slow rate at which the post '73 fiscal deficits were reduced resulted from difficulties of political management in coalition governments' (p. 903). But political reasons for ignoring real economic patterns are not limited to situations involving coalition governments; they are, perhaps, endemic to most normal democratic situations. Alesena and Tabellini (1987) argue that 'when political power alternates randomly between competing parties, each government will be tempted to leave a legacy of high debt for its successor, whose spending priorities it is not likely to share' (p. 909). With regard to the specific circumstances of the 1980s, Roulini and Sachs attribute 'the onset of large deficits to the growth slowdown and rise in unemployment after 1973, as well as the sharp rise in real interest rates after 1979' (1989, pp. 909–10). But it was not the change in the circumstances itself that caused the fiscal problem: it was the actual fiscal policies pursued in the face of the changed circumstances. Irrespective of the reasons for the policies chosen – failure to recognize the reality of the pattern, or, alternatively, the lack of the political capacity or will to choose different policies – the result was the same:

the growth of real government spending in the years just after 1973 was largely 'uncontrollable' in the sense that previous spending commitments based on pre-1973 economic conditions were politically difficult to adjust for several years . . . Another reason for induced deficits was the intentional application by some countries of Keynesian aggregate demand policies in the face of the growth slowdown . . . Right or wrong many governments are loath to raise taxes or lower government spending during a recession. (Alesena and Tabellini 1987, pp. 919–20)

Some countries – notably Germany, Japan and the UK among the major economies – did recognize the new reality and organized their fiscal affairs to stabilize the ratio of public debt to GDP; others did not.

A salient example of a country that did not adopt new policies in the face of the reality of changes in economic circumstances is Ireland. Even prior to the oil shock of 1973, Ireland had relied heavily on borrowed funds to support its development plans. As the OECD noted in 1971:

The key role of public investment in the development process has had a marked impact on public finance. With capital expenditure rising rapidly . . . a public sector deficit equivalent to some 10 to 15 per cent of GNP has had to be financed . . . In consequence, there has been a steady upward drift in outstanding national debt. (OECD 1971, p. 31)

But it was the failure to change policies in the face of the real change in the global economy that occurred in the 1970s which caused the problem to escalate. By 1975, the OECD indicated that deficits were being incurred to finance current consumption as well as capital expenditures: 'Reflecting the efforts to cushion the rise in unemployment last year and this, the public sector deficit has risen sharply to about 20 per cent of GNP' (OECD 1971, p. 5). By the early 1980s the problem had taken on sufficient magnitude that the Irish government acknowledged the need to address the fiscal imbalance; but action did not follow words. As the OECD wrote in 1982:

A principal objective of [Irish] governments since 1978 has been to tighten the setting of economic policy. But against the background of a depressed international economy the scale of retrenchment originally sought has not been achieved . . . the main explanation lies in overruns on current expenditure plans. (OECD 1982, p. 26)

The inevitable logic of the pattern took hold as debt service payments as a percentage of current expenditure rose from 17.9 in 1975 to almost 24 in 1982. The effect of compounding continued so that by the end of 1984 outstanding government debt amounted to 128 per cent of GNP with the foreign component comprising about 54 per cent of GNP (OECD 1985, p. 30). Aside from the effect on budgetary policy of the requirement to devote approximately one-third of government revenues to service the debt, the need to service the foreign component had gradually come to erase the original benefit of the foreign borrowing, namely, increased capital availability:

The initial impact of external government borrowing was to increase the resources available to the country to consume or to invest. As a result, high public sector deficits did not deprive the private sector of investible funds . . . From 1979 to 1981 new net external borrowing of the private sector minus relatively modest interest payments on earlier borrowing amounted to a cumulative 25 per cent of annual GNP (i.e. about 8 per cent each year), a hefty addition to the resources available to the country. (OECD 1985, p. 30)

Clearly, then, there were powerful incentives, shared by private and public interests alike, in accumulating capital through borrowing. However, wishes here were not determinants of economic reality, as Dupré might want us to suppose; they were thwarted by it. A policy which involved denial of the principle that an increase in a capital stock must be driven, at least at some point in the causal nexus, by increased efficiency or volume of production, ultimately ran aground because of that denial:

But maintaining a high level of borrowing for a number of years eventually means that debt service charges 'use up' all new borrowing . . . public sector net external borrowing in 1983 and 1984 did little more than finance interest charges on past debt . . . by 1984 interest payments exceeded net new external borrowing by 1 per cent of GNP. (OECD 1985, p. 31)

By this point, total government debt stood at approximately 128 per cent of GNP with the external portion representing 70 per cent of GNP; service of the external portion consumed 9 per cent of total export earnings. Driven by escalating interest costs, debt as a percentage of GNP reached 140 in 1986. By the early 1990s the debt situation limited the ability of the government to manage the economy, and was itself a destabilizing factor:

Heavy government indebtedness has the dual effect of making the public finances highly sensitive to movements in interest rates while also contributing to such movements, because it makes real interest rates more susceptible to attacks on the currency . . . Ireland remains rather vulnerable to the costs and risks of interest-rate cycles, and will probably have to continue to have to pay and risk premium on borrowing while the debt/GNP ratio remains substantially above the international amount. (OECD 1990/91, pp. 48–50)

The rest of the 1990s was dominated by the need to bring Ireland's debt to GNP ratio in line with the requirements of the new European Union Common Currency. This goal was, of course, achieved, and, happily, an Ireland that is no longer attempting to operate fiscal policy in defiance of economic reality now enjoys one of the highest rates of growth and of rising real incomes in the world.

The Irish example is a classic, and by no means unique, case of a government which, for whatever reason, acted as if the patterns of economics are not objective and are malleable in light of other political priorities. In the early stages, infrastructure development and economic growth probably were stimulated by the high level of borrowing – foreign borrowing in particular, which increased the country's ability to invest above the level its domestic savings would have supported. But ultimately, the basic pattern of compounding interest on debt limited the extent to which this policy could be pursued and eventually came to dictate much of the rest of the country's economic policy. Again, we should emphasize that our point is not that the policy choices of the Irish government were necessarily 'wrong' in any normative sense. Rather, we are simply using the Irish example to illustrate the point that certain real patterns exist at the macroeconomic level, and that these patterns will cause particular policies to have particular outcomes, regardless of the motivations of policy-makers.

As noted above, Ireland, at the time of the 1973 energy crisis, was particularly vulnerable to a debt shock by reason of its heavy state borrowing to drive publicly funded programmes of economic development. Such a policy has problems of its own if it ignores the economic reality that all resources, and capital in particular, have opportunity costs; the fact that the capital is supplied by the government does not negate this fact. This second objective pattern observable in the economic realm grows out of the fact that all economic patterns arise from the fact of scarcity. As discussed above, critics of the possibility of economic objectivity have often argued that because economics is a reaction to the fact of scarcity in the world, with the consequence that economic choices are often (if not always) about questions of distribution, objectivity is inherently unobtainable; all economics is, regardless of appearances, about values and normative choices. We claim that far from eliminating the possibility of objectivity, the fact of scarcity gives rise to a major objective feature of the economic domain: all resources have alternative uses and capital in particular, regardless of its source, is never 'free'. When it is employed in one use part of the cost of producing its output in that use is the forgone production or output that would have been obtained had it been employed in its next best alternative use.

The objective existence of opportunity cost is often implicitly (at least) denied by politicians and members of the public who argue that certain goods and services are 'public' services and should be produced and distributed free regardless of the cost of the capital required to do this. Failure to recognize or accept the reality of the pattern is often related to what *The Economist* has called 'a suspicion of profit itself' (9 December 1995, p. 66). There is a general feeling that 'social' ends and needs do not merely override the question of economic cost – i.e., make the cost worth paying – but, in fact, mean that there is no real cost when the capital is publicly provided. This is particularly true when the subsidized activity appears to be self-supporting, in that once the government provides the initial capital, the service generates sufficient funds to operate without requiring further infusions of money, although not earning profit. But, as *The Economist* says, 'When the state provides capital, or guarantees suppliers against ruin, as in the production of many public services, the risks involved are greatly reduced. But capital is still not free. Taxpayers' money has plenty of alternative uses' (ibid., p. 66). This is not to say that profit as calculated by accountants according to Generally Accepted Accounting Principles (GAAP) is necessarily an accurate reflection of the true economic return or lack thereof to capital. GAAP are designed to present the picture from the point of view of the shareholder alone and may differ from a full economic accounting. According to Jones (1981, p. 15):

Publicly relevant profit is quite different from privately relevant profit for two sets of reasons: first, publicly relevant categories are different from privately relevant categories; second, publicly relevant prices differ from privately relevant prices.

An example of the difference between profit from the perspective of a private shareholder and profit from the perspective of the economy as a whole is provided by consideration of corporate income taxes. For the corporation, these represent a cost and hence a deduction from profit; for the economy as a whole, however, they represent part of the surplus produced by capital after the costs of all inputs are paid and are, therefore, counted as part of the return on that capital. An example of the difference between privately and publicly relevant prices is the price of foreign exchange. A private entrepreneur faces the market price for foreign exchange while in reality the foreign exchange may be worth more to the economy as a result of subsidies, tariffs etc., which distort market equilibria. Similar discrepancies may obtain in labour and other factor markets.

Regardless of the need to adjust market prices to reflect underlying economic reality, the fact remains that capital has a price even when provided by governments.[8] Consequently, when it is employed for 'policy' reasons in uses where it does not earn its opportunity cost, the economy pays a price in terms of less output elsewhere in order to obtain the desired policy outcome. A good example of this is the situation that prevails in Canada with publicly owned electric utilities. In most of Canada, electricity is sold at prices below those that would generate allocative economic efficiency but at a level sufficient to allow the utility to at least break even in a financial sense (Economic Council of Canada 1986): 'As a rule, prices are set as low as possible, consistent with financial soundness. Thus revenue earned is sufficient to meet the financial requirements of the corporations' (p. 34). But financial sufficiency does not equate to economic efficiency:

In several respects, though, these requirements understate the opportunity cost of the resources used. This is particularly true of returns to capital. For the most part, little or no return on equity is earned, and the interest paid on debt is low because of government guarantees . . . In addition, the rents paid to provincial governments on water resources are minimal, and the profits earned on exports subsidize the domestic price of electricity. The consequence of this underpinning are sales of electricity for which production costs exceed returns. (p. 34)

One might object that this opportunity cost should be balanced against

---

[8] For a discussion of the calculation of the opportunity cost of capital in a Canadian context, see Jenkins (1981) and Burgess (1981).

a so-called 'social surplus' in terms of a broader welfare measure. After all, the utilities are financially self-sufficient and there are desirable policy reasons for keeping the price of electricity low. It would seem that one can achieve a socially desirable policy objective at zero cost to the taxpayer. This, however, is not the case; the opportunity cost of capital is an objective reality and the cost to society as a whole of the sub-normal rates of return can be calculated. One study (Berkowitz and Halpern 1981, table 10–9, p. 236) using 1980 figures estimated that Canadian electrical utilities earned only one-half the opportunity cost of the capital invested in them while another estimated forgone rents on water rights in 1979 at $4 billion in Ontario, Quebec, Manitoba, and British Columbia (Zucker and Jenkins 1984, table 4.1, p. 30). A third study examined the economic loss to Canada arising from the overproduction of electricity as a consequence of underpricing and the cost of investment distortion that resulted from appraising projects using interest rates that did not fully reflect the social opportunity cost of capital; the cost for the single year 1978 was estimated to be between $1.4 and $2.4 billion (Jenkins, unpublished).

It should be stressed that the above noted losses do not come about because publicly owned utilities are in any necessary sense less efficient at the production of electricity than private providers. The cost arises from a failure of allocative efficiency due to a failure to recognize and recoup the opportunity cost of the resources used in producing the electricity. It is incurred because of a desire by governments to ignore one of the objective realities of economics: scarcity is a fact, given demand schedules and budget constraints that are also facts, and this implies the objective reality of opportunity costs. As the Economic Council of Canada (1986, p. 35) notes:

the pricing and investment decisions of public firms are a reflection of government policy objectives. The distortions that have occurred under public ownership are not inherent features of this organizational mode. If provincial governments could accept pricing behaviour that was close to that required for economic efficiency, a change to private ownership would not offer any advantages in this respect.

The conclusion that can be drawn from the above discussion is that the foundation of economics in the fact of resource scarcity, far from limiting the possibility of objectivity, provides the very basis of that objectivity, a point stressed by Robbins (1932) in his classic essay on the philosophy of positive economics. Decisions about whether or not to price electricity below the rate necessary to recoup the opportunity cost of capital are indeed normative and subjective – there may be social or political reasons why such a policy may be deemed desirable. It is obviously not possible to enter directly into the minds of policy-makers and ascertain whether or not the reality of opportunity cost enters into the policy calculus. What observation surely does suggest, however, is that political discussion of such matters rarely, if ever, includes explicit recognition of the full cost of a choice to price government services below the full opportunity cost of the resource consumed. However, the fact that this choice imposes a cost on the national economy is an objective fact grounded in the reality that resources are scarce.

We will conclude our set of examples of objectively existing patterns with a brief discussion of what economists call the 'lump of labour' fallacy. This can, of course, only constitute a fallacy if there is a fact of the matter about which one can hold a fallacious view; thus its very identification depends on the idea that there are real patterns in the macroeconomic realm. The fallacy – that the output of an economy, and hence the amount of work available, is fixed – has a long history. It was Ricardo who, in 1821, was perhaps the first major economist to give credence to the idea:

the opinion entertained by the labouring class, that the employment of machinery is frequently detrimental to their interests is not founded on prejudice and error, but is conformable to the correct principles of political economy.[9] (Ricardo 1821, p. 321)

Concerns that technological innovation in the form of new products or process innovations will lead to massive unemployment are widely held at the popular level and often find support in political discourse. Opponents of this view, on the other hand, argue that the reverse is true – technological innovation creates employment. With regard to product innovation, it can certainly be argued that the invention and entry into mass use of hitherto unknown products such as home computers and microwave ovens ultimately creates new jobs, in the manufacture and service of such goods, that did not previously exist. Similarly, process innovations and the consequent improvements in productivity which they generate can be expected, ultimately, to lead to increased rather than decreased employment. While process innovation may enable a given amount of output to be produced with less labour, and hence, in the short run, lead to increased unemployment, such process innovations, like product innovations, ultimately generate increased demand. In-creased productivity reduces costs, which in turn leads to lower prices, higher wages or increased profits. The first two results increase real wages

---

[9] We are grateful to an anonymous referee for pointing out that, in falling into this fallacy, Ricardo was in fact changing his previously expressed view.

and consequently raise aggregate demand for both goods and workers. On the other hand, if higher productivity serves only to increase profits, these will ultimately drive increased investments, which will also increase output and employment.[10] This is not to deny that switching effects may occur within the ambit of a business cycle, where as the marginal productivity of capital increases during an upswing, the opportunity cost of wages rises. In this case, if wage rates are sufficiently sticky, unemployment levels may actually be increased by higher rates of capital investment. However, to whatever extent we should expect switching, we should equally well predict *re*-switching on the opposite slope of the cycle. So long as investment increases capacity faster than the growth of the labour-supply, and so long as employed labour is *fully* employed, investment-driven growth between the beginning of one cycle and the end of the next will reduce unemployment. We are unaware of any historical case where capacity growth over the full course of a cycle has been unaccompanied by a fall in unemployment except in conditions where one of the two *ceteris paribus* conditions above has been violated. Of course, this observation is very hard to test, given the basic difficulties in measuring cycles and in unambiguously demonstrating that the *ceteris paribus* conditions are satisfied. However, we claim that, given the very simple logic supporting the fundamental pattern, the burden of argument concerning its robustness should lie with the sceptic.

The literature on switching effects generally assumes a constant rate of productivity per marginal unit of capital stock. Concerns over so-called 'technological unemployment' are thus a distinct issue, though they often compound the 'lump of labour' fallacy by applying it to an analysis in which it has already been committed once *before* increasing returns to scale (either driven by technology or by efficiencies of volume) are taken into account. There are then two viewpoints as to the ultimate impact of technological innovation. The first – that of Ricardo and much popular opinion – is that technological improvements have a negative impact on employment because fewer workers can produce the same level of

---

[10] It should be noted that these remarks pertain only to the *rate* of involuntary unemployment, and not to the *structure* of unemployment. Technological change may indeed contribute, as has often been pointed out, to a situation in which a stratum of permanently unemployable people is created. If the business cycle in a sector is such that labour markets do not periodically clear, the employability of those who have been out of work longest may diminish to vanishing point, as their increasing lack of familiarity with new technology holds them constantly at the back of every job queue. If the basic insight of endogenous growth theory is correct, the existence of such a stratum may act as a brake on growth as average value of human capital in the sector diminishes. However, this fact does not somehow imply that the 'lump-of-labour' fallacy is not a fallacy.

output. The second view holds that innovation will, through increasing incomes and generating new products, lead to increasing (or at least not decreasing) levels of employment through the mechanism of consumer demand for new products and/or rising incomes being used for increased consumption. Which result will obtain in which circumstances is not a normative issue or a question of values. Rather it depends on the objective pattern prevailing in a given economy at a given time and the changes underway in that economy. What is at issue – or, at least, what ought to be at issue – are not aspects of the relative costs of supply-side factors, but rather the shape of the pattern economists call declining marginal utility of income. If the collective utility to an economy of increased income is low – i.e., most individuals don't want to consume more – then the first view may be correct. In other words, the ultimate net impact on employment levels will depend on the demand responsiveness of prices to lower costs and the elasticity of demand. In a world of fully satiated consumers with consequent total inelasticity of demand, demand would not rise to match an increase in productive capacity, and the result could be increased unemployment. But what is the evidence for one view as opposed to the other? It seems to argue overwhelmingly in favour of the conclusion that rapid technological innovation goes hand in hand with increasing rather than decreasing employment. In a study prepared for the OECD, Pascal Pettit (1995, p. 21) concludes:

Only in ceteris paribus universes is a faster increase in productivity synonymous with lower employment growth and more unemployment. The whole experience of the golden years of capitalism stresses the contrary: unprecedentedly high levels of productivity gains were accompanied by full employment.

The Economist (25 November 1995, p. 67) cites figures showing that for the last 100 years in the United States rising productivity has gone hand in hand with rising employment (and rising incomes). One can probably safely conclude that, for most economies, the marginal utility of income is not sharply declining; a flat-sloped collective marginal utility of income curve is a very plausible real pattern. This is not to say that a shift in the pattern is not possible or that some other pattern may not apply in certain economies. Again, however, real patterns are not to be identified with *nomic* generalizations. Nor is it to say that technological change will inevitably increase employment of the type for which many of those displaced by technological innovation will be suited, nor that the benefits and costs of technological innovation are in any sense 'fairly' or equitably distributed. It is just to say that there are objective patterns which exist and which cannot be ignored, dismissed or overridden by the normative aspects of economic policy-making.

Striking as these examples seem to us to be, it is problematic from the point of view of the philosophy of science to rest the case for economic objectivity mainly on instances from macroeconomics. The difficulty is that one cannot claim without controversy that macroeconomics has arrived at a theoretical consensus that would permit us to produce a stable typology of the real patterns it studies, or to measure the causal propensities of its crucial variables. (For elaboration of this point, see Ross and LaCasse 1995, pp. 474–8.) Thus the defender of objectivity in macroeconomics can only proceed, as we have done here, by suggestive enumeration of cases. We cannot seek a generic account of real macro-economic patterns through elucidation of macroeconomic foundations for the simple reason that macroeconomics *has no* settled foundations. In light of this observation, it is not surprising that reductionists and supervenience-theorists have been doubtful about the possibility of macroeconomic objectivity. The metaphysic of patterns, however, removes the need to build macroeconomic reality from foundations. Our defence of that reality may instead proceed directly: the best evidence we could have that there is an objective domain of macroeconomic patterns is simply the fact that the patterns kick back if ignored. This was the point our short stock of examples above is intended to illustrate. We doubt that an economically literate reader will have serious difficulty in adding to it.

Where microeconomics is concerned, the dependence relation between foundations and a plausible empirical reference-class for theoretical terms we find in defending a realist understanding of macroeconomics is reversed. In microeconomics, we find a consensus as strong as in any science over theoretical foundations, and a large body of impressive applications of the theory; however, it is surprisingly difficult to identify the theory's objects. The view for which one of us has argued elsewhere is that the fundamental core of microeconomics is best explicated by means of the concepts of game theory, and that, under this interpretation, games – the set of patterns to which strategic interactions converge under selection pressures of various sorts – are the basic microeconomic objects. The defence of this claim is the main subject of Ross and LaCasse (1995). Here, we will just point out that *if* the claim is accepted, then something along the lines of the real-patterns metaphysic is essential to the ambition that microeconomics be an empirical science, since possible objects that might constitute a supervenience base for games are even harder to imagine than for the macroeconomic patterns exemplified above. This is partly because game-players, that is, loci of fixed pre-ference-orderings over outcomes, can generally be token-identified only with *aspects* of objects identified from outside of the economic stance, such as people or firms, since people and firms, over the course of their biological or institutional biographies, demonstrably and frequently reverse their tastes. Worse for the defender of a token-supervenience account of microeconomics, the relation is typically many-to-many: an economic agent may be mapped with least strain on to a set of aspects of several people or firms. Worse yet, there are no individuation conditions on such putative tokens independent of the economic perspective; so the imagined token-identity would amount to nothing more than a gratuitous metaphysical flourish. Fortunately, if the metaphysic of real patterns elucidated earlier in this paper is accepted, then there is no need for resort to such ad hoc devices in support of the claim that microeconomics, like macroeconomics, tracks aspects of objective reality.

The claim that both macroeconomics and microeconomics have objectively existing domains of investigation obviously does not imply that most, or even much, work in economics is normatively disinterested. That policy problems have an overwhelming influence on which economic phenomena are chosen for investigation is surely true; but the same thing can be said of the medical disciplines and of large parts of physics and chemistry, without this impugning their claims to be positive sciences. It may also be true, as has sometimes been charged, that due to its lack of secure theoretical foundations a good deal of work in macroeconomics resembles arbitrary curve-fitting. But in this case, what we should say is that macroeconomics has not yet settled on an effective method of tracking its domain; and this is an entirely different claim from the statement that positive macroeconomics is impossible. The ideal of objective science is of immense importance as a regulating principle in research, even if in certain sciences it is rarely met. Researchers will not, however, go on respecting an ideal that they have come to believe cannot even be approximated. For this reason, if not also for the sake of truth, we should be very cautious concerning arguments for the impossibility of objectivity. It is *possible* – though, we think, highly unlikely – that societies would be better off, in some sense which welfare economics has tried, without notable success, to articulate, if economic policy choice were overtly driven by ideology rather than facts. But we would surely not be better off for mistakenly supposing that we have no other choice.[11]

[11] We would like to thank the following people for their useful comments and criticisms on earlier drafts of this paper: Chantale LaCasse, Maurice Lagueux, Uskali Mäki, Robert Nadeau, two anonymous referees, and audiences before whom versions of the paper were presented at l'Université du Québec à Montréal and at the World Congress of Logic, Methodology and Philosophy of Science in Florence, Italy. Ross is also grateful to the Social Sciences and Humanities Research Council of Canada for financial support.

References

Alesena, A. and G. Tabellini (1987) 'A Positive Theory of Fiscal Deficits and Government Debt in a Democracy', National Bureau of Economic Research, Washington, D.C., United States, working paper no. 2308.

Berkowitz, M. K., and P. J. Halpern (1981) *The Role of Crown Corporations in the Efficient Production and Use of Electricity, v. 1: An Economic Analysis of the Production, Investment and Financing Behaviour of the Canadian Electrical Utility Industry*, Toronto: Institute for Policy Analysis, University of Toronto.

Burgess, D. (1981) 'The Social Discount Rate for Canada: Theory and Evidence', *Canadian Public Policy*, 7: 344–83.

Cartwright, N. (1983) *How the Laws of Physics Lie*, Oxford: Oxford University Press.

(1989) *Nature's Capacities and their Measurement*, Oxford: Oxford University Press.

Dennett, D. (1979) 'True Believers', in A. Heath (ed.), *Scientific Explanation*, Oxford. Oxford University Press.

(1991) 'Real Patterns', *Journal of Philosophy* 88: 27–51.

(2000) 'With a Little Help From My Friends', in D. Ross, A. Brook and D. Thompson (eds.), *Dennett's Philosophy: A Comprehensive Assessment*, Cambridge, MA: MIT Press / Bradford.

Dupré, J. (1993) *The Disorder of Things*, Cambridge, MA: Harvard University Press.

Economic Council of Canada (1986) *Minding the Public's Business*, Ottawa: Supply and Services Canada.

Fodor, J. (1974) 'Special Sciences', *Synthese*, 28: 77–115.

Friedman, Michael (1979) 'Truth and Confirmation', *Journal of Philosophy*, 76: 361–82.

Friedman, Milton (1953) *Essays in Positive Economics*, Chicago: University of Chicago Press.

Harding, S. (1986) *The Science Question in Feminism*, Ithaca: Cornell University Press.

Hoover, K. (1995) 'Why Does Methodology Matter for Economics?', *Economic Journal*, 105: 715–34.

Jenkins, G. (1981) 'The Public Sector Discount Rate for Canada: Further Implications', *Canadian Public Policy*, 7: 399–407.

(unpublished) 'Public Utility Finance and Economic Waste', Harvard Institute for International Development, Harvard University, ms.

Jones, L. (1981) *Performance Evaluation of Public Enterprises*, Washington, D.C.: World Bank Discussion Paper 122.

Kim, J. (1984) 'Concepts of Supervenience', *Philosophy and Phenomenological Research*, 45: 153–76.

(1989) 'The Myth of Nonreductive Materialism', *Proceedings and Addresses of the American Philosophical Association*, 63: 31–47.

LaCasse, C. and D. Ross (1991) 'Reply to Norman, Has Rational Economic Man a Heart', *Eidos*, 8: 235–46.

Machlup, F. (1969) 'Positive and Normative Economics', in R. Heilbroner (ed.), *Economic Means and Social Ends*, Englewood Cliffs: Prentice-Hall.

Marras, A. (1993) 'Psychophysical Supervenience and Nonreductive Materialism', *Synthese*, 95: 275–304.

Myrdal, G. (1954) *The Political Element in the Development of Economic Thought*, Cambridge, MA: Harvard University Press.

(1958) 'International Integration', in P. Streeten (ed.), *Value in Social Theory: A Selection of Essays on Methodology by Gunnar Myrdal*, New York: Harper and Brothers.

Oppenheim, P. and H. Putnam (1958) 'Unity of Science as a Working Hypothesis', in H. Feigl, G. Scriven and G. Maxwell, eds., *Minnesota Studies in the Philosophy of Science*, vol. II, Minneapolis: University of Minnesota Press.

Organisation of Economic Cooperation and Development (1971, 1975, 1982, 1985, 1990/91, 1993) *Economic Surveys: Ireland*, Paris.

Pettit, P. (1995) 'Technology and Employment: Key Questions in a Context of High Unemployment', *STI Review*, 15: 13–47. Paris: OECD.

Ricardo, D. (1821) *Principles of Political Economy and Taxation*, republished in P. Sraffa (ed.), *The Works and Correspondence of David Ricardo*, vol. I, Cambridge: Cambridge University Press, 1962.

Robbins, L. (1932) *An Essay on the Nature and Significance of Economic Science*, London: Macmillan.

Rosenberg, A. (1991) *Economics: Mathematical Politics or Science of Diminishing Returns?* Chicago: University of Chicago Press.

Rosett, C. (1993) 'Rooted in Soviet Past, Russia's Central Bank Lacks Grasp of Basics', *The Wall Street Journal*, 222: 59: 3–7.

Ross, D. (1995) 'Real Patterns and the Ontological Foundations of Microeconomics', *Economics and Philosophy*, 11: 113–36.

(1999) *What People Want: The Concept of Utility From Bentham to Game Theory*, Cape Town: University of Cape Town Press.

(2000) 'Rainforest Realism: A Dennettian Theory of Existence', in D. Ross, A. Brook and D. Thompson (eds.), *Dennett's Philosophy: A Comprehensive Assessment*, Cambridge, MA: MIT Press / Bradford.

Ross, D. and C. LaCasse (1995) 'Toward a New Philosophy of Positive Economics', *Dialogue*, 34: 467–93.

Roulini, N. and J. Sachs (1989) 'Determinants of Budget Deficits', *European Economic Review*, 33: 903–33.

Savellos, E. and Ü. Yalçin (1995) *Supervenience: New Essays*, New York: Cambridge University Press.

Weston, S. (1994) 'Toward a Better Understanding of the Positive/Normative Distinction in Economics', *Economics and Philosophy*, 10: 1–17.

Zucker, R. and G. Jenkins (1984) *Blue-Gold: A Study of Hydro-Electric Rents in Canada: A Study Prepared for the Economic Council of Canada*, Ottawa: Supply and Services Canada.

Part IV

The world of economic causes

14   *Ceteris paribus* laws and socio-economic machines

1 Why economics is not allowed *ceteris paribus* laws

Economics differs from physics, we are told, in that the laws economics studies hold only *ceteris paribus* whereas those of physics are supposed to obtain universally and without condition.[1] Does this point to a metaphysical difference between the laws the two disciplines study or does it reflect merely a deficiency in the level of accomplishment of economics as compared to physics?

The conventional regularity account of laws tells us it must be the latter. On this account a theoretical law is a statement of some kind of regular association,[2] usually supposed to hold "by necessity." The idea of necessity is notoriously problematic. Within the kind of empiricist philosophy that motivates the regularity account it is difficult to explain what constitutes the difference between law-like regularities and those that hold only by accident, "nonsense" correlations that cannot be relied on. I shall not be concerned with necessity here; I want to focus on the associations themselves. These can be either universal, in which case the

* "*Ceteris Paribus* Laws and Socio-Economic Machines", Nancy Cartwright, *The Monist*, vol. 78, no. 3, pp. 276–94, Copyright © 1995, *The Monist*, La Salle, Illinois 61301. Research for this paper was sponsored by the "Modeling in Physics and Economics" project at the Centre for the Philosophy of the Natural and Social Sciences, London School of Economics. I would like to thank the members of that research group for help with this paper, as well as Mary Morgan and Max Steuer. The paper was read at a symposium on realism in the Tinbergen Institute; I would also like to thank the students and faculty who participated in that symposium for their very helpful comments.

[1] See, for instance, J. J. C. Smart, *Philosophy and Scientific Realism* (London: Routledge and Kegan Paul, 1963), who does not think even biology has proper laws.

[2] C. G. Hempel and P. Oppenheim, "Problems in the Concept of General Law," in A. Danto and S. Morgenbesser (eds.), *Philosophy of Science* (New York: Meridian Books, 1960).

law is deterministic, or they may be merely probabilistic. The regularity account is grounded in a version of empiricism that traces back to the philosophy of David Hume. Empiricism puts severe restrictions on the kinds of properties that appear in Nature's laws, or at least on the kinds of properties that can be referred to in the law-statements we write down in our theories. These must be *observable or measurable*.[3] It also restricts the kinds of facts we can learn: the only claims about these quantities that are admissible into the domain of science are facts about patterns of their co-occurrence. Hence the specification of either an equation (in the case of determinism) or of a probability distribution over a set of measurable quantities becomes the paradigm for a Law of Nature.

These two assumptions work together to ban *ceteris paribus* laws from the Nature that we study. Together they tell us that all the quantities we study are qualitatively alike. There are no differences between them not fixed either by the patterns of their associations or by what is observable or measurable about them. As a consequence it becomes impossible to find any appropriate category that would single out conditioning factors for laws from the factors that fall within them. What then could it mean to include as a law in one's theory that (to use an example I will discuss later) "In conditions C, all profitable projects will be carried out"? All that is law-like on the Humean picture are associations between measurable quantities – and that's it. The only way a condition could restrict the range of an association in a principled or nomological way would be via a more complex law involving a general association among all the quantities in question. The effect of this is to move the conditioning factor C inside the scope of the law: "All projects that are both profitable and satisfy conditions C will be carried out." That's what the Laws of Nature that we are aiming for are like. If theories in economics regularly leave out some factors like C (whatever C stands for) from the antecedents of their laws, and hence write down law claims that turn out to be, read literally, false, then economics is regularly getting it wrong. These theories need to keep working on their law-statements till they get ones that express true regularities.

I defend a very different understanding of the concept of Natural Law in modern science from the "laws = universal regularities" account I have been describing.[4] We aim in science, I urge, to discover the *natures of things*; we try to find out what powers or capacities they have and in

---

[3] Sometimes philosophers substitute for "measurable" or "observable" the requirement that the features studied be "extensional" or "occurrent" as opposed to "dispositional." To my mind the latter categories make no sense.

[4] N. Cartwright, *Nature's Capacities and Their Measurement* (Oxford: Oxford University Press, 1989); and "Aristotelian Natures and the Modern Experimental Method," in

what circumstances and in what ways these capacities can be harnessed to produce predictable behaviors. I call this the study of *natures* because I want to recall the Aristotelian idea that science aims to understand what things are, and a large part of understanding what they are is to understand what they *can do*, regularly and as a matter of course.[5] Regularities are secondary. Fixed patterns of association among measurable quantities are a consequence of the repeated operation of factors that have stable capacities (factors of this kind are sometimes called "mechanisms") arranged in the "right" way in the "right kind" of stable environment. The image is that of a machine with set components that must be assembled and shielded and set running before any regular associations between input and output can be expected. In the case of economics we can summarize this way: *regularities are a consequence of the repeated successful operation of a socio-economic machine.*

I take it that the basic information we need in economic theory is information about the characteristic behavior of the components and about how to set them running together. This information is not itself a report about regular associations between measurable quantities, although it can be used to predict regular associations. The Humean view assumes the contrary – all the information there is to learn in economic theory is immediately about the regular associations that obtain in the economy. The Humean account of laws goes naturally with a covering law theory of prediction and explanation. One set of regularities – the more concrete or phenomenological – is explained by deducing them from another set of regularities – the more general and fundamental. The distinction is like that in econometrics between structural equations and reduced-form equations.[6] The alternative theory of explanation in terms of natures rejects the covering-law account: you can't have regularities "all the way down."

The example I will present in Section 4 is one in which we cross levels of scale, or aggregation, in moving from *explanandum* to *explanans*. The model I will describe is one in which a (highly idealized) macro-economic regularity is shown to arise from the rational behavior of individual

---

J. Earman (ed.), *Inference, Explanation and Other Philosophical Frustrations* (Berkeley, CA: University of California Press, 1992).

[5] But I do not think that modern science follows the Aristotelian tradition in identifying the nature of something (what it can do) with what it is (its definition); rather it insists that the features and structures we study be identifiable independently of any specific claim about what they can do.

[6] Only note: it follows from what I shall argue in section 2 that only reduced-form equations fit the regularity account of laws; the structural equations cannot be read in the same way as genuine reports of regularities.

agents. This crossing of levels is not important to the point. We could attempt to explain macroeconomic regularities by reference to capacities and relations that can only sensibly be attributed to institutions or to the economy as a whole, with no promise of reduction to features of individuals.[7] On the other hand we could undertake – as psychologists often do – to explain behavioral or psychological regularities by reference to behavioral or psychological characteristics of the individuals involved. The point is that in all these cases it is never laws, in the sense of regularities, that are fundamental. No economic regularity, no matter how basic or important or central or universal we think it is, can stand on its own. If there are laws in the regularity sense to record in economic theories, that is because they have been created.

Ceteris paribus conditions play a special role when explanation depends on natures and not on covering laws. On the natures' picture there is a general and principled distinction between the descriptions that belong inside a law statement and those that should remain outside as a condition for the regularity described in the law to obtain. The regularities to be explained hold only *ceteris paribus*; they hold relative to the implementation and operation of a machine of an appropriate kind to give rise to them. The hypothesiss I propose in this paper is that the covering-law account is inappropriate for much of the work in modern economic theory. Economists usually talk in terms of models rather than theory. In part they do so to suggest a more tentative attitude to the explanations in question than would be warranted in a fully-fledged well-confirmed theory; and in part they do so to mark a difference in the degree of articulation: theory is a large-scale (and not necessarily formalized) outline whereas a model gives a more specified (and formalized) depiction. But I think the terminology also marks a difference of importance to the hypothesis of this paper. "Theory" suggests a set of covering laws like Maxwell's equations, laws of the kind physics' explanations are supposed to begin from. Models in economics do not usually begin from a set of fundamental regularities from which some further regularity to be explained can be deduced as a special case. Rather they are more appropriately represented as a design for a socio-economic machine which, if implemented, should give rise to the behavior to be explained. I illustrate in Section 4 with a game theory example.

---

[7] For an account of how to do non-reductionistic social science, see David Ruben, *The Metaphysics of the Social World* (London: Routledge, 1985).

2 What's wrong with regularities?

The most immediate problem with identifying natural laws with regularities is that, as John Stuart Mill observed,[8] regularities are few and far between. That is why economics cannot be an inductive science. What happens in the economy is a consequence of a mix of factors with different capacities operating in a particular environment. The mix is continually changing; so too is the background environment. Little is in place long enough for a regular pattern of associations to emerge that we could use as a basis for induction. Even if the situation were stable enough for a regularity to emerge, finding it out and recording it would be of limited use. This is the point of Trygve Haavelmo's example of the relation between the height of the throttle and the speed of the auto.[9] This is a useful relation to know if we want to make the car go faster. But if we want to build a better car, we should aim instead at understanding the capacities of the engine's components and how they will behave in various different arrangements.

The second problem with regularities is that most of the ones there are do not reflect the kind of fundamental knowledge we want, and indeed sometimes have. We want, as Mill and Haavelmo point out, to understand the functioning of certain fundamental rearrangeable components.[10] Most of what happens in the economy is a consequence of the interaction of large numbers of factors. Even if the arrangement should be appropriate and last long enough for a regular association to arise (that is, they make up a socio-economic machine) that association would not immediately teach us what we want to know about how the parts function separately. Hence the laments about the near impossibility in economics of doing controlled experiments designed especially to do this job.

But are not the laws for describing how the parts function themselves regularity statements? One central point of this paper is to urge that the answer to this question is *No*. Consider what kinds of regularity statements these would have to be. They are usually thought to record

---

[8] J. S. Mill, "On the Definition of Political Economy and On the Method of Philosophical Investigation in that Science" [1850] in *Collected Works* (Toronto: University of Toronto Press, 1967). See also "On the Logic of the Moral Sciences," *A System of Logic* [1872], also in the *Collected Works*.

[9] T. Haavelmo, "The Probability Approach in Econometrics," *Econometrica*, 12 (1944), Supplement.

[10] Parts are fundamental to the extent that their capacities stay relatively fixed over a wide (or wide enough) range of circumstances.

claims about what regularly follows if the component in question were to operate on its own. The first thing we should note is that if this is what a law is, there are very few true laws to be had, for regularities of this kind are rare indeed and the majority of these are hard won in a physics laboratory. Secondly, even if we had such regularities they could not perform the explanatory and predictive jobs that we expect of laws. The reasons for wanting a regularity account of laws quite naturally motivate a corresponding covering-law account of explanation and prediction. As noted in section 1, on the covering-law account to explain a phenomenon is to show it to be an instance of a general law, which is generally taken to mean "a general regularity." Collections of laws about what happens when mechanisms operate on their own are not then going to be able to explain the bulk of the phenomena we want them for, phenomena that result from the joint operation of a mix of mechanisms. We can of course begin to give an account here invoking "laws" or recipes for interaction. The question is, can we give an account within a purely regularity theory of laws?

Let us turn next to the idea of a mechanism operating *on its own*. We may conceive of the demand mechanism in terms of individual preferences, goals and constraints or as irreducibly institutional or structural. In either case on the regularity account of laws the law of demand records the regular behavior that results when the demand mechanism is set running alone. This paradigmatic case (which Haavelmo himself uses in talking about laws for fundamental mechanisms) shows up the absurdity of trying to describe the capacities of mechanisms in terms of regularities. No behavior results from either the supply or the demand mechanism operating on its own, and that is nothing special about this case. In general it will not make sense to talk about a mechanism operating on its own. That's because in this respect economic mechanisms really are like machine parts – they need to be assembled and set running before any behavior at all results. This is true in even the most stripped-down cases. A rigid rod, for example, must not only be affixed to a fulcrum before it becomes the Simple Machine called a "lever"; it must also be set into a stable environment in which it is not jiggled about.

The same is true in economics. Consider an analogous case, a kind of economic lever that multiplies money just as the lever multiplies force. In this example banking behavior will play the role of the rigid rod with "high-powered money" as the force on one end. The reserve ratio will correspond to where the fulcrum is located. Here is how the money-multiplying mechanism works: the "central bank" has a monopoly on making money. Following convention, let us call this *high-powered* money. The commercial banking system blows up, or multiplies, the high-powered money into the total money supply. The banks do this by lending a fraction of the money deposited with them. The larger the proportion they can lend (i.e. the smaller the reserve ratio) the more they can expand money. Two factors are at work: the proportion of high-powered money held as currency, which is one minus the proportion deposited; and the proportion lent, which is one minus the reserve ratio. Suppose, for example, that high-powered money = £100. All of it could be deposited in a bank. That bank could lend £80. All £80 could be deposited in another bank. That bank could lend £64, and so on. The total of all deposits, 100 + 80 + 64 + . . . = 500.

Assume that banks lend all they can, which as profit makers they are disposed to do. Then we can derive

$$M = (1 + cu/re + cu)\,H \tag{1}$$

where H = high powered money; re = the reserve ratio; $1 - re = li$, the lending ratio; cu = the rate of currency to deposits; M = the money stock. Equation (1) is like the law of the lever. Regularity theorists would like to read it as a statement of regular association. But that is too quick. We do not have a description of some law-like association that regularly occurs. Rather we have a description of a socio-economic machine that would give rise to a regular association if it were set running repeatedly.

This simple example illustrates both of the central points I want to argue in this paper. First, regularity theorists have the story just upside down. They mistake a sometime-consequence for the source. In certain very felicitous circumstances a regularity may occur (or, to look to the counterfactual account I will discuss briefly in the next section, it may be set ready to occur), but the occurrence – or even the possibility of the occurrence – of these regularities is not what is nomologically basic. We want to learn how to construct the felicitous circumstances where output is predictable. Our theories must tell us what the fundamental mechanisms available to us are, how they function, and how to construct a machine with them that can predictably give rise to a regular association. And the information that does this for us is not itself a report of any regular association – either a real regular association (one that occurs) or a counterfactual one (that might occur). Second, the example shows the special place of *ceteris paribus* conditions. Equation (1) holds *ceteris paribus*, that is under very special circumstances we may designate C. C does not mark yet another variable like H, M, cu and re that has mistakenly been omitted from equation (1), either by ignorance or sloth. Rather it marks the entire characterization of the socio-economic machine that equation (1) describes and that if properly shielded and run repeatedly will produce a regular rise and fall of money with deposits.

The example also reminds us that, like the rigid rod, the socio-economic lever as well must be carefully shielded to keep it intact and to ensure that it alone affects the outcome. Even in very developed models the need for shielding is often left implicit. I think that has to do with the very high level of abstraction at which theoretical models operate. Think about the rigid rod attached to the fulcrum. What counts as shielding if the rod is to function properly as a lever will be very different depending on the material of the rod and the fulcrum and the method of fixing them together. In general, if the level of abstraction is too high, about all that can be said is "ensure nothing interferes." In this case the model has not fleshed in the full set of *ceteris paribus* conditions lying behind the law derived in it but only reminded us that more still needs to be done for any real-life application.

I use the word "mechanism" in describing the money multiplier. Regularity theorists also talk about mechanisms. But for them a mechanism can only be another regularity, albeit a more "fundamental" one. "More fundamental" here usually means either more encompassing, as in the relation of Newton's to Kepler's laws, or having to do with smaller parts as in the relation between individuals with their separate behaviors and expectations on the one hand and macro-economic regularities on the other. Economics does not have any fundamental laws in the first sense. But the second sense will not help the regularity theorist either since explanations citing regularities about individuals have all the same problems as any other. When we say "mechanisms," I think we mean "mechanism" in the literal sense – "the structure or adaptation of parts of a machine."[11] The little banking model is a good case. In our banking example the rigid relationship between high-powered money that the central bank creates and the ultimate size of the money stock depends on the currency-to-deposit ratio not changing, and on every commercial bank being fully lent up, that is, being tight on, but not beyond, the legal reserve ratio. It is not immediately obvious that a group of commercial banks can "multiply" the amount of currency issued by the central bank when no one bank can lend more than is deposited with it. The banking system can lend more even though no one bank can. How much more? That is what the "law" tells us. But it is not derived by referring to a regularity, but rather by deducing the consequences of a mechanism. I illustrate the relations between economic models and regularities with another example in section 4. But first I should discuss briefly one philosophical loose-end.

11 Definition 1, *The Concise Oxford Dictionary*, 8th edn.

3 Philosophical aside

When confronted with the fact that there seem to be a lot more laws than there are regularities, regularity theorists are apt to defend their view by resorting to counterfactual regularities. Laws are identified not with regularities that obtain but with regularities that would obtain if the circumstances were right. It is fairly standard by now to go on to analyze counterfactuals by introducing an array of other "possible" worlds. Laws then turn out to be regularities that occur "elsewhere" even though they do not occur here – that is, even though they do not occur at all. As a view about what constitutes a Law of Nature this revised (or "modalized"[12]) version of the regularity account seems even more implausible than the original. A Law of Nature of this world – that is, a Law of Nature *full stop* since this is the only world there is – *consists* in a regularity that obtains nowhere at all.

There are two strategies, both I think due to David Lewis, that offer the beginnings of an account of how possible regularities can both be taken seriously as *genuine regularities* and also be seen to bear on what happens in the actual world. The first takes possible worlds not as fictional constructions but as real.[13] The second takes them as book-keeping devices for encoding very complicated patterns of occurrences in the "real" world. In this case the truth of a counterfactual (about the "real" world) will be entirely fixed by the complicated pattern of events that actually occur in the "real" world. Rather than employing this very complicated semantics directly we instead devise a set of rules for constructing a kind of chart from which, with the aid of a second set of rules, we can read off whether a counterfactual is true or false. The chart has the form of a description of a set of possible worlds with a "nearness" relation defined on them. But the description need not be of anything like a world, the "worlds" need not be "possible" in any familiar sense, and the special relation on them can be anything at all so long as a recipe is provided for how to go from genuine "occurrent," "measurable" or "observable" facts about our world to the ordering on the possible worlds. The trick in both cases, whether the possible worlds are real or only function as account books, is to ensure that we have good reasons for making the inferences we need; that is, that we are able to infer from the truth of a counterfactual as thus determined to the conclusion that if

---

[12] "Modal" because it employs concepts of necessity and possibility.
[13] This view is explicitly defended in D. Lewis, *On the Plurality of Worlds* (Oxford: Blackwell, 1986).

we really were repeatedly to instantiate the antecedent of the counter-factual (in the "actual" world), the consequent would regularly follow. This of course is immediately guaranteed by the interpretation that reads claims about counterfactual regularities just as claims about what regularities would occur if the requisite antecedents were to obtain. But then we are back to the original question: What sense does it make to claim that laws consist in these nowhere existent regularities?

The point of this question is to challenge the regularity theorist to explain what advantage these non-existent regularities have over a more natural ontology of natures which talks about causes, preventions, contributing factors, triggering factors, retardants and the like. We may grant an empiricist point of view in so far as we require that the claims of our theories be testable. But that will not help the regularity theorist since causal claims or ascriptions of capacities are no harder to test than claims about counterfactual regularities and indeed, I would argue, in many cases you can't do one without the other.[14] So far as I can see the advantage is supposed to be that the regularity account, even if it relies on regularities that are not real, does not employ any funny concepts. We use only concepts describing measurable (or "observable" or "occur-rent") quantities and their occurrence at given places and times. The propositional connectives used ("if X were to happen, then Y would happen") do not have a truth-functional semantics (by contrast with "if X then Y" which is equivalent to "not-X or Y") as they should from a strict Humean point of view. But, it seems, this is a problem that many regularity empiricists are prepared to live with (though not purists like Bas van Fraasen).

But what is funny about concepts like causality by contrast with concepts of so-called measurable or occurrent properties? David Hume had an associationist theory of concept formation that he combined with a copy theory of impressions and ideas. Our ideas are either copies of our impressions or are constructed from copies of impressions by a method much like truth-functional logic. Impressions in turn are copies of the sensory qualities of things; they are the "way-they-look" of purely sensible qualities. On this story predicates like ". . . is red" are supposed to stand for *sensible* qualities;[15] ". . . is lapping" is not sensible. So claims like "The ball is red" are supposed to make sense (to the extent that we can construct a concept of a ball from our impressions) whereas "The cat

---

[14] I have defended the first of these claims in *Nature's Capacities and their Measurement* (see n. 4, above); the second is argued in "Aristotelian Natures and the Modern Experimental Method" (also cited in n. 4, above).

[15] The other so-called "primary and secondary qualities" are supposed to be *sensible* as well.

is lapping up the milk" does not, except as a claim more or less about the locations of a sequence of color patches. Since there are no impressions derived from Nature from which we could copy causal ideas, we do not on this story really have any concept of causality. We only think we do.[16]

I do not think that any part of this story is plausible 200 years later. There is no evidence for thinking that the idea of a "sensible quality" is a reasonable one to use in our account of Nature.[17] I suspect that our concept of sensible qualities is a back formation from the Cartesian concept of an "impression," which itself is a philosophical construct with no scientific backing. Philosophers sometimes try to substitute "occurrent" instead of "sensible" but this is equally problematic. In the first place, the distinction "occurrent/dispositional" is itself questionable. But more importantly, even if it could be drawn, there is no account of why singular causings are not occurrent nor of why the occurrent is either more real than the dispositional or more epistemically accessible. The associationist theory of concept formation provided an account of epistemic access that did this job for Hume. We rightly do not hold with associationism nowadays. But there is no good alternative that shows that causings are not among what can be known.[18] The contemporary Humean attack on causation is, so far as I can see, groundless. It is an attempt to keep Hume's conclusions even though we do not accept his premises nor have any reasonable substitute for them. We may have no adequate theory of concept formation, yet it is clear that associationism cannot be maintained, and its consequent constraints on what we can sensibly think and say should not dictate our methodology.

4 An example of an economic machine

The game-theoretic model proposed by Oliver Hart and John Moore in their "Theory of Debt Based on the Inalienability of Human Capital"[19]

---

[16] Hume hypothesized that the idea of causality could be a copy of our impression of our own internal state of expectation that one event will follow another. In this case we have a concept, but it is not the concept we usually think it is.

[17] Hugh Mellor's attacks on the distinction between occurrent and dispositional properties support this point of view (H. Mellor, *The Matter of Chance* [Cambridge: Cambridge University Press, 1971]), as does Sydney Shoemaker's account of properties as nexes of causal laws (S. Shoemaker, "Identity, Cause and Mind", in *Ontological Essays* [Cambridge: Cambridge University Press, 1984]).

[18] There are, of course, a number of psychological experiments that show that we can be misled about causality, as about anything else.

[19] O. Hart and J. Moore in *Theoretical Economics Discussion Papers*, London:

provides a good example of a blueprint for a socio-economic machine. I pick this example not because it is especially representative of recent work in economic theory but rather because the analogy with machine design is very transparent in this case and the contrast with a covering-law account is easy to see. The central idea behind the model is that crucial aspects of debt contracts are determined by the fact that entrepreneurs cannot be locked into contracts but may withdraw with only small (in their model *no*) penalties other than loss of the project's assets. That means that some debt contracts may be unenforceable and hence inefficiency may result, i.e. some profitable projects may not be undertaken. Hart and Moore derive a number of results. I shall discuss only the very first (Corollary 1) as an illustration of how socio-economic machines give rise to regularities. As Hart and Moore describe, "Corollary 1 tells us that inefficiency arises only if either (a) there is an initial sunk cost of investment $K > L_0$ ($= \sum_{p_i} i = 1, \ldots, n$) and/or (b) the project's initial returns are smaller than the returns from the assets' alternative use (in particular, $r_1 < 1_1$)."[20]

The model presents a toy machine that if set running repeatedly generates an economically interesting regularity described in Corollary 1. The inputs can vary across the identity of individual players, sunk costs (K), income streams ($r_1, \ldots, r_n$), liquidation-value streams ($1_1, \ldots, 1_n$), and the initial wealth of the debtor (w_0). The output we are considering is the regularity described in Corollary 1:

R: All profitable projects which have no initial sunk costs and whose initial returns are at least as large as the returns from the alternative use of the assets will be undertaken.

The model lays out a number of features necessary for the design of a machine: it tells us (i) the parts that make up the machine, their properties and their separate capacities; (ii) how the parts are to be assembled; and (iii) the rules for calculating what should result from their joint operation once assembled. The components are two game players ("debtor" or "entrepreneur," and "creditor") who (a) have the same discount rates; (b) are motivated only by greed; (c) have perfect certainty; and (d) are perfect and costless calculators. The arrangements of the players is claustrophobic: two players set against each other with no

---

STICERD TE (1991), 1233, London School of Economics. Also in the *Quarterly Journal of Economics*, 109 (1994), pp. 841–879.

[20] Hart and Moore, 1991, p. 19. The result need mention only initial returns because of the simplifying assumption Hart and Moore make that if the return at any period is greater then the liquidation income at that period, this will continue to be the case in all subsequent periods.

possible interaction outside. Later extensions consider what happens when either the debtor or the creditor has profitable reinvestment opportunities elsewhere, but these are fixed opportunities not involving negotiations with new players. Another extension tries in a very "indirect and rudimentary fashion" (Hart and Moore 1991, p. 40) to mimic with just the two players what would happen if the debtor could negotiate with a new creditor. Other assumptions about the arrangement are described as well; for instance, as part of the proof of R it is assumed "for simplicity" that the debtor "has all the bargaining power" in the original negotiation (p. 17). The central features of the arrangement are given by the rules laid out for the renegotiation game, plus a number of further "simplifying" assumptions about the relations among capital costs, project returns and liquidation returns that contribute to the proof of R.

Rules for calculating how parts function together vary widely across domains.[21] Component forces, which have the capacity to produce motions, add vectorially. Simultaneous-equation models in econometrics suppose that when a number of mechanisms act together, the equations associated with each of them separately must all be satisfied at once. In electronics there are well-known theorems that reduce any complicated arrangements of components to a simple circuit with known behavior. And in game theory various concepts of equilibria tell us how to calculate the outcomes of the joint action of players with specified capacities (e.g. perfectly or imperfectly informed, costless calculators, etc.). For the Hart and Moore model it is supposed that the moves of the players together constitute a subgame-perfect equilibrium.

The model is less informative about the two remaining features necessary for describing the operation of a machine: (iv) what counts as shielding and (v) how the machine is set running. As we have seen, Hart and Moore describe a very closed world. There are just two players and they are locked into the very special game they are playing. The shielding conditions are implicit: nothing must occur that distorts the rules of the game and nothing must affect the choice of debt contracts other than the requirement that they constitute a subgame-perfect equilibrium. Repeated running simply means playing the game again and again. This is consistent with my suggestion earlier that models like this are described at a very high level of abstraction. The model specifies abstract functional relations between the parts that can be instantiated in various different institutional arrangements; what counts as shielding will depend heavily

---

[21] This is part of the reason it is difficult to formulate a general informative philosophical account of mechanisms and their operation.

on what the specific material instantiation is. This is especially true in game-theoretical models, where few clues are given about what real institutional arrangements can be taken to constitute any specific game.

To derive the regularity R, Hart and Moore show that in their model all subgame-perfect equilibria for their date-zero renegotiation game satisfy a set of conditions (Proposition 1) that in turn imply Corollary 1. The derivation proceeds by unpacking the concept of equilibrium in an exogenously given extensive form game. In particular the derivation employs no general laws that might be mistaken for claims about regularities. There are no empirical generalizations nor any equations on the analog of Schrödinger's or Maxwell's; there are not even any theorems of game theory written down. Rather the argument employs concepts and techniques of game theory (some of which are of course validated by reference to theorems) plus the general characterization of equilibrium to derive constraints on what the pay-offs will be from any equilibrium in the game described.

Turn now to the questions about *ceteris paribus* conditions and the regularity theory of laws. R holds (at best) only *ceteris paribus*: if conditions like those of the model were to occur repeatedly, then in those situations all profitable ventures with no sunk costs and good enough initial returns would be undertaken. On the picture of Natural Law that I have been advocating, something like the converse is true as well. If a regularity like R is to obtain as a matter of law, there must be a machine like the one modeled by Hart and Moore (or some other, with an appropriate structure) to give rise to it. *There are no law-like regularities without a machine to generate them.* Thus *ceteris paribus* conditions have a very special role to play in economic laws like R. They describe the structure of the machine that makes the laws true.

The relation of laws to models I describe is familiar in economics, where a central part of the theoretical enterprise consists in devising models in which socio-economic regularities can be derived. But it is important to realize how different this is from the regularity theory. Look back to the regularity theory. R is not a universal association that can be relied on outside various special arrangements. On the regularity theory law-likeness consists in true universality. So there must be some universal association in the offing or else R cannot be relied on at all, even in these special circumstances. If an association like R appears to hold in some data set, that cannot be a matter of law but must be viewed as merely a chance accident of a too-small sample unless there is some kind of true universal association to back it up.

The difference between an account of Natural Law in terms of nature's capacities and machines and the regularity account is no mere matter of metaphysics. It matters to method as well, both the methods used in the construction of theory and those used in its testing. *R* tells us that *ceteris paribus* all profitable ventures will be taken up – except in conditions (a) and (b). The regularity theory invites us to eliminate the *ceteris paribus* clause by extending this list to include further factors – (c) (d) (e), . . . (x) – until finally a true universal is achieved: "All profitable ventures that satisfy (a) (b), . . . (x) will be taken up." This way of looking at it points the investigation in an entirely wrong direction. It focuses the study on more and more factors like (a) and (b) themselves rather than on the structural features and arrangements like those modeled by Hart and Moore that we need to put in place if we want to ensure efficiency.

The regularity theory also carries with it an entourage of methods for testing that have no place here. When is a model like that of Hart and Moore a good one? There are a large number of different kinds of problems involved. Some are due to the fact that theirs is a game-theoretic model; these are to some extent independent of the issue raised by the differences between a regularity and a capacity view of laws. The advantage to game theory is that it makes the relationship between the assumptions of the explanatory model and laws like *R* that are to be explained in the model very tight. The results that are "derived" in the model are literally *deduced*. The cost is that the rules of the games that allow these strict deductions may seem to be very unrealistic as representations of real-life situations in which the derived regularities occur. As Hart and Moore say about their own model, "The game may seem ad hoc, but we believe that almost any extensive form bargaining game is subject to this criticism" (1991, p. 12).

Let us lay aside these special problems involving games and think about the relations between models and the results derived within them more generally. The point is that the results derived may be rendered as regularity claims, but the relationship between the structures described by the model and the regularities it gives rise to is not again itself one of regular association. So our whole package of sophisticated techniques – mostly statistical – for testing regularity claims are of no help in the decisions about choice among models. How do we decide? As far as I can see we have no articulated methodology, neither among philosophers nor among economists (though we may well have a variety of unarticulated methods). My reasons for attending to the metaphysics of economic laws stem primarily from these methodological concerns. So long as we are in the grip of the regularity view – which happens to economists as well as to philosophers – we are likely to restrict our efforts at methodology to refining ever more precisely our techniques at statistics and to leave unconsidered and unimproved our methods for model choice.

5 Three aspects of socio-economic machines

"Socio-economic laws are created by socio-economic machines." The slogan points to three distinct theses, which are separable and can be argued independently. The first, the one that I am most prepared to defend, follows Aristotle in seeing natures as primary and behaviors, even very regular behaviors, as derivative. Regular behavior derives from the repeated triggering of determinate systems whose nature stays fixed long enough to manifest itself in the resulting regularity. This feature does not point particularly to a machine analogy, though, in opposition to an organic one, as is apparent from the work of Aristotle himself.

Organic analogies usually suggest a kind of irreducible holism: the behavior of the components when separated has little to teach about how they work together in the functioning organism. By contrast, the machine analogy stresses the analytic nature of much economic thought. This is the second thesis: much of economic work is based on the hope that we can understand different aspects of the economy separately and then piece the lessons together at a second stage to give a more complete account. This idea is central to the use of idealization and correction that is common throughout economics. Bounded rationality is expected to be like unbounded but with modifications; international trade at best tends to move prices towards each other but they are often modeled as being equal; in planning models the planner is often assumed to have no other goal than social welfare just as the firm manager is assumed to maximize shareholder value of the firm; and so forth. I do not want to urge this second thesis suggested by talking of socio-economic machines as vigorously as the first. There is no guarantee that the analytic method is the right method for all the problems that economics wants to treat. But it is, I think, by far and away the one we best know how to use.

The third thesis is one about which evidence is divided. Ordinary machines do not evolve. They have to be assembled, and the assembly has to be carefully engineered. Is the same true of socio-economic machines? I do not intend in using the description to urge that the answer must be "yes."[22] One of the most clear-cut examples of a "designed" institution in economics is the International Monetary Fund (IMF),

---

[22] I owe the following discussion to Mary Morgan.

which resulted from negotiations over two radically different designs put forward for an international body to run post-Second World War international monetary arrangements. In large part the design adopted at Bretton Woods in 1944 was for a "fund" from which member countries could draw previously deposited reserves, rather than a "bank" which could create credit on deposits. Economic historians have tended to rate the institution a failure because of its design faults: (1) it was not devised to effect the transition from the war years to the peace years; (2) it ran out of reserves (as predicted by Keynes) in the 1960s and so had to create SDR (special drawing rights) to service the growth in the international economy; and (3) it was unable to bring pressure to bear on surplus countries to revalue, compromising its ability to avoid damaging currency crises and oversee orderly changes in exchange rates, leading ultimately to the collapse of the arrangements in 1971. By contrast, economic historians have tended to rate the gold standard of the pre-1914 economy as a much more effective institution – an institution which was not designed but which evolved gradually over the nineteenth century. They suggest that this institution worked well because its evolutionary character allowed it to be operated with considerable flexibility and tacit knowledge, rather than because it stuck to some supposed "rules of the game" or was operated according to some agreed-upon economic theory.[23]

6 Concluding remarks

I began with the conventional claim that the laws of economics hold only *ceteris paribus*. This is supposed to contrast with the laws of physics. On the regularity account of laws this can only reflect an epistemological difference between the two: economists simply do not know enough to fill in their law claims sufficiently. I have proposed that there is a metaphysical difference as well. Laws in the conventional regularity sense are secondary in economics. They must be constructed, and the knowledge that aids in this construction is not itself again a report of some actual or possible regularities. It is rather knowledge about the capacities of institutions and individuals and what these capacities can do if assembled and regulated in appropriate ways.

---

[23] A standard good source is J. Foreman-Peck, *A History of the World Economy: International Economic Relations since 1850* (1993).

Does this really constitute a difference between economics on the one hand and physics on the other? I think not. It is sometimes argued that quantum field theory and the general theory of relativity function like true covering-law theories. They begin with regularities that are both genuinely universal and true (or, true enough); the phenomena to be explained are just special cases of these very general regularities. Perhaps. Most of physics works differently. Like economics, physics uses the analytic method: we come to understand the operation of the parts – for example, Coulomb's force, the force of gravity, weak and strong nuclear forces, or the behavior of resistors, inductors and capacitors – and we piece them together to predict the behavior of the whole. Even physics, I would argue,[24] needs "machines" to generate regularities – machines in the sense of stable configurations of components with determinate capacities properly shielded and repeatedly set running. If this is correct then differences in the metaphysics of Natural Laws that I have been describing are not differences between economics and physics but rather between domains in which the covering-law model obtains and those in which the analytic method prevails. Economics and physics equally employ *ceteris paribus* laws, and that is a matter of the systems they study, not a deficiency in what they have to say about them.

[24] For a defense of this claim see N. Cartwright, "Fundamentalism *vs* the Patchwork of Laws," *Proceedings of the Aristotelian Society* (1994); and "Aristotelian Natures and the Modern Experimental Method" (cited in n. 4, above).

15 Tendencies, laws, and the composition of economic causes

DANIEL M. HAUSMAN[1]

John Stuart Mill is an empiricist and an inductivist. He believes that the grounds for beliefs concerning matters of fact are ultimately perceptual experiences and that generalizations are justified inductively by observation of their instances and implications. Yet Mill believes that inductive methods are not directly applicable to most subject matters. His methods of induction are suitable only to domains in which few causal factors are at work, while most subject matters involve the simultaneous action of many causal factors. The possibilities of experimental intervention increase the range of direct inductive inquiry, but that range is still limited.

Mill believes that scientific knowledge of complex subject matters can nevertheless be attained. If one is able to determine inductively the laws governing single causal factors, then one can deduce what the consequences of multiple causes acting simultaneously will be. Mill calls this procedure "the deductive method" or "the method *a priori*," but both names are misleading. The deductive method is, in fact, an indirect *inductive* method, in which the laws of individual causes are separately determined by inductive methods. The role of deduction is to determine what follows from these laws in complex circumstances. The evidence that inductively supports the premises of a deductive argument is supposed to be the inductive basis for one's belief in the argument's conclusions (1843, bk. 2, ch. 3, §3). In Mill's words:

When an effect depends on a concurrence of causes, these causes must be studied one at a time, and their laws separately investigated, if we wish, through the

[1] This essay derives from Hausman (1995). Sections 2 and 3 are largely new. Nancy Cartwright, Wade Hands, Uskali Mäki, and Elliott Sober provided helpful criticisms of earlier drafts. This work was carried out while I was the Ludwig Lachmann Fellow at the London School of Economics, and I would like to thank the Charlottenburg Trust for its support.

causes, to obtain the power of either predicting or controlling the effect; since the law of the effect is compounded of the laws of all the causes which determine it. (1843, bk. 6, ch. 9, §3)

If one wants to "obtain the power of predicting or controlling" an effect such as projectile motion through understanding its causes, one needs to investigate separately the separate causal factors (gravity, momentum, friction) and their laws.

This notion of "compounding of the laws of all the causes," of *deducing* the consequences of the concurrence of a plurality of causes, is problematic. Mill takes explanations in dynamics as paradigmatic and does not pause over the notion of adding up the effects of different causes. But the notion of "compounding" is not simple or straightforward even in the case of classical mechanics. I shall disentangle some of the principles Mill invokes in attempting to explain how scientific knowledge of complex subject matters is possible, and I shall argue that his account fails. Some of the problems in acquiring knowledge of complex subject matters arise from details of Mill's philosophy of science, but some remain for non-Millians to grapple with, too.

1 The deductive method in economics

As Mill recognized, one can find regularities in complicated phenomena. These regularities, which Mill called "empirical laws," are a valuable part of science, because they constitute data which theories should explain and because they may be of use. But empirical laws are not explanatory, and they are a precarious basis for prediction. Until they are linked to underlying causal laws, one does not know when they can be relied upon and when they are likely to break down. So scientists should not rest content with empirical laws. They should seek to uncover what Mill called "causal laws," and they cannot succeed in doing so by applying direct inductive methods to complex subject matters. When I speak of "laws," I shall be referring to causal laws.

Social phenomena are particularly inappropriate candidates for the method of "specific experience" or "the method *a posteriori*," because they are complex, available in limited varieties, and not subject to appreciable experimental manipulation. Physicists might stop there with expressions of pity for the plight of the social theorist. But social phenomena and especially economics are Mill's main interest, and he wants to explain how one can acquire scientific knowledge of them. The explanation lies in Mill's "direct" deductive method.[2] This method is not applicable to the general science of society, because there are too many causes ever to ascertain all their laws and to determine their combined effects, but it will work in subject matters such as economics in which, in Mill's opinion, there are few really significant causes.

When Mill first introduces the deductive method in Book III of *A System of Logic*, he envisions scientists deriving the laws governing complex phenomena from the laws of *all* the relevant causes. Suppose, for example, Wilson is sick, and one would like to know whether penicillin will help cure Wilson.[3] The method *a posteriori* demands an inquiry into whether others with symptoms resembling Wilson's recovered more often or more rapidly when given penicillin. The method *a priori* in contrast draws upon knowledge of the causes of Wilson's symptoms and of the operation of penicillin to decide whether penicillin will help cure Wilson. Both methods are "empirical" and involve testing. The difference is that the former attempts to use experiment or observation to learn about the complex phenomenon directly, while the latter employs observation to study the relevant component causal factors.

In an example such as this one, the deductive method seems unobjectionable, but in economics, causal factors that are known to be significant are left out of the story. As Mill was well aware, economic agents may be motivated by all sorts of passions – whether they be patriotic, malevolent, benevolent, or neurotic – which are left out of economics. Mill seems to be of two minds about whether the omission of relevant causal factors is scientifically acceptable. On the one hand, he criticizes members of the "school of Bentham" (including his father, James Mill) for theorizing about government without incorporating all the causes, whether significant or not (1843, bk. 6, ch. 8, §3). But when it comes to economics, Mill apparently recommends just the methodological practice that he condemns in his father. For the correct method of including all the causes

---

[2] The so-called inverse deductive method seems a strained attempt to defend large-scale historical speculation of the sort that Mill admired in Comte. In principle there is nothing strained or questionable about the inverse deductive method. Like the direct deductive method, one "deduces" a social regularity from the underlying causal laws and a description of the particular circumstances. What makes Mill call it the "*inverse* deductive method" is just that the social regularity is first derived from observation, rather than obtained from the deduction, so that the deduction rather than the observation serves as a verification that the regularity is indeed a derivative causal law. But in his discussion of the inverse deductive or historical method, Mill greatly relaxes the demand that the social regularity be deduced from underlying causal laws. Mill argues that merely showing that empirical social regularities are not ruled out by the causal laws is enough to lend some weight to them (1843, bk. 6, ch. 10).

[3] Compare this to Mill's own example (1843, bk. 3, ch. 10, §6).

"within the pale of the science" is not feasible. Economists must set their sights lower and aim only at a *hypothetical* science of *tendencies* which is, in Mill's view, generally "insufficient for prediction" yet "most valuable for guidance" (1843, bk. 6, ch. 9, §2).

Let us call this sort of deductive method, that so closely resembles the method of Mill's father, "the inexact deductive method," because it incorporates only some of the causes. Mill defends this method as follows:

The motive which suggests the separation of this portion of the social phenomena from the rest, and the creation of a distinct branch of science relating to them, is, that they do *mainly* depend, at least in the first resort, on one class of circumstances only; and that even when other circumstances interfere, the ascertainment of the effect due to the one class of circumstances alone is a sufficiently intricate and difficult business to make it expedient to perform it once for all, and then allow for the effect of the modifying circumstances; especially as certain fixed combinations of the former are apt to recur often, in conjunction with ever-varying circumstances of the latter class. (1843, bk. 6, ch. 9, §3)

The defences Mill offers here for employing this inexact deductive method seem to be (1) practical – there is no alternative (2) metaphysical – although the results are only hypothetical, the tendencies persist even when there are other disturbing causes, and (3) pragmatic – this is an efficient way of theorizing, and more order can be found this way than in any other.[4] I shall be questioning these defences.

In the case of economics, theorists following the deductive method first borrow basic "laws" from the natural sciences or from psychology, which Mill regards as an introspective experimental science. Then theorists deduce what follows from them in various circumstances. Finally, verification is essential (though not in order to test the basic laws, which are already established and could not be cast in doubt by the empirical vicissitudes of a conclusion deduced from a partial set of causes). It is unclear whether verification is necessary in order to regard the deductively derived generalizations as economic laws, or whether verification merely determines the applicability of these laws.[5]

---

[4] Surely Mill's father might have given the same argument in his own defense. There is an irony here in the fact that recent extensions of neoclassical economic models to politics largely recapitulate James Mill's account of political behavior. See for example Buchanan (1975).

[5] Compare Mill (1836), pp. 325–6 and Mill (1843), bk. 3, ch. 9, §3 and bk. 6, ch. 9, §1, and see De Marchi (1986) and Hutchison (1998). Mill writes, "To verify the hypothesis itself *a posteriori*, that is, to examine whether the facts of any actual case are in accordance with it, is no part of the business of science at all, but of the *application* of science" (1836, p. 325). It is not clear from the text of Mill's writings whether Mill regarded the deductive method as a distinctive method of theory appraisal or whether he regarded it as the implementation of standard inductive methods when theorizing about complex phenomena. I am indebted to Abraham Hirsch for my understanding of these problems.

Applying the deductive method in economics is even messier than the discussion so far suggests. The laws that one derives are not only inexact; they are sometimes drastically in conflict with the phenomena. These empirical inadequacies are only to be expected, since many causal factors are left out of the derivation. Furthermore the premises in the deduction do not consist exclusively of established laws and true descriptions of the relevant circumstances. Frequently included among the non-law premises are extreme simplifications, such as claims that commodities are infinitely divisible or that knowledge is perfect. Since some of the implications of such premises are bound to be wildly off the mark, one wonders what evidential weight such deduction could have. Presumably the fact that one can derive a purported causal law L for a complex system from such polyglot premises give one reason to accept L only if the simplifications are dispensable or if they are in some sense reasonable approximations in the particular domain.

2 Inexact laws

The supposed "laws" of the component causes are also problematic, since it is questionable, at least in the case of political economy, whether they are really laws at all. For example, Mill believes that the most basic law of political economy is that people seek more wealth, yet he asserts that it is absurd to maintain that people do in fact always seek more wealth (1843, bk. 6, ch. 9, §3)! What's going on?

"Laws" such as "People seek more wealth" are supposed to identify relevant *causal factors*. These may be counteracted by other factors and prevented from operating, and so, for example, people will not always seek more wealth. But a desire for more wealth remains a significant causal factor. When economists state that people desire more wealth they are stating this truth.

Exactly what truth is this? From the premise, "Desire for wealth is a causal factor," how is any conclusion about what people will do supposed to follow? One possibility is that the claim that people seek more wealth is a counterfactual claim. If other causal factors were absent, or if they were to balance, or if they were not to push too strongly in another direction, then people would always seek more wealth. One can use such a subjunctive in explaining or predicting things, if, in the circumstances involving the phenomena to be explained or predicted, other "disturbing" causal factors are absent, or they balance or they do not push too strongly in another direction. Another possibility, which differs only in its metaphysics, is that the claim that people seek more wealth is true only when qualified with a *ceteris paribus* clause: if other causal factors are absent, or they balance, or they do not push too strongly in another direction, then people always prefer a larger commodity bundle to a smaller one. When the *ceteris paribus* condition is met, such a qualified law can be used to explain and to predict phenomena.[6]

According to both proposals if some antecedent (*ceteris paribus*) condition is (or were) met, then everyone does (or would) seek more wealth. This antecedent condition is vague. One can specify some of it, but one cannot specify all of it. For example, if an agent is gagged and chained to a wall, then the antecedent condition is not met. But if an agent is competent, free, and knowledgeable about the options, the antecedent condition may still fail to be met. The set of possible interferences or "disturbing causes" is heterogeneous and impossible to specify completely. I argued that qualified laws can nevertheless have definite meanings and truth conditions and that it is possible to gather evidence that confirms or disconfirms them. In effect, I argued that inexact laws are exact laws inexactly formulated and known, and that by examining the performance of the generalization without its vague qualifications one can find reason to affirm or to deny that one has a genuine (but inexact) law (Hausman 1992, ch. 8; 1981, ch. 7).

Although I have been wedded to this picture for a long time, I have not been blind to its unsatisfactory features:

1. It is questionable whether any of the "inexact" claims of economics or of any other discipline are inexact *laws*. Is there any precise qualified or counterfactual claim that is inexactly expressed as "People prefer more wealth"?
2. Why should one believe that there are any such claims? Satisfying all the justification conditions might make the *hope* that there are such claims less unreasonable, but it is hard to see what would constitute good evidence that the claims of economics are truly inexact laws.
3. This framework sits uncomfortably with the practice of economists. When do they explore whether these generalizations meet conditions such as the ones I have formulated elsewhere? Why don't they address the question of what are the main factors that interfere or disturb the fundamental "laws" of economics? Is it only a failure of nerve and a

---

[6] Because of metaphysical qualms about counterfactuals, I preferred the non-counterfactual *ceteris paribus* construal, but the differences between regarding such claims as subjunctive or as qualified are not germane to the discussion here.

desire to dodge uncomfortable questions that leads economists so consistently to avoid the terminology of laws?

Although economists have unreasonable philosophical scruples about the explicit use of causal language, it is more natural to claim that the desire for more wealth is one of the causal factors influencing choices than to claim that there is some complicated law relating desire for wealth to choices. Since it is independently plausible to take the explanation of an event to consist in citing its causes, why not jettison the whole complicated story told above and say simply that economists explain by citing causes and predict by inferring effects from causes?

3 Tendencies and mechanisms

It is natural to describe the component causes as giving rise to "tendencies." This is the interpretation of Mill defended by Nancy Cartwright (1989, esp. ch. 4), Uskali Mäki (1992, and esp. 1993) and Geert Reuten (1996). Drawing on the work of Roy Bhasker, Tony Lawson defends a related view that science should formulate "transfactuals" that describe the "non-empirical activity" of mechanisms that are operating whether or not their operation manifests itself (1997, pp. 23, passim; see also Bhaskar 1975). On this interpretation, claims such as "People seek more wealth" express tendencies, capacities, or mechanisms rather than laws. Such tendencies sometimes give rise to regularities, and it is by virtue of the connections between tendencies and regularities that claims about tendencies can be tested. The tendencies are not, however, themselves regularities. For example, people's tendency to seek more wealth might give rise to nearly universal wealth-seeking behavior in circumstances such as those that characterize stock markets, while the tendency gives rise to little wealth-seeking behavior in Buddhist monasteries. Yet it is equally "there" in both contexts. Unlike claims concerning regularities, the tendency claim is not restricted in scope, and the tendency remains intact even when its manifestation is masked or counteracted.

If one models the principles of economics as claims about causal mechanisms, capacities, or tendencies rather than directly as inexact laws, then the deductive method would be more directly a matter of *compounding causes* rather than a matter of *deducing* (*derivative* laws). Although framing the problem of theorizing about complex systems this way may fit the language of economists more naturally, has one made any real progress? Has one escaped the task of explaining how apparently false or inexact principles can be both explanatory and a reliable basis for prediction or has one merely postponed it?

It might be argued that an advantage of jettisoning talk of laws is that one no longer faces any imperative actually to find an exact account. What counts on a causal model is identifying deep discriminating causes and discovering the mechanisms according to which they operate. To do this does not require that one produce an account that is freed from all of the inessential falsehoods of current accounts. On a view that takes the principles of economics to be inexact laws, in contrast, one does not know precisely what the principles mean until that distant ideal future when their *ceteris paribus* clauses have been filled in. Although explanations in economics can, no doubt, be improved, it seems absurd to maintain that they remain inadequate and ill-understood until their *ceteris paribus* conditions can be fully specified.

Yet, without knowing all the "disturbing causes," how confident can one be that the mechanism one identifies is really operating and responsible for the phenomena to be explained? If there is no inexact law, then on many analyses of causation, one has not correctly identified a causal factor. If one has no sense of what the inexact laws are, to what extent can one be said to understand the mechanism?

An apparently much more forceful argument can be made for the tendency construal. According to the inexact-law model, a claim such as "people seek more wealth" tells one about choice only when the *ceteris paribus* condition is met. "But that will not do . . . Even if these regularities did hold *ceteris paribus* – or, other things being *equal* – that would have no bearing on the far more common case whether other things are *not* equal" (Cartwright 1989, p. 177; see also Lawson 1996, esp. pp. 408–9).

Consider a more transparent example from simple physics. On the inexact-law view, Galileo's law tells one how bodies fall (or would fall) when there are (or if there were) no non-gravitational forces acting on them. So, by itself, Galileo's law says *nothing* about how bodies fall in the real world where other forces (such as air resistance) are always acting on them. Lawson would conclude that one should interpret Galileo's law as a transfactual describing "something that *is* going on, that is having an effect, even if the actual (possibly observable) outcome is jointly co-determined by (possibly numerous) other influences" (1996, p. 408). Cartwright rejects transfactuals, and she emphasizes instead that "part of the point of taking capacities seriously as things in the world, and not just particularly strong modalities, [is] that they should remain intact from one kind of situation to another" (1989, p. 163).

One can thus argue in favor of theorizing in terms of tendencies on the ground that, in contrast to the inexact-law model, one can talk about factors that may be intact or even "operating" even when they are canceled out or outweighed by other factors. But I think that this argument is a mistake. Rather than an objection to a qualified or subjunctive universal generalization construal, the fact that inexact laws apply only when there are no "disturbing causes" seems to me a *virtue* of talking in terms of laws rather than tendencies. Galileo's law does not suffice to make inferences about what happens when other forces are acting. One also needs principles concerning how to combine different factors. And it is worth separating the laws of the individual causes from the laws of their composition. In the case of mechanics, the principles of composition are very simple – it is just a matter of vector addition. In economics, on the other hand, principles of composition are complicated and controversial. These rules of composition should be distinguished from the individual principles of economics themselves. There are no grounds here for rejecting an inexact-law account.

In a similar vein, Nancy Cartwright has argued that "Causal interactions are interactions of causal *capacities*, and they cannot be picked out unless capacities themselves can be recognized" (1989, p. 164). If a causal law is simply a universal generalization, then the only thing that one can say about causal interaction is that the consequents in inexact laws sometimes fail to hold. There is no way to distinguish between failures due to causal interaction and failures due to errors in one's purported laws or resulting from the influence of some further disturbing cause.

Like the last objection, this one is, I believe, mistaken. As soon as one knows some of the principles of composition, one can make predictions about what will happen when causal factors are combined. When these predictions are disappointed, one can investigate whether some disturbing cause (some violation of the *ceteris paribus* condition) was responsible, or whether the factors fail to combine in accordance with the principles of composition. Only in the latter case will there be a causal interaction.

I am not sure whether one understands methodology and explanation better if one focuses on laws or if one focuses on tendencies or even whether it turns out to matter. The decision ultimately depends on what theories of scientific explanation and theory construction are most satisfactory. At a superficial level both accounts appear to be capable of explaining how people's pursuit of more wealth can be a fundamental cause, even though there is no universal law saying that people seek more wealth. I do not think that Mill's writings clearly commit him to either a tendency or a *ceteris paribus* law view of component causes, and indeed

Mill does not distinguish clearly between these interpretations of component causes. In the past I have preferred the *ceteris paribus* law view of component causes, because it is more modest metaphysically, and because I have been leery of taking the revolutionary step of demoting laws from their central role in the understanding of science. But a decision does not need to be made here, since both the law and tendency interpretations permit one to describe the difficulties that arise in "compounding" causes.

4 The composition of causes

To make possible the "deduction" of the net force in mechanics, one needs to know more than just how the causes act separately – that is, the separate force laws. One also needs to know the law governing their combination, and this law cannot be derived from knowledge of how forces act separately. To speak, as Mill does, of a deductive method, is misleading because the law governing the conjoint operation of causes cannot be deduced from the laws governing the component causes separately.

How could Mill have thought otherwise? In Book 3 of his *Logic* Mill writes:

Now, if we happen to know what would be the effect of each cause when acting separately from the other, we are often able to arrive deductively, or *a priori*, at a correct prediction of what will arise from their conjunct agency. To render this possible, it is only necessary that the same law which expresses the effect of each cause acting by itself shall also correctly express the part due to that cause of the effect which follows from the two together. This condition is realized in the extensive and important class of phenomena, commonly called mechanical, namely, the phenomena of the communication of motion (or of pressure, which is the tendency to motion) from one body to another. In this important class of cases of causation, one cause never, properly speaking, defeat or frustrate another; both have their full effect. . . This law of nature is called, in dynamics, the principle of the Composition of Forces: and, in imitation of that well-chosen expression, I shall give the name of the Composition of Causes to the principle which is exemplified in all cases in which the joint effect of several causes is identical with the sum of their separate effects. (1843, bk. 3, ch. 6, §1)

Mill is claiming that one can deduce what will happen when causes are combined from the laws of their separate action plus the principle of the Composition of Causes, which says that "the joint effect of several causes is identical with the sum of their separate effects." I shall call this principle, "the additivity assumption." In mechanical phenomena, one "adds up" the forces (or the accelerations they cause) and gets the right answer. It would be more informative to call the method Mill is espousing "compositional" rather than "deductive" for the derivation of the combined effect is a process of adding and subtracting.

If one assumes additivity, then the deductive method can work, but it is not clear what additivity means outside of the special case of mechanics. In some instances one can take it literally as, for example, when one interprets a change in quantity demanded as a sum of an income and a substitution effect.[7] But how is one supposed to "add up" the consequences for behavior of, for example, uncertainty, time preference, diminishing marginal rates of substitution and diminishing returns? What goes on in much of economics is more like deducing than adding, and it is unlike what Mill envisioned.

Even if one could make clear what was involved in "adding" causal factors in economics, it is hard to see what justification there might be for assuming that the causes of some economic phenomenon are additive. In mechanics, it seems easy to defend the assumption that causes are additive. One can alter the air-resistance and measure the change in the acceleration of a falling body. The predictions of a formula derived with the help of vector addition from Galileo's law and laws of friction are in good agreement with the data. But the same possibilities of experimentation that show that one has the correct combined law also make the deductive method unnecessary: Mill's methods of induction can be applied directly to the combined law. Proceeding by studying the component causes separately might have many advantages, but it is not needed to justify the claim that the formula combining gravitational and frictional forces is indeed a causal law.

What justifies the compositional assumption when one cannot directly establish the combined law? The effect of multiple causal factors acting together might be completely different from "sum" of their separate effects. Causal factors may interact, and Mill has provided little reason to believe that tendencies, such as the tendency to seek more wealth, are still "acting" in the presence of other causes. One might think that one could answer this skepticism about the possibility of developing economics deductively merely by successfully carrying out the steps of the deductive method. And I think that in fact Mill is confident of the possibility of developing economics deductively because of how neatly his and Ricardo's economics follows from simple and plausible premises.

---

[7] But note that demand curves are *decomposed* into income and substitution effects rather that built up from them. As I discuss below, much of economics does not in fact involve "adding" of the sort that Mill has in mind.

For example, given the capitalist's drive for profits, the worker's inclination to breed, and diminishing returns in agriculture, Ricardo and Mill held that rates of profit should decline, and population and rents should increase. But the classic argument for diminishing rates of profits and increasing population and rents is not aptly described as a procedure of adding component causes, because none of the three factors violates any of the *ceteris paribus* conditions attached to the other factors. For example, diminishing returns is not a force that needs to be added or subtracted from the drive to maximize profits, and the latter is not added to or subtracted from the propensity to propagate. One needs deductive logic rather than an additivity assumption to derive the economic conclusion concerning profits and rents, and so the success (such as it was) of an economics based on such a derivation does not support the additivity assumption.[8]

5 Can the deductive method work?

Even if Mill's economics followed his compositional method, its apparent success would not vindicate the method. Suppose that the derivation of diminishing rates of profit and increasing rents did exemplify Mill's deductive method and suppose (contrary to nineteenth century data), one found that the rate of profit did diminish and rents and population did increase. Would one then be justified in regarding this trend as a causal law? The demands of the deductive method would have been met, but what reason is there to believe that the factors mentioned *cause* the diminishing rates of profit and increasing rents? Empirical studies only establish the existence of an empirical law. To believe that one has a causal law, one has to believe that the deduction correctly displays how the individual causes act together. But this is what needs showing. Mill has no answer for those who doubt whether causal laws of complex phenomena such as economies can be deduced from the laws of the separate causes.

If the derivation of economic laws were a matter of strict logical deduction from a set of true premises, these qualms would be unfounded. But, as we have seen, the derivation of economic laws depends on

---

[8] Deductive logic is not enough. One also needs some sort of persistence or non-interaction assumption to justify the claim that the separate causal factors continue to operate in the presence of other factors. Additivity is assumed in the treatment of technological improvements, but that part of the theory is so unsuccessful that no support for the deductive method can be found in it.

incomplete premises, simplifications concerning initial conditions, and a vague additivity assumption. So there are ample grounds for doubt. A messy derivation of an economic generalization from simplifications, plausible *ceteris paribus* laws, and an additivity assumption can increase one's confidence in the correctness of the generalization, but Mill believes that science should provide inductive *proof*. Unless there are grounds to take the component causes as additive, the deductive method does not provide the sort of decisive supporting argument that Mill thought sciences ought to provide for their conclusions. Mill might appear to close this gap in his argument for a deductive economics in the following famous passage:

The laws of the phenomena of society are, and can be, nothing but the laws of the actions and passions of human beings united together in the social state. Men, however, in a state of society, are still men; their actions and passions are obedient to the laws of individual human nature. Men are not, when brought together, converted into another kind of substance, with different properties; as hydrogen and oxygen are different from water. . .Human beings in society have no properties but those which are derived from, and may be resolved into, the laws of the nature of individual man. In social phenomena the Composition of Causes is the universal law. (1843, bk. 6, ch. 7, §1)

There are two serious problems with this quotation. First, since one is not, in Mill's view, able to acquire appreciable knowledge of social phenomena without employing the deductive method, one cannot know whether Mill's claims about the relations between social phenomena and human nature are true without taking for granted what he is trying to show. Second, this passage is stronger on assertion than on argument. Mill argues only that the psychological laws governing human beings in society are the psychological laws governing individual human beings, but nothing follows from this concerning the character of social laws in general. To reach the conclusion that "the laws of the phenomena of society are, and can be, nothing but the laws of the actions and passions of human beings united together in the social state," Mill needs to show that all laws of social phenomena derive from the laws of psychology and of the natural sciences. Mill has not provided such an argument, and by addressing the different question of the relations between the *properties* of compounds and constituents, he has muddied the waters. For many properties of societies (consider, for example, social mobility or rate of increase of the money supply) resemble properties of individual human beings as little as the properties of water resemble those of hydrogen.

Mill does not believe that the additivity of effects always obtains, and he goes on immediately after the passage just quoted to write,

This principle [of the Composition of Causes], however, by no means prevails in all departments of the field of nature. The chemical combination of two substances produces, as is well known, a third substance with properties different from those of either of the two substances separately, or of both of them taken together. Not a trace of the properties of hydrogen or of oxygen is observable in those of their compound water. (1843, bk. 3, ch. 6, §1)

The composition of causes is here identified with a third principle, which one might call "the summation of properties." Mill finds that the phenomena of chemistry are not mechanical, because many of the *properties* of compounds are not "sums" of the properties of their constituents, even though they might be literally deducible from generalizations governing their constituents and how they combine. Mill slides back and forth between questions concerning (1) what can be *deduced* about complex subject matters from a knowledge of the "laws" governing individual causal factors and principles of combination (2) whether effects of causes can be "added," and (3) whether the properties of compounds are similar to those of their constituents.

Although the composition of causes is not true of all phenomena, nevertheless

The former case, that of the Composition of Causes, is the general one; the other is always special and exceptional. There are no objects which do not, as to some of their phenomena, obey the principle of the Composition of Causes; none that have not some laws which are rigidly fulfilled in every combination into which the objects enter. The weight of a body, for instance, is a property which it retains in all the combinations in which it is placed. (1843, bk. 3, ch. 6, §2)

Mill's grounds for making the general metaphysical claim of the preponderance of additivity are that all objects "obey the principle of the Composition of Causes" with regard to some of "their phenomena." This is what one would expect if physical properties are mechanical and all objects have some physical properties. But it does not follow that "The former case, that of the Composition of Causes, is the general one." And even if this conclusion were justified, it would not in turn provide a strong reason to regard the messy deductions from simplifications and psychological laws as social laws. There is nothing here to fill the gap for Mill and to justify employing the deductive method.

Someone who follows Mill's prescriptions for economics identifies a set of potentially significant causes of the phenomena of interest, ascertains their separate laws, and, assuming additivity, "adds up" their separate effects to determine their joint effects. If the results fit the data, then one concludes that one has causal knowledge of the phenomena of interest. Even in the best of cases, this method is precarious because of the additivity assumption. Deriving generalizations in this way surely gives one some further reason to believe that they are true and explanatory, but the process only provides secure justification for the derived laws when the deductive method turns out not to be necessary after all.

References

Bhaskar, Roy (1975) *A Realist Theory of Science*, Hemel Hempstead: Harvester Press.

Buchanan, James (1975) *The Limits of Liberty: Between Anarchy and the Leviathan*, Chicago: University of Chicago Press.

Cartwright, Nancy (1989) *Nature's Capacities and their Measurement*, Oxford: Oxford University Press.

De Marchi, Neil (1986) "Discussion: Mill's Unrevised Philosophy of Economics: A Comment on Hausman," *Philosophy of Science*, 53: 89–100.

Hausman, Daniel (1981) *Capital, Profits, and Prices: An Essay in the Philosophy of Economics*, New York: Columbia University Press.

(1992) *The Inexact and Separate Science of Economics*, Cambridge: Cambridge University Press.

(1995) "The Composition of Economic Causes," *The Monist*, 78: 295–307.

Hutchison, Terence (1998) "Ultra-Deductivism from Nassau Senior to Lionel Robbins and Daniel Hausman," *Journal of Economic Methodology*, 5: 43–91.

Lawson, Tony (1996) "Developments in Economics as Realist Social Theory," *Review of Social Economy*, 14: 405–22.

(1997) *Economics and Reality*, London: Routledge.

Mäki, Uskali (1992) "The Market as an Isolated Causal Process: A Metaphysical Ground for Realism," in Bruce Caldwell and Stephan Boehm (eds.), *Austrian Economics: Tensions and New Developments*, Dordrect: Kluwer, pp. 35–59.

(1993) "Isolation, Idealization and Truth in Economics," in Bert Hamminga and Neil de Marchi (eds.), *Poznan Studies in the Philosophy of the Sciences and the Humanities* 38: 147–68.

Mill, J. S. (1836) "On the Definition of Political Economy and the Method of Investigation Proper to It," repr. in *Collected Works of John Stuart Mill*, vol. 4 (Toronto: University of Toronto Press, 1967).

(1843) *A System of Logic*, London: Longmans, Green & Co., 1949.

Reuten, Geert (1996) "A Revision of the Neoclassical Economics Methodology – Appraising Hausman's Mill-Twist, Robbins-Gist, Popper-Whist," *Journal of Economic Method*, 3: 39–68.

16 Economics without mechanism

JOHN DUPRÉ

1 Mechanism

A standard and natural approach to the metaphysics of economics is to start with a careful scrutiny of economic theory and practice, or some suitable part thereof, and decide what metaphysical picture is implied by, or presupposed by, or most consistent with this theory and practice. My approach in this paper will be rather different. I shall start by presenting and motivating some broad metaphysical ideas, and then discuss the question how economics would look in the light of those ideas. The rationale for this methodology is as follows. Economics has developed in the context of a broad set of metaphysical assumptions that have existed in parallel with the last four hundred years of science. Although the metaphysical picture in question has primarily been developed in relation to the physical sciences, it has been of fundamental importance in the development of economics.[1] In a research program carried out over a number of years and culminating in my book, *The Disorder of Things* (1993), I have developed a broad critique of this metaphysical picture. An obvious sequel to this project is an examination of the implications of the rejection of this picture for various areas of science. Economics is an especially appropriate candidate for such an examination because its high status among the social sciences derives, arguably, precisely from the extent to which its practice reveals a commitment to this classical metaphysics.[2]

In *The Disorder of Things* I referred most generally to this classical

---

[1] Historians of science have recently traced the intimate connections between the rise of physical science and the development of neoclassical economics in the late nineteenth century (see e.g. Mirowski 1989).

[2] Since writing this paper I have come across Tony Lawson's important book *Economics and Reality* (1997), which applies some quite similar metaphysical ideas in some detail to

metaphysics as mechanism. Mechanism, of course, is a doctrine that has something to do with machines – in fact I have come to believe that the connections with machines are deeper and more interesting than I had appreciated when I wrote the book.[3] In the book I discuss at length three different doctrines that I take to be characteristic ingredients of mechanism: essentialism, reductionism, and (something like) determinism. One might very crudely relate these doctrines to machines in the following way: determinism says that machines are predictable and reliable: the more reliable the better the machine. The world is a perfect machine (originally it was taken to have been built by God, after all) and so is perfectly reliable. This reliable production of more or less complex behavior is achieved by the way a machine exploits the simpler reliable behavior of its parts. Thus the way to understand a machine is always in terms of a decomposition into parts, and perhaps parts of parts, and parts of parts of parts, etc. This is a form of reductionism or mereological determinism, the determination of the behavior of the whole by the behavior of the parts. Finally, the preceding doctrines presuppose that it is possible to distinguish unequivocally what the parts of a machine are. Thus, to take a familiar example, the piston is a genuine part of a car in a sense in which the dashboard, containing parts that relate to a variety of quite distinct systems, is not. This connects with a central aspect of scientific essentialism, the idea that science aims to discover an objectively real classification of things.

The debate over micro-reductionism in science concerns the extent to which science is committed to explaining the behavior of objects in terms of the behavior of their parts. An extreme and classical kind of reductionism holds that all laws governing the behavior of complex objects should be deducible from the laws of a lower-level science and thus, ultimately, the laws of all sciences should be deducible from those of particle physics.[4] Hardly anyone holds this kind of strict reductionism any more, and at least among philosophers of biology and of the social sciences, reductionism even in more moderate versions is distinctly unfashionable. While it is clear that the investigation of structural factors plays a central role in the development of science, it is generally conceded that the laws or causal knowledge to be discerned in these sciences is in some quite strong sense autonomous from any accessible facts about underlying structure. One might imagine that the decline of reductionism

economics. I discuss this book, and some minor disagreements with my own position, in Dupré (1999).
[3] The connections with Nancy Cartwright's work generally, and her contribution to this volume specifically, are obvious and not coincidental.
[4] A classic statement is Oppenheim and Putnam (1958).

would signal the decline of mechanism. But surprisingly, nothing could be further from the truth.

A fundamental issue here is the relation between reductionism and what I called "(something like) determinism." I avoid referring to determinism *tout court* for the obvious reason that much of science, and most significantly fundamental physics, is not now thought to be deterministic. Contemporary positions remain close to determinism, however, in one of two ways. First, it is often said that the indeterminism disappears at a very low level of material aggregation, so that indeterminism occurs only at a level far beneath our concern. It does seem to me obvious that it will be impossible reliably to shield macrodeterminism from the indeterminism at the microlevel, but I won't pursue this. A more important point is that an indeterministic microlevel can be just as *comprehensive* as a deterministic one. Even if it couldn't specify the behavior of each particle, it might specify the probability distribution of all possible behaviors, and do so in a way fully determined by facts at the microlevel. This is the doctrine of the causal completeness of the microlevel, of which microlevel determinism is a special limiting case, and it is a doctrine that is still widely believed.

The causal completeness of the microlevel is, of course, a necessary condition for reductionism. Reductionism hypothesizes that in the end everything will be explained by microphysics; so microphysics cannot leave anything out. It is, however, far from sufficient, as revealed by the greater prevalence of subscription to the former than to the latter. An excellent source for seeing how these positions are separated is in the recent work of Alexander Rosenberg, notably *Economics: Mathematical Politics or Science of Diminishing Returns* (1992), and *Instrumental Biology or the Disunity of Science* (1994). Rosenberg harbors no doubts as to the completeness of the microphysical, but he is also committed to the view that biology and the social sciences are irreducible to physics. According to Rosenberg, the trouble with these sciences is that their categories are physically heterogeneous. In biology this is due to natural selection. Nature selects for function not structure, and many different structures may serve the same function. In economics the problem is compounded. For not only are humans biological objects, but their properties of relevance to economics are intentional properties; and Rosenberg argues that many different physiological properties might ground the same intentional property. Thus these properties are twice removed from connectibility with the physical. But since the causal properties of an object are, nonetheless, determined by its physical structure, objects that share the same biological or economic properties will be causally heterogeneous. These sciences are, therefore, imperfect.

They are defensible as (sometimes) instrumentally useful for finite beings such as us, but more computationally and cognitively talented creatures would look directly at the physical structure of things and hence get straight to the true causal powers. It is doubtful, in fact, whether Rosenberg even sees much instrumental utility in economics.

All this is part of a familiar picture. It is the picture of mental epiphenomenalism, of the mental realm as a causally inert patina on the underlying physical – perhaps neurological – reality, and of voluntary action as mere illusion. And indeed, it is a view that makes everything macroscopic epiphenomenal, causally inert. But, finally, it is a view which philosophers driven on the one hand by an increasing realization of the hopelessness of reductionism, and on the other by admiration for physics, are frequently found to embrace.

In criticizing this view, I want to begin by attempting to allocate the onus of violating common sense. On my view things at many different levels of organization and complexity – animals, planets, plants, electrons, corporations, etc. – have autonomous causal powers.[5] "Autonomous" here means not reducible to a consequence of the causal powers of the physical particles of which they are composed. An immediate consequence of this view is that there can be no level of organization, including that of microphysics, at which the behavior of objects is completely determined by some set of laws describing only objects at that level. Levels of organization are too intimately interconnected for there to be any possible insulation of one level from the influence of other levels. But many philosophers, Rosenberg for example, find it extraordinary and implausible to deny the completeness of microphysical law for describing microphysical phenomena. My question, then, is whether we should find it more plausible to deny the completeness of physics, or to deny the ultimate causal efficacy of everything above the microphysical level. Of course I prefer the former course.

Let me elaborate a little what I see as the strangeness of Rosenberg's position. He believes that everything that happens happens in accordance with, and as determined by, the universal laws that govern the behavior of the physical particles of which everything is composed. The buzzing, blooming confusion of the phenomenal world, on the other hand, is a mere epiphenomenal froth on this underlying microphysical reality. The macrosocopic, qua macroscopic, is, for Rosenberg, causally inert. I

---

[5] This set of views, which I there describe as "promiscuous realism," is defended in detail in *The Disorder of Things*. The thesis encompasses both the autonomy of objects at different levels of structural complexity, and the necessity of diverse and independent classifications of objects at the same level (about which, see further below).

might naïvely suppose that it was the sight of the bear and my belief that bears are dangerous that causes me (perhaps foolishly) to scamper up a tree. But on Rosenberg's view it is misleading to refer here to the sight of the bear, which suggests that it is by virtue of being a bear that I react to the object as I do. On Rosenberg's picture it must be by virtue of being a certain aggregation of physical particles that the object has the causal consequences it does. Perhaps most of the aggregations of physical particles that would succeed in constituting a bear would have the relevant causal consequence, and perhaps there is a selective explanation for this happy coincidence – an explanation that might even explain why an ontology of bears is one that serves my reproductive interests well enough. But for all this, the ontology, or perhaps mythology, of bears, lions, snakes, and so on is one forced on us only by our cognitive limitations. If we were smart enough we would identify things as just the precise aggregation of physical particles that they were and predict their behavior from the laws of physics; we would certainly not hamper our thinking with the physically heterogeneous categories of biology. It is hardly necessary to spell out how central economic concepts – price, firm, market, etc. – would fare on this picture, and Rosenberg is as skeptical about economics as his metaphysics would suggest. As I have noted, he sees economics as dependent on an epiphenomenon (the intentional) of an epiphenomenon (the biological) (see Rosenberg 1992). Here it is implausible to expect even the rough correlations that we might hope for in biology between macroscopic kinds and microstructural make-up. Like Bishop Berkeley, I am unwilling to sacrifice the familiar world to a scientistic philosophy, though unlike Berkeley I am greedy enough to want to endorse the unobservable realities of physics as well. It is useful to recall that however implausible Berkeley's immaterialism may seem, he did brilliantly demonstrate that Locke's version of materialism wasn't exactly plain old common sense.

Rosenberg sometimes associates his position with empiricism (e.g. 1994, p. 10). This strikes me as remarkable. He sometimes writes as if empiricism were just whatever method best accounts for the success of physical science as, for example, when he attributes to empiricism a reliance on theoretical explanation by unification (1994, p. 11). But empiricism, which for all its admitted difficulties and necessary qualifications, I want to embrace as a cardinal empirical virtue, has something to do with grounding in experience. And surely the privileging of the unobservable over the observable is the antithesis of empiricism. I do not want to endorse the extreme empiricism of those, like Bas van Fraassen (1981), who deny that we have any reason to believe in the ontology of unobservables. But I do think the spurious adoption of the mantle of empiricism obscures the counter-intuitive nature of the kind of physicalism Rosenberg supports. And I also think that a proper recognition of the distance such a position takes us from a grounding in experience is an important part of the way in which such a physicalism violates common sense.

Rosenberg, then, defends a "materialist and mereological determinist approach to biological and, a fortiori, social systems: they are . . . 'nothing but' physical ones" (1994, p. 55). The determinist aspect of this position is obviously subject to question in view of the indeterministic aspects of quantum mechanics, but as I have said I don't think this is the crux of the matter and I shall pass over it here.[6] He concedes that the mereological determinism, the determination of the behavior of wholes by the behavior of their parts, is not an empirically supported position since we cannot in fact "systematically derive the biological from the physical" (p. 55). I suspect, however, that he thinks that mereological determinism is a condition on any materialism worthy of the name. I disagree. I consider myself a materialist but, being also an empiricist, I see no reason to believe in mereological determinism.

Before going any further, I do want to applaud one aspect of Rosenberg's position. Rosenberg thinks that microphysics describes a domain of objects that is exhaustive, in the sense at least that everything is physically composed of them and of nothing else, and that conform to universal and exceptionless laws. Rosenberg correctly concludes that the behavior of the larger things composed of these microphysical entities must be fully determined by the latter, and thus that they are in a sense mere epiphenomena of the microphysical. Acknowledging the failure of the reductionism that would substantiate this view Rosenberg, again correctly in my view, resorts to the supervenience and mereological determinism which he treats, again rightly in my view, as reductionism though only for much more computationally talented beings than we. These are ambitious claims and, as he and I agree, claims with no direct empirical support. But they are indeed consequences of his views of the microphysical and Rosenberg should be applauded for forthrightly embracing them. I emphasize this point because it often seems that philosophers want to have their cake – totalizing physics – and eat it too – higher level autonomy. I think here of a certain kind of fuzzy compatibilism about the free will question and certain appeals to both supervenience and autonomy in the philosophy of mind.

---

[6] Rosenberg takes the line that nature asymptotically approaches determinism at higher levels of aggregation (1994, p. 61). For some reason he also (erroneously) attributes this view to me.

Perhaps I also want to have my cake and eat it, because despite believing in higher-level autonomy I do consider myself a materialist, perhaps even a physicalist. I agree with Rosenberg that the microphysical realm is exhaustive: the existence of immaterial minds, souls, ectoplasm, deities, etc. strikes me as, to say the least, unlikely. Hence I believe that if somehow all the physical particles in the universe were annihilated there would be nothing left – perhaps not even empty space. Where I differ is in the commitment to universal physical laws. Thus the sense in which I agree that the biological or even economic realms are "nothing but" the physical is an extremely weak one having to do only with substantial composition. I endorse a very weak physicalism because I endorse, in a sense, only a very weak physics.

Why do so many philosophers, and presumably physicists, believe that the laws of physics are exceptionless and universal? Of course physical laws are generally expressed as universally quantified, but surely we should not be prisoners of our notation? As Nancy Cartwright has been telling us for a number of years, we know that the laws of physics are not universally true, at least as in any form in which we know how to express them (Cartwright 1983). They are true only under quite stringent conditions of the absence of any of an indefinite range of interfering factors. If, improbably, we were able to specify every such possibly interfering factor, the most we would have achieved would be a universal law with extremely restricted application. No doubt it is widely assumed that the laws of physics can always be modified in ways that specify explicitly the consequences of interaction with any possible interfering factor. But then even at the physical level we have gone far beyond what is empirically supported and are expressing mere faith in hypothetical laws that we neither possess nor have any reason to anticipate possessing.

I am aware that this line of argument is liable to produce a certain amount of exasperation. Surely, it will be said, I must admit the extraordinary successes of the physical sciences, and surely such successes would be inexplicable if the world were not in broad outline as physical scientists have supposed it to be: subject to underlying laws of complete universality and generality. It is common to emphasize here the remarkable improvements in predictive accuracy achieved by physicists over the last four centuries (see Rosenberg 1994, p. 36). But of course the fact that physicists are doing something very well doesn't imply that they have the most sophisticated grasp of what they are doing so well. (If it did there would surely be no use for philosophers of science – a consequence for which, I must admit, some enthusiasts for the physical sciences would be willing to bite the bullet.)

Arguments of the sort just mentioned begin to look rather different in the light of much recent work in the history and philosophy of physics. Nature does not pronounce positively or negatively on our theories as soon as we care to ask her. Without denying that experiments can often impressively confirm or refute theories, it has become clear that getting experiments to produce illuminating results is extremely difficult. Returning once again to the literal sense of mechanism, contemporary large-scale physics experiments most obviously, but also older simpler ones, are complex bits of machinery. Like other machines, it generally takes a great deal of work and expertise to set them up and make them work in the ways they are supposed to.[7]

This leads us to what is perhaps the most widespread basis for mereological determinism, if perhaps a less sophisticated one from a philosophical point of view than one grounded more directly in physical law. A bluff commonsensical kind of realist is liable to insist that it would be inexplicable or even miraculous that our machines could work with as much reliability as they do if the theories about the world held by the designers of those machines were not somewhere close to the truth. Would you really get on an airplane if you didn't believe that physics dealt in universal laws? The connection between mechanism and the unity of science, I believe, is intimately related to the unity of purpose and coherence of parts characteristic of a good – indeed a perfect – machine. So it seems to me appropriate that the crux of this debate should turn on a correct appreciation of the nature and significance of machines.

2 Machines and models

Most machines are not, of course, intended to demonstrate scientific theories. Indeed one of the more interesting suggestions that has come out of various parts of the history of science and technology is that the relation between these two is anything but unidirectional. It may be that much scientific theory – thermodynamics and the steam engine provide the *locus classicus* – has developed to explain the successes of engineers rather than the successes of engineers being made possible by ante-cedently established scientific theories. But in view of the point just mentioned about the machine-like nature of most experiments in physics, we can see that this point is not crucial. If physics experiments are a kind

---

[7] This point has been documented in detail by a variety of students of physics in history (Galison 1987), sociology (Pickering 1984), and even anthropology (Traweek 1988).

of machine then the laws of physics are constructed to explain the workings of machines either way. Of course there is more to it. Machines that do what we expect lead us to theories that suggest new kinds of machines, and so on. I am not denying the role of the theories, just insisting on the closure of the circle which relates physical theories to the machines that confirm and implement them, and consequently on the difficulty of arguing from this kind of support for physical laws to their universal range of application.

What I want to say, then, is that machines are very special parts of the world. For machines mereological determinism is almost true (almost, since no machines are perfect) but machines are a poor model for the world in general. Rhetorical support for this position might be gained by reconsidering William Paley's famous thought experiment of the watch found on an apparently deserted island. Paley, of course, wants us to think of the watch as similar in many respects to naturally occurring organisms. But the force of the thought experiment comes, paradoxically, from the anomalous character of the watch: it is quite *unlike* anything we might expect to find lying on the beach on a desert island. Unlike Paley, we are not led to think of a similarity because committed to the view that organisms are artifacts. According to contemporary science, watches are artifacts, plants and animals aren't. The dissimilarity between the two, apart from confirming what many believe, that the world was not created by an intelligent being, should also lead us to question the appropriateness of machines as a model for naturally occurring objects. Indeed, if the world were really a huge piece of machinery, one might wonder why useful, if more modest, machines are so hard to make.

It remains incumbent upon me to say something about what is special about machines. The first point I want to suggest is that it helps to see the behavior of machines not so much as determined but as heavily constrained. Sufficient constraint, of course, can amount to determination. Machines work when they have the capacity to do what they are intended to do, and when they are constrained from doing anything else. The simplest example might be a machine such as a lever. The rigidity of the lever and the solidity of the pivot leave the end no option but to rise when the other end is lowered. More interesting would be a relatively complex machine such as a car. A series of effectively rigid connections between the piston and the drive wheels give a car the capacity to move forward when gasoline is ignited in the cylinders. The difficulty in making a reliable car has mostly to do with blocking all other capacities – for the cylinder to burst or melt, for the piston to seize or fly out of the end of the cylinder, for various connections to fail, etc. The car runs because it has been rendered incapable of doing anything else.

Of course I do not want to deny that there must be some natural regularities to make all this possible. Many of these concern rather simple capacities of materials. Steel rods seldom break except under extreme forces; mixtures of gasoline and air almost always explode when ignited. Note that these can typically be seen as the deterministic upshots of very large numbers of indeterministic capacities exercised at the microlevel. No deterministic tendencies of hydrocarbon molecules to oxidize are required to guarantee the explosion of a cylinder full of a suitable air and gasoline mixture, nor is any deterministic tendency of any molecule to escape the gas tank required to get about the right amount into the cylinder. This provides a specific explanation of reliable regularities that offers no promise of generalization to all causal sequences. I take another similar example (though again Rosenberg (1994) has a quite different account) to be those cases of natural selection that approximate to deterministic processes.

Economists, on the whole, do not build machines but models. (I shall discuss the extent to which they may sometimes build something like machines at the end of the paper.) There is, however, an interesting parallel between model-building and machine-building. As I have noted, much of the work of building a good machine involves shielding it from the possible influence of interfering or disrupting forces. The problem with model-building, whether in economics, population genetics, sociology, or many other areas of science, is also provided by the possibility of interfering influences not considered in the model. Models, on the other hand, have a huge advantage over machines: whereas machines must find a way of actually blocking interfering forces, models simply abstract from such forces or, in other words, ignore them. Here are all the advantages of theft over honest toil.

Obviously enough, however, this advantage of models is also their great weakness. Whether they are good models depends on how important the factors the models ignore are in determining the behavior of the system being modeled. Where models fail to correspond closely with the empirical reality they aim to model – as notoriously occurs with many economic models – this may be because the elements included in the model do not have the properties attributed to them, or because other factors overwhelm the effect of those included. Popperians may note with distress that this means a model can never be refuted: we may always suppose that we have abstracted away from important factors. But this is not my main point here. Let us assume that the model is correct though perhaps incomplete; its failings, that is to say, are all of the second kind. My point, then, is that inside every model is a machine trying to get out. As long as we stick to modeling and passive observation, we can only hope to improve the model by incorporating ever more factors into it. On the other hand there is also the quite different possibility of trying to build a machine in which only the factors included in the model are allowed to operate. Others are excluded in the ways characteristic of machine-building. Thus a correct model, in the sense that the causal powers of its elements are correctly described, may be thought of as a possible machine. And a model may be correct in this sense even if it is empirically quite inaccurate. This sense in which economics is a mechanistic science, and the extent to which economists may actually aspire to be machine-builders, will be taken up in more detail later in this paper.

3 Parts and wholes

In this section I shall try to discharge one further onus clearly incumbent upon my position, an explanation of what I take to be the actual significance of structural explanation, explanation of the behavior of the whole in terms of properties of the parts. Here I want to reiterate a thesis that I suggested at several points in *The Disorder of Things*. Structural explanation, I suggest, is required to explain how a complex object has the capacities it has, but does not generally tell us which capacities will be exercised when. Thus physiology and biochemistry have provided wonderful insights into the abilities of organisms to metabolize, move, reproduce, and so on. But more is needed to determine when these capacities will be displayed. Thus even for a capacity as "mechanistic" as metabolism of food no amount of biochemistry will tell us when food to be metabolized will be introduced into the system. Here we might note an important characteristic of machines: machines typically have both relevant capacities and controls.[8]

It is true that for relatively simple organisms a behavior may be more or less deterministically elicited by features of the environment. But even in this case we cannot in principle predict the production of behavior, nor even its probability, merely from examination of the structure of the organism. The behavior of the individual can, at best, only be predicted from an extensive knowledge of the organism and its environment. Typically this will give us no more than an estimate of the probability

---

[8] I have discussed elsewhere some differences between organisms, especially humans, and machines in the context of the free will debate (Dupré 1996). One important point is that humans do not have controls.

that the organism will encounter the triggering environment. In terms of real possibilities for reductive science, it seems to me that here we have a quite sufficient obstacle to any practical reduction quite apart from Rosenberg's concerns about selection for function. In my book (1993) I elaborate such an argument in terms of the necessity of appealing to abstractions in real mereological explanations.

All explanation is partial: not everything can be explained at once. For the purposes of explanation one takes certain matters for granted, and others as in need of illumination. This elementary observation points to an important qualification of my concession that capacities are amenable to structural explanation. No doubt there are some very complex physiological facts concerning my brain and my fingers that explain my ability to write this paper. On the other hand, for the electronic traces I am producing to be *this paper*, a comparable diversity of social facts must also obtain. Starting with the social facts that give the traces, when electronically processed into words, public meanings we could move with increasing specificity towards the social practices that make possible the philosophy of science. Thus my capacity to write this paper is contingent on many social facts in addition, no doubt, to structural facts about me. I take the general dependence of language on social convention to show the same to be true for a vast range of mental facts. This joint determination of capacities by internal structure and external context makes the possession of autonomous capacities by complex objects quite unproblematic and innocent of the metaphysical mystery-mongering with which it seems sometimes to be associated. Moreover, such autonomous capacities make so-called "downward causation" the determination of parts by wholes, unproblematic.[9] It happens all the time: when, for instance, I decide to raise my arm I cause the motion of billions of physical particles. Although the case of human behavior seems to me the most compelling, I take it that the same account could be applied to much humbler systems. Indeed, in view of the indeterminism of the microphysical and the determinism of macroscopic mechanical phenomena, it seems natural to say that macroscopic mechanical movements of an object cause the movements of its microphysical parts. Needless to add, if I am right about this, there can be no possibility of the causal closure of physics.

Most philosophers, as I have said, are aware of the impossibility of

---

[9] An earlier advocate of the importance of downward causation was Campbell (1974). Kim (1993, essay 17) is another philosopher who has recognized the commitment of non-reductive physicalism to downward causation, but who thinks the idea is highly problematic, perhaps incoherent.

actual reductive explanation in many cases, and their physicalist intuitions are often defended by appeal to so-called supervenience (see again Rosenberg 1992, 1994). Indeed supervenientism has reached near epidemic proportions in recent years. Supervenience is a kind of reductionism, but not for mere mortals. To say that one domain supervenes on another is to say that the former is wholly determined by the latter such that if we had sufficiently powerful – perhaps infinite – minds, we would see everything there was to see by looking at the supervened-upon, that is microstructural, level. As supervenience buffs like to put it, once the physical is fixed, so is everything else. As indicated by the preceding discussion of context dependence, however, even in relatively simple cases, let alone cases from the human sciences, the relevant part of the supervened upon domain may be extensive. Indeed it is arguable that much of the universe would be required to provide the full basis on which many macroscopic properties supervene. Whether or not this is objectionable from a strictly ontological perspective, it is surely more than enough to substantiate my claim that the whole reductionist story is without empirical credentials. As we continue to grapple with the three body problem, a unity of science accessible only to a being capable of grasping and analyzing the microphysical state of the entire universe is not something within reach of any imaginable empirical evidence.

4 Economics

So much for the mechanical universe, the universe in which everything that happens is purely the consequence of the playing out of the laws of microphysics harnessed by the ingenious structuring of countless microphysical components. I shall now make some suggestions as to how the rejection of this metaphysical picture might bear on our understanding of the science of economics. I begin by noting that the situation described in the first part of the paper presents a very troubling dilemma for the metaphysical foundations of economics. On the one hand, it should be clear that traditional monistic physicalism problematizes the very possibility of economic phenomena. No doubt it used to be possible to suppose that economics might be more or less smoothly reduced to individual psychology, and thence through neurophysiology to chemistry and physics. But few would stake much on such a future today. The kinds of entities that figure fundamentally in economic theory – firms, consumers, physical capital, etc. – are, from a purely physical point of view, massively heterogeneous. Worse still, perhaps, many – interest rates, money supplies, etc. – do not look physical at all. Thus a plausible post-reductionist physicalist perspective on economics will be one like that of Rosenberg (1992), who sees economics as an epiphenomenon on an epiphenomenon and as, therefore, of even highly questionable instrumental utility. If the ultimate viability of an area of science depends on its connectability with fundamental physics, then surely economics is in deep trouble. I have no such expectations for science and thus my pluralistic ontology, complete with downward causation by higher-level phenomena, is in principle much friendlier to the possible reality of a domain of economic phenomena. However, I fear that not all economists will welcome my philosophical support, for several reasons.

The first such reason is the threat to objectivity, in the sense of value neutrality. It is undoubtedly a part of the self-image of economists that much of what they do is pure "positive" science; and notoriously "normative" or "welfare" economics has been perceived as something of a disciplinary backwater – not the place to seek a Nobel prize, anyhow. Economists consider themselves to be investigating an independent reality of economic phenomena, and whether their mathematical models correctly describe those phenomena depends solely on how things are out there. The metaphysical picture, of course, that would best motivate that practice would be one that applied the mechanistic metaphysics of physical science directly to economics. But it has become clear that that is impossible. Although my metaphysical position restores the possibility of genuinely causally efficacious economic entities,[10] entities that may even be linked together in quasi-mechanical ways, it does so only by severing the connection with physical science. And by doing so, I shall argue, it in turn threatens the picture of economics as an independent causal order open to fully disinterested enquiry.

The problem is that once one rejects the assumption that economic entities are physically homogeneous parts – even very complex parts – of the fabric of the cosmic machine, one is forced to look in more concrete detail at the way economic kinds are constructed. We need to examine, that is to say, the *economic* principles according to which economic entities are classified into economic kinds. And once we do this it is impossible to escape the conclusion that value judgments are deeply embedded in that constructive process. I suppose that some economists still think that the amount of work done last week in the US is as

---

[10] For more specific examples, Mäki (1990) argues for treating money and entrepreneurship as causally efficacious economic entities. General defences of the relevant kinds of causal capacities against traditional Humean objections can be found in Dupré and Cartwright (1988) and, in most detail, in Cartwright (1990).

objective a matter of fact as the amount of work done in lifting a container onto a truck – just a lot harder to measure. And as I have noted, as a historical matter it appears that the use of the same term is far from coincidental. But it is easy to show how untenable this view is. Traditionally work has been defined as activity for which some remuneration is received. But though it is easy to see the attraction of this definition from a particular interest in publicly visible processes of production, from a broader perspective the definition is entirely arbitrary. Why should my labor in raising potatoes in my back yard not count as work if the same labor provided in exchange for wages for a commercial market gardener does count as work? More generally, why should almost all domestic work – cleaning, cooking, caring for children – not count as fully as work as, say, building nuclear warheads or writing jingles for beer commercials. Some inadequacies in the simple traditional definition have been recognized in recent years, and various alterations have been made. My point here is not to criticize a particular definition nor to advocate any particular alternative. It is rather to insist that there is no unequivocal answer to such questions. Rational progress with such an issue can only be made by asking, first of all, what the point is of making such a definition in the first place, and then considering what aspects of the definition will best serve the relevant ends. It is not hard to discover such goals in the case of work, though unfortunately some of these normative views are hard to reconcile. Sometimes work is thought of as a thing to be minimized (Adam Smith's "toil and trouble," something to be contrasted with ease, leisure, relaxation). But it is also thought of as something fundamental to a person's sense of identity, and something that should be a major feature of any normal adult life. Unemployment – lack of work – is more unequivocally considered a bad thing, to be minimized subject, perhaps, to conflicting economic desiderata. Such broad normative considerations will unavoidably affect the desirability of definitions of work for economic purposes.[11]

Many, perhaps most, central economic concepts have such familiar evaluative content. GDP is generally assumed to be good, and its increase, economic growth, still better. Inflation, for reasons that are somewhat obscure,[12] is generally assumed to be very bad. And so on. Since economic policies are directed, admittedly with questionable

[11] The interrelations and conflicts between various conceptions of work, and the historical evolution of such concepts are discussed in greater detail in Gagnier and Dupré (1995) and Dupré and Gagnier (1996).

[12] Given the amount of personal debt, especially mortgage debt, in a country such as the US, it is clear that inflation would be a boon to a very large segment of the population. This point is curiously absent for most public discussion of inflation. Cynics might

success, at promoting some of these things and avoiding others, the decisions that go into defining such concepts will affect what activities public policies aim to promote. On current criteria, for instance, a major oil spill will qualify, by virtue of the economic activities involved in the attempts to clean it up, as an economic windfall. While I do not suggest that governments encourage oil spills, the typical failure to include degradation of natural resources as an item in GDP accounting is only one of several respects in which such procedures are open to debates with profound quantitative implications.[13] I am not suggesting that there is some objectively correct definition of GDP that is thereby violated, only, again, that whether a particular item is included will have large effects on how particular activities or events show up in economic outcomes, and thus, very probably, will affect which actions are carried out. Thus how economics is practiced, even at the stage of concept construction, can have important effects on the world. Since I have no reason to deny the obvious here, I take this to be an illustration of the causal autonomy of economic agents, though I do not claim that an epiphenomenalist could not tell an adequate story to take account of what I have said so far.

Unwelcome though all this may be to economists there is now direct empirical evidence of the way in which the very business of doing economics can affect the nature of economic phenomena. Some intriguing recent research has suggested that the study of economics actually makes students conform more closely to the axioms of economic man (Frank, Gilovich, and Regan 1993). At the end of an introductory economics class students were found more likely to default in prisoner's dilemma type games, and generally appeared more inclined to act according to canons of economic rationality. Economics professors were found considerably less likely to donate to charity or subscribe to public television than professors in other disciplines (though here it is hard to sort out cause and effect). Given the general currency in our present culture of economic ideas emphasizing and often applauding the pursuit of individual self-interest it is hardly improbable that such ideas could have a considerable influence on behavior far beyond the narrow confines of professional economics; and if so one cannot adequately evaluate the empirical successes, such as they are, of contemporary economic theory without considering the possibility that the behavior that generates the predicted outcomes is, to some degree, generated by the very theory used

wonder whether the official horror of inflation evident in much government policy reflects a greater concern with the interests of bankers than of the general population.

[13] For instance Waring (1988) provides a compelling account of the role of assumptions about gender in the definitions underlying national income accounting.

to predict it. Thus it is arguably impossible to separate purely empirical evaluations of the success of an economic research program from normative concerns about the desirability of the model of human nature that the program presupposes. I do not take this to be a problem peculiar to economics, though I do think the behavioral consequences of neoclassical economic ideology, to the extent that they occur, are, to say the least, unfortunate. Indeed it seems to me quite plausible that any theory of human behavior with wide currency and application will have some effect on its own subject matter. Adding the present point to my previous remarks about the unavoidable normative elements in the construction of economic concepts and the subsequent use of these concepts in guiding public policy, it seems to me clear that there is no sensible prospect of a value-free economics. The fact/value distinction, in short, should go the way of the Berlin wall.

These observations about the value-ladenness of economics relate to mechanism and the unity of science only in so far as reductive mechanism might have offered the most plausible line of resistance to them. I now come to a second respect in which I expect my ontological reassurances to meet with less than unqualified enthusiasm from economists. Although I do not believe that the preceding remarks show that economic concepts fail to refer to aspects of reality, I do believe that they show that reality does not determine a uniquely correct set of economic concepts. Normative considerations are able to gain a grip on economic concepts because the causal order alone does not determine how these concepts should be defined. I continue to insist that these concepts may reflect aspects of reality, because relative to a set of normative or other desiderata there might perfectly well be better or worse ways, even a best way, of defining a concept, such being determined by the real causal capacities of real economic agents. In *The Disorder of Things* I argued for such a pluralistic view of biology, specifically that there was no unique taxonomy of biological organisms determined by nature.[14] Here I am suggesting that the same must be true for economics, though as I hope to have made clear, this underdetermination may be of even greater practical consequence in economics. For the case of biology I argued that different taxonomic schemes would be most appropriate for different investigative purposes. For the case of economics not only will different investigative purposes call for different conceptualizations of the phenomena, but in

---

[14] Critics of this earlier view have often been unwilling to accept the compatibility of realism with the failure of uniqueness. No doubt this is related to the curiously prevalent view that the belief that scientific claims are often true is somehow incompatible with the truism that science is socially constructed.

addition the systematic adoption of a particular way of doing economics can be expected to affect, perhaps profoundly over time, the nature of the phenomena being investigated. This point makes clear the necessity of recognizing the normative dimension in the choice of a set of economic concepts. The only possible foundations for economics, I suggest, are in political philosophy.

Having worked my way down to foundations, let me return to something more superficial, ontology and the limitations of mechanism. The standard methodology of economics is, broadly speaking, mechanistic. Economic models analyze a phenomenon into a number of basic economic constituents and attempt to show how the behavior of these constituents produces a certain global behavior of the whole. One should remember, of course, that these are models, and there is some debate over how accurately models should be required to correspond to the reality they represent. On the other hand, scientists are generally realists; and, Milton Friedman[15] notwithstanding, economists had better not be instrumentalists given the rather limited empirical success that their science has enjoyed. So I shall assume that economic models, while certainly not required to mirror a complete reality (whatever that is), are surely successful only to the extent that they reflect with some fidelity some part of social reality.[16] Such a view is expressed in the best-known introduction to economics, by Samuelson (1983). "Most economic treatises," Samuelson writes, "are concerned with either the description of some part of the world of reality or with the elaboration of particular elements abstracted from reality." In the next paragraph he writes, "In every problem of economic theory certain variables (quantities, prices, etc.) are designated as unknowns, in whose determination we are interested. Their values emerge as a solution of a specified set of relationships imposed upon the unknowns by assumption or hypothesis. These functional relationships hold as of a given environment and milieu." These functional relationships, given the first quotation, describe the relationships between parts of an underlying mechanism that is assumed to generate the variables of interest. So it appears that economic practice typically assumes that the world it models is somewhat machine-like. Samuelson's remarks fit well, I take it, with my suggestion above that "inside every model is a machine trying to get out."

Here two questions immediately arise. A familiar question throughout

---

[15] Friedman (1953) provides a much discussed instrumentalist account of economics. I have added to the voluminous critical literature elsewhere (Dupré 1994).

[16] For a much more detailed analysis of the extent to which economics can be treated as a realistic science, see Mäki (1989).

the history of economics is the following: given the necessity for abstraction (admitted by Samuelson and everyone else, as far as I know) in laying bare economic machinery, how useful will the identification of such machinery be? Will the output of the machinery be recognizable against the noise of innumerable interfering phenomena? But I am interested here in a more fundamental ontological issue: Do we have any reason to believe in such economic machines at all? Here the dilemma mentioned above, that of finding a place for economics either in the monistic world of traditional mechanism or in my alternative pluralistic world, surfaces even more sharply. The economist supposes that the world contains economic machines. But the traditional mechanist believes only in physics machines. And with the failure of reductionism it seems impossible that a world full of physics machines can have any room for economic machines. My world, on the other hand, has room for all kinds of machines, even though, constantly getting in each other's way, they cannot be expected to display the absolute reliability of the mechanists' One Big Machine. I say that my world has room for all these different kinds of machines, but – and this is the other horn of the dilemma – that doesn't mean that they are really there. In a largely disordered universe there is no a priori guarantee that economics will be possible at all, at least in anything like the form currently expected of a mathematical science. How likely is it that there really are such machines?

Here two different possibilities must be distinguished. First, there is the question whether there might be naturally occurring economic machines out there in the world waiting to be discovered, and second there is the question whether people – governments, corporations, experimental economists, or whoever – might be able to build such machines. The orthodox faith among economists in the efficacy of markets might be seen as the somewhat paradoxical idea that the only good economics machines are the naturally occurring ones. The ones we try to build are seen, by contrast, as massively and chronically unreliable. Indeed one not uncommon view is that only if we resolutely refuse to tamper with naturally occurring economic machinery will it work at all. I suppose a conceivable rationale for such a view might be the analogy to biological evolution. Certainly there is little prospect of our building biological organisms better than nature, even if we can tinker with nature a bit these days. On the other hand the analogy is hardly compelling. The evidence for the exquisite adaptation of economic entities to their environment comparable to that of organisms is, to say the least, unimpressive. It is important to note, returning once again to the dilemma I have just been emphasizing, that whether one adopts a monistic physicalism like that of Rosenberg, or the kind of pluralism that I prefer, such a position is as lacking in a priori philosophical rationale as it is in empiricial support. The assumption that economic phenomena are organized throughout in a machine-like structure is plausible only in a world that is both mechanistic at the basic level, and susceptible of reductive explanation all the way down to that level. There is little reason to think we live in such a world. One wonders, even, whether the view of economics in question may not have a significant ideological component.

I certainly do not mean to deny that there is any naturally occurring economic machinery. ("Naturally occurring" here means only not deliberately contrived.) It does seem plausible that in certain geographically localized markets and in large well-organized markets for homogeneous commodities there may be quite efficient supply and demand equalizing machines. The capacity for this to happen has been well understood for over two centuries, and it is not implausible that in suitable cases no significant influences beyond economic self-interest occur to interfere with the exercise of the capacity. Such competitive markets, at any rate, are the most plausible candidates for moderately reliable naturally occurring economic machines. On the other hand with many naturally occurring markets there is a wide range of well-understood interfering factors such as varying degrees of monopoly and product differentiation and limits on the flow of information as well, of course, as a whole range of externalities that make the naturally occurring outcome, even if an equilibrium, far from optimal. Moreover, it is doubtful whether some of the social phenomena that have been theorized in this way (an example I shall mention briefly below is that of labor markets) have even the rudimentary characteristics of such machinery. A fortiori, the aggregation of all these more or less reliable more or less machines, as envisaged for example by general equilibrium theory, is unlikely to be anything at all like a machine.

What of our ability to build economic machines? Certainly there are plausible cases in which we have built quite reliable such machines. One example, which I borrow from Nancy Cartwright (this volume), is the mechanism by which central banks operate through commercial banks to attempt to control the interest rate and money supply. This is a simple mechanism, and in many cases there is good reason to believe that the intended causal connections will be strong enough to outweigh unanticipated interferences. The standard model of this process, in other words, may reflect a set of causal relations that dominate any likely interfering factors. It is also worth recalling here the familiar idea that the intention to build such a machine may well be an important causal factor in bringing about the desired result, a factor that might provide a major advantage for constructed over natural machines. On the other hand, there are grounds for skepticism about our general ability to build economic machines that will reliably serve the purposes for which they are intended. It may well be difficult or even impossible to construct economic machines that work reliably to keep a whole economy under some sort of control. Depending on the variety and prevalence of interfering factors, unpredictable or even random from an economic viewpoint, there is no reason to assume any convergence on a determinate economic outcome as we incorporate more factors into our models and attempt to control more variables.

The two models I have had in mind to this point, of discovered and constructed economic machines, might be seen as the extremes of a familiar political-economic spectrum: untrammeled competition and totalitarian central planning. There is no doubt a good deal of consensus that some point between these extremes is most desirable from a practical point of view. I now want to suggest that a pluralistic metaphysical foundation provides a plausible basis for sketching the elements of such a position. Rather than the homogeneous smoothly interconnected market mechanisms envisioned by neoclassical economics, we might rather imagine a diverse array of mechanisms, including more or less constrained market mechanisms, operating more or less predictably and reliably, and embodying more or less explicit goals. To some degree these mechanisms have been consciously engineered and to some degree they have evolved from efforts to coordinate more primitive individualistic motivations.

It is noteworthy that this picture meshes very closely with a certain conception of the agenda of institutionalist economics:

The institutionalist . . . does not have an all-encompassing, fixed analytical framework from which to analyze the world. He has no black box. The institutionalist economist is first and foremost eclectic, recognizing the importance of market forces, but at the same time concerned with the historical, institutional, and social forces that limit the role and influence of markets . . . Lacking any confining ideology the institutionalist is a tinkerer . . . He spurns as unrealistic and as inducing blindness attempts to seek one universal explanation of all events. (Mangum 1988, p. 202)

The contrast between this picture and that typically suggested by neoclassical economists is well illustrated by a consideration of the labor market. The neoclassical economist sees one dominant phenomenon, individuals selling their labor to the highest bidder, the highest bidder being the employer who can extract the largest marginal product from the individual's labor. Apparently anomalous phenomena are treated in a strictly Panglossian manner. Those who "choose" to eschew a college education do so because further education would only reduce the present value of their human capital. That others maximize this value by attending college reflects an exogenous difference in abilities which ultimately can only be explained genetically. The unemployed choose not to work because they prefer leisure (or welfare payments) to the highest offer available for their services. And so on. The labor market turns out to be a well-oiled machine. But apart from any empirical implausibility of this picture, I have argued that whether one is a monistic physicalist or a pluralist there is no a priori likelihood that such an integrated economic machine exists. If one is a monist it is unlikely that there are any economic machines; if one is a pluralist there will be too many, all liable to interact and interfere with one another.

An institutionalist picture, on the other hand, might see the labor market in close accord with the ontological picture I sketched above. There are many different job-allocating machines, loosely interconnected, partially motivated by explicit aims, and resulting in more or less predictable and more or less desirable final outcomes. Some of these machines will be such things as hiring committees and the personnel departments of firms or institutions. Others will be local or national governmental institutions providing constraints on machines of the former kind. Others again will be cultural phenomena determining the employment priorities or expectations of people from different social strata. I call all these machines because they embody certain more or less reliable causal relations and, more importantly, because mechanism is the mode in which they are assimilated into scientific understanding. But it will be obvious that such eclectic variably related bits of machinery will not be susceptible to the kind of homogenizing scientific theory that has acquired such prestige in fields from physics to economics. It will rather require local and detailed investigation appealing, as necessary, to history, cultural anthropology, sociology, and so on as well as economic theory.[17]

The crucial point, whether one is a physicalist or a pluralist, is to insist that there is no reason to expect anything like causal completeness at the economic level. What are the implications of all this for the practice of economics? I can do little more than speculate and summarize here. First, one might note the perspective on economic history. Perhaps this is the

[17] As I suggested in passing above, it is also possible that there is nothing much like a labor market anywhere. The historian William Reddy (1984) argues in detail that there was nothing like a market for labor in the eighteenth-century French textiles industry from 1750 to 1900. Reddy suggests that market discourse in this context was entirely rhetorical. It seems entirely possible that these conclusions might apply much more widely.

least controversial conclusion: economic history is history. Perhaps more coherent than just one damn thing after another, but certainly not the observable upshot of the action of universal laws. Moving from there to systematic economics, the obvious corollary is that there is little point in looking for such laws. Abstractions purporting to give a mechanistic model of an entire economy probably serve little useful purpose beyond winning Nobel prizes for their authors. Perhaps the more schematic formulations of standard macroeconomics may gesture towards some real causal capacities, though the notorious disappearing Phillips curve suggests that these may be rather transient properties of particular historical economies.

But perhaps we can still build economic machines. This is not intended as a brief for Stalinism. For one thing, I have no wish to deny that the causal interactions characteristic of a market are among the most effective causal levers we have with which to build economic machinery. Where they are usable without undesirable side-effects, markets are surely a better way of distributing goods than, say, a committee in the Ministry of Commodities. On the other hand, it strikes me as perfectly obvious that markets are tools not ends in themselves. In the many cases in which, for various reasons many well-known, they fail, we should surely be prepared to look for more appropriate tools. Not only do we have much more chance of figuring out what the likely or possible consequences of our economic actions are than we have of discovering, by abstract mathematical analysis, what will happen if we do nothing, but knowledge of the former kind is likely to be enormously more useful. By analogy with machine-making, we can hope to develop a wide range of knowledge of what can interfere with the intended consequences of our economic actions and develop ways of blocking such possible interferences. Empirical investigation of the causal capacities – and here I include, of course, historical investigation – would be essential as a foundation for such a practical, engineering-like economics. And at a policy level, none of this makes much sense without prior or at least concurrent discussion of the economic aims that we aim to promote.

There are certainly parts of economics that are practical, empirical, and value-driven. But equally certainly these are not the aspects of economics that carry the most prestige in the contemporary practice of the discipline. Nonetheless, if my philosophical analysis is correct these are the directions in which economics has most chance of making progress.[18]

---

[18] I would like to thank Uskali Mäki for a number of very helpful suggestions on a penultimate draft of this paper.

References

Campbell, Donald T. (1974) "'Downward Causation' in Hierarchically Organized Biological Systems," in F. J. Ayala and T. Dobzhansky (eds.), *Studies
in the Philosophy of Biology*, London: Macmillan Press Ltd.

Cartwright, Nancy (1983) *How the Laws of Physics Lie*, Oxford: Oxford
University Press.

(1990) *Nature's Capacities and their Measurement*, Oxford: Oxford University
Press.

Dupré, John (1993) *The Disorder of Things*, Cambridge, MA: Harvard University
Press.

(1994) "Could There Be a Science of Economics?", *Midwest Studies in
Philosophy*, XVIII: 363–78.

(1996) "The Solution to the Problem of the Freedom of the Will," *Philosophical
Perspectives*, 10: 385–402.

(1999) Review of Tony Lawson, *Economics and Reality*, *Feminist Economics*, 5:
121–6.

Dupré, John and Nancy Cartwright (1988) "Probability and Causality: Why
Hume and Indeterminism Don't Mix," *Nous*, 22: 521–36.

Dupré, John and Regenia Gagnier (1996) "A Brief History of Work," *Journal of
Economic Issues*, 30 (2): 553–60.

Frank, Robert H., Thomas Gilovich and Dennis T. Regan (1993) "Does Studying
Economics Inhibit Cooperation?", *Journal of Economic Perspectives*, 7 (2):
159–71.

Friedman, Milton (1953) "The Methodology of Positive Economics," in *Essays
in Positive Economics*, Chicago: University of Chicago Press.

Gagnier, Regenia and John Dupré (1995) "On Work and Idleness," *Feminist
Economics*, 1 (3): 1–14.

Galison, Peter (1987) *How Experiments End*, Chicago: University of Chicago
Press.

Kim, Jaegwon (1993) *Supervenience and Mind*, Cambridge: Cambridge University
Press.

Lawson, Tony (1997) *Economics and Reality*, London and New York: Routledge.

Mäki, Uskali (1989) "On the Problem of Realism in Economics," *Richerche
Economiche*, 43 (1–2): 176–98.

(1990) "Practical Syllogism, Entrepreneurship, and the Invisible Hand," in
Don Lavoie (ed.), *Economics and Hermeneutics*, London: Routledge.

Mangum, Stephen L. (1988) "Comparable Worth: The Institutional Economist's
Approach," in Garth Mangum and Peter Philips (eds.), *Three Worlds of
Labor Economics*, Armonk, NY: M. E. Sharpe, Inc.

Mirowski, Philip (1989) *More Heat than Light*, Cambridge: Cambridge University Press.

Oppenheim, Paul and Hilary Putnam (1958) "The Unity of Science as a Working
Hypothesis," in *Minnesota Studies in the Philosophy of Science*, vol. 2, ed.
H. Feigl et al., Minneapolis: University of Minnesota Press.

Pickering, Andrew (1984) *Constructing Quarks*, Chicago: University of Chicago Press.

Reddy, William (1984) *The Rise of Market Culture*, Cambridge: Cambridge University Press.

Rosenberg, Alexander (1992) *Economics: Mathematical Politics or Science of Diminishing Returns*, Chicago: University of Chicago Press.

— (1994) *Instrumental Biology or the Disunity of Science*, Chicago: University of Chicago Press.

Samuelson, Paul A. (1983) *Foundations of Economic Analysis* (enlarged edition), Cambridge MA: Harvard University Press.

Traweek, Sharon (1988) *Beamtimes and Lifetimes*, Cambridge, MA: Harvard University Press.

van Fraassen, Bas C. (1981) *The Scientific Image*, Oxford: Oxford University Press.

Waring, Marilyn (1988) *If Women Counted*, San Francisco, CA: Harper and Row.

Part V

Methodological implications of economic ontology

17 Sargent's symmetry saga: ontological versus technical constraints

ESTHER-MIRJAM SENT

Ever since the rise of rational expectations economics in the 1960s, the underlying assumption of rational expectations has both been defended for being realistic and been attacked for being unrealistic. The concept of rational expectations starts from the idea that individuals should not make systematic mistakes. Agents are not stupid, they learn from their mistakes, and draw intelligent inferences about the future from what is happening around them. While the adaptive expectations hypothesis had the disturbing implication that it allowed individuals to make systematic forecasting errors period after period, the rational expectations hypothesis asserted that people learned from their mistakes. It was based on the idea that guesses about the future must be correct on average if individuals are to remain satisfied with their mechanism of expectations formation. Rational people would take all available information into account and then discount that information into the future. If errors followed a pattern, they held information that could be used to make more accurate forecasts. The resulting predictions might still be wrong, but what mattered was that the errors would be random. People with rational expectations did still make mistakes, but not the same ones each time. Individuals could differ from one another in their expectations and still be rational if they were using different information. But when all these individual expectations were added together, errors tended to cancel out – producing an aggregate view of the future that reflected all the available information.

While some economists embraced rational expectations because it allowed a more realistic interpretation of expectations formation, others have argued that, despite the rational expectations school's insistence that expectations should be endogenous, it has dodged the crucial question of how expectations are actually formed (Arrow 1978; DeCanio 1979; Friedman 1979; Pesaran and Smith 1992). What some of these critics ignore, however, is that rational expectations economists have given different answers to the question of how we are to understand rational expectations as statements of economic reality. Hoover (1988, pp. 14–16) identifies at least two interpretations of the hypothesis. A weak form is that people do the best they can with the information they have. Some rational expectations economists, however, have called this interpretation vacuous. Moreover, it is not clear that this weak form actually implies the mathematical properties of rational expectations models. A strong form is that people actually know the structure of the model that truly describes the world and use it to form their expectations. Some rational expectations economists, though, have described this form as silly. What remains is the usual fallback position that the truth of a hypothesis does not matter as long as it generates true predictions. Unfortunately, this argument undercuts the belief of rational expectations economists that any acceptable model must incorporate rational expectations, since models with a good predictive record may meet this requirement irrespective of whether they include the rational expectations hypothesis. Complicating matters even more is the fact there are many interpretations of rational expectations. For what does it mean for individuals not to make systematic mistakes? Do they play games? Do they solve general equilibrium models? Do they fit time-series models?

According to Mäki (1994, p. 236), "[t]he most important methodological issue in economics has been and persists to be over what is called the 'realism' of theories and their 'assumptions'." Mäki argues that there is a need for reorienting the assumptions issue towards a discussion of the nature of assumptions in each specific case. This paper will analyze the nature of the rational expectations assumption. Rather than lumping all the rational expectations work together, this paper starts from the realization that there is no universal interpretation of the idea of rational expectations. Instead, it will evaluate Thomas Sargent's analysis of the rational expectations assumption. Rather than looking at his accomplishments from the perspective of orthodox philosophy of economics or conventional history of economic thought, this paper examines the stories Sargent is likely to have told when he was adopting different interpretations of rational expectations, in an attempt to understand the alternatives available to him, the choices he made, and the consequences of those decisions.

This paper will show that Sargent entertained different interpretations of rational expectations during different phases. It will further illustrate that these phases are connected through Sargent's continuous attempts to establish symmetry among agents, economists, and econometricians. Whereas Keynesian models typically posited the government as an agent with rational expectations and private agents with adaptive expectations,

Sargent felt that "[t]he people in Washington aren't all that much smarter than anybody else" (Sargent quoted by Guzzardi 1978, p. 74). Whereas the hypothesis of adaptive expectations typically posited agents who were making systematic forecasting errors period after period and economists and econometricians who were fully knowledgeable, Sargent posited agents who were inspecting and altering their own forecasting records just like economists and econometricians in their attempts to eliminate systematic forecasting errors. According to Sargent (1993, p. 21), "[t]he idea of rational expectations is . . . said to embody the idea that economists and the agents they are modeling should be placed on an equal footing: the agents in the model should be able to forecast and profit-maximize and utility-maximize as well as the economist – or should we say econometrician – who constructed the model."[1] Or: "The concept of a rational expectations competitive equilibrium . . . has the attractive property that . . . [the agents] in the model forecast . . . as well as the economist who is modeling them" (Sargent 1987a, p. 411). Hence, Sargent saw no reason for superiority of one category of individuals over another group of people. Therefore, he sought to establish symmetry among agents, economists, and econometricians in terms of the information they possess, the techniques, theories, and models they employ, and the forecasts they develop. Rather than defending this symmetry, Sargent criticized the "realism" of asymmetry and, instead, took symmetry for granted.

Since Sargent never explained the justification of symmetry among agents, economists, and econometricians, I can only speculate on this issue. First, Sargent may defend symmetry as a quality inherent in things. This has an ontic interpretation, meaning that it entails an intrinsic invariance among agents, economists, and econometricians. Second, Sargent may argue that symmetry follows from a power of recognition inherent in the mind. This interpretation is partly ontic and partly epistemic, which can be clarified by an appeal to Kantian regulative principles, implying that symmetry among economists, econometricians, and agents is an ideal of reason (see Falkenburg 1988).[2] Third, Sargent

---

[1] Also see Sargent (1987c, p. 76): "[R]ational expectations possesses the defining property that the forecasts made by agents within the model are no worse than the forecasts that can be made by the economist who has the model." Further see Sargent (1987a, p. 440): "We implement the hypothesis of rational expectations by assuming that agents' expectations about unknown random variables equal the linear least squares projections on certain information sets to be specified."

[2] Kant held that the concept of a systematic unity of nature was an ideal of reason directed towards a completeness of empirical knowledge unattainable through concepts of the understanding. Ideals of reason in Kant's sense bring about a generalization or

may claim that symmetry is a matter of metaphor. According to this epistemic interpretation, Sargent created a metaphor of the agent as an economist and econometrician (see Mirowski 1989a).[3] In order to accommodate these different justifications, I will interpret Sargent's search for symmetry as an ontological constraint on theory formation. Since this interpretation can be explained both in constructivist and realist fashions, it is neutral with respect to the different justifications of symmetry. Furthermore, the ontological constraint will gain meaning as the following sections illustrate how Sargent gave the rough notion of symmetry a more precise formulation by embedding it in different frameworks.

As we will witness in the following sections, symmetry as an ontological constraint on theory formation has guided Sargent's work on rational expectations. Each of the sections is a brief case study of how Sargent's search for symmetry resulted in different interpretations of rational expectations and kept getting obstructed by his encounters with technical constraints (for more, see Sent 1998b). The next section discusses how Sargent came to the idea of rational expectations as an econometric concept. The second one analyzes Sargent's attempts to interpret rational expectations as both an econometric and a theoretic construct. The third section evaluates his efforts to incorporate general equilibrium theory into the symmetry structure. The fourth section discusses Sargent's eventual interpretation of rational expectations as the final outcome in a learning process.

1 Phase one: rational expectations through distributed lags

This section analyzes Sargent's interpretation of rational expectations economics in the late 1960s and early 1970s. At that time, the concept of

totalization of concepts of the understanding. They do not possess objective reality, since the completeness of empirical knowledge of particulars can never be the object of objective knowledge. However, they lead to regulative principles that can guide our acquisition of knowledge to the establishment of systematic unity. Since symmetry principles enable us to discover parts of this specific systematic structure, they have a regulative character in Kant's sense.

[3] The recognition underpinning this epistemic interpretation is that we live in a world of broken symmetries and partial invariance. Foundational conservation principles are factually false and no posited invariance holds without exceptions or qualifications. However imperfect the world, human reason operates by means of assigning sameness and differences through symmetries in an attempt to force a reconciliation of constancy to change. Our very livelihoods, in the broadest possible sense, are predicated upon invariants whose existence cannot be proven but whose instrumentality renders our actions coherent.

adaptive expectations was under severe attack for fitting models that forecast better than agents, as it allows individuals to make systematic forecasting errors period after period. This was an obstacle in Sargent's search for symmetry. The hypothesis of adaptive expectations postulates that individuals use information on past forecasting errors to revise current expectations. Objections to the hypothesis included, first, that it is entirely backward-looking, and that all mechanistic backward-looking extrapolative rules allow the possibility of systematic forecasting errors for many periods in succession. Critics argued that the suboptimal use of available information is hard to reconcile with the idea of optimization that is the foundation of most microeconomic analysis. Second, no widely accepted economic theory was offered to explain the magnitude of the adjustment parameter. Some economists sought to meet these objections by using the concept of rational expectations, by taking the idea that individuals should not make systematic errors as their point of departure (Begg 1982).

Inspired by these changes in his environment, Sargent attempted to satisfy the ontological constraint of symmetry by connecting the determinism employed by neoclassical economists and the randomness advocated by econometricians through the use of rational expectations. He was troubled by the fact that there was an unclear link between time-series econometrics, in particular distributed lags, and the models that were then being used. Sargent said to Klamer (1983, pp. 63–4): "What I mean by the links not being clear is that often the models that we used had no randomness in them. They analyze individual behavior in a context in which there is no uncertainty, but they treated the data probabilistically, thus adding randomness. That procedure is not a tight one, not even an understandable one. The statistical model you're using implies that there is an environment in which there's uncertainty, whereas the economic model that you're using assumes that away. The hunch is, and it's a hunch that turned out right, that it's not just a matter of adding a random term. If there really is uncertainty, it ought to change the way you think about individual behavior." Sargent noticed that in econometrics, empirical prediction requires the use of probabilistic ideas. Once these are introduced in econometric method, connecting the work of econometricians and economists required them to be introduced in economic theory as well.

Sargent chose to approach symmetry by starting from the perspective of time-series econometrics, in particular distributed lags, and the term structure of interest rates (Sargent 1968, 1969). Through his analysis of distributed lags for interest rates, Sargent became aware of the role of expectations, because orthodox neoclassical theory stated that they influence the relationship between spot and forward rates, nominal and real rates, and short and long-term rates. Furthermore, expectations, or more specifically rational expectations, provided Sargent with an answer to how symmetry might be achieved, as they allowed him to introduce probabilistic ideas in economic theory as well. He considered rational expectations a more elegant way to resolve the separation between the randomness of distributed lags in econometrics and the determinism of neoclassical models. Since Sargent initially started from the viewpoint of econometrics, he was led to choose an econometrically motivated interpretation of the concept of rational expectations, which involved treating the econometrician and the agents in the model in a symmetric fashion.

Since he focused on interest rates, Sargent also encountered the importance of Lévy stable distributions with infinite variance and the associated problem of constructing statistical estimators. For example, Richard Roll (1970) showed that some interest rates follow a member of the class of Lévy stable distributions. Furthermore, during the late 1960s and early 1970s, Lévy stable distributions began to attract the attention of many scholars working in economics (Mirowski 1989b, 1990). Investigations showed how certain variates conformed to Lévy stable distributions, Monte Carlo studies were mounted to place some bounds on sampling behavior, and attempts were made to link estimation to the formalisms of linear programming. Roll (1970) suggested extending his work by using Sargent's spectral-method analysis of interest-rate sequences and discussed these issues with his colleague Sargent and his student Robert Blattberg at Carnegie-Mellon University. Furthermore, Lévy stable distributions promised to explain why MSAE outperformed least squares in a study of investment decisions by Sargent's thesis adviser, John Meyer (Glauber and Meyer 1964). Inspired by these developments, Sargent published a paper in 1971, together with Blattberg (Blattberg and Sargent 1971), studying the performance of various estimators where the disturbances follow distributions that have fatter tails than does the normal distribution.

The fact that distributions with infinite variance tend to have thick or heavy tails implies that large values or outliers will be relatively frequent. It means that sample variances grow unpredictably and without bound with increases in the sample size. Because the least squares technique minimizes squared deviations, it places relatively heavy weight on outliers, and their presence can lead to estimates that are extremely sensitive. If the variance does not exist, it is obviously impossible to obtain a meaningful variance estimator and the least squares estimator will not possess its usual minimum variance property, for the Gauss-Markov theorem will not hold. This in turn implies that the conventional F and t

tests on the coefficients could be very misleading, for the classical central limit theorem will not hold. If the error distribution is so thick-tailed that the mean as well as the variance does not exist, then the least squares estimator cannot be unbiased because its mean will also not exist. In the best case, stable distributions have only one moment of integral order and, therefore, estimators cannot depend on any moments higher than the first. Only in a few cases are there explicit expressions for their density or distribution functions that would enable us to concretize the algorithms for estimating the parameters and, therefore, precise statements about the sampling behavior of estimators could generally not be written down.

The upshot is that with Lévy stable distributions almost every technique of modern econometrics is useless and would have to be discarded. As a result, almost all references to stable Lévy distributions in economic variates disappeared by the mid-1970s and many of the earlier enthusiasts recanted with regard to stable Lévy distributions (Mirowski 1989b, 1990). The threat of Lévy stable distributions, which would require econometrics to search for algorithms for estimating the parameters, was averted by ignoring them, without a direct critique of the earlier findings of infinite variance. The strict deterministic stance of neoclassical theory is incompatible with economic variates following distributions that do not guarantee the existence of algorithms for estimating parameters. Hence, neoclassical econometrics is a set of techniques forged to satisfy the ontological constraint of reconciling the determinism embodied in neoclassical theory and the apparent stochastic nature of economic variates. It ignores the problems with constructing statistical estimators under stable laws, primarily by privileging the method of least squares to test or estimate its basic regression model. This requires the distribution of the random variables to be Gaussian and hence assures the existence of an algorithm for estimating the parameters. Randomness, therefore, is tamed by assuming that variances are finite.

Sargent was especially troubled by these technical constraints, for he wanted to satisfy the ontological constraint of establishing symmetry between techniques used by agents and the models developed by econometricians. In particular, his econometrically motivated interpretation of rational expectations required the availability of statistical estimators. Whereas Lévy stable distributions previously only threatened neoclassical econometrics, they could now also compromise economic theory based on rational expectations. When stable laws enter the stage, econometricians and agents would run into problems with the construction of statistical estimators. Rather than relinquishing the econometrically motivated interpretation of rational expectations through distributed lags, Sargent somewhat silently gave up Lévy stable distributions with infinite variance. Only a few explicit discussions of Lévy stable distributions can be found in his later publications. While Roll had illustrated the importance of infinite variance for his data, Sargent used the same data and assumed that the random term follows a distribution with finite variance (Sargent 1971). He subsequently extended this study and noted that "Roll argues that the evolution of bill rates is more adequately described by assuming that they are drawn from one of the stable distributions with infinite variance. While that specification is certainly an interesting one, abandoning the assumption of covariance stationarity has its costs" (Sargent 1972, pp. 75–6). Imposing covariance stationarity and ignoring stable distributions with infinite variance assured that the algorithms for estimating the parameters can be concretized, a prerequisite for the introduction of rational expectations.

In this first phase of his quest for symmetry among agents, economists, and econometricians, therefore, Sargent encountered the technical constraint that Lévy stable distributions lack an algorithm for estimating the parameters. This obstructed his attempts to connect the randomness in the models used by econometricians and agents with the determinism in the models developed by economists. Therefore, relinquishing Lévy stable distributions and their technical constraints served Sargent well in his attempts to satisfy the ontological constraint of symmetry among agents, economists, and econometricians. Yet, this led him to adopt the "unrealistic" assumption that data previously shown to have exhibited infinite variance now followed a distribution with finite variance. Hence, this phase illustrates the first instance of the intricate interplay of ontological and technical constraints in Sargent's rational expectations economics.

2 Phase two: rational expectations through vector autoregressions

While econometricians were the first promoters of rational expectations, their initial focus on methods for restricting the parameters of lag distributions subsequently changed to restricting vector autoregressions. Though the same ontological constraint of establishing symmetry among agents, economists, and econometricians guided Sargent, the change in his econometric environment led him to advocate a different connection. Whereas we saw in the previous section how Sargent tried to use rational expectations to restrict distributed lags, we will witness in this phase how Sargent, influenced by this change in his econometric environment, tried to use rational expectations to restrict vector autoregressions. Whereas Sargent had earlier tried to turn agents in economic models into econometricians using distributed lags, we will see in this section how Sargent tried to establish symmetry between agents in economic models and econometricians using vector autoregressions. The times are the late 1970s and early 1980s, the places are the University of Chicago and the University of Minnesota at Minneapolis, and the supporting roles are performed by Christopher Sims and Lars Hansen.

In his attempts to satisfy the ontological constraint of symmetry, Sargent continued to start from the viewpoint of econometrics during this phase of his work. However, rather than focusing on distributed lags, he started employing vector autoregressions. For Sargent (1987a, p. 241), "[s]tochastic processes provide a natural context in which to formulate the problem of prediction . . . When the econometric model occurs in the form of a vector version . . . it is said to be a vector autoregression." The vector autoregressive model was designed especially to forecast. It tried to overcome many of the defects of the structural approach by relying on statistical regularities only. Whereas the structural approach attempted to use economic theory and historical data to simulate the structure of the economy as a system of equations, vector autoregressions were not based on economic theories at all. Whereas large national econometric models were successful in the 1950s and 1960s, their performance hit rock bottom in the 1970s. They did not successfully predict and could not explain the simultaneous high inflation and unemployment rates. Vector autoregressions, on the other hand, seemed capable of producing forecasts that were, compared to the standard kind, more accurate, more frequent, and cheaper. It is a straightforward, powerful, statistical forecasting technique that can be applied to any set of historical data.

Some econometricians, like Christopher Sims and Sargent, responded to the evidence that naïve time-series models frequently appeared to offer better forecasting performance than other econometric models by focusing on representing the data relative to the theory (Sargent and Sims 1977). Sargent and Sims were fellow graduate students at Harvard University in the 1960s and fellow professors at the University of Minnesota in the 1970s. According to Sargent, "[l]earning from Chris Sims about time series and about Granger-Sims causality and how that fits in was fun . . . Very early on I had a hunch that Chris' stuff would fit in with rational expectations" (Klamer 1983, p. 74). Sims, one of the pioneers of vector autoregressions, believed that theoretical restrictions in statistical inference should be kept to a minimum (Sims 1980). Influenced by Sims and the change of focus in the econometrics community, Sargent concentrated on restricting vector autoregressions on the econometric side of symmetry. As before, Sargent ended up with an econometrically motivated interpretation of rational expectations. Rather than handling distributed lags, symmetry between agents and econometricians now required that agents with rational expectations fit vector autoregressions. Rather than solving structural models, agents model "without pretending to have too much a priori economic theory" (Sargent and Sims 1977) or "using methods not based on explicit economic theories" (Sargent 1979). While the theoretical background for time series was developed in statistics, the main applications arose in communications engineering. Sargent (1987b, p. xxii) claimed that in the sense that "the language that macroeconomists speak has changed . . . there has been a rational expectations revolution." But this language of applied macroeconometrics was borrowed from engineering (Sent 1998a).

In order to satisfy the ontological constraint of symmetry, Sargent sought to incorporate economic theory in the structure of vector autoregressions and rational expectations. Hence, when he adopted the method of vector autoregressions, he wanted to use the acquired statistical information to construct a theoretical model. According to Sargent, the "atheoretical" approach of macroeconomics should be used to motivate theoretical assumptions. However, a major technical constraint, in the form of observational equivalence (Sargent 1976), hindered Sargent in fully meeting the ontological end of symmetry. He discovered that models compatible with the natural rate hypothesis and models that are incompatible with it could both generate the very same time-series relations. Within any policy regime, there were an infinite number of equally accurate representations of the data. If one of these forms was invariant to changes in the policy regime, then the other forms would in general not also be invariant. The natural and non-natural rate hypotheses both generated identical observable consequences and both formed the basis for equally good forecasts, as long as the policy regime remained constant. To incorporate economic theory in his symmetry structure, Sargent felt he needed to overcome this technical constraint of observational equivalence by establishing a stronger connection between vector autoregressions and economic theory.[4]

This is where Lars Hansen enters the picture. He graduated from the University of Minnesota, Sargent's employer, in 1978 and subsequently collaborated with Sargent on many papers. Hansen and Sargent (1981a,

---

[4] I should note that while these problems led Sargent to change his approach, they never bothered Sims one bit, because Sims could care less about symmetry.

1981b) responded to the problem of observational equivalence by synthesizing structural estimation and time-series analysis and showing that time-series models were not necessarily atheoretical. Hansen and Sargent (1991b, p. 1) argued that their "goal has been to create a class of models that makes contact with good dynamic economic theory and with good dynamic econometric theory." But what is good dynamic economic theory? What is good dynamic econometric theory? Having grounded "good dynamic econometric theory" in the engineering tools of vector autoregressions, Hansen and Sargent (1990, 1991b) searched for "good dynamic economic theory" in the engineering theory of recursive dynamics and linear optimal control. The trouble was that this combination was technically not terribly successful, difficult to implement, and based on controversial assumptions. Sargent (1987b, p. 7) acknowledged that "in order to make . . . models tractable enough for macroeconomic work, their preferences, technology, and endowments have typically been so simplified, and so much has been abstracted, that it is often difficult to take their predictions seriously." Because "internal consistency [or symmetry] is always purchased with simplification and abstraction." In particular, Sargent's set-up relied on the assumptions of linear-quadratic models and time invariance on the economic-theory side and covariance stationary, linearly indeterministic models on the econometric-method side.

Though the combination of vector autoregressions, recursive dynamics or linear optimal control, and rational expectations helped Sargent to satisfy the ontological constraint of symmetry in this phase, the technical constraints he encountered led him to represent the world as being either linear quadratic and time invariant, or covariance stationary and linearly deterministic. These technical constraints illustrated that his models were technically not terribly successful and difficult to implement. Just like in the previous phase, the technical constraints led Sargent to adopt "unrealistic" representations that were based on controversial assumptions. It is important to stress that Sargent himself acknowledged that, as a result of the complex interplay between ontological and technical constraints, it is difficult to take the predictions of his models in this phase seriously.

In addition, Sargent became aware of the fact that his analysis relied on outdated engineering techniques. In particular, techniques were being developed to analyze nonstationary and nonlinear systems. At the same time, some economists started arguing that nonstationary behavior was an important aspect of the economy and that major economic variables have nonlinear relationships. Even Sargent's hero Granger began advocating the new techniques for nonstationarity and nonlinearity (Granger

1994; Granger and Teräsvirta 1993). Sargent had largely avoided questions about the way in which economic agents make choices when confronted by a perpetually novel and evolving world. This was so, despite the ontological importance of the questions, because of the technical constraint that his tools and formal models were ill-tuned for answering such questions. Changes in his environment and the appearance of a few extra technical constraints were necessary, though, to convince Sargent to move to a complexity approach to prediction, using insights from the economics workshop he attended at the Santa Fe Institute. Before discussing this final phase, the next section will outline the additional technical constraints that Sargent encountered.

3 Phase three: theoretically motivated rational expectations

This phase is centered on Sargent's eventual interpretation of rational expectations as individual rationality and mutual consistency of perceptions. From roughly the early to mid-1980s, Sargent focused on incorporating general equilibrium theory in his framework of rational expectations and vector autoregressions.[5] He believed that the true system was composed of such state variables as taste, technology, and policy, so that a model was structural if its equations were strictly linked to the deep parameters of state variables. In this interpretation, a vector autoregression was a reduced form of a system. The general equilibrium framework imposed full theoretical restrictions on the coefficients in the vector autoregression. Whereas the previous two phases in Sargent's work started with the conception of agents as little econometricians while economists were added as somewhat of an afterthought, the phase discussed in this section started with the conception of agents as little economists while econometricians were added as somewhat of an afterthought.

While Lucas had used general equilibrium theory from the start, it took Sargent until the late 1970s to move in this direction. During that time, he spent a year as a visiting professor at the University of Chicago and took two courses from Lucas. He said in his interview with Klamer (1983, p. 62): "I don't really work much with Lucas. I spent a year at Chicago. I took two courses from him. He's a very good teacher. I learn from him. I read his papers. He's been a big influence on me." His

---

[5] Sargent did not make use of Walrasian general equilibrium analysis, but he employed representative agent analysis instead.

encounters with Lucas led Sargent (1981a, p. 214) to explore the implications "of a single principle from economic theory. This principle is that
people's observed behavior will change when their constraints change."
He restricted "things so that the dynamic economic theory is of the
equilibrium variety, with optimizing agents and cleared markets."

Sargent sought to satisfy the ontological constraint of symmetry by
linking the vector autoregressions employed by econometricians and the
general equilibrium theory developed by economists through the concept
rational expectations, because "[r]ational expectations modeling promised to tighten the link between theory and estimation, because the
objects produced by the theorizing are exactly the objects in which
econometrics is cast" (Hansen and Sargent 1991a, p. 3). Besides, "Lucas
and Prescott [had done] much to clarify the nature of rational expectations as an equilibrium concept, and also pointed the way to connecting
the theory with observations" (Sargent 1987c, p. 76). Rational expectations modeling resulted in vector autoregressions: "This is an attractive
assumption because the solutions of such problems are known to imply
that the chosen variables . . . can exhibit serial correlation and cross-
serial correlation" (Sargent 1981a, p. 215). Hence, in this interpretation,
agents have expectations that are rational when these depend, in the
proper way, on the same things that economic theory says actually
determine that variable. A collection of agents is solving the same
optimum problems by using the relevant economic theory and the
solution of each agent is consistent with the solution of other agents.
Econometric methods can then be used to estimate the vector autoregressions that result from this economic model.

For Sargent, satisfying the ontological constraint of symmetry among
agents, economists, and econometricians with this set-up was facilitated
by the fact that general equilibrium theory involved an a priori bias
towards symmetry among agents. In particular, there are three pieces of
evidence in making the case that general equilibrium theory has always
had trouble with distinctly differentiated actors. First, Edgeworth's
analysis of exchange relied on keeping the number of types of agents
constant through cloning. Second, in the analysis of uniqueness and
stability, there are aggregation problems if agents are very different as
shown by the Sonnenschein–Debreu–Mantel result. Third, the existence
of general equilibrium cannot be proved in an economy in which agents
are so different that they are fully specialized and in which the possibility
of self-sufficiency is the exception rather than the rule. Unfortunately,
space limitations do not allow me to discuss these technical issues in
detail (for more, see Sent 1998b). In addition, it is difficult to explain
them in non-technical terms. Regardless, for Sargent the technical

constraints associated with general equilibrium theory led him towards symmetry not only among categories of people but also within groups of individuals.

Though Sargent had finally met the ontological end of symmetry, our narrative does not have a happy ending here. Instead, Sargent encountered new technical constraints following from the combination of rational expectations, general equilibrium theory, and vector autoregressions. First, if there is symmetry among the agents, then there is no reason for them to trade with each other, even if they possess different information. Instead of there being a hive of activity and exchange, Tirole (1982) proved that a sharp no-trade theorem characterizes rational expectations equilibria (Sargent 1993, p. 113). Second, agents and econometricians have to be different in order to justify the error term. When implemented numerically or econometrically, rational expectations models need to impute more knowledge to the agents within the model, who use the equilibrium probability distributions in evaluating their Euler equations, than is possessed by an econometrician, who faces estimation and inference problems that the agents in the model have somehow solved (Sargent 1987c, p. 79). Third, there is a need for asymmetric actors in rational expectations economics for the concept of policy recommendations to make sense. In particular, making recommendations for improving policy amounts to assuming that in the historical period the system was not really in a rational expectations equilibrium, having attributed to agents' expectations about government policy that did not properly take into account the policy advice (Sargent 1984, p. 413). A fourth problem deals with the issue of conceptualizing learning if agents are thought to be little econometricians. In particular, econometric metaphors of reasoning possess a blind spot for the process of information search and errors made in information collecting, because econometric theories of inference and hypothesis testing are applied after the data have been collected; they do not start until the variables and numbers needed for the formulas are available (Sargent 1993, p. 23). These problems, combined with the ones outlined in the previous section, eventually jointly transformed Sargent's entire program. As we will discover in the following section, Sargent tried to reimpose symmetry among agents, economists, and econometricians by making them all boundedly rational.

In this phase, therefore, technical constraints associated with general equilibrium theory led Sargent to embrace symmetry not only among but also within categories of individuals. However, due to the technical constraints he subsequently encountered in his attempt to connect the techniques used by agents, the theories constructed by economists, and the models developed by econometricians, Sargent was unable to maintain symmetry within the set-up he had developed. A "realistic" account required heterogeneous agents, an asymmetric government, and difference between agents and econometricians. Again it needs to be emphasized that Sargent himself recognized these outcomes of the involved interaction between ontological and technical constraints. In response, he sought to reestablish symmetry through the use of bounded rationality. This is the final phase in his work to which we will now turn.

4 Phase four: convergence to rational expectations

This section discusses how Sargent eventually changed his attitude towards rational expectations in response to developments in the late 1980s. During this period, Sargent became involved with the Santa Fe Institute. Complexity, intractable unpredictability, spontaneous self-organization, adaptation, nonlinear dynamics, computational theory, upheavals at the edge of chaos, inductive strategies, new developments in computer and cognitive science – these were some of the themes taken up by researchers at the Santa Fe Institute. Begun by a number of distinguished physicists at the Los Alamos National Laboratories, the Santa Fe Institute originally had nothing to do with economics. This changed with a workshop on "Evolutionary Paths of the Global Economy" from 8–18 September 1987 at the Institute campus in Santa Fe (Anderson, Arrow, and Pines 1988). The gathering was successful enough to continue the economics program at the Institute, which has anywhere from eight to fifteen researchers in residence at any given time, evenly divided between economists and physical scientists. Brian Arthur, who served as a director of the Institute's economics program "sees a 'Santa Fe approach' emerging that views the economy as a complex, constantly evolving system in which learning and adaptation play a major role. Eventually . . . this could expand the current view, much influenced by classical physics, that depicts the world as relatively simple, predictable, and tending to equilibrium solutions" (Pool 1989, p. 703).

One area that received a great deal of attention during the workshop was the specific question of how economic agents take the future into account when making decisions. The axiom of rational expectations seemed patently untrue to the physical scientists, who were acutely aware of the difficulties inherent in predicting the future.[6] The problem in

---

[6] Note that the earlier defense of rational expectations by Sargent and the current criticism of rational expectations by physicists relied on different notions of "realism." Spelling these out would take us too far from the main narrative in this paper.

developing a more "realistic" model was that if economic agents were assumed to be able to anticipate the future, but not perfectly, then it is hard to know just how imperfect rationality should be. One suggestion was to develop theoretical economic agents that learned in the way actual economic agents did. These suggestions for incorporating learning were music to Sargent's ears, because his engineering metaphors turned out to be not as convenient as he had previously thought and he had developed a keen interest in including learning in the context of rational expectations models to restore symmetry among agents, economists, and econometricians. Before analyzing Sargent's embracement of a Santa Fe-type approach, we need to first analyze prior attempts by Sargent to deal with the problems outlined in the previous two sections.

The asymmetry among agents, economists, and econometricians that followed from the technical constraints within the setting of rational expectations, general equilibrium theory, and vector autoregressions did not sit well with Sargent. In response, he was led to revise part of his framework in the mid-1980s in an attempt to satisfy the ontological constraint of symmetry. We witness Sargent (1993) relinquishing rational expectations, when he made a "call to retreat from . . . rational expectations . . . by expelling rational agents from our model environments" (p. 3) and "to create theories with behavioral foundations by eliminating the asymmetry that rational expectations builds in between the agents in the model and the econometrician who is estimating it" (pp. 21–2). Instead of starting from rational expectations, Sargent focused on agents with adaptive expectations in work mostly co-authored with Albert Marcet, who was a graduate student at the University of Minnesota during Sargent's tenure there and who subsequently followed in Sargent's footsteps by accepting an assistant-professor position at Carnegie Mellon University (Marcet and Sargent 1986, 1988, 1989a, b, c, 1992). The models they developed were adaptive in the sense in which that term is used in the control literature (but not in the macroeconomics literature). In particular, the agents were assumed to behave as if they know with certainty that the true law of motion is time invariant. Because the agents operate under the continually falsified assumption that the law of motion is time invariant and known for sure, the models do not incorporate fully optimal behavior or rational expectations.

Unwilling to relinquish rational expectations entirely, Sargent did not see learning as anything really new in economics. He saw it as a way of strengthening the standard ideas and dealing with their problems – as a way of understanding how economic agents will grope their way toward neoclassical behavior even when they are not perfectly rational (Sargent 1993, p. 23). He tried to reinforce rational expectations by focusing on convergence to this equilibrium (Marcet and Sargent 1992, p. 140). He also tried to use learning with adaptive expectations to deal with some of the problems associated with rational expectations (Sargent 1993, p. 25). Finally, incorporating learning could assist in the computation of equilibria (Marcet and Sargent 1992, p. 161).

Once he moved to restore symmetry among agents, economists, and econometricians by incorporating learning, Sargent had to figure out what version of the learning assumption he wanted to use. Since he was after symmetry in the setting of adaptive agents in economic theories and vector autoregressions in econometric models, he could only satisfy his ontological constraint if the adaptive agents were to use vector autoregressions (Marcet and Sargent 1992, p. 140). Under this rendition, then, agents used the same kind of vector autoregressions and least-squares estimation techniques as econometricians. This new framework, however, did not fully allow Sargent to satisfy the ontological constraint he had established due to encounters with new technical constraints. Agents still had to be quite smart, because "although sequential application of linear least squares to vector autoregression is not rational for these environments, it is still a pretty sophisticated method" (Marcet and Sargent 1992, pp. 161–2). In particular, agents were assumed to be almost fully rational and knowledgeable about the system within which they operate, lacking knowledge only about particular parameters in laws of motion of a set of variables exogenous to their own decisions, which they learn about through the recursive application of least squares. Thus, the representation resulting from the technical constraints was "unrealistic" in the sense that agents were assumed to have already formed a more-or-less correct model of the situation in which they were, and learning was just a matter of sharpening up the model a bit by adjusting a few knobs. Since Sargent pictured economists and econometricians as being far from rational and knowledgeable about the system they analyze, this "unrealistic" picture still left him with a rather weak attempt at satisfying his ontological constraint on theory formation.

Unhappy with the "unrealistic" interpretation of learning under adaptive expectations, Sargent wanted something closer to the way economists and econometricians learn. How could he circumvent the technical constraints that resulted in the "unrealistic" representation? Sargent (1993) thought he could restore symmetry "by expelling rational agents . . . and replacing them with 'artificially intelligent' agents who behave like econometricians. These 'econometricians' theorize, estimate, and adapt in attempting to learn about probability distributions which, under rational expectations they already know" (p. 3). Sargent had become an enthusiast for the artificial intelligence approach to learning after the first economics workshop at the Santa Fe Institute: "My interest in studying economies with 'artificially intelligent' agents was spurred by attending a meeting . . . at the Santa Fe Institute in September 1987" (p. vi). Instead of assuming that agents were perfectly rational, they could be modeled as being artificially intelligent and learning from experience like real economic agents. Instead of modeling the economy as a general equilibrium, societies of interacting artificially intelligent agents could be organized into an economy. Reluctant to give up ideas like representative agents or completed arbitrage and to renounce general equilibrium analysis, Sargent did not go all the way with Santa Fe. Rather than using artificially intelligent systems to think about populations, he saw them as models of an individual's brain. Rather than relinquishing the neoclassical notion of an equilibrium, he focused on convergence to equilibrium (Marimon, McGrattan, and Sargent 1990).

Sargent saw what he called his bounded rationality program as an effort to restore symmetry among agents, economists, and econometricians. Whereas technical constraints had earlier frustrated his attempts to satisfy this ontological constraint of symmetry through the use of rational expectations, Sargent now pictured agents, economists, and econometricians alike as being boundedly rational but converging to rational expectations. Ironically, however, the move to artificial intelligence came along with technical constraints that left Sargent with a new asymmetry between him and the agents in his models. When Sargent made the agents more bounded in their rationality, he had to be smarter because his models became larger and more demanding econometrically. According to Sargent (1993), "an econometric consequence of replacing rational agents with boundedly rational ones is to add a number of parameters" (p. 168) because there "are many choices to be made in endowing our artificial agents with adaptive algorithms" (p. 134) and we "face innumerable decisions about how to represent decision making processes and the way that they are updated" (p. 165). Furthermore, artificial intelligence did not allow Sargent to fully establish symmetry, because the proliferation of free parameters in the bounded rationality program left him with an asymmetry between economists and econometricians: "Bounded rationality is a movement to make model agents behave more like econometricians. Despite the compliment thereby made to their kind, macroeconometricians have shown very little interest in applying models of bounded rationality to data. Within the economics profession, the impulse to build models populated by econometricians has come primarily from theorists with different things on their minds than most econometricians" (pp. 167–8).

This final phase illustrates how Sargent's attempts at satisfying the ontological constraint of symmetry continued to be frustrated as a result of his encounters with technical constraints. Sargent himself acknowledged that neither learning through adaptive expectations nor learning through artificial intelligence established the symmetry he sought. Whereas the technical constraints associated with adaptive expectations excluded agents from the symmetry structure, the technical constraints associated with artificial intelligence continued to exclude agents from the symmetry structure and further left Sargent with an asymmetry between economists and econometricians. Will Sargent ever be able to satisfy the ontological constraint of symmetry among economists, econometricians, and agents? Will he continue to encounter technical constraints that keep him from establishing symmetry? How will the ontological and technical constraints interact? We will have to wait and see.

5 Conclusion

An evaluation of the "realism" of the rational expectations assumption must be seen in context. One of the individual contributors, Thomas Sargent, entertained different interpretations of rational expectations in different periods. This paper has outlined four case studies of Sargent trying to establish symmetry among agents, economists, and econometricians. The first one was staged in the late 1960s through early 1970s. The events explored in the second case study took place in the late 1970s through early 1980s. The third one was set in the early to mid-1980s. The events discussed in the final case study took place in the late 1980s through early 1990s.

Sargent's community in the late 1960s through early 1970s consisted of his thesis adviser Meyer, his colleague Roll, and his student Blattberg. In this setting, Sargent made the initial decision to focus on the randomness of time-series econometrics, the determinism of neoclassical economic theory, connecting economic theory and econometric method through rational expectations, and the term structure of interest rates. As a result of those decisions, Sargent was led to adopt an econometrically motivated interpretation of rational expectations and to acknowledge the importance of Lévy stable distributions. The technical constraints he ran into were that for Lévy stable distributions there was no general estimation method and the properties of estimators could only be investigated in an indirect way. He accommodated these problems by giving up Lévy stable distributions despite the evidence in favor of their "realisticness." Sims and Hansen were Sargent's collaborators in the late 1970s through early 1980s. Influenced by his colleague Sims and a change in his economic environment, Sargent tried to employ rational expectations for restricting vector autoregressions and to use the acquired statistical information to construct a theoretical model. The trouble was that the technical constraint of observational equivalence implied that the natural and non-natural rate hypotheses both generated identical observable consequences and both formed the basis of equally good forecasts. When Sargent tried to get rid of this technical constraint by collaborating with Hansen on recursive dynamics and linear optimal control models, he found new technical constraints in that his models were technically not terribly successful and difficult to implement. Furthermore, these constraints led Sargent to develop models based on "unrealistic" assumptions. In the early to mid-1980s, Sargent hung out with Lucas. In this environment, he initially decided to focus on general equilibrium theory, vector autoregressions, and rational expectations. This promised to allow him to establish symmetry not only among but also within categories of individuals. However, he found that asymmetry appeared as a consequence of the no-trade theorems, incorporating information gathering, error term justification, and making policy recommendations. Sargent tried to accommodate these technical constraints and restore symmetry by adopting adaptive expectations and artificial intelligence. Marcet and the Santa Fe Institute were part of Sargent's environment in the late 1980s through early 1990s. In these surroundings, Sargent first focused on adaptive rather than rational expectations. This reduced the asymmetry among agents, economists, and econometricians, but technical constraints prohibited Sargent from fully satisfying the ontological constraint of symmetry. Sargent tried to incorporate a more "realistic interpretation of learning by finally adopting a version of artificial intelligence that was limited to convergence with representative agents. Yet, technical constraints continued to frustrate Sargent's search for symmetry since he was left with asymmetry between himself and agents and between economists and econometricians.

Sargent entertained different interpretations of rational expectations in different periods. In the late 1960s through early 1970s, he used an econometrically motivated interpretation of rational expectations with a focus on restricting distributed lags. In the late 1970s through early 1980s, this emphasis changed to restricting vector autoregressions. During both these phases, Sargent started with the conception of agents as little econometricians while economists were added to the symmetry picture as somewhat of an afterthought. In the early to mid-1980s, Sargent focused on how rational expectations in a general equilibrium framework could lead to vector autoregressions. During this phase, he started with the conception of agents as little economists while econome-tricians were added as somewhat of an afterthought. In the late 1980s through early 1990s, Sargent tried to show convergence to rational expectations through learning by agents, economists, and econometri-cians alike through the use adaptive expectations or artificial intelligence. Furthermore, Sargent's choices were partly inspired by his social environ-ment; Meyer, Roll, and Blattberg in the late 1960s through early 1970s, Sims and Hansen in the late 1970s through early 1980s, Lucas in the early to mid-1980s, and Santa Fe and Marcet in the late 1980s through early 1990s. It was further shown that as a result of each interpretation of rational expectations, Sargent had to deal with different technical constraints. He quietly relinquished Lévy stable distributions when they turned out to be too threatening. He resorted to convenient engineering metaphors in his quests for rationality and a more scientific macro-economics. He was unable to retain symmetry within the rational expectations framework. Finally, he took the convenient way out by wreaking all kinds of travesties upon the standard Santa Fe approach.

Rather than analyzing rational expectations economics in general, this paper has followed one rational expectations economist, Sargent, around. Rather than criticizing or defending his work based on evalua-tions in terms of realism, this paper has shown how Sargent's own attempts to satisfy the ontological constraint of symmetry resulted in different interpretations of rational expectations and kept getting ob-structed by his encounters with technical constraints. Rather than imposing outside standards, this paper has illustrated that Sargent was unable to meet his own standards as a result of the intricate interplay of ontological and technical constraints. This kind of analysis provides an alternative to the many different, simple, and equally (un)compelling stories about the rational expectations revolution that have been circu-lating in the methodology and history of thought communities up until now.

References

Anderson, Philip W., Kenneth J. Arrow, and David Pines (eds.) (1988) *The Economy as an Evolving Complex System*, Redwood City: Addison-Wesley.

Arrow, Kenneth J. (1978) "The Future and the Present in Economic Life," *Economic Inquiry*, 16(2): 157–69.

Begg, David K. H. (1982) *The Rational Expectations Revolution in Macroeco-nomics*, Baltimore: Johns Hopkins University Press.

Blattberg, Robert and Thomas J. Sargent (1971) "Regression with Non-Gaussian Stable Disturbances: Some Sampling Results," *Econometrica*, 39(3): 501–10.

DeCanio, Stephen (1979) "Rational Expectations and Learning from Experience," *Quarterly Journal of Economics*, 93(1): 47–57.

Falkenburg, Brigitte (1988) "The Unifying Role of Symmetry Principles in Particle Physics," *Ratio*, 1(2): 113–34.

Friedman, Benjamin M. (1979) "Optimal Expectations and the Extreme Information Assumptions of 'Rational Expectations' Macromodels," *Journal of Monetary Economics*, 5(1): 23–41.

Glauber, Robert R. and John R. Meyer (1964) *Investment Decisions, Economic Forecasting, and Public Policy*, Boston: Harvard Business School.

Granger, Clive W. J. (1994) "Forecasting in Economics," in Neil A. Gershenfeld and Andreas S. Weigend (eds.), *Time Series Prediction: Forecasting the Future and Understanding the Past*, Reading, MA: Addison-Wesley.

Granger, Clive W. J. and Timo Teräsvirta (1993) *Modeling Nonlinear Economic Relationships*, Oxford: Oxford University Press.

Guzzardi, Walter (1978) "The New Down-to-Earth Economics," *Fortune*, 21 December: 72–9.

Hansen, Lars P. and Thomas J. Sargent (1981a) "Formulating and Estimating Dynamic Linear Expectations Models," in Robert E. Lucas and Thomas J. Sargent (eds.), *Rational Expectations and Econometric Practice*, Minneapolis: University of Minnesota Press.

(1981b) "Linear Rational Expectations Models for Dynamically Interrelated Variables," in Robert E. Lucas and Thomas J. Sargent (eds.), *Rational Expectations and Econometric Practice*, Minneapolis: University of Minnesota Press.

(1990) "Recursive Linear Models of Dynamic Economies," National Bureau of Economic Research Working Paper No. 3479.

(1991a) "Introduction," in Lars P. Hansen and Thomas J. Sargent (eds.), *Rational Expectations Econometrics*, Boulder: Westview Press.

(1991b) "Recursive Linear Models of Dynamic Economies," unpublished manuscript. Stanford University, Hoover Institution.

Hoover, Kevin D. (1988) *The New Classical Macroeconomics*, New York: Basil Blackwell.

(2001) "Is Macroeconomics for Real?", this volume, pp. 225–45.

Kim, Kyun (1988) *Equilibrium Business Cycle Theory in Historical Perspective*, Cambridge: Cambridge University Press.

Klamer, Arjo (1983) *Conversations with Economists*, Savage: Rowman and Littlefield.

Latour, Bruno (1987) *Science in Action*, Cambridge, MA: Harvard University Press.

Lawson, Tony (1994) "A Realist Theory for Economics," in Roger E. Backhouse (ed.), *New Directions in Economic Methodology*, London: Routledge.

Lucas, Robert E. (1987) *Models of Business Cycles*, Oxford: Basil Blackwell.

Lucas, Robert E. and Thomas J. Sargent (1979) "After Keynesian Macroeconomics," *Federal Reserve Bank of Minneapolis Quarterly Review*, 3 (Spring): 1–16.

(1981) "Introduction," in Robert E. Lucas and Thomas J. Sargent (eds.), *Rational Expectations and Econometric Practice*, Minneapolis: University of Minnesota Press.

Mäki, Uskali (1994) "Reorienting the Assumptions Issue," in Roger E. Backhouse (ed.), *New Directions in Economic Methodology*, London: Routledge.

Marcet, Albert and Thomas J. Sargent (1986) "Convergence of Least Squares Learning Mechanisms in Self-Referential Linear Stochastic Models," Hoover Institution Working Papers in Economics E-86–33.

(1988) "The Fate of Systems With 'Adaptive' Expectations," *American Economic Review*, 78(2): 168–72.

(1989a) "Convergence of Least Squares Learning Mechanisms in Self-Referential Linear Stochastic Models," *Journal of Economic Theory*, 48(2): 337–68.

(1989b) "Convergence of Least Squares Learning in Environments with Hidden State Variables and Private Information," *Journal of Political Economy*, 97(6): 1306–22.

(1989c) "Least Squares Learning and the Dynamics of Hyperinflation," in William Barnett, John Geweke, and Karl Shell (eds.), *Economic Complexity: Chaos, Sunspots, and Nonlinearity*, Cambridge: Cambridge University Press.

(1992) "The Convergence of Vector Autoregressions to Rational Expectations Equilibrium," in Alessandro Vercelli and Nicola Dimitri (eds.), *Macroeconomics: A Strategic Survey*, Oxford: Oxford University Press.

Marimon, Ramon, Ellen McGrattan, and Thomas J. Sargent (1990) "Money as a Medium of Exchange in an Economy with Artificially Intelligent Agents," *Journal of Economic Dynamics and Control*, 14(2): 329–74.

Mirowski, Philip E (1989a) *More Heat than Light*, Cambridge: Cambridge University Press.

(1989b) "'Tis a Pity Econometrics isn't an Empirical Endeavor: Mandelbrot, Chaos, and the Noah and Joseph Effects," *Richerche Economiche*, 43(1–2): 76–99.

(1990) "From Mandelbrot to Chaos in Economic Theory," *Southern Economic Journal*, 57(2): 289–307.

Muth, John F. (1960) "Optimal Properties of Exponentially Weighted Forecasts," *Journal of the American Statistical Association*, 55: 299–306.

(1961) "Rational Expectations and the Theory of Price Movements," *Econometrica*, 29: 315–35.

Pesaran, M. Hashem and Ron Smith (1992) "The Interaction Between Theory and Observation in Economics," *The Economic and Social Review*, 24(1): 1–23.

Pickering, Andrew (1992) "From Science as Knowledge to Science as Practice," in Andrew Pickering (ed.), *Science as Practice and Culture*, Chicago: University of Chicago Press.

Pickering, Andrew and Adam Stephanides (1992) "Constructing Quaternions: On the Analysis of Conceptual Practice," in Andrew Pickering (ed.), *Science as Practice and Culture*, Chicago: University of Chicago Press.

Pool, Robert (1989) "Strange Bedfellows," *Science*, 245: 700–3.

Roll, Richard (1970) *The Behavior of Interest Rates*, New York: Basic Books.

Sargent, Thomas J. (1968) "Interest Rates in the Nineteen-Fifties," *Review of Economics and Statistics*, 50(2): 164–72.

— (1969) "Commodity Price Expectations and the Interest Rate," *Quarterly Journal of Economics*, 83(1): 127–40.

— (1971) "Expectations at the Short End of the Yield Curve: An Application of Macaulay's Test," in Jack M. Guttentag (ed.), *Essays on Interest Rates*, vol. 2, Columbia University Press, for the NBER.

— (1972) "Rational Expectations and the Term Structure of Interest Rates," *Journal of Money, Credit, and Banking*, 4(1): 74–97.

— (1976) "The Observational Equivalence of Natural and Unnatural Rate Theories of Macroeconomics," *Journal of Political Economy*, 86(6): 1009–44.

— (1979) "Estimating Vector Autoregressions Using Methods Not Based On Explicit Economic Theories," *Federal Reserve Bank of Minneapolis Quarterly Review*, 3(3): 8–15.

— (1981a) "Interpreting Economic Time Series," *Journal of Political Economy*, 89(2): 213–48.

— (1981b) "Lecture Notes on Filtering, Control, and Rational Expectations," unpublished manuscript, University of Minnesota, Minneapolis.

— (1984) "Autoregressions, Expectations, and Advice" (with discussion), *American Economic Review*, 74(2): 408–21.

— (1987a) *Macroeconomic Theory*, 2nd edition, Boston: Academic Press.

— (1987b) *Dynamic Macroeconomic Theory*, Cambridge, MA: Harvard University Press.

— (1987c) "Rational Expectations," in John Eatwell, Murray Milgate, and Peter Newman (eds.), *The New Palgrave*, London: Macmillan.

— (1993) *Bounded Rationality in Macroeconomics*, Oxford: Oxford University Press.

Sargent, Thomas J. and Christopher A. Sims (1977) "Business Cycle Modeling without Pretending to Have Too Much A Priori Theory," in Christopher A. Sims (ed.), *New Methods in Business Cycle Research: Proceedings From a Conference*, Federal Reserve Bank of Minneapolis.

Sent, Esther-Mirjam (1998a) "Engineering Dynamic Economics," *History of Political Economy*, 29, special issue: 41–62.

— (1998b) *The Evolving Rationality of Rational Expectations: An Assessment of Thomas Sargent's Achievements*, Cambridge: Cambridge University Press.

Sims, Christopher A. (1980) "Macroeconomics and Reality," *Econometrica*, 62: 540–52.

Tirole, Jean (1982) "On the Possibility of Speculation under Rational Expectations," *Econometrica*, 50(5): 1163–82.

18 Two models of idealization in economics

ALAN NELSON[1]

Economics and social sciences in general can be troubling because of their lack of utility in making accurate quantitative predictions. The trouble cannot be simply written off to the complexity of the phenomena to be predicted because physical phenomena are at least as complex on most sorts of complexity metrics that one might try to imagine. Modern physics is able to work through complexity by means of idealizations which enable us to simplify our analyses to the point where they have quantitative results that actually prove useful. Let us examine the suggestion that idealization in economics is different from idealization in physics (which is not yet to suggest that the difference implies a fault) to see whether we might get some perspective on the quantitative performance of economics.

The nature of idealization in science is, of course, not fully understood – not even in physics. There are, however, some aspects which have been well understood since the time of Newton and Leibniz. Physics, for example, postulates such ideal *entities* as point masses, ideal gases, and frictionless planes. One reason that the name *ideal* is appropriate for these entities is that they clearly differ from any real massive body, sample of gas, or surface of an object. And the difference is not restricted to the fact that point masses have less volume than actual bodies, ideal gases less intermolecular attraction, and frictionless planes less friction than their real counterparts. It is quite impossible that there be a massive body with no volume, gas molecules that exert no attractive forces on each other, and surfaces without friction.

There is an explanation of why the impossibility of these entities does

[1] Talks partly based on the material in this paper were given at the Erasmus University of Rotterdam, and at the 1996 meeting of the American Economic Association. I am grateful to both audiences for useful comments and to Uskali Mäki for criticism of the written version.

not detract from their utility. We have quantitative laws that apply in a perfectly exact way to these ideal entities. These laws do not work so well – sometimes hardly at all – in the same form for many actual entities. Why do we nevertheless regard them as true and, in some ways, fundamental? The answer is that the behavior of real entities that are very similar to the ideal ones in the relevant respects is very closely approximated by the exactly calculated behavior of the ideal. What is more, the closer the real entities are in the relevant respects to the ideal, the more closely the ideal approximates their own behavior. And finally, if we examine the relationship between, on the one hand, the degree of similarity of the real to the ideal and, on the other hand, the accuracy with which the behavior of the ideal approximates the behavior of the real, we find a function that is continuous and may have other nice properties as well. Suppose, for example, that we do experiments with surfaces having a wide range of coefficients of friction and record the error we get by applying the law for a frictionless surface. We will find that the error smoothly approaches zero as the coefficient of friction approaches unity. The great seventeenth-century philosopher Leibniz thought that these remarkable facts could be deduced from a great metaphysical Principle of Continuity, but for physicists, it is enough that they are true.

The concept of idealization under discussion has it that the behavior of real objects nicely approaches the behavior prescribed by ideal laws as the real objects nicely approach ideal objects in the relevant respects. Let us call this Standard Idealization. It is very tempting to suppose that Standard Idealization operates in economics just as it does in the physical sciences. Indeed, comparisons with frictionless planes and the like are frequently encountered in textbooks. One reads that the perfectly maximizing consumer is like an ideal gas molecule, or that the assumption of perfect information is like the assumption of a perfect vacuum, or that economic general equilibrium is like the equilibrium of a sample of gas, and so on. It is generally realized that people are not perfect maximizers, that perfect information is impossible, and that economies are never in general equilibrium (though this last one is, perhaps, somewhat controversial). It also seems to be generally assumed, however, that in common situations where people behave nearly like perfect maximizers, etc., that the results of idealized economic reasoning will make a good quantitative fit with reality. In other words, it seems to be generally assumed that Standard Idealization is prevalent in the application of economic theory or in the theory itself.

There is another concept of scientific idealization that is important to consider even though it does not seem to play a role in modern physical sciences.[2] It should be called *Cartesian Idealization* because it was described and developed by the great scientist, mathematician, and philosopher René Descartes in the seventeenth century, though it has not received much attention. I shall argue that this neglect is unwarranted because its application to economics is illuminating.

In his work *Principles of Philosophy*, Descartes derives three funda-mental laws of physics – they bear some resemblance to Newton's more famous (and successful) three laws. The laws are derived from metaphy-sical principles concerning matter (it has only the geometrical properties of extension) and God (He is immutable). In retrospect, we easily see this commitment to substantive metaphysical principles as the root of Descartes's eventual failure in physics. It was largely through attention to observed phenomena that Newton found the critical concept of mass and the computational device of the center of mass which is so important for the quantitative success of Newton's laws.

Descartes's laws are miserably inadequate for empirical application.[3] Descartes himself was well aware that his laws could not be applied to give quantitative predictions, but this left him quite undaunted. There were at least two reasons for his attitude. One reason is that Descartes thought it completely impossible to have quantitative laws exactly describing the kinematics of bodies. His universe is absolutely full of indefinitely small particles whose effects on the bodies we actually observe are not at all negligible. The mechanical world is much too complex for any actual behavior to be described in quantitative detail not even by laws that are known to be true. It is ironic that Descartes's laws could apply exactly and quantitatively to observable bodies only if these were situated in the complete simplicity of a vacuum. Vacuums, too, turn out to be utterly impossible in Cartesian metaphysics because of the famous dictum that any extension whatsoever is nothing other than body. Why do the "laws" have the status of laws if they are empirically useless? This brings us to the second reason that Descartes was unperturbed by the quantitative inapplicability of his laws. It is that such calculations were not even among the goals of the scientific enterprise. This requires some explanation.

Descartes was a mechanistic scientist. This means that all phenomena which admit of any scientific explanation at all must be explicable solely

---

[2] There is a large literature on the methodology of idealization in economics. A good place to find recent contributions is Hamminga and de Marchi (eds.) (1994).

[3] They seem to predict, for example, that a speeding bullet will be repulsed by a ripe watermelon. Descartes's problem, of course, is with his concept of matter as consisting in extension. This means that he cannot have the concept of density (quantity of matter per unit volume) and hence cannot have the crucial concept of mass.

in terms of matter and its motion. Mechanistic science was, in part, a reaction to scholastic philosophy which posited various forces and influences that were regarded as "occult" by the mechanists. One of the principal challenges to mechanism was the existence of phenomena that seem to defy purely mechanical explanation such as gravitation, magnetism, and the functioning of sensory organs. Descartes was usually satisfied in his scientific writings and correspondence if he could tell a mechanistic story about such phenomena which showed how it was *possible* that they were the manifestations of nothing more than matter in motion. So when he proposed that magnets attract iron because they emit invisibly small screw-shaped particles which screw into appropriately shaped orifices in the iron, he thinks with the famous Cartesian perfect certainty that this account had to be completely true. Since he had given a metaphysical proof that some kind or other of mechanical story must be true, establishing the mere possibility of a particular account sufficed to defeat the claim that it was impossible for mechanism to deal with this or that phenomenon.

One result of this project of furthering the mechanistic revolution in science is that Cartesian physics runs on two tracks. The first track consists of laws that are known to be true of the world since they are deduced with perfect certainty from metaphysical first principles. These laws are quite literally *ideal* since they follow from our divinely guaranteed innate ideas of body and of God. They are, in a later philosophical terminology, *a priori*. Even though the laws are true they are, as already noted, completely useless for accurate predictions of the behavior of physical objects. Since these ideal laws do not directly explain anything, Cartesian science requires another track. This consists in qualitative and schematic accounts of mechanisms which *could* underlie the phenomena of interest, and which are not downright inconsistent with the ideal laws.[4]

This can all be summarized by saying that Cartesian Idealization makes the fundamental laws absolutely true since they are derived from certainly true ideas. The truth of the laws does not mean, however, that they can be used to produce accurate quantitative descriptions. Euclidean geometry is true of three-dimensional shapes, but one does not use it to produce the most perspicuous description of the shape of a rose. It is, in fact, physically impossible that there be a physical object that is a perfect Euclidean solid. Similarly, one does not use the laws of motion to describe accurately the mechanical universe; one instead gives qualitative descriptions of mechanisms that are compatible with the laws. It is,

---

[4] This interpretation of Descartes is developed in Nelson (1995).

moreover, impossible in Cartesian physics that the fundamental laws of physics yield accurate quantitative results.[5]

Now it might seem disingenuous to suggest that Cartesian Idealization can help us as we turn to questions about how to understand economics. Descartes's physics, despite the popularity it enjoyed well into the eighteenth century, did not stand up to comparison with Newton's. Today, we might even hesitate to confer upon it the honorific term, *Science*, because of its explicit reliance on metaphysical principles. Nevertheless, the failure of Descartes's physics does not necessarily reflect badly on its attendant conception of idealization. Unless we are committed to the assumption that any science must resemble physics in all methodological respects, we must consider independently which concept or concepts of idealization fit best with economics.

The project of understanding economics through Cartesian Idealization is not as outlandish as it might seem; in fact, in some respects it is not even entirely original. The illustrious economic methodologist Lionel Robbins can be interpreted as advocating something quite similar. Robbins has been described as a "platonist" and an "a priorist" (and worse!), and we are now in a position to understand how there is some justice in these attributions. But we are also in a position to understand his contribution more sympathetically. Let us reexamine what his view was. One prominent aspect of Robbins's methodological doctrine was his insistence that economics should form a deductive system.[6] For this reason he is also sometimes considered to be allied with logical postivists. In the second, 1935 edition of *An Essay on the Nature and Significance of Economic Science*, Robbins wrote:

As we have seen, [the propositions of Economics] are deductions from simple assumptions reflecting very elementary facts of general experience. If the premises relate to reality the deductions from them *must* have a similar point of reference. (Robbins 1935, p. 104, emphasis added)

Deductive systems in science have virtues of elegance and clarity, but they are, perhaps, mainly motivated by the consideration mentioned here by Robbins. If we can be sure of the truth of the axioms, or premises, then we can be similarly sure of what we deduce from them. In economics, there is a special concern about whether the deductions from

---

[5] The laws could apply exactly only if the bodies in question were perfectly isolated from all others (i.e. in a vacuum) and perfectly elastic (i.e. absolutely hard). Both of these conditions are physically impossible – in fact, they involve logical contradiction (see Nelson 1995).

[6] It is unlikely that Robbins was directly influenced by Descartes's presentation of physics. Blaug describes the connection between Robbins's methodological writings and those of J. S. Mill and, especially, J. E. Cairns (Blaug 1980, pp. 86–91).

the premises relate to reality because economics performs so badly in quantitative predictions.

This concern leads, through an interesting twist, to the methodological doctrine associated with Milton Friedman. This doctrine has it that the job of economic theory is to find premises for deductions which in fact result in good predictions. These premises, or "assumptions" are then instrumentally justified whether or not they are realistic. Here, "realistic" means something like "quantitatively applicable." The concept of Cartesian Idealization separates quantitative applicability (or realism) from truth. So economists influenced by Friedman and employing Standard Idealization might say that good economic premises are false. An economist impressed by Cartesian Idealization wants premises that are true even though they might not be realistic or quantitatively applicable.

Robbins fully realized these concerns about quantitative prediction, but did not think they reflected badly on either the premises or the deductions of economics. He wrote:

But to recognise that Economic laws are general in nature is not to deny the reality of the necessities they describe . . . having delimited the nature and the scope of such generalizations we may proceed with all the greater confidence to claim for them a complete necessity within this field.

Economic laws describe inevitable implications. If the data they postulate are given, then the consequences they predict necessarily follow . . . Granted the correspondence of [the analytic method's] original assumptions and facts, its conclusions are inevitable and inescapable. (Robbins 1935, pp. 121–2)

The laws of economics are, therefore, absolutely true of real economic phenomena. Robbins did not mean, however, that they can be quantitatively applied in any exact way. This is only something we have been thoroughly conditioned to expect because of faulty comparisons between physics (and Standard Idealization) and economics (and Cartesian Idealization). True laws that have no quantitative application seem paradoxical if one has in mind Standard Idealization, but after studying Descartes we know better. Descartes shows under what conditions it is possible to have true laws that are quantitatively almost worthless. Robbins also knew better. Concerning money, for example, he wrote:

We are not justified in asserting, however, as has been so often asserted in recent years, that if the exchanges fall, inflation *must* necessarily follow . . . We know that governments are often foolish and craven and that false views of the functions of money are widely prevalent. But there is no *inevitable* connection between a fall in the exchanges and a decision to set the printing presses working.

A new human volition interrupts the chain of "causation."[7] (Robbins 1935, p. 128)

This example shows that the goals of economic science do not generally include accurate quantitative prediction. Instead, the real goals of economics could be taken to be threefold:

(1) To provide deductions of propositions that are absolutely true of the world.

(2) To provide qualitatively predictions that are accurate most of the time.

And perhaps,

(3) To provide *post hoc* reconstructions of historical events, usually recent events. Sometimes these reconstructions can be expected to fit the historical record with considerable quantitative precision.

Robbins himself (and Descartes for that matter) does not seem to have recognized (3), but it is not inconsistent with this concept of idealization and since it does describe a very large proportion of research in economics, it should be included in the descriptive methodological concept being developed. Robbins also does not have much to say about (2), though we have seen that Descartes does. Here, however, it would seem that Descartes's important objective of providing qualitative mechanistic explanations has a clear analogue in much of contemporary economics. A good deal of macroeconomics has qualitative explanation and prediction as an explicit goal. And microeconomics is often defended against critics by pointing out that it too can sometimes provide useful qualitative predictions – as useful anyway as those provided in such sciences as meteorology and seismology.

If (1)–(3) can be accepted as the goals of economics, then envy of (post-Cartesian) physics should not discourage economists faced with these failures of quantitative prediction. As Robbins noted:

It may be admitted that our knowledge of the facts which are the basis of economic deductions is different in important respects from our knowledge of the facts which are the basis of the deductions of the natural sciences. It may be admitted, too, that from this reason the methods of economic science – although not the tests of its logical consistency – are often different from the methods of

---

[7] The reference here to "human volition" strikingly parallels one of the sources of unmanageable complexity in Cartesian physics. Descartes made thinking substances and physical substance utterly distinct, but was notoriously very vague on how the two kinds of substance interact. Insofar as physical substance is affected by minds, the laws of physics will fail to be accurate in particular applications.

natural sciences . . .

In Economics, as we have seen, the ultimate constituents of our fundamental generalizations are known to us by immediate acquaintance . . . There is much less reason to doubt the counterpart in reality of the assumption of individual preferences than that of the assumption of the electron. (Robbins 1935, pp. 104–5)

So economics is actually in a better situation than physics with respect to its basic assumptions. It is not even necessary to justify them either by direct empirical test, or by Friedman-style reference to the usefulness of the theorems that can be proved from them.

These [the most basic postulates of economics] are not postulates the existence of whose counterpart in reality admits of extensive dispute once their nature is fully realized. We do not need controlled experiments to establish their validity: they are so much the stuff of our everyday experience that they have only to be stated to be recognized as obvious. (Robbins 1935, p. 79)

Moreover, since the structure of economics is deductive, the deductive consequences of the premises also have superior epistemological status to those of physics. Physics comes off better only with respect to quantitative applications. Robbins repeatedly advises caution about the prospects of quantitative laws in economics, writing:

Perhaps, indeed, this is another of the methodological differences between the natural and the social sciences. In the natural sciences the transition from the qualitative to the quantitative is easy and inevitable. In the social sciences, for reasons which have already been set forth, it is in some connection almost impossible, and it is always associated with peril and difficulty. (Robbins 1935, p. 111)

Let me summarize the positive part of this paper's argument. Consider what economics is indisputably strong at. One would include rigorous deductions from elegant mathematical premises, *qualitative* predictions that are sometimes used to good effect by governments and firms, and quantitative retrodictions. These are exactly the things one would expect if we understand economics as making use of Cartesian Idealization. Now consider where economics is indisputably weak, or at least not so strong as physics etc.

Economics is weak at making accurate quantitative predictions concerning phenomena of interest to economic agents. Given Standard Idealization, this is a very serious and puzzling problem for the entire enterprise of economic science. In Cartesian Idealization, however, accurate quantitative prediction is not to be expected. On the contrary, we are free to embrace the powerful arguments that have been given (by Robbins and many others) for why we should not expect accurate quantitative prediction: crucial parameters change unpredictably, exogenous causal factors intrude inevitably, and so on. In short, Cartesian Idealization seems clearly superior as a *descriptive* tool for understanding what actually gets done by economists. Saying it is a "descriptive tool" means that it makes sense of the activity of economists. It explains why they are interested in (and good at) (a) finding elegant premises that permit the deduction of interesting theorems and (b) describing rough mechanisms that enable qualitative forecasting. Saying that Cartesian Idealization describes economics is not to say that it fits with most economists' self-image, or that most economists would naturally formulate it as an answer to the interviewer's question: "What are you doing?" Many, perhaps most economists, who consider the question explicitly would naturally come up with the picture of Standard Idealization which describes physics so well.

One can also imagine that an understanding of Cartesian Idealization could have prescriptive value for economics. It could help focus the efforts of economists in those arenas where there is progress to be made: proving interesting theorems, and suggesting mechanisms that produce good qualitative predictions. Such a prescription would not be taken kindly, however, by those whose careers are invested in trying to do what the Cartesian concept entails is not part of the goal of economics in the first place – making quantitative predictions.

It is possible to put a negative spin on the argument of this paper. There is some tension in both Descartes's and Robbins's thought between the idea that science proceeds by deduction from principles that are extremely simple and evident, and the fact that the principles are not at all trivial to discover. Descartes convinced very few, for example, that the easily introspectible innate idea of body reveals that the essence of body is nothing but geometrical extension. Worse, in historical retrospect we see that his physics was superseded by another that showed the ideas that seemed so certain and innate to Descartes himself were flatly wrong.

Regarding the simple fact that people have well-behaved preferences, Robbins writes:

The business of discovery consists not merely in the elucidation of given premises but in the perception of the facts which are the basis of the premises. The process of discovering those elements in common experience which afford the basis of our trains of deductive reasoning is economic discovery just as much as the shaking out of new inferences from old premises . . . But the great discovery, the Mengerian revolution, which initiated this period of progress, was the discovery of the premises themselves . . . The perception and selection of the basis of economic analysis is as much economics as the analysis itself. (Robbins 1935, pp. 105–6)

I suppose it is true that some principles which are completely obvious once stated are extremely difficult to discover, but there is a competing hypothesis. It is always possible that the obviousness of the principles that are discovered with so much labor is more a matter of ideology and indoctrination than a matter of absolute truth. Three hundred years later, we can see that is how it was with Descartes, anyway. Perhaps we should ask ourselves the same kinds of hard questions about the basic postulates of economics that Newton asked when faced with the basic postulates of Cartesian physics. Consider the propositions that Robbins himself considered fundamental. Do individuals really have "preferences" that can be "arranged in order" in the senses of those terms that are required by economics? Can we separate and count "factors of production" in the same sense and then see that they must be subject to diminishing returns? A consideration of the Cartesian, or Robbinsian concept of idealization would ultimately refocus methodological investigations on these kinds of questions.[8]

References

Blaug, Mark (1980) *The Methodology of Economics*, Cambridge: Cambridge University Press.

Descartes, R. (1644/1983) *Principles of Philosophy* (trans. V. Miller and R. Miller), Dordrecht: Reidel Publishing Company.

Hamminga, B. and N. de Marchi (eds.) (1994) *Idealization in Economics*, special issue of *Poznan Studies in the Philosophy of the Sciences and the Humanities*, 38.

Nelson, Alan (1990) "Are Economic Kinds Natural?," *Minnesota Studies in the Philosophy of Science*, vol. 14: 102–35.

  (1995) "Micro-chaos and Idealization in Cartesian Physics," *Philosophical Studies*, 77: 377–91.

Robbins, Lionel (1935) *An Essay on the Nature and Significance of Economic Science* (2nd edn.), London: Macmillan.

---

[8] One approach to answering these questions is developed in Nelson (1990).

19 The way the world works (www): towards an ontology of theory choice

USKALI MÄKI

1 Introducing the ontology of theory choice

Economists choose theories and they choose ways of pursuing theories, and they leave others unchosen. Why do economists choose the way they do? How should economists choose? What are the objectives and what are the constraints? What should they be? The questions are both descriptive and prescriptive.

There are two broad classes of "criteria of choice" that have been somewhat systematically considered in the recent literature on economic methodology:

1. **Empirical criteria**. There are several possible ways of incorporating empirical criteria in one's theory of science. The respective methodology of theory assessment may be static or dynamic, it may be deductivist or inductivist, it may include various ideas of what constitutes empirical evidence, and so on. What they all share is the general idea that scientific theories are, or are to be, checked against empirical evidence according to some rules, and that this determines the choice of theory.

2. **Social criteria**. Again, there are several options. The social criteria may be related to the social interests of scientists or larger social collectives, they may be based on the persuasiveness and tradition-boundedness of theories, they may involve social or moral norms, they may be derived from various costs and benefits of holding a theory in a given research community, and so on. If they involve

Earlier versions of this paper have been presented at a seminar at the High Council of Scientific Research of Spain and at Erasmus Institute for Philosophy and Economics. Acknowledgements to the two audiences for inspiring reactions and in particular to Jack Vromen and Frank Hindriks for detailed comments.

empirical data, it is the social aspects of the data that matter. What all these views share is that scientific theories are taken to have social attributes (functions, consequences) that play or should play a major role in theory choice.

In the field of economic methodology, most of the research and discussion during the era of "Popperian dominance" (see Mäki 1990a) was devoted to examining the empirical criteria and to assessing theories and larger theoretical constellations in terms of such criteria (e.g., Latsis 1976; Blaug 1980; Weintraub 1985). This research led to the discovery that empirical criteria play only a limited role in theory development and in discriminating between rival fundamental theories (e.g., chapters in de Marchi 1988; de Marchi and Blaug 1991; de Marchi 1993). Theories turn out to be severely underdetermined by empirical evidence so that the Duhem–Quine problem is taken to be particularly difficult in economics.

Partly in response to the failure to establish a systematic relationship between theory choice and empirical criteria, attempts have recently been made to look at the social dynamics of theory choice in economics. Given that theory choice is taken to be radically underdetermined by empirical tests, it is suggested that various social factors adopt the role as determinants, complementing or replacing or shaping the conventional empirical criteria. Some of the key categories used for depicting the allegedly powerful social factors in play have been "conversation," "rhetoric," "social construction," and more specifically, "sunk costs," "path dependence," "physics envy," "gender bias," and others (e.g., Klamer 1983; McCloskey 1985; Mirowski 1989; Weintraub 1991; Mäki 1992d, 1993a, 1999; Hands 1994; Ferber and Nelson 1993; Zamora 1999). Many of the possible directions and issues within this class of factors remain to be examined.

My view is that there is an important third class of criteria which should be invoked both in descriptive and normative considerations of theory choice in economics:

3. **Ontological criteria**. These may be related to various conceptions about the basic constituents of social reality, their causal capacities, relations of causal and other kinds of dependence between them, and mechanisms of change among them. More particularly, these criteria may be based on some more or less fundamental and more or less well-articulated visions concerning human beings in regard to notions of rationality, and the social arrangements of their lives in regard to individualism, collectivism, as well as conceptions of social causation and evolution. What all such ideas share is that consistency with conceptions of the structure and functioning of the world serves as a criterion of, or a constraint on, theory choice.

I believe there is no doubt that, as a matter of actual fact, ontological criteria play an important role in constraining actual theory choices made by economists. I also believe they should play such a role. Given these two claims, a third one is suggested: too little systematic analysis has been done on the ontological grounds of theorizing by economic methodologists. Some interesting work has been done on the ontology of economics, though. Among the examples are the argument from the folk psychological foundations of microeconomics (Rosenberg 1992); work on causal powers and tendencies in the economy (Cartwright 1989; Mäki 1990b, 1992c; Lawson 1997); work on causal processes and mechanisms (Mäki 1992c, 1998a; Salmon 1998); study on Dennettian real patterns (Ross 1995); and a study on universals in economics (Mäki 1997). One may also translate notions such as "physics envy" and "gender bias" into ontological claims. Few of the works in the above list explicitly construe ontological notions as criteria of theory choice or as constraints on theorizing. This is where the focus of the present essay lies (this draws upon earlier work with a similar focus: Mäki 1998d; 1998e; see also Mäki 1992c).

I will introduce a generic ontological notion, that of *the way the world works*, or *www* for short. My descriptive claim is that many economists invoke this idea with an intention of providing a constraint on theorizing. I will call this ontological constraint *the www constraint*. Economists invoke this constraint either implicitly or explicitly. I am also inclined to hold the normative claim that economists are on the right track when they, at least in some important instances, invoke such a constraint. My arguments in this paper are for the descriptive claim.

Let us suppose that it is of the essence of science that scientists pursue an understanding of the world. Let us also suppose that understanding the world amounts to understanding how the world works, the way the world functions. Let us further suppose that at least to a large extent, the world's workings are a matter of causal processes being in place. Let us finally suppose that an understanding of the world is sought by means of theories. All this means that scientific theories are – and are to be – constructed and employed with the purpose of depicting the causal processes that constitute the ways the world works. One of the prominent recent philosophical statements of this time-honored general idea has been put forth by Wesley Salmon: "To understand the world and what goes on in it, we must expose its inner workings. To the extent that causal mechanisms operate, they explain how the world works" (Salmon 1984, p. 133). Explanatory understanding is dependent on description, or theoretical redescription: the events and their co-occurrences and sequences, as well as the entities involved in them, are redescribed in terms of theory as what they are believed to be, namely as manifestations of "underlying" entities and processes. Thus answers to why? questions are dependent on answers to how? questions (see Mäki 1990c, 1992c). In Salmon's words: "Causal processes, causal interactions, and causal laws provide the mechanisms by which the world works; to understand *why* certain things happen, we need to see *how* they are produced by these mechanisms" (Salmon 1984, p. 132). There is a sense in which adequate explanations *are* adequate descriptions of goings-on in the world.

Here is how the *www* constraint often works: if it is the case that we understand the world by way of theories which describe its causal functioning, then any doubt about the capacity of a given theory to expose the major elements of such causal functioning amounts to a doubt about its capacity to render parts of the world understandable. Such doubts may lead to various responses, ranging from outright rejection to relative lack of attention. In such cases, the constraint functions negatively: beliefs about its non-satisfaction serve as grounds for exclusion. Even though this negative role of the constraint in providing grounds for exclusion may be particularly important, this does not rule out its positive role in providing supportive grounds for a theory. The general point is that the *www* constraint serves a function in determining the merits and demerits of a theory.

We will next look at an example of the negative function of the constraint. The model of perfect competition will serve as our case. While this model enjoys an established status in most textbooks of economics, there are economists who believe the model to be fatally misguided as a picture of the competitive market economy. We will see how skepticism about the model of perfect competition as expressed by certain economists is based on invoking the *www* constraint. These economists have doubts about the non-satisfaction of the constraint, and these doubts serve as grounds for exclusion. Their reasoning may be put in terms of unrealisticness: all models are unrealistic; this model is unrealistic in a wrong way.

2 The way the world won't work: perfect competition

The purpose of the present section is not to add anything novel to some of the customary complaints about the model of perfect competition, nor to try to persuade the advocates that the criticisms are sound. My purpose is rather to show that some of these criticisms amount to what I have set out to argue in this paper: some such criticisms are a matter of

(1) invoking an ontological *www* constraint on economic theorizing, and to (2) arguing that the perfect competition model does not meet this constraint. I cite three economists – George Richardson, Ronald Coase, and James Buchanan – as evidence in support of the two claims. Notice also that I will not have to be very precise about what the target of such criticisms is (nor is the textual evidence I employ very precise about this); it is enough for my case to show that the *www* constraint *is* being invoked in an argument against *something*.

In each case, the reasoning is the same, exhibiting the same pattern:

1. Acknowledge the unavoidability of excluding much in one's theory: any theory or model is necessarily relatively narrow and simple.
2. Argue that the model of perfect competition is narrow in a wrong way, in that it excludes items that should not be excluded.
3. Suggest that the grounds for the claim of faulty narrowness, and, more generally, for judging what to include and what to exclude in one's model, are based on one's conception of the way the world works.

Narrowness of theory

It is a standard criticism of a model or theory to blame it for excluding something from consideration. This suggests a common form of unrealisticness: a theory is unrealistic if it is unjustifiably "narrow" – that is, if it excludes from consideration factors that are deemed important. This notion is entertained also by Coase and Richardson. Both think that conventional textbook theory is unrealistic in this sense: it excludes factors that should be included in the theory. To put it in other words, conventional neoclassical theory isolates from factors that should be explicitly theorized; thus, the theory should be de-isolated so as to incorporate these factors (see Mäki 1992a, 1994a, 1994b).

However, and this is where Coase and Richardson part company, they do not share the details of *where* to start de-isolating the theory, that is, *what* precisely to include that was excluded from consideration, and in what order. Any theory excludes an enormous number of elements in reality. From this set of excluded elements, one may then only choose for inclusion a small subset comprising those that are found most important. Coase and Richardson choose somewhat differently. For Coase, the most important element to be included is transaction costs; for Richardson it is the process of information acquisition that will ensure the satisfaction of what he calls the "informational requirements."

For Coase, the incorporation of positive transaction costs required the relaxation of the assumption of zero transaction costs, which "is, of course, a very unrealistic assumption" (Coase 1960, p. 15). By relaxing this assumption, the theory could be broadened by way of theoretical de-isolation. The item thereby incorporated is what he calls "the missing element" in economic theory (Coase 1993c, p. 62). This is not the only missing item, however: "No doubt other factors should also be added" (Coase 1988b, p. 30).

Richardson stresses his main theme by saying that economists "should take account of informational considerations that have generally been neglected" and then goes on by suggesting that "there are yet other relevant considerations which cannot be brought into formal analysis" (Richardson 1998, p. 21). There is a lot that has been neglected, but not all of these factors can be incorporated into formal theory. "Economic theory is an indispensable instrument of analysis, but effective only when we are aware of its limitations" (p. 21). Yet, much that has been excluded, can and should be included. Among them are product and process innovations. Richardson blames standard theory for "[c]hoosing to set aside, or assume away, the fact that products and processes are subject to continuous development" (p. 3). This is not an innocent exclusion, since "the habit of abstracting from product development, the pace of which has been accelerating, may have led economists to view the real world as much less competitive than business men know it to be" (p. 14).

Coase is explicit that some of the excluded factors are those that characterize the internal organization of the business firm, thus leading to a notion of the firm as a black box:[1]

The concentration on the determination of prices has led to a narrowing of focus which has had as a result the neglect of other aspects of the economic system. [. . .] What happens in between the purchase of the factors of production and the sale of the goods that are produced by these factors is largely ignored. [. . .] The firm in mainstream economic theory has often been described as a "black box." And so it is. This is very extraordinary given that most resources in a modern economic system are employed within firms, with how these resources are used dependent on administrative decisions and not directly on the operation of a market. Consequently, the efficiency of the economic system depends to a very considerable extent on how these organizations conduct their affairs, particularly, of course, the modern corporation. Even more surprising, given their interest in

[1] The exclusion of internal characteristics of the objects under study (such as the internal organization of business firms) amounts to "internal isolation" in contrast to "external isolation" which is a matter of excluding characteristics of the system surrounding the object (such as other markets in partial equilibrium analysis) (see Mäki 1992a for details).

the pricing system, is the neglect of the market or more specifically the institutional arrangements which govern the process of exchange. (Coase 1993 [1992], p. 229)

Richardson shares the belief that price theory gives an overly narrow if not distorted picture of economic reality; he also thinks that its prominence may be based on the mechanical analogy borrowed from physics. This suggests that conventional price theory is set up to conform to a wrong ontological constraint:

if we are led to study the informational aspects of social systems only in terms of a rigid conceptual framework borrowed from physics, we shall certainly obtain a distorted picture. Prices, for example, and particularly the current values of prices, assume from this point of view an undeserved prominence, because it is in terms of them that a quasi-physical signalling mechanism can be elaborated and given mathematical expression. (Richardson 1960, p. 41)

Coase puts some of the blame on the conception of economics as a theory of choice which has contributed to the exclusion of the human and institutional "substance" of the economy from theoretical consideration. The resulting picture is ontologically suspect:

This preoccupation of economists with the logic of choice [. . .] has nonetheless had, in my view, serious adverse effects on economics itself. One result of this divorce of the theory from its subject matter has been that the entities whose decisions economists are engaged in analyzing have not been made the subject of study and in consequence lack any substance. The consumer is not a human being but a consistent set of preferences. The firm to an economist [. . .] "is effectively defined as a cost curve and a demand curve [. . .]". Exchange takes place without any specification of its institutional setting. We have consumers without humanity, firms without organization, and even exchange without markets. (Coase 1988b, p. 3)

No doubt economists have an amazing variety of grounds for thinking of a given theory as unrealistic, but a major one is certainly the perception of the theory as excessively narrow or partial or isolative. As we have seen, this is also one of Coase's and Richardson's critical perceptions of standard neoclassical theory. They insist on the de-isolation of the theoretical picture of the economy by incorporating neglected elements into the theory.[2] But we have not said enough; our picture of their views on narrowness is still too narrow.

---

[2] More precisely, we are here talking about "horizontal de-isolation" – de-isolation at a given level of abstraction or vertical isolation (Mäki 1994a). In contrast to Coase's quest for horizontal de-isolation, he also insists on vertical de-isolation, that is, lowering the level of abstraction by engaging oneself in empirical case studies (Mäki 1998b).

The missing "imperfections": Richardson

Having listed some successes of the market system in adjusting to changes, and before providing an exposition of aspects of general equilibrium theory to account for these successes, Kenneth Arrow makes this claim: "All these phenomena show that by and large and in the long view of history, the economic system adjusts with a considerable degree of smoothness and indeed of rationality to changes in the fundamental facts within which it operates" (Arrow 1974, p. 254). Richardson agrees that the market system has the capacity of coordinating activities and adjusting to changes. However, referring to the theory of general equilibrium, Richardson makes a somewhat blunt statement:

We therefore need to find a better explanation of how, and in what conditions, coordination through market transactions, which we know from experience can work, does in fact work. Men stir up a dust . . . and then complain that they cannot see. And it is indeed through the creation of a model with perfect competition, perfect mobility (and, sometimes, perfect knowledge, whatever that means) that we obscure the actual process of adjustment. (Richardson 1995, p. 1492)

"Men stir up a dust and then complain that they cannot see." This sounds like a rather harsh judgement about economists holding certain theories. In what follows, we try to understand what Richardson means by the expressions "stirring up a dust" and "cannot see." This much should be clear to begin with: one does not "stir up a dust" by making just any unrealistic assumptions. The very first page of Richardson's *Information and Investment* hints at the possibility of *harmless* unrealistic- ness in the case of the perfect competition model:

The conditions which define it, as everyone knows, are rarely, if ever, character- istic of the real world, but it can be argued that this divergence represents no more than the normal degree of abstraction associated with general theoretical models. (Richardson 1960, p. 1)

Coase is more explicit about what makes unrealisticness justified, or, in Richardson's words, what determines "the normal degree of abstraction":

. . . our assumptions should not be completely realistic. There are factors we leave out because we do not know how to handle them. There are others we exclude because we do not feel the benefits of a more complete theory would be worth the costs involved in including them. [. . .] Again, assumptions about other factors do not need to be realistic because they are completely irrelevant. (Coase 1988c, p. 66)

In other words, Coase is comfortable with a theory being isolative in general, provided there are good reasons for this such as the ones he cites above.[3] However, there are limits to unrealisticness: beyond these limits, one would "stir up a dust." There are some items that just cannot be excluded without obscuring the view: if you exclude them, you "cannot see." This is the fundamental message endorsed by Richardson and Coase. They also hold a shared idea of what determines these limits. These limits, they believe, are determined by our conception of the way the world works. They not only believe that the conventional picture is narrow, but that it is harmfully narrow in unduly excluding important factors. The question is to ask, what is it that makes those factors *important*? Why are they claimed to be *unduly* excluded? Why should *precisely they*, and not some other factors, be included? In order to answer these questions something else is needed. In the case of Coase and Richardson this something else amounts to the invocation of the ontological constraint. Plenty of documentation can be provided in support of this suggestion.

The subtitle of Richardson's main work, *Information and Investment*, is accurate: *A Study in the Working of the Competitive Economy*. Indeed, it is a recurring theme of the book that it is the task of economics to give an account of how the economy "works." Richardson's persistent critique of the perfect competition model is telling. The second page of *Information and Investment* summarizes his critique of the model precisely for failing to account for the world's workings:

Perfect competition, I shall affirm, represents a system in which entrepreneurs would be *unable* to obtain the minimum necessary information; for this reason, it cannot serve as a model of the *working* of actual competitive economies. (Richardson 1960, p. 2; emphases added)

Here is the claim put in more specific terms:

I feel convinced that one of the *essential* elements of any adequate account of the attainment of equilibrium has not been provided; for the most part, indeed, the need for it has been ignored. No explanation has been given of how, in the conditions which define the perfectly competitive model, entrepreneurs *could* obtain the information on which their expectations, and therefore the investment plans required for equilibrium, would have to be based. (Richardson 1960, pp. 23–4; emphases added)

Note that Richardson says that considerations of information are supposed to provide "one of the essential elements" involved in the process of "the attainment of equilibrium" and that the model under

---

[3] For arguments that show why an economist espousing realism as a theory of theories is entitled or even required to use unrealistic assumptions, see Mäki (1994a, 1994b).

criticism fails to incorporate this essential element. Richardson puts the idea explicitly in terms of the working of the world:

Whatever insights the theory of perfect competition may have given us, it fails to provide . . . a convincing account of how free enterprise economies in fact work. . . . And this failure results from its neglect of what we may call the informational requirements of any workable system, the conditions that must be realized, that is, in order that those within it can have sufficient knowledge to take investment decisions. (Richardson 1998, p. 2)

He goes on by explaining why he thinks the model of perfect competition fails in accounting for the way the system works – why its advocates have "stirred up a dust":

By abstracting from some of the circumstances of real economic life, we have, paradoxically, made it more difficult, if not impossible, to explain how the system works. I have argued elsewhere that markets generally operate not despite, but because of, some "imperfection" of competition, because of the existence, that is, of circumstances which, although excluded by definition from the perfect competition model, fullfil the informational requirements of the system by endowing the business environment with a high degree of stability sufficient to make informed investment decisions possible. (Richardson 1998, p. 2)

The "imperfections" that Richardson refers to – in his 1960 book he called them "restraints" – are institutional features of economies, including forms of information sharing such as price agreements, vertical integration, and signaling, as well as reputation and trust. Such "imperfections" reduce the cost of information and constitute commitments, and thereby facilitate the coordination of competitive and complementary investments. The "imperfections" are among the essential elements in the way the world works. To understand the workings of the economic world one has to understand such institutional features. Such understanding is not provided by the model of perfect competition:

Coordination through market transactions is only possible . . . by virtue of the existence, in the real world, of circumstances which set bounds to what can happen. And these *enabling circumstances*, which exist naturally (such as differential capabilities) or which may be contrived through collective action (such as market sharing arrangements), *all represent deviations from the pure competition model*. (Richardson 1995, p. 1492; emphases added)[4]

---

[4] "Perfect competition earned its reputation as an ideal market structure because of the belief that, to the extent that the conditions defining it were realized, resources would be allocated so as to exhaust all profit opportunities. No one, in my view, ever provided a fully satisfactory explanation of how this was to come about . . . the conditions favourable to successful adjustment are not those laid down in the perfectly competitive model" (Richardson 1964, pp. 160, 161).

Richardson argues that to understand (even the possibility of) successful adjustment through market transactions, we need to incorporate various institutional features into our picture of the economy. This can be done by relaxing assumptions such as those of perfect information, atomistic firms, and homogeneous goods, and of paying attention to the ways in which the "informational requirement" is met. In the imperfect information world, institutions matter. There is a parallel logical structure in Coase's account. By relaxing the zero transaction cost assumption, that is, by incorporating positive transaction costs into his account Coase was not only able but also forced to incorporate institutional features that were previously neglected from systematic analysis. In the positive transaction cost world, institutions matter.

We cannot yet pretend to fully understand the notion of the world's working as it appears in Richardson. What does it mean, precisely? Why does one theory fail and why does another theory succeed as a potentially adequate representation of the way the world works? A complete account would be impossible to pursue here, but one observation can be provided. An element of ontic necessity – necessity *de re* rather than just *de dicto* – appears to involved. Richardson puts the idea variously, including references to "conceivable" systems and to some elements being "essential" or "necessary" for the functioning of the system. Here is an example:

> Irreducible uncertainty, as a factor in any *conceivable* economic system, owes its existence, in part to incomplete information about preferences and production functions. In much of economic theory, this incompleteness is ignored . . . But where the object is to study the working of a competitive economy, the question of the availability of information *cannot* thus be pushed aside. (Richardson 1960, p. 81; emphases added)

He also says that "some market imperfections may be *essential* to the process of successful economic adjustment" (p. 38; emphasis added) and that "the conditions which define the system of perfect competition are not such as would *permit* the economic adjustments required" (p. 10; emphasis added). As Brian Loasby puts it, Richardson's "conclusion is that in perfecting the model of perfectly competitive equilibrium, economists have refined away the essential mechanism" (Loasby 1986, p. 152). Here is yet another way of formulating the idea:

> By assuming, overtly or tacitly, that [the optimum strength for these restraints] is zero, and therefore by neglecting the whole problem of information, the perfect competition model condemns itself not only to unrealism but to *inadequacy even as a hypothetical system*. (Richardson 1960, p. 69; emphasis added)

The following may be taken as an explanation of what Richardson means by "inadequacy even as a hypothetical system":

It is no defence to appeal, moreover, to the analogy of mechanical statics which, though neglecting friction, can still identify the equilibrium position of a system of forces, for we cannot demonstrate that economic systems have such positions of rest without reference to expectations and information which *could not* be presumed to be available in the absence of restraints. (Richardson 1960, p. 69; emphasis added)

Thus, "inadequacy even as a hypothetical system" can be taken to mean something like "ontic impossibility". This can then be taken to imply that there are some ontically *necessary* features that a real system has to possess in order for its theoretical picture to count as *adequate* "even as a hypothetical system." This suggests that it is in the character of hypothetical pictures that they represent systems that are at least possible – even though perhaps not fully actual. One further piece of evidence appears to support this reading. Ontic necessities and impossibilities have entailments regarding empirical actualities. The following can be read in this light:

It is not by accident that the markets in the real [actual] world that are closest to pure competition, namely commodity markets, are usually subject to some kind of regulation, or to disarray or, very commonly, to both. There is absolutely no presumption that either the presence of a large number of competitors, or the homogeneity of the products they offer, are, as the theory of perfect competition would lead us to suppose, conditions favourable to efficient allocation. (Richardson 1995, pp. 1492–3)

To sum up, there seem to be two ontically necessary connections envisaged by Richardson. One is that information is necessary for adjustment. The other is that "restraints" are necessary for information. And since these restraints appear in the form of institutions – "customs, conventions, and the laws" (1960, p. 69) – this implies that a theory about the working of the competitive economy has to incorporate institutions. This is a theoretical necessity suggested by the two ontic necessities.

Missing category of costs, missing institutions: Coase

Consider then Coase's version of the idea of the world's workings. We have already cited Coase's complaint about economics which theorizes "consumers without humanity, firms without organization, and even exchange without markets" (Coase 1988b, p. 3). Let us try to see what grounds Coase has for this complaint. Such grounds are far from intuitively obvious given that there are highly respected scientific theories that study planets without extension, planes without friction, and molecules without color. Why are some exclusions suspicious while some others are not?

Coase explains that it took him a long time to realize that "the whole of economic theory would be transformed by incorporating transaction costs into the analysis" (Coase 1993c, p. 62). The somewhat revolutionary tone in this judgement can only be understood as reflecting the idea that transaction costs constitute a major factor in economic reality and that its inclusion in theory has major consequences for economics. But what does "major" mean here? It does not just designate the idea that here we have another "factor" which has a large impact on economic phenomena and therefore had better be included in explanations. More is involved than just causal relevance, namely what we might call *ontic indispensability*: the element to be added is not just causally influential, it is necessary for the functioning of the system. The introduction of positive transaction costs in the theory brings with it new kinds of entities, namely institutions, such as legal rules and contractual structures. If it is held that such institutions play *both an indispensable and a powerful* role in the functioning of the economy, it would be inexcusable to exclude them from the analysis.

This suggestion is based on a central idea that occurs frequently in Coase's writings, namely that it is the task of economic theory to provide "insight into how the system works" (Coase 1988c, p. 64). He argues that "realism [i.e. realisticness] of assumptions is needed if our theories are ever to help us understand why the system works in the way it does" (p. 65). Of course, by this he must mean realisticness subject to the ontological constraint – and this leaves room for plenty of legitimate unrealisticness.

The idea that there is a way in which "the economic system works" suggests that the complaint about a "missing element" in theory is in effect a complaint about an indispensable *missing link* in the working of the real system; without this link, the system would not function as it does – or would not function at all. Therefore, this link has to be theorized in order to understand how the system works. Coase's view here is akin to Richardson's, amounting to the suggestion that some sort of necessity is involved: "The solution was to realize that there were costs of making transactions in a market economy and that it was *necessary* to incorporate them in the analysis" (Coase 1993a, p. 46; emphasis added). In this somewhat essentialist spirit, he says that the point of theorizing is "to get to the essence of what [is] going on in the economic system" (Coase 1988c, p. 68).

The missing endogenous process: Buchanan

Our final witness is James Buchanan. He puts forth a familiar complaint:

The basic flaw in this model of perfect competition is not its lack of correspondence with observed reality; no model of predictive value exhibits this. Its flaw lies in its conversion of individual choice behavior from a social-institutional context to a physical-computational one . . . but surely this is nonsensical social science, and the institutionalist critics have been broadly on target in some of their attacks. (Buchanan 1979, p. 29)

Buchanan then goes on to put forward his favored position; it is in terms of endogenous process. Here is a lengthy passage:

A market is not competitive by assumption or by construction. A market *becomes* competitive, and competitive rules *come to be* established as institutions emerge to place limits on individual behavior patterns. It is this *becoming* process, brought about by the continuous pressure of human behavior in exchange, that is the central part of our discipline, if we have one, not the dry rot of postulated perfection. A solution to a general-equilibrium set of equations is not predetermined by exogenously determined rules. A general solution, if there is one, *emerges* as a result of a whole network of evolving exchanges, bargains, trades, side payments, agreements, contracts which, finally at some point, ceases to renew itself. At each stage in this evolution toward solution there are *gains* to be made, there are exchanges possible, and this being true, the direction of movement is modified. (Buchanan 1979, p. 29)

Buchanan concludes that it is "for these reasons that the model of perfect competition is of such limited explanatory value except when changes in variables exogenous to the system are introduced. There is no place in the structure of the model for internal change, change that is brought about by the men who continue to be haunted by the Smithean propensity [to truck, barter, and exchange]" (Buchanan 1979, pp. 29–30). We may paraphrase these remarks by saying that, according to Buchanan, the model of perfect competition fails to meet an important *www* constraint, namely it fails to depict the way the competitive economy works in terms of endogenous causal process.

4 Concluding remarks

I have used a class of criticisms against the model of perfect competition as evidence in support of the descriptive claim that at least some economists invoke ontological constraints in their arguments for or against particular theories or lines of theorizing. This limited evidence does not yet give us much of an idea about the proportion, weight, and likely context of ontological arguments in the argumentative practices of economists. It remains a task for empirical investigation to determine such matters. For example, it is obvious that the ontological arguments in relation to the model of perfect competition far from exhaust all the relevant and popular arguments there are about this model. Indeed, many economists are unimpressed by such arguments and justify their use of the model in non-ontological terms. To them, the model was never intended as an account of the way the competitive economy works. And they often say this explicitly so as to discourage others to assess the model by what they regard as wrong standards. Does this mean that these economists do not have conceptions of the *www*, or more precisely, consequential conceptions of the *www*? Not at all, on the contrary. The very fact that they often explicitly speak out their view that the perfect competition model *is not*, and *is not intended as*, a description of the way the competitive economy works implies that *they do have* consequential views of the workings of the world.

All theories are bound to be unrealistic in the trivial sense of excluding much, in being isolative or narrow. All economists think that there are limits to narrowness. Many economists think that the appropriate isolations have to meet an ontological constraint provided by conceptions of the way the economic system works. Some economists believe that the model of perfect competition does not meet the constraint, and therefore cannot be taken as an adequate representation of the core or essence of the competitive economy – not even as a hypothetical possibility. The need for de-isolation – that is, the need for incorporating institutional "imperfections" – is ontologically grounded. The idea is not the simple one that these "imperfections" are real and causally influential, and therefore should be included – for example in order to improve the fit of the predictive implications of the model. The idea is rather the stronger one that the imperfections play a necessary or essential role in the working of the world, and that therefore they should play an indispensable role in theory.

No complete account of the workings of the *www* constraint can be attempted here. I will just list a few features that would appear to be characteristic about it. It is the task of future research to revise and refine these suggestions.

1. The *www* constraint is an ontological constraint on theory choice. It is to the merit of a theory to meet the constraint, and to its demerit to fail to meet it. Good theories are believed to depict the way the world works

and thereby to make the world understandable to us. Reasons to think that a given theory has failed to conform to the constraint are reasons to think that the theory will not help us understand. Economists have beliefs about the *www*, and these beliefs serve as, or give rise to, reasons to think of a theory favorably or unfavorably. Not all economists invoke such reasons all the time, but some economists invoke them some of the time.

2. The *sources* of such reasons may range across a broad spectrum of ideas, such as the contents of the theory itself, other scientific theories, metaphysical theories, everyday experience, commonsense accounts, and systematically gathered empirical evidence. The *www* constraint on theories draws upon such sources which may be either explicitly acknowledged or implicitly presupposed. These sources will constitute something like a hierarchy. On the top, there may be some general metaphysical visions such as a generic causal process theory (think of Einstein's determinism and the locality principle); below it, there may be alternative more specific metaphysical theories such as versions of the generic causal process theory at various levels of specificity (think of Salmon's formulations of the notion of causal process close to the highest such level; and Richardson's ideas about competition close to the lowest level). These may set boundaries within which other sources selectively take over – such as other scientific theories, commonsense experience, previous research, and so on. These "lower-level" sources may, in turn, feed back to the higher-level sources of ontological beliefs.

3. Theorizing involves making choices, including choices between theories. Every theory candidate includes "unrealistic" elements. It is therefore never going to be a sound criticism of any given theory to claim that the theory is unrealistic. However, supposing that all theories are not equally bad, or equally good, it must be that some elements of unrealisticness are all right, while some others are less so. The problem of theory choice is also a problem of choosing between good and bad unrealistic elements. The suggestion pursued here is that the *www* constraint is there to help scientists resolve this choice problem. Putting the thought in terms of truth, we may say the following. Falsehood is not sufficient for making a theory bad. Truth is not sufficient for making a theory good. Yet, truth and falsehood should matter. For them to matter, we have to be able to distinguish between harmful and harmless falsehoods on the one hand, and between significant and insignificant truths on the other. Good theories avoid harmful falsehoods and contain significant truths. These distinctions are based on the *www* constraint. Good theories are true about the *www* and can survive falsehoods that

are not big enough to stop the world (see Mäki 1998e). In our example, Richardson believes that the assumptions of very large numbers, atomistic firms (price signals in the market being the only vehicle of contact between them), and perfect information, are harmful falsehoods: under these assumptions, the competitive economy cannot possibly work.

4. The *www* constraint is characteristically not able to constrain the theory choice so that only one unique optimal theory option remains to be "chosen." Rather, the constraint typically functions as a weaker *exclusion device*: it helps exclude theory candidates which depict the world in such a way that we have reason to believe that the world *does not* function that way, or, more strongly, that it *cannot* function that way, or, still more strongly, that it cannot function at all, given what we know about it. This is the thrust of the arguments against the model of perfect competition that we have dealt with; they serve the purpose of excluding the model but do not uniquely determine the best alternative model. We may say that theory choices are underdetermined by the ontological constraint just as they are underdetermined by empirical tests and by various social criteria. We may also say that the three classes of constraints – empirical, social, and ontological – may combine in various permutations and with different weights of impact so as to reduce the degree of overall arbitrariness in theory choice.

5. Among other things, two philosophical positions are involved in this notion. One is *ontic realism*: the world and its constituent sub-systems have a characteristic way of functioning. The solar system, the earth's ecological system, the human organism, your computer – they all have a definite way of working. We may say that they function in the way they do because they are what they are – because they are made of certain kind of stuff, because they have such and such constituents and such and such a structure. We may also say, at least in some cases such as Richardson's conceptions about the workings of the competitive economy, that *modal* elements are involved: our conceptions of the *www* suggest that there are ontic necessities and impossibilities in the world. This view is *ontic* realism, since it characterizes a feature of reality. It is ontic *realism*, since this feature – the way the world works (or the way it necessarily works or cannot possibly work) – is supposed to be a characteristic the world has independently of what we believe of it or how we represent it.

6. The other philosophical position is *theoretical realism*: good theories are purportedly true descriptions of the way the world works. This runs counter to instrumentalist conceptions of theories according to which

theories are not attempts to capture the inner workings of the world, but rather – and no more than – instruments of organizing data or of attaining some practical goals. The realist will allow for unrealistic assumptions, but will hold that it is inexcusable not to be realistic about those elements that are necessary for the functioning of a given system, while it is permissible and advisable to leave out some others that are not.

In his critique of Coase's methodology, Posner put forth an instrumentalist view, namely that "[a] model can be a useful tool of discovery even if it is unrealistic, just as Ptolemy's astronomical theory was a useful tool of navigation [. . .] even though its basic premise was false" (Posner 1993, p. 77). Given Coase's interest in how the system under study functions, he would not be content with Ptolemyan theory. He would prefer Copernican heliocentrism to the false geocentrism, even if the Copernican theory has many minor details wrong and may therefore fail in predictions. "Faced with a choice between a theory which predicts well but gives us little insight into how the system works and one which gives us this insight but predicts badly, I would choose the latter [. . .]" (Coase 1988c, p. 64). Coase's rejection of the instrumentalist conception of theories is explicit: "But a theory is not like an airline or bus timetable. We are not interested simply in the accuracy of its predictions. A theory also serves as a base of thinking. It helps us to understand what is going on [. . .]" (p. 64). While bus timetables may help us predict the behavior of buses and thus to serve as "inference tickets," they fail to give us any idea about the mechanisms and processes that keep buses running as they do.[5] As Salmon puts it, "[a] detailed knowledge of the mechanisms may not be required for successful prediction; it is indispensable to the attainment of genuine scientific understanding" (Salmon 1984, p. 133).

References

Arrow, Kenneth J. (1974) "General Economic Equilibrium: Purpose, Analytic Techniques, Collective Choice," *American Economic Review*, 64: 253–72.
Blaug, Mark (1980) *The Methodology of Economics*, Cambridge: Cambridge University Press.
Buchanan, James (1979) *What Should Economists Do?* Indianapolis: Liberty Press.
Cartwright, Nancy (1989) *Nature's Capacities and their Measurement*, Oxford: Clarendon Press.

---

[5] For a critique of Posner's critique of Coase, see Mäki (1998c).

Coase, R. H. (1937) "The Nature of the Firm," *Economica*, 4 (n.s.): 386–405.

(1960) "'The Problem of Social Cost," *Journal of Law and Economics*, 3: 1–44.

(1988 [1946]) "The Marginal Cost Controversy," *Economica*, 13 (n.s.). References are to the reprint in Coase (1988a).

(1988a) *The Firm, the Market, and the Law*, Chicago: University of Chicago Press.

(1988b) "The Firm, the Market, and the Law," in Coase (1988a): 1–31.

(1988c) "How Should Economists Choose?" in *Ideas, Their Origins, and Their Consequences*, Washington DC: American Enterprise Institute: 63–79.

(1993 [1992]) "The Institutional Structure of Production," *American Economic Review*, 82. References are to the reprint in Williamson and Winter (1993): 227–35.

(1993a) "The Nature of the Firm: Origin," in Williamson and Winter (1993): 34–47.

(1993b) "The Nature of the Firm: Meaning," in Williamson and Winter (1993): 48–60.

(1993c) "The Nature of the Firm: Influence," in Williamson and Winter (1993): 61–74.

de Marchi, Neil (ed.) (1988) *The Popperian Legacy in Economics*, Cambridge: Cambridge University Press.

(1992) *Post-Popperian Methodology of Economics*, Boston: Kluwer.

de Marchi, Neil and Mark Blaug (eds.) (1991) *Appraising Economic Theories*, Aldershot: Edward Elgar.

Ferber, Marianne and Julie Nelson (1993) *Beyond Economic Man: Feminist Theory and Economics*, Chicago: University of Chicago Press.

Hands, Wade (1994) "The Sociology of Scientific Knowledge," in *New Developments in Economic Methodology*, ed. Roger Backhouse, London: Routledge: 75–106.

Klamer, Arjo (1983) *Conversations with Economists*, Totowa: Rowman and Allenheld.

Latsis, Spiro (ed.) (1976) *Method and Appraisal in Economics*, Cambridge: Cambridge University Press.

Lawson, Tony (1997) *Economics and Reality*, London: Routledge.

Loasby, Brian (1986) "Competition and Imperfect Knowledge: The Contribution of G. B. Richardson," *Scottish Journal of Political Economy*, 33: 145–58.

Mäki, Uskali (1989) "On the Problem of Realism in Economics," *Ricerche Economiche*, 43: 176–98. Reprinted in *The Philosophy and Methodology of Economics*, ed. Bruce Caldwell Aldershot: Edward Elgar.

(1990a) "Methodology of Economics: Complaints and Guidelines," *Finnish Economic Papers*, 3: 77–84.

(1990b) "Mengerian Economics in Realist Perspective," *History of Political Economy*, Annual Supplement to vol. 22: 289–310.

(1990c) "Scientific Realism and Austrian Explanation," *Review of Political Economy*, 2: 310–44.

(1992a) "On the Method of Isolation in Economics," *Idealization IV: Intellig-*

ibility in Science, ed. Craig Dilworth, special issue of *Poznan Studies in the Philosophy of the Sciences and the Humanities*, 26: 319–54.

(1992b) "Friedman and Realism," *Research in the History of Economic Thought and Methodology*, 10: 171–95.

(1992c) "The Market as an Isolated Causal Process: A Metaphysical Ground for Realism," in *Austrian Economics: Tensions and New Developments*, ed. Bruce Caldwell and Stephan Boehm, Kluwer Publishers: 35–59.

(1992d) "Social Conditioning of Economics," in *Post-Popperian Methodology of Economics*, ed. N. de Marchi, Kluwer Publishers: 65–104.

(1993a) "Social Theories of Science and the Fate of Institutionalism in Economics," in *Rationality, Institutions and Economic Methodology*, ed. U. Mäki, B. Gustafsson, and C. Knudsen, London: Routledge: 76–109.

(1994a) "Isolation, Idealization and Truth in Economics," in *Idealization in Economics*, ed. Bert Hamminga and Neil de Marchi, special issue of *Poznan Studies in the Philosophy of the Sciences and the Humanities*, 38: 147–68.

(1994b) "Reorienting the Assumptions Issue," in *New Developments in Economic Methodology*, ed. Roger Backhouse, London: Routledge: 236–56.

(1996) "Scientific Realism and Some Peculiarities of Economics," *Boston Studies in the Philosophy of Science*, 169: 425–45.

(1997) "Universals and the *Methodenstreit*: A Reexamination of Carl Menger's Conception of Economics as an Exact Science," *Studies in History and Philosophy of Science*, 28: 475–95.

(1998a) "Mechanisms, Models, and Free Riders," in *Economics and Methodology: Crossing the Boundaries*, ed. R. Backhouse, D. Hausman, U. Mäki, and A. Salanti, London: Macmillan: 98–112.

(1998b) "Is Coase a Realist?" *Philosophy of the Social Sciences*, 28: 5–31.

(1998c) "Against Posner Against Coase Against Theory," *Cambridge Journal of Economics*, 22: 587–95.

(1998d) "On the Issue of Realism in the Economics of Institutional Organization: Themes from Coase and Richardson," in *Beyond Keynes*, ed. S. Dow and J. Hillard.

(1998e) "Aspects of Realism About Economics," *Theoria*, 13: 301–13.

(1999) "Science as a Free Market: A Reflexivity Test in an Economics of Economics," *Perspectives on Science*, 7: 486–509.

McCloskey, Donald (1985) *The Rhetoric of Economics*, Madison: University of Wisconsin Press.

Mirowski, Philip (1989) *More Heat than Light*, Cambridge: Cambridge University Press.

Posner, Richard A. (1993) "The New Institutional Economics Meets Law and Economics," *Journal of Institutional and Theoretical Economics*, 149: 73–87.

Richardson, G. B. (1960) *Information and Investment. A Study in the Working of the Competitive Economy*, Oxford: Oxford University Press.

(1964) *Economic Theory*, London: Hutchinson.

(1972) "The Organization of Industry," *Economic Journal*, 82: 883–96.

(1995) "The Theory of the Market Economy," *Revue économique*, 6: 1487–96.

(1998) "Innovation, Equilibrium and Welfare," in *Beyond Keynes*, ed. S. Dow and J. Hillard.

Rosenberg, Alex (1992) *Economics – Mathematical Politics or a Science of Diminishing Returns*, Chicago: University of Chicago Press.

Ross, Don (1995) "Real Patterns and the Ontological Foundations of Micro-economics," *Economics and Philosophy*, 11: 113–36.

Salmon, Pierre (1998) "Free Riding as Mechanism," in *Economics and Methodology: Crossing Boundaries*, ed. R. Backhouse, D. Hausman, U. Mäki, and A. Salanti, London: Macmillan: 62–87.

Salmon, Wesley (1984) *Scientific Explanation and the Causal Structure of the World*, Princeton: Princeton University Press.

Weintraub, E. Roy (1985) *General Equilibrium Analysis*, Cambridge: Cambridge University Press.

(1991) *Stabilizing Dynamics. Constructing Economic Knowledge*, Cambridge: Cambridge University Press.

Williamson, Oliver E. and Sidney G. Winter (eds.) (1993) *The Nature of the Firm: Origins, Evolution, and Development*, Oxford: Oxford University Press.

Zamora Bonilla, Jesus P. (1999) "Verisimilitude and the Strategy of Economic Theory," *Journal of Economic Methodology*, 6: 331–50.

Name index

Subject index